One Hundred Years of American Women Writing, 1848–1948

THE MAGILL BIBLIOGRAPHIES

The American Presidents, by Norman S. Cohen, 1989
Black American Women Novelists, by Craig Werner, 1989
Classical Greek and Roman Drama, by Robert J. Forman, 1989
Contemporary Latin American Fiction, by Keith H. Brower, 1989
Masters of Mystery and Detective Fiction, by J. Randolph Cox, 1989
Nineteenth Century American Poetry, by Philip K. Jason, 1989
Restoration Drama, by Thomas J. Taylor, 1989
Twentieth Century European Short Story, by Charles E. May, 1989
The Victorian Novel, by Laurence W. Mazzeno, 1989
Women's Issues, by Laura Stempel Mumford, 1989
America in Space, by Russell R. Tobias, 1991
The American Constitution, by Robert J. Janosik, 1991
The Classical Epic, by Thomas J. Sienkewicz, 1991
English Romantic Poetry, by Bryan Aubrey, 1991
Ethics, by John K. Roth, 1991
The Immigrant Experience, by Paul D. Mageli, 1991
The Modern American Novel, by Steven G. Kellman, 1991
Native Americans, by Frederick E. Hoxie and Harvey Markowitz, 1991
American Drama: 1918-1960, by R. Baird Shuman, 1992
American Ethnic Literatures, by David R. Peck, 1992
American Theatre History, by Thomas J. Taylor, 1992
The Atomic Bomb, by Hans G. Graetzer and Larry M. Browning, 1992
Biography, by Carl Rollyson, 1992
The History of Science, by Gordon L. Miller, 1992
The Origin and Evolution of Life on Earth, by David W. Hollar, 1992
Pan-Africanism, by Michael W. Williams, 1992
Resources for Writers, by R. Baird Shuman, 1992
Shakespeare, by Joseph Rosenblum, 1992
The Vietnam War in Literature, by Philip K. Jason, 1992
Contemporary Southern Women Fiction Writers, by Rosemary M. Canfield Reisman and Christopher J. Canfield, 1994
Cycles in Humans and Nature, by John T. Burns, 1994
Environmental Studies, by Diane M. Fortner, 1994
Poverty in America, by Steven Pressman, 1994

One Hundred Years of American Women Writing, 1848–1948

An Annotated Bio-Bibliography

Jane Missner Barstow

Magill Bibliographies

The Scarecrow Press, Inc.
Lanham, Md., & London
and
Salem Press
Pasadena, Calif., & Englewood Cliffs, N.J.
1997

SCARECROW PRESS, INC.

Published in the United States of America
by Scarecrow Press, Inc.
4720 Boston Way
Lanham, Maryland 20706

4 Pleydell Gardens, Folkestone
Kent CT20 2DN, England

British Library Cataloguing in Publication Information Available

Library of Congress Cataloging-in-Publication Data

Barstow, Jane Missner.
    One hundred years of American women writing, 1848–1948 : an
annotated bio-bibliography / Jane Missner Barstow.
        p. cm. — (Magill bibliographies)
    Includes index.
    ISBN 0–8108–3314–X (cloth: alk. paper)
    1. American literature—Women authors—Bio-bibliography—
Dictionaries. 2. American literature—19th century—Bio-bibliography—
Dictionaries. 3. Women authors, American—19th century—Biography—
Dictionaries. 4. American literature—20th century—Bio-bibliography—
Dictionaries. 5. Women authors, American—20th century—Biography—
Dictionaries. 6. Women and literature—United States—History—Dictionaries.
I. Title. II. Series
PS151.B37 1997
810.9'9287—dc21   97–4001
[B]

ISBN 0–8108–3314–X

♾ The paper used in this publication meets the minimum requirements of
American National Standard for Information Sciences—Permanence of
Paper for Printed Library Materials, ANSI Z39.48–1984.
Manufactured in the United States of America.

This book is dedicated to interlibrary loan librarians everywhere and especially to Julie Aldrich, head librarian at Hartford College for Women, and Kim Farrington, director of ILL at the University of Hartford.

CONTENTS

Contents

INTRODUCTION

This bibliography is based on two major premises: first, that over the last twenty-five years, there has been a sea change in thinking about what is meant by "American literature"; second, that American women writing in a variety of genres played major roles in the growing fields of book and periodical publication by the mid-nineteenth century. The sixty-six writers who are the major subjects of the critical studies annotated here represent a wide diversity of genres and experiences; they are poets and novelists, journalists and authors of political treatises, founders of religions and birth control clinics; they are conservatives and radicals, Southerners and New Englanders, heterosexuals and homosexuals, wives and widows. Many never married or had no children; others had large families. All were born or raised in the United States and wrote in English. Most are middle-class and white, though there are a few representatives of America's new immigrant groups and a significant number of African American writers. All of these writers were well-known in their own times; all published book-length works between 1848 and 1948; all were born between 1805 and 1905; all have been subject to a major revival since the 1970's because of new information and new perspectives on their lives and works.

The mid-nineteenth century is a key period in American literary history in general and women's literary history in particular. In an 1837 lecture, reprinted as "The American Scholar," Ralph Waldo Emerson argued that the United States had come of age as a country; after a "long apprenticeship to the learning of other lands," it was now ready to develop its own literature and its own bards who would sing distinctly American songs and would "lead in a new age." The most obvious response to this clarion call was the publication of Walt Whitman's *Leaves of Grass* (1855), with its larger-than-life persona who ecstatically celebrates his own sensual self as a representation of America's assertive new spirit. At about the same time, Emily Dickinson was writing her first poems, which were equally fresh and original, but could not have been more different in form, with their tightly compressed four-line stanzas, intricate off-rhymes, and complex ironies. The dramatic contrast between the expansive egotism of Whitman's poetry and the meditative inwardness of Dickinson's, between Whitman's efforts at self-promotion and Dickinson's decision to keep her poems in a drawer, offers a tempting, if somewhat extreme, metaphor for the very different life experiences of nineteenth century men and women increasingly segregated in their separate spheres.

1

One could argue that America already had a national literature of its own by the 1850's given the publication of *The Scarlet Letter* in 1850 and *Moby Dick* in 1851, and the founding of *The Atlantic Monthly* in 1857, which would become the major literary outlet for many American writers, male and female. By the 1850's women writers had come to dominate the market for popular fiction, leading to Nathaniel Hawthorne's infamous complaint about a "damned mob of scribbling women" taking away the readers that were rightfully his. Though *The Scarlet Letter* was, in fact, a commercial success, its sales lagged far behind Susan Warner's *A Wide, Wide World*, published the same year and soon to become the first American book to sell a million copies in its author's lifetime. Though no serious literary scholar would question the literary superiority of Hawthorne over Warner, today we evaluate Warner's work in the context of the kind of domestic fiction it exemplifies and for what it tells us about the desires and concerns of its readers. We also consider the importance of literature in providing middle-class women with an accepted way to earn a living without violating the separation of public and private spheres. Women may have flocked to writing fiction as a legitimate way to help support their families; they also turned reading into a major leisure-time activity for the middle class. It has been estimated that by 1870 as many as two-thirds of all novels published in the United States were written by women.

The most important landmark of the mid-nineteenth century for scholars of women's history and literature is the first women's rights convention at Seneca Falls in 1848. Elizabeth Cady Stanton's Declaration of Sentiments, a paraphrase of the Declaration of Independence, begins, "We hold these truths to be self-evident: that all men and women are created equal," and proceeds to list a series of twelve resolutions, including "that all laws which prevent woman from occupying such a station in society as her conscience shall dictate, or which place her in a position inferior to that of man, are contrary to the great precept of nature, and therefore of no force or authority"; "that the objection of indelicacy and impropriety, which is so often brought against woman when she addresses a public audience, comes with a very ill-grace from those who encourage, by their attendance, her appearance on the stage, in the concert, or in feats of the circus"; and "that it is the duty of the women of this country to secure to themselves their sacred right to the elective franchise." Slowly but surely, these words, reinforced by the popular lectures Stanton and other suffragists delivered throughout the country, began to challenge basic American assumptions about the rights and proper roles of women.

The year 1848 marks a time of dramatic change throughout the western world, not just in America. People took to the streets in Europe and England to demand fulfillment of liberal democratic rights promised by the French and American revolutions, and Marx and Engels published the *Communist Manifesto*. The physical landscape of America was also undergoing transformation during these years of rapid industrialization and urbanization in the East, and ongoing exploration and settlement of the West (the Gold Rush began in 1848 with the discovery of gold flakes at Sutter's Mill). By 1850 there were one million workers in the labor force, one quarter of whom were women. The Fugitive Slave Law was passed in 1850, leading to the publication in 1851 of Harriet Beecher Stowe's *Uncle Tom's Cabin*. As the country moved inexorably toward civil war, supporters of women's rights continued to hold annual conventions, and small victories were chalked up in state courts reforming property rights and divorce laws. For many activists, however, the most important concerns were abolition and the work of the Underground Railroad, with all agitation for women's rights virtually at a standstill by 1861. Though, on one hand, the war interrupted the work of women's rights, on the other hand, it would create countless new opportunities for women called to take the place of men in schools, factories, and government offices.

There were, of course, far more women weeping over the domestic novels of the nineteenth century than convening on behalf of women's rights. Still, careful reading of nineteenth century fiction shows that revolutionary ideas about woman's position in the family, about her intellectual and physical capabilities, and about her potential contributions to society if granted more freedom and independence were beginning to permeate the thinking of even the most traditional of wives and mothers. In general, between 1848 and 1948 the progress of women as writers and in terms of their own rights as individuals can be divided into three major periods. The first, which roughly ends in the 1870's following the Civil War, is marked by increasing consciousness of women's issues and the increasing popularity of women's fiction. The second, which culminates in the 1920 passage of the Nineteenth Amendment granting full suffrage to women, is marked by great gains in access to education and entry into the professions, countered by increased professionalization of many fields and thus the limiting and devaluing of women's contributions. In other words, at the same time that women's writing, for example, was gaining in sophistication, literary critics were beginning to define the "essence" of American literature in ways that almost inevitably excluded women. The third period, which begins as liberated female writers and artists joined the bohemian colonies of Paris and Greenwich Village, continues through the Depression and ends after the Second World War. It is usually considered a low point in women's history. Recent studies, however, have begun to unearth more examples of female achievement in all fields; certainly women writers were becoming increasingly diverse during these years in terms of the kind of work they produced and in terms of their own ethnic backgrounds.

This bibliography ends in 1948, one hundred years after Seneca Falls. Though the date seems arbitrary, as are the foregoing divisions to some degree, it does conveniently precede several key milestones which prefigure the women's and civil rights movements of the 1960's. Simone de Beauvoir began writing her two-volume *The Second Sex* in

1948; it was published in France in 1949, and in the United States in
1953. Margaret Mead published *Male and Female: A Study of the Sexes
in the Changing World* in 1949. De Beauvoir's work separated the
biological fact of being a female from other aspects of the feminine that
she identified as not necessarily innate. She then analyzed how
femininity was learned and why it had become a source of oppression.
Mead's work examined western definitions of the family and gender-
based assignment of roles and functions in society, concluding that
these were not universal since other cultures had quite different
divisions of labor. By 1963, with Betty Friedan's publication of *The
Feminine Mystique*, the earlier intellectual discussions moved into the
daily realm of the suburban housewife who found herself frustrated and
unhappy despite the material comfort of her life. Friedan helped found
the National Organization for Women (NOW) in 1966 with its political
agenda for a new American Dream based on the equality of women and
men both at home and in the workplace. Soon after, the first generation
of avowedly feminist historians and literary critics were beginning the
work of recovery and revision which would challenge traditional
literary scholarship and lead to the hundreds of articles and books on
which this bibliography is based.

While the foregoing historical overview provides a context for the
bibliography and a rationale for its boundaries, the writers represented
also reflect a major reconsideration of what is meant by American
literature, the sea change described in the first paragraph of this
introduction. It is important to note that this change goes far beyond
the inclusion of more women in the so-called canon. Certainly, the first
task for feminist scholars writing in the 1970's was to uncover the
many important women whose works had been forgotten and then to
identify the commonalities which justified establishment of a women's
tradition with its own history and aesthetics. Later, as the post-modern
theories derived from linguistics, psychoanalysis, Marxism, and
deconstruction began to leave their mark on the practice of literary
analysis, the boundaries between genres and disciplines began to
dissolve. The interpretation of literature came to be seen as an open
process with any attempt to establish set patterns and traditions
understood to be problematic. Post-modern critics warned that if
women's literature were defined in terms of particular themes and
techniques, those writers whose work did not conform would find
themselves excluded from future anthologies and discussions, much as
earlier definitions of American literature were used to exclude most
women. We now understand that changing literary tastes and the
personal preferences of editors have as much to do with the survival of
particular nineteenth and early twentieth century works as does intrinsic
merit. Today's scholars may themselves unwittingly devalue or
overlook certain texts because they do not fit the particular theory or
collective description they are trying to promote.

This bibliography is intended for a broad audience. Teachers may find it helpful in diversifying a curriculum, getting ideas about how to teach a particular writer, or deciding which secondary sources to put on a suggested reading list. Students may use it as a source of paper topics and for a quick overview of the kinds of perspectives from which a particular writer has been considered since 1970. Scholars may use these listings as a point of departure for their own research, or as a source of ideas for dissertation topics.

The bibliography is divided into six chapters. Chapters 1 through 5 focus on sixty-six writers, with groupings dictated to a large extent by the parameters of major secondary sources. In other words, given the many critical studies that focus on women poets, on women journalists, on the nineteenth century novel, or on African American writers, in particular, it makes sense to group individual writers accordingly. Each of these five chapters covers major figures about whom a great deal has been written as well as a few less well-known writers ripe for further study. The chapter introduction establishes literary and historical context, identifies general studies and relevant journals, and also makes reference to writers not included, yet worthy of note. For each individual writer there is a brief biographical entry, a listing of reissued editions of her writings, and annotations of a broad range of scholarly articles, book chapters, and full-length books on her life and work. The final chapter looks at critical and bibliographic studies of groups of writers rather than individuals. The Asian American, Jewish American, Latina, and Native American writers referenced, with a few notable exceptions, are most often discussed in the context of emerging ethnic traditions and as the historical foremothers of popular contemporary writers such as Amy Tan, Cynthia Ozick, Sandra Cisneros, and Leslie Silko.

The choice of late nineteenth and early twentieth century writers represented reflects in large part the interests of the critics and historians who study the women of this period. Not surprisingly, many scholars tend to write about writers with whom they can identify; women write about women, lesbians write about lesbians, African Americans write about African Americans, Southerners about Southerners, Asian Americans about Asian Americans, and (in a few cases) mystery writers about mystery writers. There are scholars of American literature throughout the world; the majority, however, are themselves American. The best scholars use their subjectivity to enhance rather than limit their understanding of a work; those writing with personal experience of a particular culture can often correct past misreadings and establish important contexts for future readers. I hope that this bibliography will help students and teachers learn about a diversity of writers and works whose life experiences may differ widely from their own.

One final note on the considerations which were behind the inclusion or exclusion of particular writers. All wrote the bulk of their work before 1948; almost all were born in the nineteenth century. With the exception of a few of the writers referred to in chapter 6, all wrote in English and were raised in the United States. All have been the subject of at least three major books and/or articles written since 1970; most have been the subject of important studies published since 1980. All have works currently in print. In other words, these are the writers whose lives and works have been attracting critical attention as a direct result of the "sea change" in thinking about American literature referred to earlier. Appendix A which lists over 150 writers by genre and birthdate, includes many women who published between 1848 and 1948 but whose work may not fit the above criteria.

In choosing which sources to annotate, I have tried to include those most frequently cited by other critics and easily accessible at the average college or university library, with a little help from interlibrary loan. For less well-known writers I have been able to include almost all sources published since 1970; for major figures I have tried to choose a cross section of the most recent, most influential, and most general sources with a limit of approximately twenty annotations each. The length of annotations varies considerably, with short annotations for standard reference works and longer annotations to summarize complex critical arguments.

The general studies listed at the end of this introductory chapter fall into three different categories. The reference books included (Barker-Benfield, Davidson, Davis, Duke, James, Magill, Mainiero, and Sicherman) reflect the major work of recovery provided by historians. Other texts (Banner, Bell, Chodorow, Degler, Hartman, Mumford, Smith-Rosenberg, Welter, Wheeler, and Zinsser) provide background on relevant topics, such as changing notions of the family, women's diseases, and female beauty, reported from psychological, sociological, and historical perspectives. Finally, several texts (Ammons, Baym, Davidson, Fox-Genovese, Gilbert and Gubar, Lauter, Nelson, Showalter, and Williamson) directly address or are derived from new perspectives on American literature.

Two sources, in particular, are often credited with initiating women's literary studies—Patricia Meyer Spacks's *The Female Imagination* (1972) and Ellen Moers's *Literary Women* (1976). Moers established the history of a female literary subculture from the eighteenth century to the 1970's. Spacks raised important issues—what it means to a woman to write, in what ways women do and do not challenge "man-created myths," the degree to which women's creative expression reflects female points of view—which continue to be debated by later generations of feminist critics. Both discuss a wide range of well-known British and American writers; Moers also includes European writers. I have not annotated them here since they do not deal primarily with American literature. However, several of the general works listed below clearly build on their pioneering work.

Countless standard reference works also contain useful information on many of the women writers in this bibliography. Among the most comprehensive and easily accessible are *Contemporary Authors, The*

Dictionary of Literary Biography, Nineteenth Century Literary Criticism, Twentieth Century Literary Criticism, and *Contemporary Literary Criticism.* These sources contain basic biographical information as well as a review of each author's critical reputation. The last three also contain lengthy excerpts from books, reviews, and scholarly articles. Scholars interested in a particular writer should also be aware of newsletters and periodicals such as *Cather Studies, The Journal of the Edna St. Vincent Millay Society,* and *The Edith Wharton Review*; significant articles from these specialized sources are often reprinted in major literary journals and essay collections.

GENERAL STUDIES

Ammons, Elizabeth. *Conflicting Stories: American Women Writers at the Turn into the Twentieth Century.* New York: Oxford University Press, 1991.

Ammons sees the forty-year period between 1890 and 1930 as a particularly rich one for women writers in terms of both the quantity and quality of their publications. She has chosen seventeen women from a variety of ethnic and racial backgrounds in order to establish the "shared historical context" of their work. Despite real differences in "education, money, privilege, and opportunity," many of these writers fit the profile of the "new woman" of the Progressive Era and express a similar feminist belief in the abilities and rights of women. Ammons is particularly interested in the impact of the "cult of true womanhood" on black women whom it forced to prove they were ladies and on white ladies whom it forced to prove they were women.

See also: Elizabeth Ammons, "Men of Color, Women, and Uppity Art at the Turn of the Century," in *American Realism and the Canon,* eds. Tom Quirk and Gary Scharnhorst, Newark: University of Delaware Press, 1994, which briefly summarizes the same material covered in the above book.

Banner, Lois W. *American Beauty.* Chicago: University of Chicago Press, 1983.

Banner traces the development of cultural ideals of beauty from Colonial times through the twentieth century. She looks at changes in fashionable body images over time and the impact of the women's movement on notions of beauty. She also looks at the role of beauty contests, famous actresses, and particular consumer goods in the commercialization of beauty. The text includes illustrations and a selected bibliography.

Barker-Benfield, G. J., and Catherine Clinton. *Portraits of American Women: From Settlement to the Present.* New York: St. Martin's Press, 1991.

These well-illustrated biographies, grouped by historical era, include discussion of each woman's impact on her contemporaries.

Baym, Nina. "Melodramas of Beset Manhood: How Themes of American Fiction Exclude Women Authors." *American Quarterly* 33, no. 2 (Summer 1981): 123-139.

In reviewing the many reasons behind most women writers' exclusion from literary history, Baym notes that current theories (from the 1950's to the 1970's) define American literature as "essentially male." For example, Leslie Fiedler in his 1960 book, *Love and Death in the American Novel*, describes women writers as creators of "flagrantly bad best-sellers" whose popularity made it more difficult for serious writers (all male in his examples) to find an audience. Other critical works, including ones by Henry Nash Smith and R. W. B. Lewis, define American literature in terms of myths about the "virgin" land with female characters cast as "entrappers" or "impediments" to male freedom. Women, who are not themselves misogynist, are unlikely to write books which fit such a definition. Baym's final point is that the writer has come to be seen as an "Adamic creator," the reincarnation of the pioneer exploring unmapped territory, a role from which women, once again, are necessarily excluded.

Bell, Susan Groag, and Karen M. Offen, eds. *Women, the Family, and Freedom: The Debate in Documents*, 2 vols. Stanford: Stanford University Press, 1983.

This comprehensive anthology includes essays, speeches, legal briefs, fictional excerpts, and other writings from 1750 to 1950 which are grouped by historical period. Together, they trace the evolution of western thought on women, their position in the family, and their social and political rights. Subtopics within each period include men's authority in the family, women's political consciousness, and the debates over suffrage and education for women. There are introductions to each section and a bibliography and suggested reading list for each volume.

Chodorow, Nancy. *The Reproduction of Mothering: Psychoanalysis and the Sociology of Gender*. Berkeley: University of California Press, 1978.

This revision of Freudian psychology focuses on a girl's ongoing identification with her mother as a crucial shaping influence on her development, in contrast to a boy's need for separation and individuation. Rather than shifting allegiance from mother to father as Freud believed, girls, according to Chodorow, learn to "reproduce" their mothers' nurturing behavior and to bond with other women. Moreover, girls emerge from their childhood with a basis for "empathy" built into their sense of self in a way that boys do not. Because they are parented by a person of the same gender, girls experience themselves as less differentiated than boys, as more continuous with the external object-world. This identification is not without its problems given that the mother may be seen as passive and dependent, resulting in the daughter's unconscious devaluation of herself.

Davidson, Cathy N., ed. *The Oxford Companion to Women's Writing in the United States*. New York: Oxford University Press, 1995.

This encyclopedic collection of essays covers a wide variety of topics and individual authors. There are entries on abolition and anarchism, as well as on female anthropologists. There are essays on genres and periods, for example one on poetry from 1850-1976 and one on domestic fiction. There are essays on most ethnic groups, including Latina, Asian American, and Native American, with six separate essays on African American literature, plus one on African American reading networks. Each essay is followed by a bibliography. There are also two timelines appended, one of social history and one of primary texts. All of the writers in this bibliography are included, with the exception of Mary Baker Eddy, the founder of Christian Science.

Davidson, Cathy N., and E. M. Broner. *The Lost Tradition: Mothers and Daughters in Literature*. New York: Frederick Ungar, 1980.

This is a collection of twenty-four essays, including ones on Emily Dickinson (chapter 3), and Ellen Glasgow, Willa Cather, Edith Wharton, and Anzia Yezierska (chapter 2), which grew out of a 1976 workshop at the Midwest Modern Language Association Convention. The essays are grouped by broad topical divisions such as "The Lost Mother," "Daughters of the Patriarchy," and "Mother as Medusa." The editors also present a preliminary bibliography organized by genre; the drama and poetry sections, in particular, emphasize early twentieth century American women writers.

Davis, Cynthia J., and Kathryn West. *Women Writers in the United States: A Timeline of Literary, Cultural, and Social History*. New York: Oxford University Press, 1996.

This comprehensive chronology includes detailed information on the career paths of many of the writers referenced in this bibliography.

Degler, Carl N. *At Odds: Women and the Family in America from the Revolution to the Present*. New York: Oxford University Press, 1980.

Noting that the historic family has depended on women's subordination, Degler traces the evolution of the "modern" family in the context of women's search for greater autonomy. In addition to demographic and economic statistics, Degler turns to letters, diaries, and literary sources for evidence about the family. Much of the book focuses on the nineteenth century; Degler pays special attention to new roles for women as companions to their husbands, moral guardians of the family, and nurturers of children. He also examines changing attitudes about female sexuality and birth control, the special problems faced by African American and immigrant families, and transformations in patterns of women's work.

Duke, Maurice, Jackson R. Bryer, and M. Thomas Inge. *American Women Writers: Bibliographical Essays.* Westport, Conn.: Greenwood Press, 1983.

The collection contains fourteen essays on writers whom the authors consider important historically. Each essay is prefaced by a listing of primary sources, including editions, manuscripts, and letters. Following are surveys of biography and criticism reviewed chronologically and by topic. Twenty-four writers are covered, including Sarah Orne Jewett, Mary E. Wilkins Freeman, Kate Chopin, Edith Wharton, Gertrude Stein, Djuna Barnes, Ellen Glasgow, Katherine Anne Porter, Zora Neale Hurston, Pearl Buck, and Marianne Moore.

Fox-Genovese, Elizabeth. "Between Individualism and Fragmentation: American Culture and the New Literary Studies of Race and Gender." *American Quarterly* 42, no. 1 (March 1990): 7-34.

Fox-Genovese offers a complex argument for acknowledgment of both diversity and a common culture in the study of American literature. Race and gender should enjoy privileged positions because they are at the core of our sense of self. As for the so-called dominant culture, we need to understand that it is based on the power of a privileged elite, a power that may have marginalized and silenced many voices, but which also had prestige in the eyes of those it excluded. Fox-Genovese offers examples of women whose work demonstrates a kind of "bilingualism," the double consciousness first defined by W. E. B. Du Bois. These include Harriet Jacobs, Nella Larsen, Edith Wharton, and Willa Cather, all of whom managed to criticize the attitudes and institutions that limited their lives without jettisoning the dominant culture's standards of excellence.

Gilbert, Sandra M., and Susan Gubar. "Toward a Feminist Poetics," in *The Madwoman in the Attic: The Woman Writer and the Nineteenth Century Literary Imagination.* New Haven: Yale University Press, 1979.

Gilbert and Gubar define an "anxiety of authorship" derived from "complex and often only barely conscious fears" on the part of nineteenth century women writers, who believed that in "daring to write" they were defying their own femininity and behaving like monsters, rather than the angels they were supposed to be. This anxiety manifested itself in images of "enclosure and escape," fantasies of "maddened doubles," and "metaphors of physical discomfort" which frequently recur in their work. Despite access to a rich female literary subculture which enabled them to read and respond to each other's works, nineteenth century women struggled to break free of the narrow and repressive social and literary sphere to which they felt themselves confined. It is thanks to their struggles in "isolation that felt like illness" and "alienation that felt like madness" that contemporary women have been able to write with authority and trust in their own right to claim the status of artist.

Hartman, Mary, and Lois Banner, eds. *Clio's Consciousness Raised.*
New York: Harper & Row, 1974.
   This is a collection of fourteen papers which were first presented at a
conference of women historians held at Douglass College in 1973.
Topics include the beginnings of the birth control movement, the
treatment of "women's" diseases, the impact of the washing machine on
women's lives, and the cycle of women's lives from puberty to
menopause. The focus throughout is on the lives of ordinary people and
the effects of myths about women's nature on the behavior of women
and men in a variety of social contexts.

James, Edward T., ed. *Notable American Women, 1607-1950: A
Biographical Dictionary.* Cambridge, Mass.: Belknap Press, 1971.
   This three-volume encyclopedia was the first large-scale scholarly
work of its kind dedicated to women's history in America, a project
begun at Radcliffe College in connection with the Schlesinger Library.
Each biographical entry provides a comprehensive overview of the life
and career of its subject followed by a brief list of references.
Biographies are divided by field in the index for each volume,
including listings for radicals, social reformers, translators, editors and
publishers, general writers of literature, and children's authors.

Lauter, Paul. "The Literatures of America: A Comparative Discipline,"
in *Redefining American Literary History*, eds. A. LaVonne Brown
Ruoff and Jerry W. Ward, Jr. New York: The Modern Language
Association of America, 1990.
   Lauter argues for a comparative approach to study of the "many and
varied" literatures of the United States that would allow us to view
diverse works through "critical lenses" other than those used for
mainstream texts. Such an approach would also make it clear that
Anglo-European male writing represents only one of the many voices
which comprise the "chorus" of American culture. Literary history, as
Lauter sees it, should acknowledge the uneven development of literary
cultures and not compare the early work of a new immigrant group to
the increasingly sophisticated products of writers from highly
privileged backgrounds. It should also note that the thematic concerns
of a particular group, the burning questions its writers seek to answer,
may differ widely from one group to the next. A woman writer might
speak of how the weak can achieve a degree of power or about the
importance of community in the face of poverty while her male
counterpart writes of escape and adventure. Moreover, literary history
should not necessarily value one set of literary conventions over
another, privileging, for example, "denseness and speculative play" over
"immediacy of language" and intense symbolism. Finally, Lauter
recommends that we look to oral traditions and to linguistics and social
history to help us learn to see literature comparatively and thus
appreciate it in all its richness and diversity.

See also: Paul Lauter, *Canons and Contexts*, New York: Oxford University Press, 1991.

Magill, Frank N., ed. *Great Lives from History: American Women Series*. Pasadena, Calif.: Salem Press, 1995.

This set of five volumes contains biographical essays on 409 women from a wide variety of fields of achievement. Each entry provides an overview of the subject's early life and her adult work, a summary of her major contributions and significance, and a bibliography. Indices list subjects by birthdates and group them by field of endeavor.

Mainiero, Lina, ed. *American Women from Colonial Times to the Present*. New York: Frederick Ungar, 1979-1982.

This is a four-volume encyclopedia which covers more than one thousand writers from all disciplines. Each entry provides basic biographical information, a critical assessment of major works, and a bibliography of primary and secondary sources.

Mumford, Laura Stempel. *Women's Issues*. Pasadena, Calif.: Salem Press, 1989.

This annotated bibliography includes a listing of general studies of women's issues and nine chapters on topics such as "history, politics, and education," "health issues and sexuality," and "religion and spirituality." Each chapter is divided into several sections with, for example, "literature," visual arts," music," and "popular culture" under the general heading of "Women and The Arts." The two dozen sources on literature include anthologies, studies of major writers such as Emily Dickinson and Willa Cather, and influential theoretical texts, several of which focus on Native American and African American women writers.

Nelson, Nancy Owen, ed. *Private Voices, Public Lives: Women Speak on the Literary Life*. Denton: University of North Texas Press, 1995.

Each of the essays in this collection is written in the first person from the perspective of a reader whose personal and professional lives have been affected by the study of particular texts. Several of the writers discuss how their "love" of Willa Cather, Katherine Anne Porter, or Laura Ingalls Wilder (chapter 2) has helped them define their own female identities; others write about Emily Dickinson (chapter 3), Harriet Beecher Stowe (chapter 1), or Edith Summers Kelley (chapter 2) as providing mirrors to the self. The text is followed by brief contributor biographies.

Showalter, Elaine, ed. *Feminist Criticism: Essays on Women, Literature, & Theory*. New York: Pantheon Books, 1985.

This is a collection of essays, most of which previously appeared in feminist journals in 1980 and 1981. Showalter has chosen them to represent a broad range of theoretical perspectives. Nina Baym's "Melodramas of Beset Manhood," annotated above, and pieces by Jane

P. Tompkins and Deborah E. McDowell, annotated in later chapters, are included. Showalter's introduction points out the progression in feminist criticism from revelations of the "misogyny" behind literary images of women and the exclusion of women from the literary canon, to the establishment of the thematic and aesthetic bases for a female literary tradition, to an increasingly sophisticated theorizing about the production of literary texts and the conceptual grounds for literary study.

_____. *Sister's Choice: Tradition and Change in American Women's Writing*. Oxford: Clarendon Press, 1991.

Showalter has attempted to offer a "new" literary history of American women's writing which will consider "various themes, images, genres, and cultural practices" while avoiding assumptions of uniqueness and coherence. Her own idiosyncratic choices include four individual writers: Margaret Fuller, Louisa May Alcott, Kate Chopin, and Edith Wharton, a chapter on the 1920's and 1930's which focuses on women poets and the black women writers Fauset, Larsen, and Hurston, and a chapter on the American version of the gothic from Charlotte Perkins Gilman to Joyce Carol Oates. Showalter concludes by tracing the literal and literary history of quilting which she sees as a metaphor for a multifaceted, multicultural, ever-changing and unequal sisterhood of writers united ever so tenuously by a "yearning for community and continuity."

Sicherman, Barbara, and Carol Hurd Green, eds. *Notable American Women: The Modern Period: A Biographical Dictionary*. Cambridge, Mass.: Belknap Press, 1980.

This supplement to the original three-volume encyclopedia (see James above) adds women raised in the twentieth century who died between 1951 and 1975.

Smith-Rosenberg, Carroll. *Disorderly Conduct: Visions of Gender in Victorian America*. New York: Alfred A. Knopf, 1985.

This is a collection of nine essays, five of which had been previously published, including "The Female World of Love and Ritual: Relations Between Women in Nineteenth Century America," which appeared in the inaugural issue of *Signs* (1975) and which is widely quoted for its discussion of women's culture and female friendships. Smith-Rosenberg's other topics include religious protest, the role of the American Medical Association in restricting women's roles, and the rhetoric of the American Female Moral Reform society. New to this volume is an attention to "women's words" as expressed in letters and diaries, and a discussion of the author's own work as a social historian.

Welter, Barbara *Dimity Convictions*. Athens: Ohio University Press, 1976.

Welter begins with an analysis of female adolescence in the nineteenth century, which she sees as marked by an obsession with death and chastity, and ends with a portrait of Margaret Fuller, the female intellectual who in her life and work attempted to bridge the gap between the mind and the heart, and who died tragically in 1850. The book's best known chapter, "The Cult of True Womanhood," analyzes the advice meted out by nineteenth century women's magazines in terms of four cardinal virtues: piety, purity, domesticity, and submissiveness. Other chapters discuss the feminization of American religion, the rise of female detective novels, and what life was like for a merchant's daughter.

Wheeler, Kenneth W., and Virginia Lee Lussier. *Women, the Arts, and the 1920's in Paris and New York.* New Brunswick, N.J.: Transaction Books, 1982.

This collection of fifteen essays describes the lives and achievements of many writers, including Louisa May Alcott, Louise Bogan, Willa Cather, Jessie Fauset, Hilda Doolittle (H. D.), Zora Neale Hurston, Nellie Larsen, Edna St. Vincent Millay, Marianne Moore, Gertrude Stein, and Edith Wharton. Wheeler and Lussier believe the convergence of suffrage and time-saving devices for housewives made the 1920's a particularly productive decade for liberated self-expressive women. Greenwich Village, Harlem, and Paris were the undisputed centers of an artistic, literary, and general cultural revolution in which these women played a major role. Photographs of Fauset, Millay, Stein, and Wharton are among the illustrations the text contains.

Williamson, Marilyn L. "Toward a Feminist Literary History." *Signs* 10, no. 1 (Autumn 1984): 136-147.

Williamson calls for feminist literary critics to pay more attention to women's nontraditional writings, which can best be understood in terms of their "social, historical, and cultural contexts." For example, critics need to know what kind of language was "assigned to women" in a particular historical period in order to evaluate the literature produced by women of that era. Rather than focusing on women's failures in the writing of great poetry, feminist critics might turn to their achievements in the domestic novel. Williamson concludes that literature, like history, has begun to broaden its scope and now includes "business letters, film, slave narratives, radical popular poetry" and other nontraditional forms. An "historical, ideological" approach to women's writing should, therefore, prove one of the many acceptable ways to "organize and study a great variety of texts."

Zinsser, Judith P. *History and Feminism: A Glass Half Full.* New York: Macmillan, 1993.

This is a general study of the impact feminism has had on historical scholarship and the teaching of history, as well as on the profession itself—its graduate programs, professional organizations, publications, and politics. There are separate chapters dedicated to "men's history" and to "women's history." Zinsser highlights the contributions of many writers referenced in this bibliography, with special attention to the role of Mary Ritter Beard (chapter 4), whom she identifies as the most important advocate for women's history from the 1930's on. There is also an annotated listing of major sources.

Chapter 1
LATE NINETEENTH CENTURY FICTION WRITERS

The writing and reading of novels in the second half of the nineteenth century was truly a female enterprise. Literary historians estimate that as many as two-thirds of novels published in the late nineteenth century were written by women. Several factors can be cited in explanation of this phenomenon: a growing leisure class with the money to buy books and the free time to read them, increasing dissatisfaction with a dominant ideology that restricted white, middle-class women to a domestic sphere, messages from the suffrage movement that encouraged women to search for new role models, and unstable economic situations which led many women raised in more prosperous circumstances to turn to writing as one of the few acceptable ways to help support themselves and their families. The mid-nineteenth century also saw the rise of periodicals marketed to national audiences. *Godey's Lady's Book*, edited by Sarah Hale from 1837 to 1877 and considered the forerunner of today's home magazines, and *The Atlantic Monthly*, founded in 1857 and considered the nation's first "serious" literary magazine, both published serialized novels and short stories by most of the writers included here.

Though earlier in the century women had established themselves as popular writers, "the female cultural industry" can be viewed as taking off in 1850 with the publication of Susan Warner's *The Wide, Wide World*, which sold 40,000 copies in its first year and a million copies in Warner's lifetime, earning it the epithet "America's first best-seller." Harriet Beecher Stowe's *Uncle Tom's Cabin* (1852) soon followed, selling 300,000 copies in its first three years and several million in Stowe's lifetime. Other best-sellers included Maria Cummins's *The Lamplighter* (1854) and Fanny Fern's *Ruth Hall* (1855). Though the publication and readership of novels declined during the Civil War, soon after, Louisa May Alcott's *Little Women* (1868) inaugurated the March family novels with phenomenal sales at home and abroad. This same period saw vastly increased circulation figures for journals and literary magazines that published the serialized novels and stories of women writers. E. D. E. N. Southworth, one of the most popular writers of the 1870's and 1880's, for example, helped boost the circulation of the *N.Y. Ledger* and *The Saturday Evening Post* to half a million readers.

Women writers of the second half of the nineteenth century are generally seen as belonging to two large groups. The earlier writers, including Alcott, Stowe, Warner, and Rebecca Harding Davis, are identified with the tradition of sentimental romance and the cult of "true womanhood." The later writers, including Mary Wilkins Freeman, Sarah Orne Jewett, Elizabeth Stuart Phelps, Grace King, and Kate Chopin, are classified as regional realists or local color writers. Though the regionalists received more critical respect than the sentimentalists, both were considered to be writers of "popular" rather than "serious" literature; until recently, women's literature by virtue of the gender of its authors was considered less "artistic" and less "universal" than its male counterpart. Feminist scholarship still identifies domestic and regional novels as women's genres, but these are now interpreted more positively as forms which allowed women to describe worlds they knew well and to express their own moral sense of women's condition. Rather than devaluing the narrowness of such genres, modern critics acknowledge that nineteenth century women could not write about epic adventures, given the severely restricted lives they were forced to live, and that they should be admired for daring to pick up their pens in a world that often ridiculed the lives and works of women authors.

Despite the enormous popularity of these writers in their own time, much of their work was lost or simply forgotten in the first sixty years of the twentieth century. The work of recovery on the part of feminist critics since the 1970's has resulted in reissued editions of the novels of many nineteenth century writers. If one can talk about a female cultural industry in the second half of the nineteenth century, one can also identify a related academic industry which has emerged one hundred years later. Articles about lesser known nineteenth century women writers now appear regularly in feminist journals, such as *Women's Studies* and *Signs,* and in literary journals, such as *American Literature, American Transcendental Quarterly,* and *Studies in American Fiction.* Of special interest is *Legacy: A Journal of American Women Writers,* first published in 1984, which includes in each issue the text of two "lost" stories and profiles of their writers. Though the work of recovery continues, scholars in the 1990's have several new projects. Some consider women's texts as products of a particular cultural moment and use them as historical documents to explore the lives, personal experiences, and beliefs of both writers and readers. Others look at what the novels are trying to accomplish, to explain their popularity with readers, and to evaluate them on their own terms rather than against male norms. Still others try to establish new criteria for judging artistic merit and to look at characters, plots, themes, and imagery as defining a particular female counter-tradition. The shared aim of all of these approaches is nothing less than a redefinition of what constitutes American literature.

Given the dominance of women in the late nineteenth century publishing industry and the relative absence of women in anthologies of nineteenth century American writers, it is not surprising that feminist scholars have dedicated so much attention to this critical period in women's literary history. This chapter cannot begin to cover all the writers whose work has been recovered and reevaluated in the last twenty years. For example, Rose Terry Cooke, who has been identified as one of the leaders of the New England regionalists, and Elizabeth Barstow Stoddard, whose idiosyncratic style earned her praise from critics but did not result in many sales, are both frequently referenced but had (as of 1996) fewer studies devoted to their work alone than the other writers included here. Moreover, Maria Cummins and E. D. E. N. Southworth, though as popular as Susan Warner, have received less critical attention, perhaps because *The Wide, Wide World* was identified as the "first" best-seller. More attention has been paid to New England writers in general than to writers from other regions, partly because New England was the center of nineteenth century intellectual life, and partly because the numbers of New England writers encourage the study of relationships and influences.

Please note that chapters 1 and 2 separate the twentieth century writers from their nineteenth century predecessors. Though several of the general studies annotated below cover writers referenced in both this chapter and the next, the majority of these studies are limited to the nineteenth century since in itself it has provided such a wealth of material for literary historians and feminist critics. Those few general studies which refer only to twentieth century writers are included in chapter 2. Because scholarship on women writers of fiction makes a clear distinction between two traditions—one white, one black—African American novelists are covered in chapter 5. Both writing and reading in the late nineteenth and early twentieth centuries was, of course, a middle-class phenomenon. Literacy rates were still low for new immigrants, and few working-class Americans had the leisure or the inclination to read for pleasure. Still, there is an ongoing concern to identify non-mainstream writers who may have had a readership in their lifetimes (see, for example, the reference to the Native American writer Zitkala-Sa under Wexler below). I have included the Jewish writer Anzia Yezierska in chapter 2, and a study of Asian American and Latina writers in chapter 6. Also note that I have included Charlotte Perkins Gilman and Fanny Fern in the chapter on intellectuals, journalists, and reformers, though both were also well-known as novelists; and I have included Helen Hunt Jackson here because she is best known for her novel, *Ramona*, though she qualifies as both a reformer and a poet as well.

GENERAL STUDIES
Baym, Nina *Woman's Fiction: A Guide to Novels by and about Women in America, 1820-1870.* Ithaca, N.Y.: Cornell University Press, 1978, 2nd ed. 1993.

Baym looks at the plots of more than 100 novels by women that tell the story of a heroine who is forced to rely on her own intelligence and resourcefulness to find her way in the world. Though some writers tried to fit other concerns, such as abolition, into this plot, the most successful stuck close to the formula. Baym sees Harriet Beecher Stowe as a special case in that her women are not personally threatened and she is asking them to deal with institutions beyond the family. By the late 1860's women's fiction, as Baym defines it, had run its course and serious writers were looking for new forms. Though more esthetically sophisticated, post-Civil War literature by women was also less socially progressive and optimistic than that of the earlier generation.

Brodhead, Richard H. "Regionalism and the Upper Class," in *Rethinking Class: Literary Studies and Social Formations*, eds. Wai Chee Dimock and Michael T. Gilmore. New York: Columbia University Press, 1994.

Brodhead is interested in the historical reasons for regionalism's popularity and its role as a "career vehicle" for countless writers who would not have had access to publication in previous generations. Regional fiction, because of its conventional formulas and straightforward style, made it possible for "untrained" writers, including women and African Americans, to publish their first stories. Public demand for regional literature derived from an imagined nostalgia for old-fashioned traditions in a country becoming increasingly industrialized, urban, and national. The upper classes, in particular, with their new leisure developed an "elite need" for what they perceived as the "primitive"; regional stories were often printed next to advertisements for rustic vacation spots in popular journals. Regionalism thus made it possible for writers "from nowhere" to achieve "high cultural status" writing for readers who wanted to "purchase" stories about the lives of the marginal and lower class.

Carpenter, Lynette, and Wendy K. Kolmar. *Haunting the House of Fiction: Feminist Perspectives on Ghost Stories by American Women.* Knoxville: University of Tennessee Press, 1991.

In their introduction, the editors review the history of the ghost story in England and America, focusing on the ways in which women writers have "reconceived the genre" and on the particular influence of Ann Radcliffe's gothic novels and Charlotte Brontë's *Jane Eyre*. Men's ghost stories are based on a dualistic perception of the world with scientific rationality seen in opposition to Christian faith. Women's ghost stories portray the rational and the irrational, the natural and the supernatural, along a continuum of experience, and they view "sympathy" rather than reason as the key human interpretive faculty. Women's ghost stories are about young girls and wives victimized by violence in their own houses; they are filled with images of captivity and freedom. The text contains twelve essays on American women writers of ghost stories from the nineteenth and twentieth centuries, including Jewett, Freeman, Gilman, Wharton, and Glasgow, as well as a bibliography and examples of illustrations from the original stories.

Donovan, Josephine. *New England Local Color Literature: A Women's Tradition*. New York: Frederick Ungar, 1983.

Donovan identifies a "school of writers" which includes Harriet

Beecher Stowe, Rose Terry Cooke, Elizabeth Stuart Phelps, Sarah Orne Jewett, and Mary E. Wilkins Freeman. These writers, aided by the rise of regional literature that encouraged them to focus on the worlds they knew best, created a "women's literary realism" in opposition to the sentimental romances of previous generations. Donovan includes a biographical essay on each of the five that focuses on her major contribution to this new "school" of writing and her influence on the others. She also describes the role of Annie Adams Fields, Jewett's domestic partner and a key figure in Boston publishing circles, whose network of writers helped bring these women in touch with each other. The Jewett and Freeman chapters are annotated below.

_____. "Women and the Rise of the Novel: A Feminist Marxist Theory." *Signs* 16, no. 3 (Spring 1991): 441-462.

Donovan believes that upper middle-class women turned to novel writing because of their "economic displacement" with the rise of capitalism in the eighteenth century. Novel writing was accessible to women because it did not require extensive classical training; moreover, the novel was close to non-literary forms such as letters, diaries, and family biographies in which women had some practice. It was an easy transition from useful domestic work with an artistic value such as knitting, baking, or quilting, to the writing of fiction. Women brought to the novel an ironic point of view derived from their position outside the capitalist exchange system and their own roles as commodities in the marriage market. They also brought to the novel a "use-value ethos" that recognized the emotional importance of human activities in contrast to the dominant "exchange value ethos" that saw even human relationships in terms of quantity rather than quality.

Douglas, Ann. *The Femininization of American Culture.* New York: Knopf, 1977.

Douglas dates the beginning of American mass culture with the public embrace of Stowe's Little Eva as an "infantile heroine." She sees the rise of sentimentalism and nostalgia as the unfortunate result of nineteenth century ministers and women writers attempting to promote "matriarchal values" in opposition to the repressive dogmatism of Calvinism. Women, as the majority of church-goers and readers and as the prime consumers, began to dominate culture at the same time as American Protestant churches began to care more about "attendance" than "adherence." Together they created an anti-intellectual environment which defeated the more formal "humanistic, historically-minded romanticism" represented by Herman Melville and Margaret Fuller.

Fetterly, Judith, and Marjorie Pryse. *American Women Regionalists, 1850-1910: A Norton Anthology.* New York: W. W. Norton, 1992.

This is a collection of stories and excerpts from novels by fourteen writers, including Stowe, Jewett, Freeman, Chopin, and King, as well as Alice Dunbar-Nelson, Sui Sin Far, and Zitkala-Sa.

Harris, Susan K. "'But is it any good?': Evaluating Nineteenth Century American Women's Fiction." *American Literature* 63, no. 1 (March 1991): 43-61.

Given new interest in nineteenth century women's novels that had earlier been dismissed by the critical establishment, Harris argues the need for establishing new criteria to discriminate among them. These criteria should encompass three levels: the contextual to consider the works within their own time, the rhetorical to analyze use of language and narrative technique, and the retrospective to identify the work's significance in terms of literary history. For example, critics might question an author's degree of political awareness and the artistic choices she makes in expressing her views, or they might evaluate a text's "rereading" of earlier works and its role as a precursor of later works. Harris elaborates on these criteria through application to works by Stowe, Fern, Stoddard, Warner, and Southworth.

_____. *Nineteenth Century Women's Novels: Interpretive Strategies.* Cambridge, England: Cambridge University Press, 1990.

This collection of eight essays includes discussions of Alcott, Chopin, Fern, Jewett, Phelps, Stoddard, Warner, and Willa Cather, a few of which are annotated here. The focus throughout is the relationship between "cover stories" based on cultural conventions and "subtexts" whose subversive messages emerge despite ambiguous narrative voices. Harris's introduction looks at diaries and letters for evidence of the way nineteenth century female readers understood the subtexts of the novels they read and their particular interest in models of outstanding women. The introduction also provides an overview of major twentieth century studies of nineteenth century American writers which may have interpreted women's novels very differently than their original readers did.

Hovet, Grace Ann, and Theodore R. Hovet. "*Tableaux Vivants*: Masculine Vision and Female Reflection in Novels by Warner, Alcott, Stowe, and Wharton." *American Transcendental Quarterly* 7, no. 4 (December 1993): 335-356.

The authors begin by explaining how the Emersonian rhetoric of vision empowers the male gaze and how his concept of female transparency then "effaces" the feminine so that it may reveal a higher masculine reality. If the male gaze is "blocked" by a sexual desire to possess its object, the perceiver is considered to be suffering from a perceptual disorder and the "opaque blocking object" is itself labeled "a tramp." The Hovets analyze key scenes in novels by Warner, Alcott, Stowe, and Wharton in which their protagonists are compared to works of art (Madonna or Madame Recamier, for example) and attempt to protect themselves from "erasing or accusatory gazes." These scenes demonstrate how aware these writers were of the psychological effects of the "male gaze" on women. Moreover, *My Wife and I* (1871) by Stowe and *Little Women* (1868) by Alcott assert that an "honest disclosure" of how men have constructed images of women can disrupt the "rhetoric of vision" in ways that are liberating for both male and female.

Huf, Linda. *A Portrait of the Artist as a Young Woman: The Writer as Heroine in American Literature.* New York: Frederick Ungar, 1983.
Huf notes that few novels by women celebrate their struggles to become writers, perhaps because artists display the unfeminine traits of ambition and self-love. When women do create artist heroes, they are generally "stalwart, spirited, and fearless," unlike their male counterparts, who are "passive, sensitive, and shy." Female artist heroes must choose between their sexuality and their profession; male artist heroes between their spiritual aspirations and immersion in daily life. Male artist heroes idealize women as muses; female artist heroes often have men who stand in their way. Moreover, in the woman's *Kunstlerroman* images of entrapment abound, with the artist's failure to escape her double bind symbolized by birds falling and planes crashing, unlike the successful flights to escape of their male counterparts. Among the works that Huf considers to demonstrate the characteristics of this genre are *Ruth Hall* (1855) by Fanny Fern, *The Story of Avis* (1877) by Elizabeth Stuart Phelps, *The Awakening* (1899) by Kate Chopin, and *The Song of the Lark* (1915) by Willa Cather.

Jones, Anne Goodwyn. *Tomorrow Is Another Day: The Woman Writer in the South, 1859-1936.* Baton Rouge: Louisiana State University Press, 1981.
Jones provides a history of the "ideal of southern womanhood" and the ways in which it informed the lives and fiction of upper middle-class white women into the twentieth century. Beginning with the development of a slave-owning planter class in the seventeenth century and continuing well after the Civil War, the purity and vulnerability of southern women was used to justify slavery and the southern way of life. Despite the fact that no part of the image conformed to the reality of their lives, most women accepted their appointed roles as arbiters of public morality and kept on a "mask" of dependency, submissiveness, and sexual inaccessibility in deference to white male supremacy. Jones looks at the work of seven writers—Augusta Evans, Grace King, Kate Chopin, Mary Johnson, Ellen Glasgow, Frances Newman, and Margaret Mitchell—to see how these women wrestled both privately and publicly with the internal ambiguities and contradictions they experienced as southern ladies.

Kelley, Mary. *Private Woman, Public Stage: Literary Domesticity in Nineteenth Century America.* New York: Oxford University Press, 1984.
Kelley examines the lives and writings, both published prose and private diaries, of twelve women, including Fanny Fern, Harriet Beecher Stowe, and Susan Warner, who were raised to lead traditional lives, yet

found themselves thrust on a public stage as authors of best-selling novels. Most of these women responded to their new status with frustration and ambivalence. Domesticity was the central reality of their lives; though they may have yearned to extend the spheres in which they lived, they were held back by deep inner restraints. They devalued their own roles as professional writers and rationalized their work as "doing good" for the larger human family. Kelley sees their history as both unique and representative of nineteenth century women who searched for ways to lead lives of significance. Her text is divided into three major divisions. The first looks at the development of a "substantial literary marketplace" which made possible the extraordinary popularity of these writers. The second analyzes the personal circumstances that led these women to write and their failed attempts to maintain anonymity. The third considers their responses to the larger feminist issues of their time.

Lang, Amy Schrager. "Class and the Strategies of Sympathy," in *The Culture of Sentiment: Race, Gender, and Sentimentality in Nineteenth Century America*, ed. Shirley Samuels. New York: Oxford University Press, 1992.

Lang argues that the American response to class divisions, unlike the European revolutions of 1848, was increasingly to promote and embrace images of harmony as symbolized by the idealized middle-class home. The harmony to be found inside the home was based not on economic conditions, but on the divine differentiation of the sexes. Lang looks to domestic fiction for evidence of the ways in which such harmony was promoted with Maria Cummins's 1854 best-seller *The Lamplighter* as her model. She then compares Harriet Beecher Stowe's *Uncle Tom's Cabin* (1852) and Rebecca Harding Davis's *Life in the Iron Mills* (1861) as works which "diverge" from this model because of their concern with the plight of a group of people whose enslavement prohibits upward mobility.

See additional annotation under Rebecca Harding Davis.

Romines, Ann. *The Home Plot: Women, Writing & Domestic Ritual*. Amherst: University of Massachusetts Press, 1992.

Romines defines the "home plot" as a "complex of narrative strategies" which, in contrast to the traditional male plot, emphasizes continuity over dramatic climax and life-preserving community values over individual achievement. She argues that "domestic ritual" became particularly significant for women writers following the Civil War during a period of "oppressively separate spheres." While earlier sentimental novels by women were plotted similarly to novels by men, by the 1870's women were turning the rhythms of domestic life into the central focus of very different kinds of fictions. Romines examines the work of five writers—Harriet Beecher Stowe, Sarah Orne Jewett, Mary Wilkins Freeman, Willa Cather, and Eudora Welty—who both achieved canonical status and produced a substantial body of domestic fiction, and whose work raises important questions about the meaning of women's lives.

Tompkins, Jane. *Sensational Designs: The Cultural Work of American Fiction, 1790-1860.* New York: Oxford University Press, 1985.

Tompkins hopes to "loosen the hold" that a small group of master texts has had on American literary criticism by revealing the "historical contingencies" that contributed to their canonization and by bringing to light the merits of other texts that have been forgotten or devalued. In particular, she focuses on the novels of Harriet Beecher Stowe and Susan Warner as well as on the work of Charles Brockden Brown and James Fenimore Cooper, all writers who wrote to influence large numbers of readers rather than to impress literary critics. Tompkins proposes a new kind of historical criticism which will help modern readers understand the original impact of such writers through consideration of the "religious beliefs, social practices, and economic and political circumstances" which informed their work. She also argues that we should value literature which does real "cultural work" by "providing society with a means of thinking about itself," rather than speaking solely to a cultural elite.

See additional annotation under Harriet Beecher Stowe.

Toth, Susan Allen. "'The Rarest and Most Peculiar Grape': Versions of the New England Woman in Nineteenth Century Local Color Literature," in *Regionalism and the Female Imagination*, ed. Emily Toth. New York: Human Sciences Press, 1985.

Toth looks at the diverse representations of the American "new woman" which began to appear in popular magazines in 1865 with special attention to the contributions of New England writers Harriet Beecher Stowe, Rose Terry Cooke, Mary E. Wilkins Freeman, Sarah Orne Jewett, and Alice Brown. During this period New England still dominated American intellectual life and the New England woman was thought to be especially strong in will and body, as well as rather eccentric. Toth's writers provided an array of characters: community leaders, shy spinsters, widows who reject a second marriage, wives who endure unhappy relationships, women who cling to their mothers, most of whom anticipate the independent and aggressive "new women" of twentieth century-fiction.

Warren, Joyce W., ed. *The (Other) American Tradition: Nineteenth Century Women Writers.* New Brunswick, N.J.: Rutgers University Press, 1993.

This collection of both new and reprinted essays contains discussions of individual writers, including Fanny Fern, Harriet Jacobs, Harriet Beecher Stowe, and Harriet Wilson; groups of writers, including Jewish women writers and northern African American antebellum writers; and unusual topics such as the literature of philanthropy.

Westbrook, Perry D. *A Literary History of New England.* London: Associated University Presses, 1988.

This encyclopedic text contains brief biographical sketches of dozens of New England authors and analysis of their most regional works. It includes chapters on Emily Dickinson, Harriet Beecher Stowe, Louisa May Alcott, Elizabeth Stuart Phelps, and Edith Wharton, as well as a grouping of six regionalists, including Rose Terry Cooke, Mary E. Wilkins Freeman, and Sarah Orne Jewett. Westbrook notes that Stowe, Alcott, and Phelps all wrote about New England villages and small towns in rather idyllic terms as compared to the more realistic depictions of economic, social, and moral decline in the works of Freeman, Jewett, and Cooke.

Wexler, Laura. "Tender Violence: Literary Eavesdropping, Domestic Fiction, and Educational Reform," in *The Culture of Sentiment: Race, Gender, and Sentimentality in Nineteenth Century America,* ed. Shirley Samuels. New York: Oxford University Press, 1992.

This essay begins by summarizing the Douglas-Tompkins debate over the literary value of American domestic fiction (see annotations above). According to Wexler, Tompkins highlights "sentimental power" as an alternative to patriarchal Calvinism; Douglas sees it as "destructive" to intellectual rigor and as the precursor to a debased American mass culture. Despite their disagreement, both speak with mildly ironic and well-educated middle-class voices; neither notes the consequences of sentimental pietism for people outside the American mainstream. To demonstrate the disabling impact of this ideology, Wexler looks at the case of Zitkala-Sa (Gertrude Bonnin), a Dakota Sioux, whose mother was persuaded to send her eight-year-old daughter far away from home to a missionary school where she was educated according to the tenets of middle-class domesticity. After writing one of the first personal narratives by a Native American, Zitkala-Sa was embraced and feted by white women. Suddenly, after three years of playing the role of white women's pet Indian, she married a Dakota Sioux, moved back to her reservation and became an activist lobbying in Washington, D.C. for the rights of her people.

LOUISA MAY ALCOTT
1832-1888

Born in Germantown, Pennsylvania, Alcott, the second of four sisters, was raised in Concord and later lived in Boston, Massachusetts. Her father, Bronson Alcott, a transcendentalist philosopher and educator, was a close friend of Ralph Waldo Emerson and Henry David Thoreau, who were important presences in Louisa's life. Bronson's idealistic activities, such as the creation of a utopian community called "Fruitlands," combined with his own inability to earn a living, left the family on the edge of poverty. Following the influence of her strong, self-sacrificing mother, Louisa spent almost all of her adult life providing emotional and financial support to her family. Several years after the publication of several gothic thrillers written under the pseudonym A. M. Bernard, a collection of *Hospital Sketches* (1863) based on her brief experience as a nurse during the Civil War, and a first novel entitled *Moods* (1865), Alcott was persuaded by her father and publisher to write a cheery book for girls. The phenomenal success of *Little Women* (1868) and its several sequels, including *Little Men* (1871) and *Jo's Boys* (1886), helped lift the family out of their financial straits. In addition to her prolific writings, Alcott held a variety of jobs during her life, from seamstress to lady's companion, which she described in her novel *Work* (1873) and in several other volumes. Alcott continued to care for her father and for an orphaned niece years after the death of her mother. She and her father grew old and ill together with her death following his a mere two days later.

Reissued Editions

The Alternative Alcott, ed. Elaine Showalter. New Brunswick, N.J.: Rutgers University Press, 1988.

The Best of Louisa May Alcott. New York: Outlet Book Company, 1994.

Freaks of Genius: The Unknown Thrillers of Louisa May Alcott, eds. Daniel Shealy and Madeleine B. Stern. Knoxville: University of Tennessee Press, 1992. This is the fourth collection of Alcott's thrillers to be reissued; *Behind a Mask* (1975), *Plots and Counterplots* (1976), and *A Double Life* (1988) are also available.

Hospital Sketches. New York: Garland Publishers, 1984.

The Journals of Louisa May Alcott, eds. Joel Myerson and Daniel Shealy. Boston: Little, Brown, 1989.

Little Women, Good Wives, Little Men. New York: Octopus Books, 1978.

A Long Fatal Love Chase. New York: Random House, 1995.

Louisa May Alcott's Fairy Stories and Fantasy Stories, ed. Daniel Shealy. Knoxville: University of Tennessee Press, 1992.

Louisa May Alcott: Selected Fiction, eds. Daniel Shealy, Madeleine B. Stern, and Joel Myerson. Boston: Little, Brown, 1990.

A Modern Mephistopheles and Taming a Tartar, ed. Madeleine B. Stern. New York: Praeger Publishers, 1987.

Moods. New Brunswick, N.J.: Rutgers University Press, 1991.

The Selected Letters of Louisa May Alcott, eds. Joel Myerson and Daniel Shealy. Boston: Little, Brown, 1987.

Transcendental Wild Oats and Excerpts from the Fruitlands Diary, ed. William Henry Harrison. Cambridge: Harvard Common Press, 1981.

Work: A Story of Experience. New York: Schocken, 1977.

Biography and Commentary
Note: In addition to the book-length studies and journal articles annotated below, there are often discussions of Alcott's work in such children's journals as *The Lion and the Unicorn*.

Auerbach, Nina. "*Little Women* and *Pride and Prejudice*," in *Communities of Women: An Idea in Fiction*. Cambridge: Harvard University Press, 1978.
     Auerbach believes that Alcott's work, unlike Jane Austen's, depicts a world without men as complete and self-sufficient; her circle of women is a harmonious and well-balanced one. Laurie in *Little Women*, who plays a similar role to Bingley in *Pride and Prejudice*, envies the March family harmony rather than contributing to it. Despite pressure from her publisher, Alcott refused to marry Jo to Laurie. Auerbach suggests that she would have liked to end the novel with Beth surviving "to preside over a self-sustaining sisterhood."

Bassill, Veronica. "The Artist at Home: The Domestication of Louisa May Alcott." *Studies in American Fiction* 15, no. 2 (Autumn 1987): 187-197.
     Bassill sees both Jo March and the protagonist of the Alcott story, "Psyche's Art," as women torn between the desire to create and the desire to serve. Both works reflect Alcott's deep-seated ambivalence about her own stature as an artist and her father's success at linking love and self-sacrifice in his daughter's mind. Though these works depict fathers as comforting but subordinate figures, Alcott's gothic thrillers portray evil older men who threaten orphans. Her fiction viewed as a whole then both upholds and subverts Bronson Alcott's teaching.

Bernstein, Susan Naomi. "Writing and *Little Women*: Alcott's Rhetoric of Subversion." *American Transcendental Quarterly* 7, no. 1 (March 1993): 25-43.
     Bernstein examines the role of writing in *Little Women* as a metaphor for the novel's apparent contradictions. Jo's writing is connected with her desire both for independence and to be of service to her family; it derives from a mix of sentimentality and feminism; and it is an expression of uncontrollable passion as well as a vehicle for channeling her energies. Jo's poems, in particular, demonstrate how the

physical act of writing can free the inner life from the bonds of the conscious self.

Chapman, Mary. "Gender and Influence in Louisa May Alcott's *A Modern Mephistopheles.*" *Legacy* 13, no. 1 (1996): 19-37.
  Alcott's repeated comparisons of women and works of art in her juvenile fiction take on a "sinister aspect" in her gothic thrillers, according to Chapman. The complex plot of this novel exposes the way women artists can be misled into believing they have real power when, in fact, they have been reduced to "objets d'art" in bondage to the male gaze. The androgynous model of artistry then offers the only hope for women to become subjects rather than objects.

Dalke, Anne. "'The House Band': The Education of Men in *Little Women.*" *College English* 47, no. 6 (October 1985): 571-578.
  Dalke criticizes Auerbach's reading of the novel for focusing only on the first half in order to make its point. Dalke argues that there are two journeys in *Little Women*, the first leading to individual development, the second to recognition of communal values and the significance of relationships. It is during this second journey that the novel's fathers, husbands, and sons are taught to value nurturance and families. This subplot becomes the main story in both *Little Men* and *Jo's Boys*.

Douglas, Ann. "Mysteries of Louisa May Alcott." *New York Review of Books* 25 (September 28, 1978): 60-63.
  Douglas sees Martha Saxton's "dark" biography of Alcott as a "major step" in the necessary reappraisal of Alcott's life and work. Douglas herself points out additional contradictions: Alcott's support for women's rights versus her life of self-sacrifice, her "cheery" children's books versus her "melodramatic' stories of "deception and discovery." She also sees Bronson Alcott as a more positive figure than Saxton describes—not just the irresponsible, self-indulgent eccentric, but a true "prophet" who managed to be at peace with himself and for whom recognition and success as a writer finally came in the last decades of his life. Louisa drew upon both her father's serenity and her mother's passion. However, the extremes never really came together for Alcott or her characters, whose lives change drastically as if by metamorphosis rather than by real development or growth.

Elbert, Sarah. *A Hunger for Home: Louisa May Alcott and Little Women.* Philadelphia: Temple University Press, 1984.
  This critical biography focuses on the relationship between Alcott's family life and her work. Elbert sees Alcott as a product of the nineteenth century reform tradition and a key contributor to the debate over the proper role of women.

Fetterly, Judith. "*Little Women*: Alcott's Civil War." *Feminist Studies* 5 (Summer 1979): 369-370, 381-383.

Fetterly believes Alcott's thrillers provide an important context for understanding the subversive anger and political messages in *Little Women*. According to Fetterly, Alcott was herself ambivalent about Jo's marriage to Professor Bhaer, which was clearly a betrayal of her own preference to remain an independent, economically self-sufficient single woman.

MacDonald, Ruth K. *Louisa May Alcott*. Boston: Twayne Publishers, 1983.

MacDonald offers a thorough review of Alcott's life and work, including her gothic short stories, the March family stories, five less well-known juvenile novels, and her so-called adult fictions. For each work, MacDonald provides a brief synopsis, identifies its significance within the total oeuvre, and comments on critical reception. She concludes that Alcott's adult novels are "remarkably good" in terms of character development and that they explore in greater depth than the juvenile works contemporary social issues, including unhappy marriages and women's education. Despite reliance on conventional happy endings, Alcott's work succeeds in expressing sincere optimism rather than clichéd sentimentalism.

Marsella, Joy A. *The Promise of Destiny: Children and Women in the Short Stories of Louisa May Alcott*. Westport, Conn.: Greenwood Press, 1983.

Marsella summarizes and analyzes the sixty stories published in five volumes of Alcott's "Scrap Bag" series. She sees the stories as typical of nineteenth century domestic fiction, narrated by a warm, loving maiden aunt who teaches the basic values of "labor, love and hope." Marsella also looks to these stories for evidence of Alcott's attitudes about "domestic culture" and the ongoing debate about public and private roles for women.

Moers, Ellen. "Money, Jobs, Little Women: Female Realism," in *Literary Women*. New York: Doubleday, 1976.

Alcott's novel, *Work: A Story of Experience*, offers a surprisingly modern tribute to women's solidarity and the significance of real work. Its message is that menial and humble work should be "shouldered manfully—by women, little and big." This is a very different message, argues Moers, from the one Mark Twain would present to young boys a decade later in *Tom Sawyer*.

Murphy, Ann B. "The Borders of Ethical, Erotic, and Artistic Possibilities in *Little Women*." *Signs* 15, no. 3 (Spring 1990): 562-585.

Murphy reviews twenty years of scholarship on Alcott to demonstrate *Little Women*'s continuing fascination for feminist critics. She herself sees the novel's power as resulting from its truthful exposition of the contradictions inherent in female experience. The book is "memorable" for young girls because it warns of the "enforced silencing of voice, eroticism, and anger" for those who quest for independence and artistic achievement. Jo's refusal of Laurie, her most important act of assertion, though a rejection of her society's romantic fictions, results in her later entrapment in an even more confining fiction, marriage to a "nonerotic father-figure and tutor."

Saxton, Martha. *Louisa May: A Modern Biography of Louisa May Alcott.* Boston: Houghton Mifflin, 1977.
  Saxton's biography opens with a grim portrait of a thirty-five-year old Louisa, her thin hair grayed by disease. This sets the tone for Saxton's account of an existence based on self-sacrifice. Saxton provides background on the childhoods and young adult lives of both of Alcott's parents before focusing on their unhappy marriage. She blames the father, in particular, for Louisa's self-disgust and sense of her own worthlessness. *Little Women*, the book Louisa wrote to please her father, represents a regression from earlier, more fanciful works and the first of her attempts to recreate her past as it should have been in her parents' sentimental view of the world. In the end, Louisa made her peace with her father, dying two days after his death. It was a lonely existence but an active one; despite self-doubt, Alcott never quit writing.

Showalter, Elaine. "*Little Women*: The American Female Myth," in *Sister's Choice: Tradition and Change in American Women's Writing.* Oxford: Clarendon Press, 1991.
  Showalter discusses *Little Women's* impact on several generations of readers from Simone de Beauvoir to the female governors of Alabama and Nebraska. She sees Jo, in particular, as a "cherished sister," a role model, not of "unattainable genius," but of independence with the freedom to make choices about her own life. The novel has endured, she argues, because of its "memorably American and personal voice." Feminist critics writing at the end of the twentieth century have found Alcott and her work a fertile field to examine "the relationship between patriarchal culture and women's culture" and to consider issues of canonization and female literary identity. Showalter builds on the insights of these critics in reviewing Alcott's life and career.

Sicherman, Barbara. "Reading *Little Women*: The Many Lives of a Text," in *U.S. History as Women's History: New Feminist Essays*, eds. Linda K Kerber, Alice Kessler-Harris, and Kathryn Kish Sklar. Chapel Hill: University of North Carolina Press, 1995.
  Sicherman uses the novel to get at the relationship between reading and female identity for adolescent girls of "diverse class, culture, and historical era." For example, in the early twentieth century white middle-class girls identified with Jo's quest for personal autonomy, while Jewish immigrant readers saw the portrait of family life as a model for assimilation. Sicherman quotes Charlotte Perkins Gilman, Ida

B. Wells, Simone de Beauvoir, and other less well-known readers to demonstrate the novel's consistent appeal over time. She also provides a history of Alcott's rising celebrity and establishes her importance as a role model for young women seeking literary careers. Ultimately, *Little Women* has survived because it is an "open" text with "multiple reference points and voices" and because of its continuing relevance to the lives of its millions of readers.

Stern, Madeleine B. *Critical Essays on Louisa May Alcott.* Boston: G.K. Hall, 1984.

Stern has collected dozens of contemporaneous reviews of Alcott's work plus critical essays dating from 1889 to 1994; several of the latest essays were written expressly for Stern's book. In her introduction, Stern traces Alcott's critical reception from her first review in 1854 for *Flower Fables,* a book of fairy tales, to the feminist reappraisals of the 1970's and 1980's. The *Little Women* centennial in 1968 resulted in a "floodgate" of criticism; moreover, each decade since her death has produced its own biographies and critiques. Stern lists many of these and the various bibliographies which followed.

_____. "Introduction," in *Behind a Mask: The Unknown Thrillers of Louisa May Alcott.* New York: Morrow, 1975.

Stern describes the detective work involved in discovering Alcott's thrillers and briefly analyzes the four narratives included in the anthology. She also focuses on several aspects of Alcott's life—for example, her brief but humiliating experience as a servant to a Dedham lawyer, which helped provide fuel for her frightening tales. Stern concludes that Alcott wrote thrillers out of both financial and psychological necessity.

Strickland, Charles.*Victorian Domesticity: Families in the Life and Art of Louisa May Alcott.* Tuscaloosa: University of Alabama Press, 1985.

Strickland discusses Alcott's life and literature in the context of Victorian values and sentimentality. The book begins with an analysis of how the "sentimental revolution" determined popular attitudes about family life and relationships between the family and the larger social world. It then traces Alcott's childhood and young womanhood, the impact of feminism on her sense of self and her characters, and the varieties of family life she depicts in her fiction. Despite her commitment to "moral uplift" and her own personal struggles, Alcott lacked understanding of the lower classes and the nature of poverty, according to Strickland. And though she transcended sentimentality in her portraits of male/female relationships, she wholeheartedly supported the cult of domesticity in her prescriptions for child nurture.

FRANCES HODGSON BURNETT
1849-1924

Burnett was born in Manchester, England. Following the death of her father, her mother and the five children moved to rural Tennessee where they lived with an uncle for three years before settling in Knoxville. By the age of twenty, Burnett was writing five or six stories a month to help support her siblings. In 1873 she married an eye doctor with whom she had two sons. Following her divorce from him in 1898 and increasing celebrity as a writer, she married a young actor whom she had met in London while working on stage productions of her stories; they divorced after seven years. Though best known today for her highly successful children's stories, Burnett began her writing career with love stories and novels about fashionable society. *Little Lord Fauntleroy* (1886), her first best-seller, was modeled on her son Vivian. It was followed by *A Little Princess* (1905) and *The Secret Garden* (1911); all three of these children's classics have been made into Hollywood films.

Reissued Editions
Note: There are dozens of new editions of *A Little Princess* and *The Secret Garden* as well as audio and video cassettes; there have also been at least four editions of *Little Lord Fauntleroy* since 1981. No more than two editions per book are listed below.

The Land of the Blue Flowers. Gearheart, Oreg.: Starseed Press, 1991.

Little Lord Fauntleroy. Boston: Godine, 1993; New York: Dell, 1986.

A Little Princess. New York: Puffin Books, 1994; New York: Random House, 1994.

The Lost Prince. New York: Puffin Books, 1986.

Racketty Packetty House. Westminster, Md.: Outlet Books, 1992.

The Secret Garden. New York: Puffin Books, 1994; New York: Scholastic, 1987.

Biography and Commentary
Bixler, Phyllis. *Frances Hodgson Burnett*. Boston: Twayne, 1984.
   Bixler offers a well-researched and thoughtful study of Burnett's life and work. She considers Burnett's adult fiction, her discussion of women's issues, her use of dialect, and her interest in the folktale, as well as her famous children's stories. Bixler sees the adult fiction as particularly useful in understanding the development of Burnett's art and her interest in certain political and social themes. She also sees her career as significant in the development of both the American and British female traditions.

Evans, Gwyneth. "The Girl in the Garden: Variations on a Feminine Pastoral." *Children's Literature Association Quarterly* 19, no. 1 (Spring 1994): 20-24.

Evans sees Burnett's secret garden as the model for other children's stories in which a "child is brought into a healing and restorative relationship with nature." In all of these stories the garden is secret and forbidden and more powerful than any of the characters.

Phillips, Jerry. "The Mem Sahib, the Worthy, the Rajah and His Minions: Some Reflections on the Class Politics of *The Secret Garden*." *The Lion and the Unicorn: A Critical Journal of Children's Literature* 17, no. 2 (December 1993):168-194.

Phillips sees *The Secret Garden* as "rich" in "ideological dissonance," and very clearly reflective of the decline of the British Empire. The use of the "child orphan," who is also a "migrant" and a "displaced person," highlights issues of social identity; the great country house is "a laboratory of class relations"; and the garden represents "dreams of social perfection." Moreover, the little Indian room is itself a "tribute to the British imperial spirit" with despotism defined as Oriental, rather than acknowledged as deriving from the arrogance of the colonial ego.

Plotz, Judith. "Secret Garden II; or *Lady Chatterly's Lover* as Palimpsest." *Children's Literature Association Quarterly* 19, no. 1 (Spring 1994): 15-19.

Despite the obvious differences between Lawrence's very adult work and Burnett's "safe" story for young girls, Plotz identifies several important affinities between them. Most obvious is the focus on "triangular relationships" in which a female character has to deal with two male figures, one upper-class, one lower-class. Both works also suggest that "life springs from a secret source" and both associate rebirth with the use of dialect and the sensuality of spring flowers. Plotz concludes that *The Secret Garden* was just the kind of fable Lawrence needed to help him get past his own preoccupation with death. And, though he probably knew of Burnett's story, it is not surprising that he would fail to acknowledge the influence of a powerful "matriarch."

Richardson, Alan. "Reluctant Lords and Lame Princes: Engendering the Male Child in Nineteenth century Juvenile Fiction." *Children's Literature* 21 (1993): 3-19.

Richardson uses Nancy Chodorow's theories on the gender conflicts young boys experience in developing a male identity to discuss two late nineteenth century children's classics—Dinah Maria Craik's *Little Lame Prince* and Frances Hodgson Burnett's *Little Lord Fauntleroy*. According to Richardson, the transatlantic Fauntleroy "cult" proves the significance of the "mama's boy" for Victorian readers. He believes such a "fantasy" may have softened the increasingly rigid masculine roles of the period, thus helping the child deal with his anxiety over separating from his mother.

KATE CHOPIN
1850-1904

Kate O'Flaherty, daughter of an upper-class French woman and an Irish merchant, was raised in St. Louis and educated to be a southern belle. After her graduation from Sacred Heart Academy, Kate married Oscar Chopin, moved to New Orleans, and gave birth to six children—five sons and a daughter—in their first ten years of marriage. Oscar died two years later. After moving back to St. Louis and following the death of her mother, Chopin decided to pursue a career as a writer to help support herself. Though her first novel, *At Fault* (1890), was published at her own expense, her stories were soon being accepted by major literary magazines. By 1894 she had published her first collection of short stories, *Bayou Folk*; this was followed by *A Night in Acadie* (1897) and *The Awakening* (1899), the novel which shocked the male critical establishment of her day and which became a feminist classic following its reissue in 1964 and in 1972. Chopin wrote little else after *The Awakening* and died a few years after its publication.

Reissued Editions
Note: There are frequent reprintings of *The Awakening* and of *The Awakening and Selected Stories* by Dover Press and Bantam Books, as well as of a Norton Critical Edition which includes scholarly essays and pieces on the novel's biographical and historical contexts. Also available are audiocassettes of the novel and of several Chopin stories, and the following books:

A Matter of Prejudice and Other Stories by Kate Chopin. New York: Bantam Books, 1992.

A Vocation and a Voice: Stories by Kate Chopin. New York: Penguin Books, 1991.

Biography and Criticism
Birnbaum, Michele A. "'Alien Hands': Kate Chopin and the Colonization of Race." *American Literature* 66, no. 2 (June 1994): 301-323.

Birnbaum looks at the role played by racial, ethnic, and lower-class "others" in the personal liberation of Edna Pontellier, the heroine of *The Awakening*. Though Edna and her husband seem to ignore the degree to which their servant, an unnamed quadroon, has actual responsibility for the care of their children, without her Edna's journey would be impossible. Moreover, Edna is attracted to the untrammeled sexuality she locates in women of color; in effect, Mariequita functions as Edna's alter ego and as a competitor for the love of men. Edna feels that she has been invaded by something "foreign," precisely because she accepts the exotic stereotypes of "other" women; it is no accident that her awakening begins in cottages that were once slave quarters. Readers may celebrate Edna's sexual liberation but should also be critical of her "imperial self," which can complain of too many servants while ignoring both her dependence on them and their own individuality and humanity.

Boren, Lynda S., and Sara deSaussure Davis, eds. *Kate Chopin Reconsidered: Beyond the Bayou.* Baton Rouge: Louisiana State University Press, 1992.
This collection includes a bibliography, three biographical studies, three discussions of Chopin's less well-known-known fiction, and eight analyses of various aspects of *The Awakening.* Several of these are adaptations of papers presented at the 1990 Kate Chopin International Conference and at the 1988 MLA convention in New Orleans.

Cutter, Martha. "Losing the Battle but Winning the War: Resistance to Patriarchal Discourse in Kate Chopin's Short Fiction." *Legacy* 11, no. 1 (1994): 17-36.
Cutter notes that most of Chopin's stories focus on "repression of the female voice" and the various ways women try to make themselves heard whether through a "voice of insubordination," through silence, through overt or covert resistance, or even through "mimicry of patriarchal language." Earlier stories emphasize the way women are punished or labeled as a result of attempting to speak out; later stories written from 1894 on depict women who are more aggressive and vocal yet still end up "effaced." These more daring works are the ones which have proved most lasting and which ensure that Chopin's voice, unlike those of her characters, will continue to be heard.

Dyer, Joyce. *The Awakening: A Novel of Beginnings.* New York: Macmillan, 1993.
This text, part of the *Twayne Masterworks* series, includes a chronology and annotated bibliography. Dyer analyzes the symbolism of the parrot and the background characters, and of the three key mythic scenes in which Edna appears as Diana/Artemis, Eve, and Venus/Aphrodite. Dyer also reviews the novel's critical history and various interpretations of the ending. She herself sees Edna's suicide as the only way she was able to dissolve attachment to her children and be "absolutely alone." Motherhood is the focus throughout the last chapters; it is "motherhood" which drives Edna into the sea.

Elfenbein, Anna Shannon. "Kate Chopin: From Stereotype to Sexual Realism," in *Women on the Color Line: Evolving Stereotypes and the Writings of George Washington Cable, Grace King, Kate Chopin.* Charlottesville: University Press of Virginia, 1989.
Elfenbein sees Chopin as a writer who raises important questions

about race and gender. Though Chopin does use racist imagery in conventional and stereotypic ways, she also demonstrates how women are victimized by stereotypes. Many of her stories, including "Desiree's Baby," "La Belle Zoraid," "At the 'Cadian Ball," and "The Storm," examine the "genteel stereotype of the tragic octoroon" and the ways in which it ultimately alienates women from each other. As a "sexual realist," Chopin understands the association of sexual freedom with "foreign, lower-class, or ethnically 'tainted' women." Edna Pontellier in *The Awakening* may be more self-aware than other Chopin protagonists but, because bound by sex, class, and race, is unable to empathize fully with the many different "types" of women who surround her.

Emmitt, Helen V. "'Drowned in a Willing Sea': Freedom and Drowning in Eliot, Chopin and Drabble." *Tulsa Studies in Women's Literature* 12, no. 2 (Fall 1993): 315-332.
    Emmitt begins with the pronouncement that "drowning in literature is gendered." Water represents "self-fulfillment for women," rather than the "narcissistic mirror" or "devouring female" it generally symbolizes for men. For Edna the sea is the perfect lover. Edna is unwilling to be an old maid or to define herself wholly in relation to her children. She has tried out both fantasy and social transgression only to discover that the men in her society cannot offer her what she needs. Her death is not a conscious suicide; she "drifts" into a "familiar unknown," her only means of escape from a world "in which she cannot see herself."

Gilbert, Sandra M. "The Second Coming of Aphrodite: Kate Chopin's Fantasy of Desire." *Kenyon Review* 5, no. 3 (Summer 1983): 42-66.
    Gilbert suggests a "mythic" reading as an alternative to the more common realistic ones. In such a reading *The Awakening* becomes a romantic fantasy about the metamorphosis of a wife and mother into a powerful goddess of love and art. The ending of the novel, which returns to the seaside where it began, might then be interpreted, not as a suicide, but as a resurrection. Gilbert places her admittedly hyperbolic analysis in the context of other versions of the Aphrodite/Venus story, comparing Chopin to Flaubert, Whitman, Dickinson, Baudelaire, Woolf, Cather, H. D., and others who have responded more or less sympathetically to the visionary freedom from the restraints of realism offered by serious identification with a powerful and erotic myth.

Jones, Suzanne W. "Place, Perception, and Identity in *The Awakening*." *The Southern Quarterly* 25, no. 2 (Winter 1987): 108-119.
    Jones analyzes Chopin's use of two very different settings, the city New Orleans and the Creole world of the island in the gulf, to get at her ambivalence about women's roles. For Edna, the island brings awareness of the relativity of manners and morals; there are repeated references to "sight" and to her new perceptions. The island experience seems to represent the rich development of Edna's inner life, though it creates problems in her social life. Edna needs relationships with other

people, unlike Mlle. Reisz, yet cannot escape being surrounded by hypocrites rather than kindred spirits. From the urban perspective, her island rebirth looks like a self-indulgent adolescent fantasy.

Keesey, Donald. *Contexts of Criticism.* Mountain View, Calif.: Mayfield, 1994.
This textbook for students of literature uses *The Awakening* as one of three case studies. It contains the full text of the novel as well as reprints of seven critical essays (1970-1990) chosen to represent diverse theoretical perspectives. The Gilbert, Stange, Walker, Wolff, and Yaeger articles annotated here are included.

Rowe, John Carlos. "The Economics of the Body in Kate Chopin's *The Awakening*," in *Perspectives on Kate Chopin, Proceedings from the Kate Chopin International Conference* (April 6, 7, 8, 1989). Natchitoches, La.: Northwestern State University Press, 1990.
Rowe offers a Marxist reading of the novel in which he interprets Edna's various awakenings and final swim as a search for the value of her own body apart from its significance as a "means of exchange." Unlike the romantics, Edna can experience her body only in its alienation from nature; she cannot see it in transcendental terms. Her passivity and exhaustion are typical of the alienated worker who despairs over the value of his labor; her erotic titillation in response to Robert and Alcee is not unlike the thrill of the investor who risks his own capital in highly speculative ventures.

Showalter, Elaine. "*The Awakening*: Tradition and the American Female Talent," in *Sister's Choice: Tradition and Change in American Women's Writing.* Oxford: Clarendon Press, 1991.
Showalter sees *The Awakening* as the product of a particular moment in American literary history when local colorists and New Women writers were beginning to be noticed and the legacy of the domestic novel was waning. Though the local colorists mythologized the disappearing women's culture, the New Women criticized it as "boring and restrictive." Chopin's work seems to mark the transition. Both Edna Pontellier and her author "oscillate" between traditional definitions of femininity and their desire to lead emancipated, independent lives.

Skaggs, Peggy. *Kate Chopin.* Boston: G. K. Hall, 1985.
This volume, part of *Twayne's United States Authors* series, includes a review of Chopin's life and critical reputation, a discussion of each of her major works, and a chronology and annotated bibliography. Skaggs concludes that in all of her work Chopin demonstrates that humans need three things: a place in the social order where they feel they belong, the love of other people, and a sense of individual sovereignty. As literature, her work was far ahead of its time and defies easy classification.

Stange, Margit. "Personal Property: Exchange Value and the Female Self." *Genders* 5 (July 1989): 106-119.

Stange interprets the novel in terms of economic theories of "conspicuous consumption" and the late nineteenth century reformist agenda for women's property rights, voluntary motherhood, and general self-ownership of one's own body. Edna's hands are particularly significant in that they are proof of her leisure-class status and, therefore, a demonstration of her husband's wealth. The ring she wears is an additional sign of her status as "surplus wealth" and of her role as wife, hence as her husband's property. Edna wants to have her own property and to have the freedom to give or withhold herself sexually as she wishes. In the end, she withholds herself from future motherhood by withholding herself from life itself, the most extreme prerogative of the self-ownership she craves.

Toth, Emily. *Kate Chopin*. New York: William Morrow, 1990.

This comprehensive biography includes a chronology, photographs, bibliographies of Chopin's published and unpublished works and secondary sources, and documentation with respect to the "alleged banning" of *The Awakening*. Toth quotes extensively from Chopin's diaries and her poems to support her portrait of the author as a somewhat unconventional woman whose lifestyle was always considered a bit scandalous by her peers. The biography covers Chopin's childhood with emphasis on the important influence of her grandmother, her education and the books she read, her relationships with men, including her husband and the man with whom she is assumed to have had a passionate adulterous affair, and the sources of key characters and events in her fiction. Toth concludes that Chopin, unlike her famous protagonist and most other women writers of her generation, was able to achieve a creative and autonomous existence without much external support and without sacrificing her female self.

Walker, Nancy. "Feminist or Naturalist: The Social Context of Kate Chopin's *The Awakening*." *The Southern Quarterly* 17, no. 2 (1979): 95-103.

Walker reads the novel as typical of naturalism in that Edna has little control over her destiny and seems unconcerned about the significance of her actions. Edna's "awakening" results from her exposure to a culture in which sensual pleasures—music, color, food, and sex—are valued openly, not because of feminist doctrines. It is the clash of Creole and Puritan cultures which ultimately determines her fate.

_____, ed. *Kate Chopin: The Awakening*. Boston: St. Martin's Press, 1993.

This volume is part of Bedford Books' Case Studies in Contemporary Criticism. It includes the full text of the novel, an introduction to Chopin's life and work, bibliographic information organized by critical perspective, and five essays, including the ones by Stange, Wolff, and Yaeger annotated here. There are also a glossary of literary terminology and brief explanations of the theories represented: psychoanalytic criticism, deconstructionism, new historicism, feminist criticism, and reader-response criticism.

Wolff, Cynthia Griffin. "Thanatos and Eros: Kate Chopin's *The Awakening.*" *American Quarterly* 25, no. 4 (1973): 449-471.

Wolff offers a detailed psychological analysis of Edna as a "schizoid personality" who is afraid of genuine emotional involvement. This psychological state is symbolized by the background figures of the lovers and the woman in black who has apparently withdrawn from all personal interaction. Though Edna attempts to internalize the contradictions she experienced as a middle child sandwiched between her two sisters—the vixen Janet and the matron Margaret—she does so in immature, sometimes infantile ways. Her "libidinal appetite" is fixated at the oral level as expressed by her desire for "limitless fusion with the external world." Unlike Mlle. Reisz, who can control and create, Edna is most comfortable as a "receptive vessel." She enjoys being caressed by Adele as if a little girl, and often seems preoccupied with eating and sleeping. Her suicide then, in Wolff's interpretation, is the ultimate regression; in her final thoughts she is a child once more.

Yaeger, Patricia S. "'A Language Which Nobody Understood': Emancipatory Strategies in *The Awakening.*" *Novel: A Forum on Fiction* 20, no. 3 (Spring 1987): 197-219.

Yaeger sees Edna as a woman in search of a language which will allow her to express her unspoken needs, not one controlled by the men in her life. For the most part, Edna can only think about herself in the subject/object terms her society has taught her. Her delightful conversations with Robert are liberating to some degree, but ultimately fanciful. Edna comes closest to true emancipation during "unstable" moments of self-questioning and dialogue with other women, which lead her into areas of the mind that are not well-mapped. In the end she is left stumbling for words, unable to answer Dr. Mandalet's questions and unable to accept his interpretation of how she feels.

REBECCA HARDING DAVIS
1831-1910

Davis was born to a prosperous family in Pennsylvania and raised in Virginia. The oldest of five children, she continued to live at home and to help with the education of her siblings after graduating from a female seminary. *Life in the Iron Mills*, her first novella, was accepted for publication by *The Atlantic Monthly* in 1861 and was soon followed by several dramatic stories about the Civil War and a longer work serialized in the *Atlantic* and later published in book form as *Margret Howth* (1862). These publications were the beginning of Davis's friendship with James T. Fields, the editor of the *Atlantic*, and his wife

Annie. Davis married a reader-admirer in 1863 and settled in Philadelphia. Though she continued to write and published several stories and novels, her life was increasingly dominated by arduous domestic duties and illness. Nonetheless, she managed to raise two sons and a daughter and to work as a contributing editor to the *New York Tribune* while her husband became more involved in abolitionist activities and his own position as editor of the *Philadelphia Public Ledger*.

Reissued Editions
Life in the Iron Mills and Other Stories. Old Westbury, N.Y.: Feminist Press, 1985.

Margret Howth: A Story of Today. New York: Feminist Press of City University of New York, 1990.

Biography and Commentary
Harris, Sharon M. *Rebecca Harding Davis and American Realism*. Philadelphia: University of Pennsylvania Press, 1991.

Harris looks at fifty texts, including novels, stories, and essays as well as correspondence, to demonstrate that Davis was a "materialist" committed to developing a "fiction of the commonplace" in order to expose harsh realities and to advocate for reform. Davis was not an "unconscious writer," but rather one with well-developed ideas about ways to challenge conventional literary modes and values. Harris's critical evaluation of her work establishes Davis as a transitional writer who, along with Stowe, Alcott, Phelps, Freeman, and others, synthesized sentimentalism and regionalism with realism in the service of strong social criticism.

―――――――――. "Redefining the Feminine: Women and Work in Rebecca Harding Davis's 'In the Market.'" *Legacy* 8, no. 2 (Fall 1991): 118-121.

This issue of *Legacy* includes both the text of the story and Harris's introduction to it. Harris sees "In the Market" (1868) as representing a turning point in Davis's work toward stronger feminist depictions of women's potential to be productive, contributing members of society. The story compares the fate of two sisters, one of whom forsakes all sense of self with marriage, the other of whom becomes a leading business person without sacrificing a solid marriage and family. The story was also the first that Davis published in *Peterson's Magazine*, a "ladies" journal, rather than in *The Atlantic Monthly*.

Hood, Richard A. "Framing a 'Life in the Iron Mills.'" *Studies in American Fiction* 23, no. 1 (Spring 1995): 73-84.

Hood offers a detailed analysis of the novel's narrative frame, focusing on Davis's "brilliant use" of a "strangely doubled point of view." The narrative voice frequently addresses the reader in an antagonistic tone that implicates her directly in an ongoing dialogue, yet also mocks her as an outsider who can only learn second-hand about the mill-town which the narrator herself knows intimately. Though Hood agrees with Shurr (see below) that the narrator is a character in the story, he argues that Deborah is a far better candidate than Mitchell, since she alone can "claim both the experience of the story and the ability to tell about the story." The linking of narrator and character in Deborah allowed Davis to distinguish between the "thwarted" lives of middle-class female artists and those of working-class mill-hands, Hood concludes.

Lang, Amy Schrager. "Class and the Strategies of Sympathy," in *The Culture of Sentiment: Race, Gender, and Sentimentality in Nineteenth Century America*, ed. Shirley Samuels. New York: Oxford University Press, 1992.

Lang contrasts *Life in the Iron Mills* with *Uncle Tom's Cabin* to explain why Davis had difficulty sentimentalizing her protagonist, Hugh Wolfe, and persuading readers of his ability to transcend his condition. Davis's narrator is far more ambivalent about Hugh than Stowe's is about Uncle Tom; the former literally has trouble seeing Hugh clearly. Though both men are given feminine characteristics, Hugh's debilitate rather than ennoble him; he is a figure of human waste rather than of human potential. Even as an artist, Hugh remains mute while his sculpture is invested with the power of speech. In a sense, art appropriates his life just as the mill owner appropriates his labor. The hostile narrator tries to chide the reader into emotional identification with the "victim of industry," but is herself unable to enter imaginatively into his world. Readers resist belief in the transcendent truth of Hugh Wolfe's life because the narrator has taught us too well that the grim fate of the ironworker is inescapable.

Molyneux, Maribel W. "Sculpture in the Iron Mills: Rebecca Harding Davis's Korl Woman." *Women's Studies* 17 (1990): 157-177.

Molyneux sees Davis's portrayal of industrial brutality as well as her resistance to suggestions that she make the novel more romantic as "radical" acts for a privileged woman who wrote in secret partly because of a fear of rejection. Davis was able to transform her own anxiety about literary achievement into the image of the Korl woman who gives form to the unfinished work both of the narrator and of Hugh, "a thinly disguised surrogate for the woman artist." The novel also brings into focus the special problems of women who work in traditionally male fields—the factory or the social documentary.

Pfaelzer, Jean. "The Sentimental Promise and the Utopian Myth: Rebecca Harding Davis's 'The Harmonists' and Louisa May Alcott's 'Transcendental Wild Oats.'" *American Transcendental Quarterly* 3, no. 1 (March 1989): 85-100.

Pfaelzer reads these two stories as critiques of the "sentimental" view of gender separation behind male-defined utopian communities. Davis's story depicts a man on the run from civilization "still marked as women's space." His utopia fails, in Davis's version, because it is unnatural, particularly in its treatment of children. In the end, the androgynous protagonist reclaims his son whom he had earlier surrendered to the community. Davis thus anticipates the psychoanalytic theories of Nancy Chodorow and others in illustrating how individualism ultimately denies the kind of "connection" necessary for a true utopia.

See also: Jean Pfaelzer, "Subjectivity as Feminist Utopia," in *Utopian and Science Fiction by Women*, eds. Jane L. Donawerth and Carol A. Kolmerten, Syracuse, N.Y.: Syracuse University Press, 1994.

Rose, Jane Atteridge. "The Artist Manqué in the Fiction of Rebecca Harding Davis," in *Writing the Woman Artist: Essays on Poetics, Politics, and Portraiture*, ed. Suzanne W. Jones. Philadelphia: University of Pennsylvania Press, 1991.

In this biographical essay Rose examines the "double bind" Davis faced throughout her life and the choices she was forced to make as woman and artist that ultimately left her dissatisfied. The fiction Davis wrote over a forty-year period, as analyzed by Rose, dramatizes the three stages of her personal struggle: as a young woman she was frustrated by social expectations, as a mature woman she attempted to reconcile domestic and artistic identities, and as an older woman she felt unfulfilled, having earlier renounced art in favor of marriage and motherhood. Rose plots the chronology of her artist characters against the story of Davis's life to demonstrate the way in which she used fiction to "exorcise" her "illicit desire."

See also: Jane Atteridge Rose, "Images of Self: The Example of Rebecca Harding Davis and Charlotte Perkins Gilman." *English Language Notes* 29, no. 4 (June 1992): 70-78, on "The Wife's Story" and "The Yellow Wallpaper," both quasi-autobiographical accounts of their authors' experience of the infamous "rest cure."

——————. "Reading *Life in the Iron Mills* Contextually: A Key to Rebecca Harding Davis's Fiction," in *Conversations: Contemporary Critical Theory and the Teaching of Literature*. Urbana, Ill.: National Council of Teachers of English, 1990.

Rose argues that in order to understand Davis's work, one must be aware of its relationship to the "ideology of domesticity," including its basic tenet: "the doctrine of gender spheres, idealism, sentimentalism, and evangelicalism." Davis's response to this ideology was to "mediate gender" by assuming a masculine narrative voice and by "bifurcating" the role of her protagonist, for example, splitting the focus in "Iron Mills" between Hugh and Deborah, each representing a different sensibility. Other Davis characters defy social norms and promote social reform based on "feminine" spiritual ideals, rather than political action.

Davis deals with the problem of unfeminine "egoistic artistic desire" by "creating fictional projections of herself as artist and then negating their power." Though Davis aspired to the "objectivity of realism" and the "autonomy of authorship," she remained deeply ambivalent about her role as a writer and "thoroughly enmeshed" in the beliefs of her time.

Shurr, William H. *"Life in the Iron Mills*: A Nineteenth Century Conversion Narrative." *American Transcendental Quarterly* 5, no. 4 (December 1991): 245-257.

Though most critics have assumed the gender and identity of Davis's narrator cannot be determined, Shurr offers strong evidence that the narrator is someone within the tale. He establishes the characteristics of the narrator: "a thoughtful and perceptive person," "androgynous with an artistic temper," and "a zealot with a message"; he then considers three possible candidates: Mitchell, Kirby, and Dr. May. Shurr concludes that Mitchell must be the narrator because of his ability to know the details of the story and because of his conversion from "aloof esthete" to "intensely personal Christian utopianism." Assuming that Mitchell is the narrator helps explain why Davis's "field of reference" seems more religious than socialist. Shurr also provides background on mid-nineteenth century liberal Christianity and concludes that Mitchell fits its philosophy in his role as "ministering artist-savior" living among the poor.

Yellin, Jean Fagan. "The Feminization of Rebecca Harding Davis." *American Literary History* 2, no. 2 (Summer 1990): 203-219.

Yellin examines the publishing history of Davis's first novel, *Margret Howth,* for evidence that her failure to continue to write overtly about themes of social protest may have been the result of editorial influence rather than her own sentimentality. The novel was originally submitted to *The Atlantic Monthly* with the working title *The Deaf and the Dumb* and an explanation by Davis that it was about the inarticulate cry of the poor for bread (both real and spiritual), a cry which remained unheard by those with power and resources. After the novel was rejected because it was too "grim," Davis completely rewrote it, saving its flawed hero from death and providing a happy, if improbable, ending. Through a close reading of the revised version and Davis's letters to James T. Fields, the *Atlantic* editor, Yellin guesses what the original must have been like and assumes it would have been a better book more in line with *Life in the Iron Mills.*

MARY WILKINS FREEMAN
1852-1930

Freeman was born into an old New England family in Randolph, Massachusetts, and spent her adolescence and young adulthood in Brattleboro, Vermont. Her other siblings all died in infancy or youth, and she herself was not a healthy child. After her mother's death, Freeman kept house for her father and then, after his death, she returned to Randolph, where she lived with the family of her childhood friend, Mary Wales. In 1902, following ten years of friendship, she married Dr. Charles Manning Freeman, from whom she was later separated and divorced as a result of his institutionalization for alcoholism. Freeman's writing was well-received during her lifetime. She first established herself as a writer of children's poems and stories in the early 1880's, though she had published a prize-winning story for adults as early as 1882. Her first major book, *A Humble Romance and Other Stories*, was published in 1887 and her most important novel, *Pembroke*, in 1894. In her forty years of writing primarily about New England "characters" and the appalling poverty of many of their lives, she published more than a dozen collections of stories, fifteen novels, poetry, prose, and one play. In 1926 she was awarded the William Dean Howells Gold Medal for distinction in fiction and was elected to the National Institute of Arts and Letters.

Reissued Editions
Pembroke, ed. Perry Westbrook. New Haven, Conn.: College and University Press, 1971.

The Revolt of Mother and Other Stories, ed. Michelle Clark. Old Westbury, N.Y.: Feminist Press, 1974.

Selected Stories of Mary Wilkins Freeman, ed. Marjorie Pryse. New York: W. W. Norton, 1983.

The Short Fiction of Freeman and Jewett, ed. Barbara H. Solomon. New York: American Library, 1979.

Biography and Criticism
Apthorp, Elaine Sargent. "Sentiment, Naturalism, and the Female Regionalist." *Legacy* 7, no. 1 (Spring 1990): 3-21.
    Apthorp contrasts *McTeague* (1899), a novel by Frank Norris, with "A Mistaken Charity" (1887), a story by Mary Wilkins Freeman, to demonstrate the difference between the social protest fiction of the "naturalists" and that of the literary "daughters" of Stowe and Davis. Naturalists insisted on maintaining a distance from their characters that would allow them to evaluate and define; Freeman, Jewett and other female "realists" believed in the power of sympathetic imagination. As artists the naturalists saw themselves exempt from the ignorance and naiveté of their characters; the female realists accepted their own subjectivity and the commonality of experience they shared with their characters. Naturalists used irony to express a determinist world view; female realists in the tradition of Stowe and Davis expressed a spirit of outrage and urgent appeal for reform.

Blum, Virginia L. "Mary Wilkins Freeman and the Taste of Necessity." *American Literature* 65, no. 1 (March 1993): 69-94.

Freeman, who wrote both serious fiction and "formulaic consignment stories," was torn between her desire for both "profits" and "artistic achievement." Like many of her contemporaries, she "imbibed" the language of necessity and believed that art written for money couldn't possibly be any good. Blum sees Freeman's "ambivalence" about her own artistry reflected in her equation of food and literature. Her stories depict the "character altering capacity of food" and the relationship between class and food. They are filled with starving elderly women and young women who endure deprivation to feed others. Blum, punning freely as she proceeds, highlights Freeman's elaborate descriptions of her characters' diets, critical evaluations of her work, and Freeman's comments about herself. Blum's conclusion: Freeman's stories are about their own "edibility"; in effect, they, like their author, "crave our consumption."

Cutter, Martha. "Frontiers of Language: Engendering Discourse in 'The Revolt of Mother.'" *American Literature* 63, no. 2 (June 1991): 279-291.
Cutter sees the male and female "linguistic universes" in Freeman's story as structured around totally opposed systems of value. For the father the barn symbolizes the value of money, commerce, and success; for the mother the house symbolizes the value of people, family, and generativity. Generally such an opposition would result in a "speaking" man and a "silent" woman; however the mother, in moving the home into the barn, manages to communicate her values and to undermine the father's authority, rendering him "inarticulate." This is a hopeful ending, in Cutter's eyes, offering the promise for a real merger in which "linguistic and sexual peace" might be able to prevail.

Donovan, Josephine. "Mary E. Wilkins Freeman and the Tree of Knowledge," in *New England Local Color Literature*. New York: Frederick Ungar, 1983.
Donovan identifies Freeman as the "last" of the New England local-color writers whose work marks the death of a woman-centered world. Donovan briefly discusses dozens of Freeman's stories and novels in terms of several major themes: intense mother-daughter relationships, strong women who revolt against female roles, and the destructive force of an overpowering will. In all of these stories, Freeman depicts the defeat of matriarchal values by the "imperialism of masculine technology and patriarchal institutions."

Fisken, Beth Wynn. "'The Faces of Children That Had Never Been': Ghost Stories by Mary Wilkins Freeman," in *Haunting the House of Fiction: Feminist Perspectives on Ghost Stories by American Women*, eds. Lynette Carpenter and Wendy K. Kolmar. Knoxville: University of Tennessee Press, 1991.
Fisken looks at four of Freeman's stories in the context of her life. The first two—"A Gentle Ghost" and "A Little Maid at the Door"—

are about the "forlorn little girl" Freeman saw herself as having been. These are "mock" ghost stories populated with specters of the characters' grief and loneliness. "Wind in the Rose Bush" and "The Lost Ghost" are more horrifying and nightmarish tales in which children are subject to criminal neglect and abuse. Despite her ambivalence toward the ghost story form, its conventions allowed Freeman to express obliquely the guilt and grief she felt over the deaths of her sister, mother, and father, and her own late marriage and lack of children, Fisken concludes.

Getz, John. "'Eglatina': Freeman's Revision of Hawthorne's 'The Birthmark,'" in *Critical Essays on Mary Wilkins Freeman*, ed. Shirley Marchalonis. Boston: G. K. Hall, 1991.

In her lifetime, Freeman was often compared to Hawthorne, with whom she shared a common ancestry and positive critical reputation. Getz offers evidence of Freeman's resistance to these comparisons, which sometimes "diminished" her work even while presumably praising it. "Eglatina," a realistic, feminist version of "The Birthmark," may have been written as a direct response to Hawthorne. Aylmer, the arrogant scientist, who uses his genius to remove his wife's imperfection, ultimately poisoning her in the process, is Hawthorne's protagonist. Freeman's story focuses instead on a woman who is effectively "silenced" by her fear that her blind fiancé will reject her after surgery corrects his eyesight.

Grasso, Linda. "'Thwarted Life, Mighty Hunger, Unfinished Work': The Legacy of Nineteenth Century Women Writing in America." *American Transcendental Quarterly* 8, no. 2 (June 1994): 97-118.

Grasso compares Mary Wilkins Freeman's "The Poetess" (1880) and Constance Fenimore Woolson's "Miss Grief" (1891) as examples of works which continue the "unmasking" of the writing woman's anger, first revealed "accidentally" by Rebecca Harding Davis. Both stories are about writing women destroyed both in body and spirit by publicly sanctioned authority figures, and both decry the waste of the sacrificed female self. Freeman's poetess writes on acceptable female subjects and does not seek fame; she only hopes to be of value and to offer comfort to her readers. Though an old and frail spinster, she is far more than a stock figure. The closing image of a caged canary is a rich symbol of both her powerlessness and her triumph. Ultimately, her suicide is an act of survival. Grasso asks today's readers to free Freeman's anger from the story by keeping its memory alive.

Marchalonis, Shirley, ed. *Critical Essays on Mary Wilkins Freeman*. Boston: G. K. Hall, 1991.

This is a collection of original reviews, two essays by Freeman herself, ten reprints of articles dating from 1903 to 1986, and several new essays. Included are the Getz, Meese, Pryse, and Reichardt pieces annotated here.

Meese, Elizabeth. "Signs of Undecidability: Reconsidering the Stories of Mary Wilkins Freeman," in *Crossing the Double-Cross: The Practice of Feminist Criticism*. Chapel Hill: University of North Carolina Press, 1986.

Meese views critical disagreements about Freeman's work in terms of new theories of "misreading" and as "displaced reenactments" of conflicts and ambiguities in the stories themselves. For example, some readers of "A New England Nun" have interpreted the story as about Louisa's "self-mutilative" life; others have seen it in terms of Louisa's positive attempt to achieve a measure of personal fulfillment. Meese argues that neither group of readers has been attentive to the full ambiguity of the text. Other of Freeman's stories also "stage" the drama of their own misreading. Freeman herself contributed to the misreading of "The Revolt of Mother" by denying the story's truthfulness in response to criticism of its apparent feminist message.

Pryse, Marjorie. "An Uncloistered 'New England Nun.'" *Studies in Short Fiction* 20 (Fall 1983): 289-295.

Pryse argues that most studies of Freeman's story reflect their own biases about solitary women and a belief that manifest destiny and the flight from domesticity are the exclusive themes of American literature. Freeman's protagonist, Louisa, rather than being a foolish and pathetic woman, appears heroic, wise, "even transcendent," when viewed in the context of her own world. In effect, she discovers that when "sexuality and sensibility mutually exclude each other," becoming a hermit may be a price worth paying. In the end her imaginative freedom and ability to ward off chaos more than compensate for her solitude and celibacy.

Reichardt, Mary R. "Mary Wilkins Freeman: One Hundred Years of Criticism." *Legacy* 4, no. 2 (Fall 1987): 31-44.

This bibliographic essay is divided into two sections. The first covers criticism during Freeman's lifetime which praised her perceptive characterizations of women. The second reviews articles written since the 1960's which focus on her rebel figures but exclude discussion of her painterly style and her important work for children. Reichardt sees Freeman as a writer whose feminine subject matter fell into disfavor with the rise of "naturalism" and whose work is still waiting for the full reevaluation it merits.

Westbrook, Perry D. *Mary Wilkins Freeman* (revised edition). Boston: G. K. Hall, 1988.

This text includes a chronology and bibliography, a biographical essay, and analysis of Freeman's major writings (stories, novels, one play, prose) in the context of her life and of New England religious and social culture. It also includes a discussion of Freeman's literary reputation pre- and post-1960. Westbrook sees Freeman as the "most truthful recorder in fiction" of New England village life, with the ability to express "universalities" with both pathos and humor. He is particularly interested in Freeman's depiction of the "overdeveloped Calvinistic will," which he sees as a direct result of her own religious upbringing.

HELEN HUNT JACKSON
1830-1885

Jackson was born in Amherst, Massachusetts, and raised under the strict Calvinistic authority of her father, Nathan Fiske, a Congregational clergyman and philosophy professor. As a young adult she traveled extensively and finally settled in San Francisco. After the deaths of her first husband, Lieutenant Edward Bissel Hunt, and her nine-year-old son, Jackson turned to writing as a solace, publishing articles, poems, sketches, and novels. She married a wealthy Quaker financier, William S. Jackson, in 1875 and published her most famous novel, *Ramona*, in 1884. Before *Ramona*, which was hailed by the Women's National Indian Association as a strong voice for Indian reform, Jackson had published several well-researched texts on the plight of American Indians, including *Century of Dishonor* (1881). She also engaged in a persistent letter-writing campaign on behalf of Indian land rights. In her own time Jackson was also considered one of America's best poets.

Reissued Editions

A Century of Dishonor: A Sketch of the United States Government's Dealings with Some of the Indian Tribes. Norman: University of Oklahoma Press, 1995.

Ramona. New York: New American Library, 1988.

Westward to a High Mountain: The Colorado Writings of Helen Hunt Jackson. Denver: Colorado Historical Society, 1994.

Biography and Criticism

Banning, Evelyn. *Helen Hunt Jackson.* New York: Vanguard Press, 1973.

This illustrated biography is based on the 1939 study by Ruth Odell and newly revealed correspondence between Emily Dickinson and Jackson. Banning makes extensive use of Jackson's own words in establishing the three major roles she played in her life—army wife, mother, and society woman; literary person, poet, essayist and writer of fiction; and woman with a "cause." The text includes a bibliography, a list of Jackson's publications in periodicals, and a detailed discussion of her less well-known works.

Coultrap-McQuin, Susan. "'Very Serious Literary Labor': The Career of Helen Hunt Jackson," in *Doing Literary Business: American Women Writers in the Nineteenth Century.* Chapel Hill: University of North Carolina Press, 1990.

Jackson began her literary career as an expression of personal grief and ended it as an advocate for Indian rights; she began as a protégée of Thomas Wentworth Higginson and ended by encouraging Higginson's prize pupil, Emily Dickinson, to publish her poems. During the course of this career she developed a professional life-style based on serious literary study, superb business skills, and mentorship of other writers. She believed writing well required time and effort and conscientious attention to detail. *Ramona* was her attempt to write a novel like *Uncle Tom's Cabin* that would draw attention to the plight of American Indians. Ultimately, Jackson's work has been undervalued because of her use of pseudonyms. Coultrap-McQuin sees Jackson as an enigmatic figure whose two pen names may have been a "hedge against market failure" rather than the product of female modesty.

Mathes, Valerie Sherer. *Helen Hunt Jackson and Her Indian Reform Legacy.* Austin: University of Texas Press, 1990.
This work looks at Jackson as both a writer and a reformer, and provides an overview of American Indian history. Mathes emphasizes the role of women in the Indian reform movement. She also points out that Jackson, like most other well-meaning reformers, wanted to "civilize" Native Americans without ever asking them whether or not they wanted to be "civilized."

May, Antoinette. *Helen Hunt Jackson: A Lonely Voice of Conscience.* San Francisco: Chronicle Press, 1987.
This comprehensive biography offers a lively account of Jackson's life from early childhood to death.

Schmudde, Carol E. "Sincerity, Secrecy, and Lies: Helen Hunt Jackson's No Name Novels." *Studies in American Fiction.* 21, no. 1 (Spring 1993): 51-66.
Examination of Jackson's early novels—*Mercy Philbrick's Choice* (1876) and *Hetty's Strange History* (1877)—demonstrates her ongoing exploration of the "tricky borderline between sincerity and deception." Moreover, Jackson's decision to publish all of her early work under two separate pseudonyms—H. H. and Saxe Holm—reflects her desire to protect her privacy and free herself from responsibility for her own creations. Once Jackson embraced the cause of the Indians, she began to understand that truth-telling was no longer a game and chose to drop the mask of anonymity, Schmudde concludes.

Walker, Cheryl. "Tradition and the Individual Talent: Helen Hunt Jackson and Emily Dickinson," in *The Nightingale's Burden: Women Poets and American Culture Before 1900.* Bloomington: Indiana University Press, 1982.
Walker sees both women as products of the same female literary tradition. She compares their literary development and considers their influence on each other. Jackson was better suited to the world of her times than Dickinson. She was also one of the first writers to recognize

Dickinson's genius. Much of Jackson's own poetry, like Dickinson's, is about secret grief and reveals her ambivalent feelings about women. Though she was unwilling to speak publicly about women's issues, Jackson refused to marry her second husband until he agreed to allow her the freedom to write.

Whitaker, Rosemary. "Legacy Profile: Helen Hunt Jackson." *Legacy* 3, no. 1 (Spring 1986): 56-62.
This brief overview of Jackson's life and work focuses on her relationship with Emily Dickinson and is followed by an excerpt from *Ramona*.

SARAH ORNE JEWETT
1849-1909
The second of three daughters, Jewett was born and raised in southern Maine in a distinguished New England family. Despite several years of formal schooling, Jewett credits her father, a respected local doctor, for most of her education and her knowledge of literature, nature, and country life. Jewett published her first story, "The Flag of Our Union" (1868), when she was eighteen years old. By 1877 she had published a collection of sketches (*Deephaven*) which had previously appeared in *The Atlantic Monthly*. Following her father's death in 1878, Jewett deepened her important friendship with Annie Fields, wife of the *Atlantic* editor, James T. Fields. Sustained by Fields's support and that of other intimate female friends, Jewett continued to write throughout her life and to earn critical acclaim. *The Country Doctor*, her first novel, appeared in 1884, followed by *A White Heron and Other Stories* in 1886 and *The King of Folly Island* in 1888. Jewett's "masterpiece," *The Country of the Pointed Firs*, was published in 1896 and her last major work, *The Tory Lover*, in 1901. Jewett was awarded an honorary doctorate of letters by Bowdoin College in recognition of a career which contributed nineteen volumes of much-loved stories and novels to American letters.

Reissued Editions
Notes: A centennial conference on Jewett was held in Portland, Maine, June 21-23, 1996; papers from it should be available in 1997. In addition to the editions below, many of Jewett's stories are available on audio-cassette.

Best Stories of Sarah Orne Jewett. Augusta, Maine: Lance Tapley, 1988.

A Country Doctor. New York: New American Library, 1986.

The Country of the Pointed Firs and Other Stories. New York: Anchor Press, 1989.

The Irish Stories of Sarah Orne Jewett. Carbondale: Southern Illinois University Press, 1996.

Novels and Stories of Sarah Orne Jewett. New York: Penguin Books, 1994.

A White Heron, illustrated edition. Gardiner, Maine: Tilbury House, 1990.

Biography and Criticism

Ammons, Elizabeth. "Jewett's Witches," in *Critical Essays on Sarah Orne Jewett*, ed. Gwen L. Nagel. Boston: G. K. Hall, 1984.

    Ammons provides evidence that Jewett, like many of her contemporaries, believed in the spirit world and was fascinated by the possibility of extrasensory communication with both the living and the dead. Some of her stories use the occult in quite conventional ways; others depict witches as guides and healers rather than destroyers. Ammons examines five of the most interesting: "Lady Ferry" (1879), "The Courting of Sister Wisby" (1887), *The Country of the Pointed Firs* (1896), "The Foreigner" (1900), and "The Green Bowl" (1901). All of these fictions celebrate female psychic power; "The Green Bowl," in particular, is "aggressively modern" in depicting the "ancient power" and wisdom of a witch as compatible with a woman's life in modern America.

Blanchard, Paula. *Sarah Orne Jewett: Her World and Her Work.* Reading, Mass.: Addison-Wesley, 1994.

    This volume in the *Radcliffe Biography* series includes illustrations and a bibliography. Blanchard begins with Henry James's characterization of the last quarter of the nineteenth century as "our ancient peace." She sees Jewett, along with James and H. D. Howells, as the keeper of this peace, an artist whose works and life expressed the "generation's civility and its increasingly beleaguered idealism." A superb stylist and chronicler of women's lives and conversations, Jewett was both a "citizen of the world" and a "country doctor's daughter." Blanchard attempts to place Jewett in the context of the New England literary and artistic life of her time, suggesting that the Jewett "world" can be seen in the works of the era's best known painters such as John Singer Sargent and Mary Cassatt.

Donovan, Josephine. "Sarah Orne Jewett and the World of the Mothers," in *New England Local Color Literature*. New York: Frederick Ungar, 1983.

    Donovan credits the power of Jewett's work to a tension between her realistic depiction of a "fallen" world and her utopian vision of a supportive community. The theory of literature behind her artistic creation derives from French symbolism and the "doctrine of correspondences" popularized by Emmanuel Swedenborg, whose theosophy Jewett studied. Jewett was also interested in the "conflicting attractions of rural and urban life" and the relationship between individualism and community. Donovan refers to dozens of Jewett's stories to demonstrate how Jewett's "greatest" works, beginning with "A White Heron" in 1886, used "imaginative realism" to create a symbolic universe in which the everyday world comes to represent a "spiritual" and "matriarchal" landscape.

See also: Josephine Donovan, "Jewett and Swedenborg," *American Literature* 65, no. 4 (December 1993): 731-750, in which Donovan examines more deeply Swedenborg's influence on Jewett, emphasizing, in particular, how his philosophy helped her to see "value" rather than "selfishness" in her decision to be a writer instead of serving others directly as women of her generation were supposed to do.

Held, George. "Heart to Heart with Nature: Ways of Looking at 'A White Heron.'" *Colby Quarterly* 18 (1982): 55-65.

Held considers this story in the context of Jewett's life and career: her concern that the story was too romantic for the times, her developing friendship with Annie Fields following the death of her father, Sylvia's resemblance to Jewett herself and to a young Nan Price in *A Country Doctor*. Though the story has been criticized for its didactic ending, Held finds its message a key to Jewett's symbolism; the heron comes to represent anything precious a girl might be tempted to give up for the sake of a man. The story in Held's reading "reverberates" with such issues as the socialization of girls, the balance of power between sexes, and the need for a woman to be true to her nature.

Howard, June. "Unraveling Regions, Unsettling Periods: Sarah Orne Jewett and American Literary History." *American Literature* 68, no. 2 (June 1996): 365-384.

Howard notes that feminist critics overemphasize Jewett's similarity to women today and literary historians overemphasize her distance from contemporary life. Both are guilty of oversimplification of the total body of her work and of neglecting consideration of stories that do not fit their theories.

Leder, Priscilla. "Living Ghosts and Women's Religion in Sarah Orne Jewett's *The Country of the Pointed Firs*," in *Haunting the House of Fiction*, eds. Lynette Carpenter and Wendy K. Kolmar. Knoxville: University of Tennessee Press, 1991.

Leder contrasts the ghost story told by Captain Littlepage in "Firs" with Edgar Allan Poe's *The Narrative of Arthur Gordon Pym of Nantucket* (1838) to show how Jewett "reappropriates the classic American encounter with a terrifying wilderness." While Poe's characters are paralyzed and in danger of being swallowed up by the chasm they face, Littlepage's sailors "take conscious fright and are able to flee." Moreover, Poe presents his narrative as "literal," while Jewett presents hers as "literary"; Jewett's tale within a tale is judged by its "human usefulness" rather than its "truth." "Through her presentation of Captain Littlepage's account and her women characters' response to it, Jewett reveals that the other realm is not the chaotic antithesis of this one." Poe writes of "alienation and discontinuity"; Jewett writes of "continuity and community."

Mobley, Marilyn Sanders. *Folk Roots and Mythic Wings in Sarah Orne Jewett and Toni Morrison.* Baton Rouge: Louisiana State University Press, 1991.

This critical study demonstrates how two women of different races and generations both turn to the cultural roots of their people for much of their inspiration. It analyzes the use of myth and folklore in key works of each.

Nagel, Gwen L. *Critical Essays on Sarah Orne Jewett.* Boston: G. K. Hall, 1984.

This collection contains reviews of Jewett's work written at the time of publication, reprinted essays primarily from the 1980's, including the Held piece annotated here, and several original essays, including the Ammons piece annotated here. Nagel's introduction summarizes the history of Jewett's critical reception and provides basic bibliographic information.

Pennell, Melissa McFarland. "A New Spiritual Biography: Domesticity and Sorority in the Fiction of Sarah Orne Jewett." *Studies in American Fiction* 18, no. 2 (Autumn 1990): 193-206.

Pennell analyzes two Jewett stories—"Miss Tempy's Watchers" and "The Passing of Sister Barsett"—as precursors of *The Country of the Pointed Firs.* Like much of Jewett's work, these stories portray older women whose ordered lives and domestic achievements provide models of hope and survival. These are women whose spiritual ties are with each other, rather than with men and male institutions. Jewett makes good use of a traditional New England form, the "spiritual biography," to dramatize their exemplary existences.

Roman, Margaret. *Sarah Orne Jewett: Reconstructing Gender.* Tuscaloosa: University of Alabama Press, 1992.

Roman examines almost all of the stories found in the nineteen volumes Jewett published during her lifetime in terms of Jewett's own personal development and her belief that both men and women need to break free of restrictive gender norms. The text is divided into three parts: the first considers youthful characters who either live in denial of gender norms or are able to escape from them; the second considers the shadowy "malformed" figures in Jewett's work who live dismal existences according to prescribed roles; the third considers a group of "robust, nurturing women" and a few "redeemed men" who represent positive alternatives to the prevailing patriarchal system. These last, more optimistic works, are surprisingly modern in their view that men and women should be encouraged to develop along whatever paths prove most natural for them.

Sherman, Sarah Way. *Sarah Orne Jewett, an American Persephone.* Hanover, N.H.: University Presses of New England, 1989.

Sherman's book, which includes illustrations and a bibliography, discusses Jewett's life and career in terms of the female culture that defined her womanhood, with special attention to its values and its symbols. She looks, in particular, at Rose Terry Cooke's stories and Harriet Beecher Stowe's *Pearl of Orr's Island* (1862), which promoted a "female world of love and ritual," and at Walter Pater's essays, which spoke of a pastoral, matriarchal consciousness. Jewett's first novel, *Deephaven,* reveals their influence, but also an ambivalence about the pastoral world and feminine modes of communication. With her masterpiece, *The Country of the Pointed Firs,* Jewett's maternal figures are clearly priestesses rather than eccentrics, and rural Maine the reincarnation of pastoral Greece.

Silverthorne, Elizabeth. *Sarah Orne Jewett: A Writer's Life.* Woodstock, N.Y.: Overlook Press, 1993.

This illustrated biography draws upon Jewett's unpublished letters and diaries to portray the range of intellectual and personal influences behind Jewett's work. Though the author does not provide source notes, there is a selected bibliography.

Wittenberg, Judith Bryant. *"Deephaven:* Sarah Orne Jewett's Exploratory Metafiction." *Studies in American Fiction* 19, no. 2 (Autumn 1991): 153-163.

Wittenberg identifies Jewett's first novel as a "metafiction" because in it Jewett overtly considers issues of narrative technique including the relationship of a writer to her material and the "psychosocial function" of literature. In their quest to find and "reconstitute" various stories about the lives of people in a small town in Maine, the narrator Helen and her friend Kate mirror the creative process of perceiving, understanding, and recording experience. The novel itself dramatizes different approaches to narration (oral versus written), different types of stories (capsule biographies versus dramatic tales of conflict), and a wide variety of types of storytellers. It also establishes the power of fiction to bring coherence and meaning to experience, to reorder the "troublesome" aspects of life and reinforce the "beneficent."

GRACE KING
1852-1932

The oldest of four girls in a family of eight children, King was raised in New Orleans and as an adult writer became known as a spokeswoman for its history and culture. King was a conservative supporter of the South whose consciousness was dominated by her experience of civilian life during the Civil War and Reconstruction. She began writing in hopes of achieving some degree of financial independence and in order to counteract George Washington Cable's negative portrayals of Creole society. Her first story, "Monsieur Motte," was published in 1886, her first collection of stories in 1888. King's most productive period followed a trip to Europe in 1892 and led to the publication of six volumes of history and fiction: *Tales of a Time and Place* (1892) and *Balcony Stories* (1893), her second and third short-story collections; *Jean Baptiste Le Moyne* (1892), a biography of the Canadian founder of New Orleans; *A History of Louisiana* (1893); *New Orleans: The Place and the People* (1895); and *DeSoto and His Men in the Land of Florida* (1898). She also wrote introductions for many of the French writers included in the thirty-volume *Library of the World's Best Literature* (1896-1897). In the last two decades of her life King wrote two novels, *The Pleasant Ways of St. Medard* (1916) and *La Dame de Sainte Hermaine* (1924), and one work of history, *Creole Families of New Orleans* (1921). King was decorated by the French government in 1918 for her writings. Her autobiography, *Memories of a Southern Woman of Letters*, was published posthumously in 1932.

Reissued Editions
Balcony Stories. New York: Gregg Press, 1968.

Grace King of New Orleans: A Selection of Her Writings, ed. Robert Bush. Baton Rouge: Louisiana State University Press, 1973.

Memories of a Southern Woman of Letters. Salem, N.H.: Ayer Co. Pubs., Inc., 1977.

Monsieur Motte. Salem, N.H.: Ayer Co. Pubs., Inc., 1977.

New Orleans: The Place and the People. Westport, Conn.: Greenwood Press, 1968.

Tales of a Time and Place. Delray Beach, Fla.: Garrett, 1969.

Biography and Commentary
Bush, Robert. "Grace King: The Emergence of a Southern Intellectual Woman." *The Southern Review* 13, no. 2 (April 1977): 272-288.

In this biographical essay, Bush identifies the key figures in the development of King's intellectual life. For example, despite her ridicule of Bostonian abolitionists, she was clearly influenced by the feminism of Julia Ward Howe and eagerly joined the Pan Gnostics literary club Howe formed while in New Orleans to head the Woman's Department of the Cotton Centennial Exposition. Most significant was the influence and friendship of Charles Dudley Warner, the editor and literary critic who encouraged her writing and helped publish her first stories. Bush calls King the first southern woman to write history of importance, and concludes she is more important as a "symbol" of the South than for her regional fiction.

See also: *Grace King: A Southern Destiny*, Baton Rouge: Louisiana State University Press, 1983, Bush's full-length illustrated biography of King.

Elfenbein, Anna Shannon. "Grace King: Ingenues on the Color Line," in *Women on the Color Line: Evolving Stereotypes and the Writings of George Washington Cable, Grace King, Kate Chopin*. Charlottesville: University Press of Virginia, 1989.

Elfenbein believes that King demonstrated more ambivalence toward black women and less blatant racism in her fiction than she did in her other writings, perhaps because of a subconscious identification with the oppression experienced by her own characters. King's essay, "Heroines of Novels" (1855), strongly criticized the stereotypic depiction of women in most French, German, and American novels and called for more novels with characters as complex as a Jane Eyre or a Maggie Tulliver. Her best stories, such as "Monsieur Motte" (1886) and "The Little Covenant Girl" (1893), portray the unfulfilling lives of women trapped in traditional roles and suggest that black and white women must struggle together against the tyranny and ineptitude of men.

Jones, Anne Goodwyn. "Grace King: That Great Mother Stream Underneath," in *Tomorrow Is Another Day: The Woman Writer in the South, 1859-1936*. Baton Rouge: Louisiana State University Press, 1981.

Jones reviews King's life and career in the context of New Orleans Creole society, though King was not a "born to the blood" Creole herself. In her person, King embodied the dependence, deference, and stoicism of a southern lady. She was quick to withdraw from any potentially controversial situation, though her memoirs often reveal the hypocrisy she saw and the ambivalence she felt. In her stories King removes the "mask" and writes about women, white and black, who begin the journey toward womanhood, but are forced to stop short. Jones offers a detailed interpretation of the best of these, "Monsieur Motte" and its sequels, "Bonne Maman" (1886) and "The Little Covenant Girl," in which King was able to remove the mask of the southern lady to some degree.

Kirby, David. *Grace King*. Boston: G. K. Hall, 1990.

This volume in the Twayne United States Authors series is the first full-length study of King and includes a chronology and bibliography. Kirby begins with a psychological sketch of King's life, followed by detailed summaries and analyses of her short stories, novels, and historical writings. He concludes with a review of King's critical reputation and consideration of the historical and literary context in which her work emerged. According to Kirby, King's major contribution as a writer was her perceptive portraits of southern women robbed of their place in life and struggling to adapt to new roles.

Taylor, Helen. "The Case of Grace King." *The Southern Review* 18, no. 4 (October 1982): 685-702.

Taylor sees King as unusual among women writers "in the enormous range of acquaintances she had among writers, editors, and public figures in the United States and Europe." In considering the influence of these acquaintances, Taylor concludes that the male defenders of a "genteel literary tradition," including Charles Dudley Warner, had a negative, repressive impact on King's early career, whereas several women writers were "liberalizing and liberating" forces in her life. For example, despite his objections, King sought out the company of Isabella Hooker while visiting Warner in Hartford. Soon she became part of an international network of female writers and educators who encouraged her to challenge traditional thinking on gender issues and who allowed her to develop her own female voice.

_____. "Grace King," in *Gender, Race, and Region in the Writings of Grace King, Ruth McEnery Stuart, and Kate Chopin.* Baton Rouge: Louisiana State University Press, 1989.

Taylor discusses King's life and career in the context of other postbellum southern writers. She then provides a brief synopsis and interpretation of key stories from King's four major collections and of her final novel, *La Dame de Sainte Hermaine* (1924). Taylor sees King as one of the few writers to confront issues of race and gender within a specifically regional context. Moreover, she credits her with attempting to get at the "truth of her region, class, and sex" by experimenting with a wide variety of narrative voices. In her fiction, in particular, King moved toward feminism and revealed her own contradictory feelings about the "lived experience" of women.

ELIZABETH STUART PHELPS
1844-1911

Phelps was born and raised in Andover, Massachusetts, where, as the oldest daughter, she was expected to serve tea and help take care of her father and four younger brothers. Her mother, who died in childbirth at the age of thirty-six, was herself a successful novelist who sacrificed her career for her family. Phelps took her mother's name (she was christened Mary Gray) presumably as an expression of solidarity with her mother's frustrations and difficult life. Because her father, a minister and professor of sacred rhetoric, disapproved of non-domestic work for women, Phelps was forced to write in an unheated attic "as if she were a burglar." Phelps achieved popular success with the publication of *The Gates Ajar* (1868), the first book in her utopian trilogy. *A Silent Partner*, her first "career" novel, was published in 1871, *The Story of Avis*, a quasi-fictional account of her mother's life, was published in

1877, and *Dr. Zay*, the only other of her career novels reissued for modern readers, in 1882. Despite her reputation as a shy spinster, Phelps married Herbert Dickinson Ward, a man seventeen years her junior, in 1888. She died in 1911 having published fifty books, including a memoir memorializing her father and a carefully edited autobiography.

Reissued Editions
Chapters from a Life. New York: Arno, 1980.

Dr. Zay. New York: Feminist Press of City University of New York, 1987.

The Silent Partner (includes the short story "The Tenth of January"). Old Westbury, N.Y.: Feminist Press, 1983.

The Story of Avis. New Brunswick, N.J.: Rutgers University Press, 1985.

Biography and Commentary
Albertine, Susan. "Breaking the Silent Partnership: Businesswomen in Popular Fiction." *American Literature* 62, no. 2 (June 1990): 238-265.
     Albertine looks at two works—Phelps's *The Silent Partner* (1871) and Margaret Deland's *The Iron Woman* (1911)—for evidence of American ambivalence about women in business. By the time Phelps wrote her novel, women were beginning to work in a growing variety of occupations—more than five hundred were listed in an 1864 encyclopedia. Still, Phelps writes from a conservative middle-class perspective that wants to both "enlarge and preserve" the traditional woman's sphere. She understands the "bonds of gender" and how sexism and marriage may work against women's active participation in business, but is quite naive about class barriers and the sources of the dismal workplace conditions she criticizes. The novel ends with a call for a millennial spiritual rather than political reformation.

Fetterly, Judith. "'Checkmate': Elizabeth Stuart Phelps's *The Silent Partner*." *Legacy* 3, no. 2 (Fall 1986): 17-29.
     Fetterly analyzes the role of class and gender in determining who has the power of speech in Phelps's novel, how those who are silenced express themselves, and how those who have access to speech use it. Perley Kelso is a sentimental heroine; by virtue of class, she is a lady who uses her status to silence others. This willingness to invoke class privilege in silencing others makes her complicit in her own silencing, Fetterly concludes.

Huf, Linda. "Scenes from a Marriage, by Elizabeth Stuart Phelps," in *A Portrait of the Artist as a Young Woman*. New York: Frederick Ungar, 1983.

This analysis of *The Story of Avis* begins by reviewing the hostile press the book received when first published and the relationships between the novel and Phelps's own life. Huf sees the novel as typical of women's *Kunstlerromane* in its use of flying imagery and in its portraits of a weak husband "puffed with self-importance," its use of a female foil who represents the "sunny" ideal of womanhood, and its use of a mother/stepmother/aunt who looks darkly on the heroine's ambitions. Though the novel is "unremittingly cheerless," Huf judges it worth reading for its "engrossing" message that gifted women must avoid marriage and motherhood until the time when husbands agree to provide for wives the same services wives provide for them.

Kessler, Carol Farley. "A Literary Legacy: Elizabeth Stuart Phelps, Mother and Daughter." *Frontiers* 5, no. 3 (1981): 28-33.
    Kessler compares the major writings of both of the Phelpses to demonstrate how the "narrow and ambivalent feminism" of the mother is "enhanced" in the daughter's unqualified assertions of "women's right to achievement and fulfillment." The fiction of the elder Phelps offers realistic depictions of women's daily lives that implicitly criticize the social system of separate spheres; the daughter insists on the need for self-fulfilling activity for women whether combined with marriage or not. The daughter blamed her mother's premature death and "aborted career" on "suppressed longings" and "despised capacities" and took it upon herself to carry on her writings and her quarrel with the world.

Lang, Amy Schrager. "The Syntax of Class in Elizabeth Stuart Phelps's *The Silent Partner*," in *Rethinking Class: Literary Studies and Social Formation*, eds. Wai Chee Dimock and Michael T. Gilmore. New York: Columbia University Press, 1994.
    Lang uses Phelps's novel as an example of the difficulty nineteenth century writers had in writing about class, and of how the language of class ends up displaced by the language of gender. The novel sets up a contrast between Perley, the wealthy self-indulgent belle, and Sip, the honest working girl who has given up her "femininity" in her struggle for survival. The key scene occurs when Perley invites the mill girls to a "soiree" where they demonstrate their "common humanity" by dressing up and talking about art "produced by a leisure class to which they do not belong." This scene, according to Lang, demonstrates Phelps's middle-class desire to harmonize the potential for class conflict by rendering class differences inessential. Ultimately, the novel will insist that the real problem is not the opposition between capital and labor, but rather between men and women.

Masteller, Jean Carwile. "The Women Doctors of Howells, Phelps, and Jewett: The Conflict of Marriage and Career," in *Critical Essays on Sarah Orne Jewett*, ed. Gwen L. Nagel. Boston: G. K. Hall, 1984.
    Three well-known writers published novels centered on a woman doctor at about the same time. W. D. Howells in *Dr. Breen's Practice*

(1881) presents a woman who gives up her career in order to marry; Sarah Orne Jewett in *A Country Doctor* (1884) presents a woman who chooses to continue her career and not marry; Elizabeth Stuart Phelps alone in *Dr. Zay* (1882) presents a woman who marries and continues to practice medicine. Even Phelps, however, who was committed to careers for women, allows her heroine to marry only when suffering from illness and overwork. Like the mythic Atalanta whose name she bears, Dr. Zay is "defeated" in a moment of weakness. In the end, readers are left unsure of whether or not her husband will forgo his advantage and continue to consent to his wife's career even when it "conflicts with his comfort."

Morris, Timothy. "Professional Ethics and Professional Erotics in Elizabeth Stuart Phelps's *Dr. Zay.*" *Studies in American Fiction* 21, no. 2 (Autumn 1993): 141-152.

Phelps's doctor is quite modern in her love of science; she works because she wants to, not because she must support herself. Despite such a "radical view" of women's capabilities, Phelps makes it clear that her doctor is a "lady," not an abortionist, and that she is heterosexual, not "unnatural," in order to prove that she does not conform to negative nineteenth century stereotypes about women doctors. Phelps's feminism is limited by class and by conservative attitudes about sexuality; in effect, she writes with two voices, Morris concludes.

Ward, Susan. "The Career Woman Fiction of Elizabeth Stuart Phelps," in *Nineteenth Century Women Writers of the English Speaking World*, ed. Rhoda B. Nathan. Westport, Conn.: Greenwood Press, 1986.

Ward sees Phelps's work as historically important because she espoused liberal feminist ideas without rejecting conservative Christian morality and the conventional formulas of nineteenth century domestic fiction. Clearly she was influenced by the women's rights movement and espoused many of its ideas in the nonfiction articles she wrote in the 1870's. Between 1870 and 1909 Phelps published at least eight short stories and three novels which focused on women and careers. In most of these the heroines are unsubmissive or undomestic, but still traditional in other ways. The plots follow typical patterns, with poor and abandoned women questing for a way to survive; however, in Phelps's stories they are saved by their own business acumen rather than by a man. This mix of the conventional and the new made Phelps's work palatable to her readers, Ward concludes.

HARRIET BEECHER STOWE
1811-1896

Stowe was born in Litchfield, Connecticut, the seventh of nine children, all of whom were raised with the Calvinist values of their father, the prominent Congregational minister Lyman Beecher, for a life of public service in the church or the home. She married Calvin Stowe, a professor of biblical literature, in 1836 and began to write to help supplement his meager salary. In 1850, after the death in infancy of her sixth child, and with a seventh child on the way, the Stowes moved to Maine, where Calvin had taken a job at Bowdoin College. Stowe's first collection of stories, *The Mayflower*, was published in 1843; her first novel, *Uncle Tom's Cabin*, in 1852 (it appeared serially in 1851). An overnight success, the novel was equally popular in England and Europe. Stowe responded to the storm of protest the novel generated with *A Key to Uncle Tom's Cabin* (1853), in which she documented the sources for the horrors of slavery she had described, and another novel, *Dred: A Tale of the Great Dismal Swamp* (1856), that depicts the terrible impact of slavery on white families. Throughout the rest of her life, Stowe continued to help support her family through her writings. *The Minister's Wooing* (1859), *The Pearl of Orr's Island* (1862), *Oldtown Folks* (1869), *Pink and White Tyranny* (1871), *Sam Lawson's Oldtown Fireside Stories* (1872), and *Poganuc People* (1878) are New England fictions which highlight women's roles as domestic saviors. Stowe also wrote children's stories, housekeeping manuals, and newspaper articles. Her complete works, collected in twenty volumes, along with forty-two translations of *Uncle Tom's Cabin* and a bust of the author, were exhibited at the World's Columbian Exposition in Chicago seven years after her death.

Reissued Editions
Note: There are frequent reprintings of *Uncle Tom's Cabin* by Penguin Books, Bantam, G. K. Hall, Macmillan, and other major publishers, as well as of a Norton Critical Edition which includes scholarly essays and pieces on the novel's biographical and historical contexts. Also available are audiocassettes of the novel and the following books:

The Harriet Beecher Stowe Reader. Hartford: Stowe-Day Foundation, 1993.

The Minister's Wooing. Hartford: Stowe-Day Foundation, 1978.

Oldtown Folks. New Brunswick, N.J.: Rutgers University Press, 1987.

The Pearl of Orr's Island. Hartford: Stowe-Day Foundation, 1979.

Pink and White Tyranny: A Society Novel. New York: New American Library, 1988.

Poganuc People. Hartford: Stowe-Day Foundation, 1977.

Biography and Commentary
Ammons, Elizabeth, ed. *Critical Essays on Harriet Beecher Stowe*. Boston: G. K. Hall, 1980.

This is a collection of essays on Stowe by literary critics and feminist scholars.

Anderson, Beatrice A. "Uncle Tom: A Hero at Last." *American Transcendental Quarterly* 5, no. 2 (June 1991): 95-108.
Anderson sees Uncle Tom, not as the stereotypic, passive, and submissive follower of a white man's imposed religion, but rather as a "strong, vital character whose motivations, while uncomplicated, are noble and heroic and not solely religious." She revisits key events in the novel—Tom's refusal to rebel against his sale from the Shelby estate, his rescue of Little Eva, and his endurance of Legree's abuse—to demonstrate the nature of Tom's true character. She also examines his religious beliefs in the context of slave religious practice which, as Stowe knew, differed from white Christianity in significant ways. Tom's incredible resilience, competence, and unwavering morality, despite years of abuse, was intended to persuade readers that slaves were human beings and to inspire the antislavery movement.

Banks, Marva. "*Uncle Tom's Cabin* and Antebellum Black Response," in *Readers in History: Nineteenth Century American Literature and the Contexts of Response*, ed. James L. Machor. Baltimore: Johns Hopkins University Press, 1993.
Banks provides examples of comments made about Stowe's novel in the antebellum black press in the years immediately following its publication and identifies these as products of a particular historical moment marked by the Fugitive Slave Law, a revitalized American Colonization Society, and rampant "political, economic, and social oppression" in both the North and the South. Most of the more than two hundred articles which appeared between 1852 and 1855 focused on the novel's political and social issues, not its artistry, and were often appended to discussions of larger issues such as education and employment. At first, there was general appreciation of the novel as a powerful piece of propaganda that would help fuel the antislavery movement and the underground railway. Soon, however, there was criticism of Stowe's support of colonization, especially in the novel's "Concluding Remarks," and of her use of racial stereotypes, especially in her characterization of Tom's Christian piety and submisssiveness. Banks notes that these are the same accusations James Baldwin would level against the novel one hundred years later in his 1949 essay, "Everybody's Protest Novel."

Bellin, Joshua D. "'Up to Heaven's Gate, Down in Earth's Dust': The Politics of Judgment in *Uncle Tom's Cabin*." *American Literature* 65, no. 2 (June 1993): 275-293.
Bellin uses this phrase of Augustine St. Clare to represent the two conflicting energies within Stowe's novel: the power of the individual human will that struggles to resist oppression, and the powerlessness of the individual seeking to comprehend his/her place in a universe

controlled by God. These contradictory visions are mirrored in the novel through the contrasting of characters and philosophies; for example, the two St. Clares (Augustine and Alfred) or Uncle Tom and George Harris; and the two major journeys, the Harris's north toward freedom and Uncle Tom's south toward greater enslavement. Augustine St. Clare is himself both the spokesman and the symbol of these oppositions, since he dies before he is able to transform his ideas into actions, thus leaving the fate of his slaves to the mercy of God. Ultimately, Stowe's novel abandons any scheme for active resistance and contents itself with waiting for the Day of Judgment.

Boyd, Richard. "Models of Power in Harriet Beecher Stowe's *Dred*." *Studies in American Fiction* 19, no. 1 (Spring 1991): 15-30.

Boyd sees the "problem" of the novel as exemplified by the debate between Anne's sentimental appeal to "elevated feelings" and Frank's cynical response that "we're all slaves to one thing or another." This cynicism casts its shadow over even the most idealized scenes of domestic harmony. Stowe understands the power of imitation and hopes her readers will be inspired to imitate her exemplary mothers rather than the male perpetrators of violence. Milly, the most saintly character in the novel, however, is too exceptional to serve as such a model; in the end she is herself marginalized, illustrating the futility of Stowe's vision.

Brown, Gillian. "Getting in the Kitchen with Dinah: Domestic Politics in *Uncle Tom's Cabin*." *American Quarterly* 36, no. 4 (Fall 1984): 503-523.

Brown argues that Stowe was advocating a new economic order symbolized by Rachel Halliday's kitchen. Stowe's utopian domestic economy is a home "divested of men, markets, and desire," the evils epitomized by Simon Legree's capitalistic program of self-advancement. Rachel's home represents the polar opposite of the southern plantation; it is a place where maternal love and generosity combine with political and moral action. Slavery's greatest evil was its corruption of the family, according to Stowe; Brown believes Stowe sought not just the abolition of slavery but the total reformation of "domesticity" itself.

Crumpacker, Laurie. "Four Novels of Harriet Beecher Stowe: A Study in Nineteenth Century Androgyny," in *American Novelists Revisited: Essays in Feminist Criticism*, ed. Fritz Fleischmann. Boston: G. K. Hall, 1982.

Crumpacker traces the evolution of Stowe's thinking through four novels. *Uncle Tom's Cabin* depicts pious mothers, both black and white, and preaches domestic feminism. *The Minister's Wooing* proposes a redefinition of Calvinism so that women could play public roles as reformers, mystics, and preachers. *Pearl of Orr's Island* emphasizes the importance of education to child-rearing and the development of sensitive human beings. Finally, in *Oldtown Folks*

Stowe describes an ideal community as a place which nurtures androgynous individuals.

Gosset, Thomas F. *Uncle Tom's Cabin and American Culture.* Dallas, Tex.: Southern Methodist University Press, 1985.
    This illustrated text includes a bibliography, extensive notes, a history of productions of the Uncle Tom play between 1865 and 1940, and a review of the novel's critical reception from the 1940's to the 1980's. Gosset begins with an examination of Stowe's early life and the circumstances that led her from a largely introverted and withdrawn adolescence to a major public role in the antislavery struggle. He then chronicles the actual writing of *Uncle Tom's Cabin* and explains the cultural and personal sources of its major themes; in particular, he examines Stowe's ideas on race. He also considers the different reactions to the novel in the North and the South, its popularity abroad, and provides examples of "anti-Uncle Tom" literature.

Harris, Susan K. "The Female Imaginary in Harriet Beecher Stowe's *The Minister's Wooing.*" *New England Quarterly* 66, no. 2 (June 1993): 179-197.
    Harris sees this novel as containing an important subtext which highlights women's lives and abilities, despite its apparent adherence to the cover story of subordination couched in romance and the history of New England Calvinism. This "covert" tale is set in "female territory" expressed through scattered images of eggs, nests, shells, pearls, and other objects which, along with repeated references to the sea and to women sewing and spinning, form a "feminine iconography."

Hedrick, Joan D. *Harriet Beecher Stowe: A Life.* New York: Oxford University Press, 1994.
    This Pulitzer Prize-winning biography includes extensive notes, a bibliography, and a selection of photographs from *The Schlesinger Library* and the *Stowe-Day Foundation.* Hedrick sees Stowe as an "odd and whimsical woman" driven by the Beecher family sense of mission. The biography attempts to place her in the context of the mores of her times with emphasis on the powerful influence of the cult of "true womanhood." For example, Hedrick documents how middle-class families dealt with high rates of infant morality and how the death of her own eighteen-month-old son "mobilized" Stowe to speak to other mothers about the pain of losing a child. Hedrick also provides a literary history of America which chronicles the role both of the parlor societies that nourished Stowe's literary talents and of journals such as *The Atlantic Monthly* (which Stowe helped found) in espousing a professionalized "high" culture that ultimately devalued her work.
    See also: Joan D. Hedrick, "Parlor Literature: Harriet Beecher Stowe and the Question of 'Great Women Artists,'" *Signs* 17, no. 2 (Winter 1992): 275-303.

Karcher, Carolyn L. "Reconceiving Nineteenth Century American Literature: The Challenge of Women Writers." *American Literature* 66, no. 4 (December 1994): 781-793.

Karcher believes that Stowe's work, especially *The Minister's Wooing* (1859), as well as the work of Lydia Maria Child and Susan Ridley Sedgwick, is proof of the need to rethink conventional wisdom about the nature of American literature. Stowe and other women writers of her time wrote social novels rather than romances in order to delineate the real problems of their day. They were far more active reformers than their male peers, and they wrote more or less openly about women's right to sexual pleasure despite the assumption that it was the prudishness of female readers that prevented male writers from a frank portrayal of sexuality.

Lang, Amy Schrager. "Slavery and Sentimentalism: The Strange Career of Augustine St. Clare." *Women's Studies* 12 (1986): 31-54.

Lang argues that it is Stowe's rigid separation of public and private spheres that causes the problematic "femininity" of *Uncle Tom's Cabin*. Stowe's inability to transcend gender types results from her adherence to the sentimentalist view of women and blacks as by nature more Christian, more affectionate, more sympathetic, and more just than white men. Though Stowe's women have the capacity to sympathize with the oppressed, they are unable to translate that sympathy into action as symbolized by the premature death of the "feminine" St. Clare before he was able to free Tom.

Levine, Robert L. "*Uncle Tom's Cabin* in Frederick Douglass' Paper: An Analysis of Reception." *American Literature* 64, no. 1 (March 1992): 71-93.

Levine examines Douglass' own commentary on the novel and other discussions of it he chose to publish, including the letters of Martin Delany, with whom he engaged in an open debate about Stowe's "racist" support of colonization. Despite critiques of Douglass' naiveté in supporting Stowe, especially after her initial opposition to black suffrage, Levine believes that Douglass had genuine respect for her ability to sympathize with the oppression of others and that, in effect, he was appropriating the novel to make sure that it did the work "it announced itself as doing." Knowledge of the dialogue between Stowe and Douglass provides hope for communication between blacks and whites and can help critics in the 1990's to "historicize" their own feelings about the novel.

MacFarlane, Lisa Watt. "'If I Get to Where I Can': The Competing Rhetorics of Social Reform in *Uncle Tom's Cabin*." *American Transcendental Quarterly* 4, no. 2 (June 1990): 135-147.

MacFarlane identifies three vocabularies, each associated with the journey of one of the major characters: Eliza and domestic ideology, George and republicanism, and Tom and Christian evangelicalism.

These languages interact and sometimes contradict each other; in analyzing the conflicts among them, MacFarlane reveals the limitations of the ideologies they articulate. Inherent in Stowe's novel are "all the reasons the Civil War failed as social reform" and left behind a legacy of racism.

Schultz, Nancy Lusignan. "The Artist's Craftiness: Miss Prissy in *The Minister's Wooing.*" *Studies in American Fiction* 20, no. 1 (Spring 1992): 33-44.
   Schultz sees Miss Prissy not just as a stereotypic comic confidante, but as a metaphor for the "subtle but subversive" power of female artists in a patriarchal culture. Miss Prissy is a dressmaker and a gossip who likes to construct stories; Stowe treats both these art forms with a mix of irony and seriousness and credits them with unraveling the forces that threaten the happiness of the main protagonists. Miss Prissy and not the narrator speaks the novel's "last words," in effect writing the proper comic outcome.

Stepto, Robert B. "Sharing the Thunder: The Literary Exchanges of Harriet Beecher Stowe, Henry Bibb, and Frederick Douglass," in *New Essays on Uncle Tom's Cabin,* ed. Eric J. Sundquist. Cambridge, England: Cambridge University Press, 1986.
   Stepto identifies two slave narratives by Henry Bibb and Josiah Henson, both published in 1849 and widely discussed, as sources for Stowe's "bifurcated" hero. Tom, dark and meek, has close connections to Henson; Harris, fair and aggressive, combines elements of Bibb and Frederick Douglass, with whom Stowe regularly corresponded. Stepto also compares Douglass's "The Heroic Slave" (1853) with *Uncle Tom's Cabin,* noting their many similarities including the use of the vernacular, their presentation of the "geography" of slavery, and the contrast between home and tavern as symbolic representations of good and evil. Douglass, however, differs from Stowe in that his hero is much more skeptical about the role of the Christian church in aiding abolition and he sends him to live in the British Bahamas rather than Liberia in support of his belief that American blacks should stick together in the New World. In effect, Douglass's hero, Madison Washington, renders Tom "visible" by giving him some of Harris's characteristics: "a body promising action and a voice promising speech."

Sundquist, Eric J. *New Essays on Uncle Tom's Cabin.* Cambridge, England: Cambridge University Press, 1986.
   This collection includes two essays on the role of women in Stowe's novel, one on the Calvinist and gothic sources of the novel, and two on the relationship between the novel and black cultural history; these last two by Stepto and Yarborough are annotated here. Sundquist's introduction provides a history of the novel's critical reputation over the years; he looks at the reasons behind black calls for the novel to be

banned and summarizes feminist reevaluations. In his own analysis of *Uncle Tom's Cabin*, Sundquist concludes that the novel failed to go "all the way" in its condemnation of racism, and that its final vision of a new Christian nation in Africa is partly a response to northern fears about the potential mixing of races following emancipation.

Szczesiul, Anthony E. "Catholic Hagiography and *Uncle Tom's Cabin.*" *American Transcendental Quarterly* 10, no. 1 (March 1996): 59-72.

Stowe was criticized by the Catholic Church for her apparent appropriation of Catholic doctrine. Szczesiul believes that Stowe intentionally looked to Catholic hagiography for its emphasis on the supernatural and because of her own dissatisfaction with Calvinism. The portraits of Tom and Eva, in particular, seem to draw upon the lives of Catholic saints and to reflect Stowe's belief in an active, caring God who aids Christians on earth as they mobilize to achieve a new world order.

Tompkins, Jane. "Sentimental Power: *Uncle Tom's Cabin* and the Politics of Literary History." *Glyph* 8 (1981): 79-102. Reprinted in: Jane Tompkins, *Sensational Designs*. New York: Oxford University Press, 1985.

Tompkins sees Stowe's novel as "the most important book of the century" and as a "brilliant" example of nineteenth century America's favorite plot: "the story of salvation through motherly love." It is a work which should be evaluated as a "political enterprise, halfway between sermon and social theory," rather than in terms of "stylistic intricacy" or other formalistic criteria. The story of Little Eva's death, for example, rather than being mocked for its overwrought sentimentalism, should be understood in terms of Christian theology which teaches that "the highest human calling is to give one's life for another." The book can also be understood as a "jeremiad," fusing theology and politics effectively enough to persuade the country to go to war and free its slaves. Stowe's ultimate goal, expressed in "the Quaker Settlement," was to bring about a kingdom of heaven guided by a matriarch who rules with loving kindness, dispensing "holy communion" from her kitchen.

Wolff, Cynthia Griffin. "'Masculinity' in *Uncle Tom's Cabin.*" *American Quarterly* 47, no. 4 (December 1995): 595-618.

According to Wolff, by 1850 the Puritan definition of "manliness" based on a balance between individualism and civic duty was being challenged by the "ruthless pursuit of money and property," with self-sacrifice and sensitivity devalued as "feminine." Stowe's depiction of Uncle Tom was consciously intended to emphasize his "heroic, loving, and manly" qualities in keeping with abolitionist and reformist thinking about the importance of fraternal love. St. Augustine, as the passive and "feminized" opposite of Tom, represents the distortion of this ideal. And Legree represents a "violent cartoon" version of the aggressive and competitive masculinity embodied by George.

Yarborough, Richard. "Strategies of Black Characterization in *Uncle Tom's Cabin* and the Early Afro-American Novel." in *New Essays on Uncle Tom's Cabin*, ed. Eric J. Sundquist. Cambridge, England: Cambridge University Press, 1986.

Yarborough sees Stowe's novel as the "epicenter" of a massive cultural phenomenon; her characters "leaped" into the status of cultural archetypes that dominated the fictional treatment of Afro-Americans by black and white writers for several generations. Stowe herself relied heavily on popular stereotypes, including the darky figures of the minstrel stage. Yarborough illustrates, for example, how Topsy's famous dance reflects the odd notion whites held of Afro-American folk music and dance. He also highlights the distinctions Stowe makes between full- and mixed-blood blacks that reflect nineteenth century prejudicial concepts of race; the heroism of George and Eliza is closely aligned with their "whiteness." Though most twentieth century African American writers have tried to distance themselves from everything *Uncle Tom's Cabin* represents, northern blacks in the 1850's saw it as a "godsend" to mobilize white sentiment against slavery, and black writers up until World War I followed Stowe's lead.

SUSAN WARNER
1819-1885

Born in New York City, Warner was raised on a small island in the Hudson River where the family was forced to move following her father's business losses. Susan and her younger sister Anna were ultimately responsible for supporting themselves, their father, and a paternal aunt who stayed with them following the death of their mother. Both sisters became prolific writers, though their earnings were not enough to return the family to prosperity. Susan's first novel, *The Wide, Wide World* (1850), became the nation's first "best-seller" and was translated into many languages. Her second novel, *Queechy* (1852) was almost as popular. In her lifetime, Warner published more than twenty-five books and collaborated on children's works with her sister, as well.

Reissued Editions
The Wide, Wide World. New York: Feminist Press of City University of New York, 1987.

Biography and Commentary
Dobson, Joanne. The Hidden Hand: Subversion of Cult Ideology in Three Mid-Nineteenth Century Women's Novels." *American Quarterly* 38, no. 2 (Summer 1986): 223-242.

Dobson establishes the basic tenets of the "ethos of domestic femininity" and then considers how this ethos is reflected in the work of E. D. E. N. Southworth, A. D. T. Whitney, and Susan Warner, writers whose popular novels "subvert feminine ideals" despite following the conventional sentimental pattern of tracing an abandoned female child's progress from girlhood to marriage. On the surface, *The Wide, Wide World* is about Ellen Montgomery's education into non-rebellion in the face of suffering. However, a "strong emotional undertow" pulls the reader in the opposite direction through the cumulative weight of abuse and tyranny she experiences. Even the "prince" that comes to Ellen's rescue has the potential to be abusive as implied in his skill at breaking in horses. Ultimately, the novel is about survival and the price one pays for it; Ellen, like the female protagonists of other novels of the period and unlike Huckleberry Finn, cannot simply run away from her oppression.

Hovet, Grace Ann, and Theodore R. Hovet. "Identity Development in Susan Warner's *The Wide, Wide World*: Religion, Performance, and Construction." *Legacy* 8, no. 1 (Spring 1991): 3-16.
    The Hovets see Warner's novel as a key text in the "story of white middle class women's efforts to construct a meaningful identity in American culture" that would stress "interdependence" as an alternative to Emerson's self-reliance and autonomy. They identify three stages to female identity formation: the development of a "relational self" in childhood, passage to a "performing self" who experiments with different roles and learns to mask displeasing modes of self-expression in adolescence, and the maturation of an "adult self" who learns to negotiate between the needs of self-expression, role expectations, and pleasing others. Ellen Montgomery, the heroine of *The Wide, Wide World*, in her willingness as a wife to continue to perform and to silence her own voice, represents a regression from this model of which Warner was "not unaware."

Schnog, Nancy. "Inside the Sentimental: The Psychological Work of *The Wide, Wide World*." *Genders* 4 (March 1989): 11-25.
    Schnog looks to Warner's novel as a key document in the debate over the politics and mechanics of sentimentality and as an "invaluable" resource in the study of "women's psychosocial condition" in the nineteenth century. She considers the often criticized "tearful scenarios," not as a melodramatic exaggeration of human feelings, but as an honest effort on Warner's part to represent "real emotional and psychological experiences." Warner's religious females were not "duped buyers" of a system of belief that exacted their submission, but "generators" of a system of belief that helped them cope with the separations and isolation that often marked their lives, Schnog concludes.

Stewart, Veronica. The Wild Side of *The Wide, Wide World*." *Legacy* 11, no. 1 (1994): 1-16.
    Stewart agues that readers interested in the connections between

Warner and her novel should consider the character of Nancy Vawse as well as the protagonist, Ellen Montgomery. Nancy may represent the "more subversive and creative" side of Warner's personality. With her "chaotic lawlessness" and her "defiant" spirit of rebellion, she briefly disrupts the novel's dominant messages. In the end, as Nancy's power recedes, Ellen represses her delight in nature and turns to God for direction and authority.

White, Isabelle. "Anti-Individualism, Authority, and Identity: Susan Warner's Contradictions in *The Wide, Wide World.*" *American Studies* 31, no. 2 (Fall 1990): 31-41.

White sees Warner's novel as focused on the conflict between the individual and authority. Ellen Montgomery, the novel's protagonist, learns submission to male authorities so she can finally submit to God's authority. Warner's ideology, domesticity, and evangelical Christianity opposed American individualism and materialism and promised women compensation in the next world for their sacrifices in this one. Despite these apparent messages, the novel inadvertently encourages individualism and rewards its author and protagonist with power and material goods. White supports this analysis through consideration of an additional chapter included in the 1987 Feminist Press edition which "makes explicit what the original version only implies," that Ellen Montgomery in the end has internalized authority and thus earned a room of her own and a husband who will no longer oppose her wishes.

Williams, Cynthia Schoolar. "Susan Warner's *Queechy* and the *Bildungsroman* Tradition." *Legacy* 7, no. 2 (Fall 1990): 3-16.

Williams sees *Queechy* as similar in plot but broader in context than *The Wide, Wide World.* Though the heroine is "morally and spiritually perfect" at the beginning, from chapter 17 on, the novel follows the five stages of the *Bildungsroman* structure in interesting ways. Williams looks at each of these stages and how they compare with the traditional male version. The most important difference occurs in the final stage when, instead of embarking on a new life, the heroine seems entrapped and without prospects. The novel then requires a *deus ex machina* in the form of a male lover. His secret influence on the heroine's life, once revealed, returns the novel to the female domestic tradition and away from the "worldliness" implied by Warner's use of the *Bildungsroman* form.

Williams, Susan S. "Widening the World: Susan Warner, Her Readers, and the Assumption of Authorship." *American Quarterly* 42, no. 4 (December 1990): 565-586.

Williams argues that Warner was driven to write the kind of sentimental fiction she did by the expectations of her readers and her need to support herself. Critics who equate Warner with her heroine, Ellen Montgomery, miss the authorial distance she maintains. Warner originally published under the pseudonym Elizabeth Wetherell and resisted public desire to know more of her. Examination of original manuscripts reveals, however, that she soon began to edit out the more worldly and less domestic scenes in order to ensure strong sales. There is also evidence in the manuscripts that Warner, despite sincere devotion to her sister, found their famous relationship restrictive. Had Warner not been financially dependent on a particular public, she would clearly have written quite different novels, Williams concludes.

CONSTANCE FENIMORE WOOLSON
1840-1894

Woolson was the sixth of nine children, and the grand-niece of James Fenimore Cooper. She was born in New Hampshire and raised in Cleveland, Ohio, where her family moved following the death of her three older sisters from scarlet fever. Woolson never married; following the death of her mother in 1879, she and her sister traveled in Europe. Woolson died in Venice, a possible suicide, after living in Italy for many years and achieving some recognition for her regular contributions to *The Atlantic Monthly*. Her first collection of stories, *Castle Nowhere: Lake Country Sketches* (1875), based on family summers spent on Mackinac Island, was favorably compared to the work of Sarah Orne Jewett. Her second volume of stories, *Rodman the Keeper: Southern Sketches* (1880), deals sympathetically with the Reconstruction period. Her novels include *Anne* (1882), *For the Major* (1883), *East Angels* (1886), *Jupiter Lights* (1889), and *Horace Chase* (1894). Two collections of her Italian stories were published posthumously.

Reissued Editions
Anne. Salem, N.H.: Ayer, 1977.

Castle Nowhere: Lake Country Sketches. New York: AMS Press, 1971.

Horace Chase. New York: Irvington, 1986.

Jupiter Lights: A Novel. Irvine, Calif.: Reprint Services, 1992.

Rodman the Keeper: Southern Sketches. New York: Irvington, 1986.

Women Artists, Women Exiles: "Miss Grief" and Other Stories. New Brunswick, N.J.: Rutgers University Press, 1988.

Biography and Commentary
Brehm, Victoria. "Island Fortresses: The Landscape of the Imagination in the Great Lakes Fiction of Constance Fenimore Woolson." *American Realism* 22 (1990): 51-66.

Brehm looks at Woolson's use of remote settings in more than twenty of her early stories as an imaginative projection of her own need to escape the expectations of feminine domesticity in both her life and her fiction. These stories divide into two groups—the first ten are literally set on Great Lakes islands, the second ten in wilderness clearings isolated by a lake on one side and "impenetrable timber" on the other. Brehm focuses on "Ballast Island" (1873) as typical of the first group in its portrait of a woman who survives a hostile world and achieves independence. Woolson's spinster sacrifices her own happiness for a greater good and starts life in a new place strengthened by her struggle. Woolson's later stories set in the South depict characters who no longer run away, but live as outsiders within a society of close family traditions.

Dean, Sharon L. "Homeward Bound: The Novels of Constance Fenimore Woolson." *Legacy* 6, no. 2 (Fall 1989): 17-28.
   Dean sees concerns with home and homelessness as a primary theme in Woolson's novels. Though her artists may choose independent and lonely existences, her major female characters almost always choose marriage for the sake of a home. Dean looks at Woolson's girl-women who need marriage and her more complex heroines who, like Woolson herself, search for other forms of "rootedness" in five of her novels. The last of these, *Horace Chase* (1894), is the only one with a heroine able to get a home without abandoning her independence; it is also the only Woolson novel in which the unmarried woman is not treated comically.

—————————. "Women as Daughters, Women as Mothers in the Fiction of Constance Woolson," in *Critical Essays on Constance Fenimore Woolson*, ed. Cheryl B. Torsney. New York: G. K. Hall, 1992.
   Despite not having been a mother herself, Woolson was clearly a close observer of parent-child interactions. Dean looks at her depictions of father-daughter, mother-son, and mother-daughter relationships and finds them "remarkably consistent with modern sociological and psychological theory." Dean also notes the connections between these stories and Woolson's own life, in particular the changed focus in her stories following the deaths first of her father, and later of her mother. Though Woolson's women "brood" over the choices they must make as mothers, Woolson herself was the product of a close family and lamented her own lack of "connectedness."

Gebhard, Caroline. "Constance Fenimore Woolson Rewrites Bret Harte: The Sexual Politics of Intertextuality," in *Critical Essays on Constance Fenimore Woolson*, ed. Cheryl B. Torsney. New York: G. K. Hall, 1992.
   Woolson was attracted to Harte's work because of its "uncouth characters and rugged scenes" which freed her from the confines of the female literary mode. Her early stories have a more somber tone than Harte's, but the influence is clear. In "The Lady of Little Fishing" (1874) Woolson consciously revises the male fantasy of Harte's "The

Luck of Roaring Camp" (1870), inserting a "female voice" and "female desire" into a male text. Gebhard offers a detailed comparison of the two works to demonstrate how Woolson has "rewritten" nineteenth century culture from a woman's point of view. Though the Lady suffers the same abandonment and death as does Harte's silent prostitute, the story is radical in its articulation of a woman speaking her desire. After this story Woolson soon dropped Harte as a literary model, but continued to write about sexual politics.

Torsney, Cheryl B. *Constance Fenimore Woolson: The Grief of Artistry.* Athens: University of Georgia Press, 1989.

Torsney examines Woolson's life in the sociocultural context of her life as a nineteenth century daughter, woman, and writer. She also looks at her work in relation to the development of the *Kunstlerroman* among women writers. Intelligent and unhappy artist heroines, "always marginal to society," appear in much of Woolson's work. Her "best" story, "Miss Grief," shows how artistry leads to the "grief of silence, of having something important to say and then having it suppressed."

See also Torsney's "The Traditions of Gender: Constance Fenimore Woolson and Henry James," in *Patrons and Protegees: Gender, Friendship, and Writing in Nineteenth Century America,* ed. Shirley Marchalonis, New Brunswick, N.J.: Rutgers University Press, 1988.

_____, ed. *Critical Essays on Constance Fenimore Woolson.* New York: G. K. Hall, 1992.

This volume contains an introductory history of Woolson criticism and reprints of contemporaneous reviews of her work and of analytic essays that appeared in journals and books on American literature between 1915 and 1990; there are also four new essays. The Brehm, Dean, Gebhard, and Weimer pieces annotated here are all included.

Weimer, Joan Myers. The 'Admiring Aunt' and the 'Proud Salmon of the Pond': Constance Fenimore Woolson's Struggle with Henry James," in *Critical Essays on Constance Fenimore Woolson,* ed. Cheryl B. Torsney. New York: G. K. Hall, 1992.

Weimer traces the history of the personal and professional relationship between Henry James and Woolson, concluding that it was productive for James, but ultimately destructive for Woolson. Though both "adapted images and situations from each other's work, built characters around one another's personal traits, and considered writing a play together," both also wrote stories which revealed how each was threatened by the other. Woolson tried to play the role of "admiring aunt" to James, which meant repressing her literary and sexual identities, according to Weimer. Worse yet, James's criticism of her work, though intended to be generous and supportive, was sometimes condescending and "misread" her, perhaps out of a subconscious need to see her as a "conservative woman" whose characters make heroic sacrifices for their men. Weimer compares *East Angels* (1886) with

James's *The Europeans* (1878) to demonstrate how Woolson transforms James's comedy of manners into an ironic tragedy and to argue for a reading of Woolson's work as a critique, rather than an endorsement of the heroine's self-immolation, as James described it.

_____. "Women Artists as Exiles in the Fiction of Constance Fenimore Woolson." *Legacy* 3, no. 2 (Fall 1986): 3-15.

Weimer sees Woolson as "of particular interest" to women's literary history because of her acute awareness of her "situation as a woman writer." Many of her female characters are exiles in one form or another—from their homes, from their feelings, from their own art—as Woolson was herself an exile for much of her life. Many of her stories depict the "excruciating dilemmas" of women artists. "Miss Grief," for example, is the portrait of a woman writer whose genius is incomprehensible to her readers. Though several of her contemporaries also depicted the struggles of women artists, none wrote fictions as "powerful or complex" as Woolson's, Weimer concludes.

Chapter 2
EARLY TWENTIETH CENTURY FICTION
WRITERS

This chapter is in many ways a sequel to the previous one. Several of the authors straddle both centuries, and many of the general studies annotated in chapter 1 include references to writers discussed here. Many late nineteenth century trends continued and intensified in the years preceding and following passage of the Nineteenth Amendment. With the rise of the "new woman" and the backlash against her (see Patterson below), twentieth century women found themselves facing an anomalous mix of opportunities and obstacles in almost every career move they made. This is especially true of literature, where so-called professionalization of standards led to the devaluation of "popular" writers, mostly women, despite achievement of important literary recognition. In fact, half of the first twenty-four Pulitzer Prizes awarded for fiction (1918-1943) went to women, including Edith Wharton (1920), Willa Cather (1922), Margaret Wilson (1924), Edna Ferber (1925), Julia Peterkin (1929), Margaret Ayer Barnes (1931), Pearl Buck (1932), Caroline Miller (1934), Josephine Winslow Johnson (1935), Margaret Mitchell (1937), Marjorie Kinnan Rawlings (1939), and Ellen Glasgow (1942). Over the next twenty-four years (1943-1967) only three women were so honored: Harper Lee (1961), Shirley Ann Grau (1965), and Katherine Anne Porter (1966).

As the century progressed, critics and academics defined "modernism" as the reigning literary movement, a movement which privileged irony, literary experimentation, complex use of symbolism, and cynicism toward traditional values. Good literature was increasingly expected to be "difficult" and in need of "decoding." Writers whose fiction was conventional and easily accessible to an unsophisticated audience were, therefore, dismissed as pandering to the public. Nowhere is this value system more evident than in the scorn accorded to Pearl Buck following her Nobel Prize in 1931. And though most readers would agree that Buck's work simplifies and romanticizes Chinese life, its enormous influence on American attitudes is also beyond dispute. Frequent references to Edith Wharton as a lesser Henry James also reflect the devaluation of the popular female writer. For example, Alfred Kazin in *On Native Grounds* (1942), a "classic" study of American literature, states that Wharton lacks James's power to "excite the literary mind," despite the fact that she speaks "plainly," "with a force he (James) could never muster."

Both Wharton and Buck made small fortunes from their best-selling books; this too was held against them. Another female writer who made a fortune from her best-sellers was the mystery writer Mary Roberts Rinehart, the best-paid writer in the United States for almost fifty years. Despite this success and the fact that her books have never gone out of print, she was completely forgotten by the critical establishment following her death in 1958. Rinehart and her peers, unlike previous generations of women writers, saw themselves as professionals whose lives were dedicated to their careers, though they made occasional public pronouncements to the contrary. Their productivity was immense: Buck, Cather, Glasgow, Rinehart, and Wharton wrote dozens of novels, scores of stories, and countless essays. Writing was a full-time occupation accompanied by public appearances, philanthropic activities, and participation in professional literary circles. Rinehart and Buck also each raised several children.

Most of the women who achieved success as writers came from middle- and upper-middle-class backgrounds and wrote about the lives of women not unlike themselves. However, the growing urbanization of America also created interest in immigrant culture and the lives of the poor. Especially during the Depression, there was an audience for both the ghetto melodramas of Anzia Yezierska, who wrote from personal experience, and the proletarian novels of Josephine Herbst, who wrote from the perspective of a political activist and journalist. Few women chroniclers of the working class achieved the success of their male peers Frank Norris, John Dos Passos, or John Steinbeck, perhaps because women were still expected to write romances with acceptable endings— happy or tragic. Edith Summers Kelley is included here as an example of a writer whose work, despite critical acclaim, was considered too grim to gain much of a readership in its own time. The Feminist Press reissue of her novel, *Weeds*, and of Agnes Smedley's *Daughter of Earth* (see chapter 4) reflects a growing interest in women writers who participated in the radical and progressive movements of the 1920's, 1930's, and 1940's. There is also new interest in Marjorie Kinnan Rawlings's portraits of the Florida poor and Mari Sandoz's historical fiction about Native Americans.

Another type of work, the young adult novel, has played an increasingly important role in the twentieth century. It is only quite recently that children's books have been identified as a separate genre; I have intentionally included them in the two chapters on the novel because I believe they merit serious literary consideration. The extraordinary popularity of Louisa May Alcott in the 1870's and 1880's and of Frances Hodgson Burnett at the turn of the century was matched by Laura Ingalls Wilder in the 1930's and 1940's. Moreover, the film and television versions of these writers' works have ensured their continued popularity.

Finally, let me refer to two popular writers not annotated in this chapter because their work as of 1996 had not yet been the subject of serious critical reevaluation. Edna Ferber (1885-1968) published thirteen novels, eight plays, and several collections of short stories. *So Big* (1924), *Show Boat* (1926), *Cimarron* (1929), *Saratoga Trunk*

(1941) and *Giant* (1952) were all made into films. Ferber also collaborated with George S. Kaufman on several popular plays, including *Royal Family* (1928), *Dinner at Eight* (1932), and *Stage Door* (1936). Elizabeth Seifert (1897-1983), sometimes referenced under her married name Gasparotti, published more than eighty novels, mostly medical romances such the famous *Young Doctor Galahad* (1938). At least half of these are regularly reprinted often in large print format for elderly readers.

Clearly, women continued to play active roles in American literature in the early twentieth century, as they had at the end of the nineteenth, yet there are few general studies which reflect their contributions. Only Willa Cather and sometimes Edith Wharton are regularly referenced. Despite their absence in general studies of the modern novel, women writers are often the central focus in studies of particular ethnic groups (Jewish women writers, Asian women writers) or of more specialized genres (science fiction, utopias, humor). I have included here a few books and articles which offer a broad overview of the period or focus on a small group of writers. However, most of the annotations are of critical works on individual writers. *American Literature, Modern Fiction Studies, Studies in Short Fiction,* and *Studies in the Novel* occasionally contain articles on Cather, Glasgow, Porter, and Wharton, the most "respected" of the writers here; *Women's Studies* has published articles on almost all of them.

GENERAL STUDIES

Brown, Dorothy. *Setting a Course: American Women in the 1920's.* Boston: G. K. Hall, 1987.

This volume in Twayne's American Women in the Twentieth Century series focuses on the "New Woman" and her relationship to the rapidly changing cultural and political life of the 1920's. Brown looks at political reform work, education, religion, family life, and literature during the period. Also included is a brief biographical essay.

Donovan, Josephine. *After the Fall: The Demeter-Persephone Myth in Wharton, Cather, and Glasgow.* University Park: Pennsylvania State University Press, 1989.

Donovan believes that this myth can be used to allegorize the transformation from a "matricentric preindustrial culture" represented by Demeter to an industrial realm of "patriarchal captivity" represented by the abduction of Persephone and her eating of the pomegranate seed despite her mother's warning. The first two chapters of the text examine the role of social Darwinists and sexologists in bringing about the "fall" of women's culture, and the work of Mary E. Wilkins Freeman, Charlotte Perkins Gilman, and Sarah Orne Jewett as a reflection of changing ideologies with respect to women's lives and identities. The rest of the text focuses on Edith Wharton, Willa Cather, and Ellen Glasgow, three "major" writers linked by gender, race, class, nationality, and their personal genius. Donovan traces how their handling of the myth was influenced by their historical relationship with the women writers of their mother's generation, how each treated the myth differently at different stages of her career, and how each ultimately returned to a matriarchal vision late in life.

Gelfant, Blanche H. *Women Writing in America: Voices in Collage.* Hanover, N.H.: University Press of New England, 1984.

This is an eclectic collection of essays on twentieth century writers, including Willa Cather, Katherine Anne Porter, Anzia Yezierska, Mary Austin and Meridel LeSueur. Gelfant pairs these writers in unusual ways in order to hear their voices more clearly. She notes the "intersection" of American motifs with women's themes, and the degree to which even "traditional" writers subvert conventional expectations about women's roles. In her discussion of urban novels, she highlights images of survival, focusing on female characters who are "not mad, suicidal starving, raging, or sinking into inanition." Throughout these essays, Gelfant demonstrates the "strength" of women writers, despite the "exigencies" which threatened to silence them.

Gilbert, Sandra M., and Susan Gubar. *No Man's Land: The Place of the Woman Writer in the Twentieth Century.* New Haven: Yale University Press, 1988.

This is a three-volume history of the ongoing literary battle of the sexes, which Gilbert and Gubar see as one of the major "meta" stories of the twentieth century. Two key assumptions mark their thinking: that authors are "gendered" human begins whose writings will necessarily reflect their own experience of male-female relationships, and that the late nineteenth century rise of feminism and fall of Victorian concepts of femininity fueled the sexual battle. The first volume, *The War of the Words,* looks at literary modernism as practiced by British and American, male and female writers, from Tennyson to Woolf, and from Hemingway to Plath. The second volume, *Sexchanges,* offers detailed readings of the lives and works of Cather, Wharton, Gilman, and other writers associated with either World War I or the emergence of a lesbian literary tradition. The final volume, *Letters from the Front,* considers the flowering of feminist modernism in such writers as H. D., Marianne Moore, and Zora Neale Hurston. Together the three volumes are intended "to illuminate the radical transformations of culture" that have made the "territory of literature," as well as the institutions of marriage and the family, of education and the professions, into a "vexed" terrain where men and women seem constantly in conflict.

Hapke, Laura. *Daughters of the Great Depression: Women, Work, and Fiction in the American 1930's.* Athens: University of Georgia Press, 1995.

Hapke looks at reports from the Department of Labor, articles in business magazines, and images from films and fiction for evidence of the conflicts and tensions affecting women wage earners during the

Depression. Despite the fact that women needed to work more than ever in order to help support themselves and their families, women who did so were often depicted as "harlots or bad mothers," and blamed for taking jobs away from men. The fiction of the period documents the "collective guilt" expressed by women, whether stenographers, teachers, domestics, or factory workers. Hapke notes that even "radical" writers like Meridel Le Sueur and Agnes Smedley portrayed working women as "overburdened mothers," rather than as "champions of the proletariat." Only a few writers, such as Josephine Herbst, created women characters who find salvation in a good job, rather than a good man.

Kessler, Carol Farley, ed. *Daring to Dream: Utopian Fiction by U. S. Women before 1950*, 2nd ed. Syracuse, N.Y.: Syracuse University Press, 1995.
This updated version omits several pieces from the first 1984 edition which are now readily available. The second edition includes three full-length stories and excerpts from five novels.

Levy, Helen Fiddyment. *Fiction of the Home Place: Jewett, Cather, Glasgow, Porter, Welty, and Naylor*. Jackson: University Press of Mississippi, 1992.
Levy sets up a definition of the "homeplace" and its primary characteristics based on Charlotte Perkins Gilman's *Herland* (see chapter 6 of Levy's book); it is an ideal pastoral domestic setting presided over by an elder wise woman who embodies the care and wisdom associated with maternity. The "homeplace" is egalitarian and cooperative, existing in a "seamless" relationship with the natural environment, and thus stands in opposition to the male literary spaces of forest and marketplace. Levy traces a progression from the language of competitive individualism to a mythic and almost telepathic communication in the late work of the six writers she studies. In the process of rejecting patriarchal narrative forms, these writers all arrived at an appreciation of their own "artistic tasks" and the legacy of their "mothers," Levy concludes.

Patterson, Martha. "'Survival of the Fitted': Selling the American New Woman as Gibson Girl, 1895-1910." *American Transcendental Quarterly* 9, no. 2 (June 1995): 73-87.
Patterson believes that the Gibson Girl images (the Beauty, the Boy-girl, the Flirt, the Sentimental, the Convinced, and the Well-Balanced), which appeared in *Collier's Weekly, Life*, and other popular magazines at the turn of the century, "legitimized, democratized, and commercialized" the so-called "new woman." Charles Dana Gibson, their creator, was able to co-opt the most threatening aspects of the new woman and make them palatable to a mass market; the "Gibson Girl might play golf, but she certainly didn't play politics." Those women who did participate in the suffrage movement were portrayed as humorless and unattractive. Patterson quotes from Chopin, Wharton,

and Gilman to demonstrate the power and pervasiveness of these images. She concludes that Gibson Girls did offer women a degree of freedom from the "strictures of Victorian femininity" while at the same time serving the needs of consumer capitalism by persuading women to invest substantially in the packaging and marketing of their own appearance.

Wagner-Martin, Linda. *The Modern American Novel, 1914-1945.* Boston: G. K. Hall, 1990.

This volume in Twayne's Critical History of the Novel series includes a bibliography and a chronology which lists major publications and deaths of significant writers from 1909 to 1945. Wagner-Martin's focus is a reconsideration of literary "modernism" as a much more diverse movement in terms of its writers, themes, and styles than has generally been assumed. Beginning with the evolution of modernism, she looks at the contributions of Cather, Glasgow, Wharton, and Gertrude Stein (see chapter 3). She then singles out as a high point in literary history the year 1925, which saw the publication of Cather's *The Professor,* Glasgow's *Barren Ground,* Wharton's *The Mother's Recompense,* Stein's *The Making of Americans,* and Yezierska's *The Bread Givers,* as well as novels by Fitzgerald, Dreiser, Hemingway, Dos Passos, and Sinclair Lewis. Other chapters discuss the Harlem Renaissance, including the work of Larsen and Hurston (see chapter 5) and the "proletarian realism" of the 1930's, including the work of Meridel Le Sueur and Herbst. Common to all these writers is a pessimism about modern American culture; seldom do their novels describe positive relationships among women or a woman's capacity to achieve a fulfilling life.

GERTRUDE ATHERTON
1857-1948

Atherton was born in San Francisco and raised by her mother and maternal grandparents following her parents' divorce when she was three. In 1876 she eloped with George Atherton, who had previously been her mother's suitor. The couple had two children, the first of whom died of diphtheria in 1882, the year Atherton published her first novel, *The Randolphs of Redwoods.* Serialized anonymously in the *Argonaut,* a San Francisco weekly, it was later published as *A Daughter of the Vine* (1899). Following George's death in 1887, Atherton left her daughter with her mother and moved to New York City, where she wrote a weekly column, "Letter from New York," for the *Argonaut* and published her second novel, *What Dreams May Come* (1888). During a trip to Europe Atherton wrote *Los Cerritos* (1890), her first California novel. She then returned to San Francisco and began visiting historic missions and interviewing local inhabitants in order to gather material for future novels. This period also marked the beginning of her friendship with Ambrose Bierce, the *San Francisco Examiner's* most influential and acerbic critic. Bierce helped promote

The Doomswoman (1892), the California love story Atherton hoped would establish her reputation as a novelist. Atherton spent the next twenty-five years in New York, England, and Europe writing journalistic pieces and novels and reporting on World War I for *The New York Times*. During the last two decades of her life in San Franciso, she presided over the local chapter of the writers' organization PEN, was elected to the National Institute of Arts and Letters, and received a Gold Medal from the city. When she died at the age of ninety, Atherton was working on a novel about quicksilver mining in California to add to the more than fifty books, mostly novels, she had already produced.

Reissued Editions
Adventures of a Novelist. Salem, N.H.: Arno Press, 1980.

Los Cerritos. Ridgewood, N.J.: The Gregg Press,1968.

The Doomswoman. Upper Saddle River, N.J.: Literature House, 1970.

The Foghorn Stories. Salem, N.H.: Books for Libraries Press, 1970.

The Spinners Book of Fiction (a posthumous collection). Boston: G. K. Hall, 1979.

Biography and Commentary
Bradley, Jennifer. "Woman at the Golden Gate: The Last Works of Gertrude Atherton." *Women's Studies* 12, no. 1 (1986): 17-30.
 Bradley focuses on Atherton's writings during the 1930's and 1940's, when Atherton's apparent preoccupation with California history led some critics to complain that she was trapped in the past.

Leider, Emily Wortis. *California's Daughter: Gertrude Atherton and Her Times*. Stanford: Stanford University Press, 1991.
 This illustrated biography includes a chronology and a bibliography. Leider believes Atherton's importance lies in her achievements as a social historian rather than as a creative artist. Atherton's first novels were considered scandalous for their frank eroticism and brought their author a celebrity which she thoroughly enjoyed. Throughout her career she actively sought personal publicity. Leider highlights key events and friendships in Atherton's turbulent career, and notes that she herself became known as the embodiment of the robust competitive spirit of the California her novels described.

McClure, Charlotte S. *Gertrude Atherton*. Boston: G. K. Hall, 1979.
 This volume in Twayne's United States Authors series includes a chronology, a bibliography, an overview of Atherton's critical reputation, and a biographical essay. McClure divides Atherton's work into five periods and offers her own analysis of the major elements and

overall significance of her novels in relation to each other. Atherton, according to McClure, was a social historian whose critical observations were based on her own understanding of the relationship between human nature and culture.

Weir, Sybil. "Gertrude Atherton: The Limits of Feminism in the 1890's." *San Jose Studies* 1 (1975): 24-31.
Weir examines the relationship between Atherton's analysis of stereotypes and her fictional portrayals of women. She concludes that Atherton's characterizations of men and women were to some degree limited by the expectations of her female readers.

PEARL SYDENSTRICKER BUCK
1892-1973

Buck was born in West Virginia to missionary parents who took her to China when she was three months old. With the exception of her time as a student at Randolph-Macon's Woman's College, Buck spent most of her first forty years in China. In 1917 she married John Lossing Buck, who had gone to China to teach modern farming methods. Buck published her first book, *East Wind: West Wind*, in 1929, followed by *The Good Earth* in 1931, which was an overnight success and received the Pulitzer Prize for fiction. Buck divorced her husband to marry her publisher, Richard Walsh, in 1935. By this time she had decided to live permanently in the United States where her retarded daughter could receive the special care she needed. Buck bought a large country estate and she and Richard soon adopted four Amerasian children. In 1938, after having published seven additional books, Buck received the Nobel Prize for literature, which cited her "epic portrayals of Chinese life" and her "masterpieces of biography": *Fighting Angel* (1936) about her father, and *The Exile* (1936) about her mother. Though Buck continued to write, publishing more than eighty-five works of fiction and nonfiction throughout her life, her philanthropic activities assumed greater importance in the years following the Nobel Prize. She and Richard founded the East-West Association in 1941 to help promote human understanding, and Welcome House in 1949 to care for the children of Asian women and American soldiers. In the 1950's and 1960's, Buck spoke passionately about the dangers of the Cold War, the rights of disabled children, and the needs of women for greater freedom; she also started a new foundation to support abandoned Amerasian children in their own countries. Following her death, Buck's extraordinary life was commemorated with a special U. S. postage stamp.

Reissued Editions
The Big Wave. New York: HarperCollins, 1986.

The Child Who Never Grew. Rockville, Md.: Woodbine House, 1992.

East Wind: West Wind. Mount Kisco, N.Y.: Moyer Bell Ltd., 1993.

The Enemy. Mankato, Minn.: Creative Education, 1986.

The Good Earth. New York: Pocket Books, 1994.

The House of Earth Trilogy: The Good Earth, Sons, & A House Divided. Mount Kisco, N.Y.: Moyer Bell Ltd., 1995.

Little Red. Mankato, Minn.: Creative Education, 1987.

The Living Reed. Mount Kisco, N.Y.: Moyer Bell Ltd., 1990.

Mandala: A Novel of India. Mount Kisco, N.Y.: Moyer Bell Ltd., 1995.

The Old Demon. Mankato, Minn.: Creative Education, 1982.

The Oriental Novels of Pearl Buck Series including *Dragon Seed, Imperial Woman, The Three Daughters of Madame Liang.* Mount Kisco, N.Y.: Moyer Bell Ltd., 1991-1992.

Pavilion of Women. Mount Kisco, N.Y.: Moyer Bell Ltd., 1994.

A Pearl Buck Reader. New York: Reader's Digest Press, 1985.

Sons. Mount Kisco, N.Y.: Moyer Bell Ltd., 1992.

Biography and Criticism
Bellman, Samuel. "Popular Writers in the Modern Age: Constance Rourke, Pearl Buck, Marjorie Kinnan Rawlings, and Margaret Mitchell," in *American Women Writers: Bibliographical Essays,* eds. Maurice Duke, Jackson R. Bryer, and M. Thomas Inge. Westport, Conn.: Greenwood Press, 1983.
　　Bellman offers an annotated survey of available primary and secondary sources. He notes that Buck, like other "popular" women writers, has received little critical attention; this is partly because of the "gargantuan" amount of writing she did and the uneven quality of her fiction. What is needed, he suggests, is a comparative study that would contrast native Chinese and Taiwanese narratives of Chinese life with the "uncomplicated" pictures Buck provided.

Conn, Peter. "Pearl S. Buck and American Literary Culture," in *The Several Worlds of Pearl S. Buck: Essays Presented at a Centennial Symposium, Randolph-Macon Woman's College, March 26-28, 1992,* eds. Elizabeth J. Lipscombe, Frances E. Webb, and Peter Conn. Westport, Conn.: Greenwood Press, 1994.
　　Conn sees Buck as a writer of "homespun" conventional novels, several of which are worthy of critical reappraisal. *The Good Earth* and

The Townsman (1945) are both typical Depression stories which celebrate the soil and hard work. Buck published *The Townsman* under the pseudonym John Sedges because she believed her work had been devalued by both literary nationalism and sexism; positive reviews and substantial sales proved her right. Conn offers his reading of the novel, comparing it to the work of Sherwood Anderson and Sinclair Lewis.

Doyle, Paul A. *Pearl Buck.* Boston: G. K. Hall, 1980.
  This volume, part of the Twayne United States Authors series, is a revision of Doyle's 1963 text. It provides a comprehensive review of Buck's life and literary career, including discussion of her major works and her humanitarian activities. A chronology and bibliography are included. Doyle sees Buck as an "intermediary" between East and West and argues that she wrote three significant books, the biographies of her mother and father and *The Good Earth*, despite the disapprobation of the critical community. Doyle discusses the various reasons for her lack of critical success, the mixed response she received after winning the Nobel Prize, the influence of her missionary parents and her early reading on her literary theories, and the education she received from her Chinese nurse and tutor.

Haiping, Liu. "Pearl S. Buck's Reception in China Reconsidered," in *The Several Worlds of Pearl S. Buck: Essays Presented at a Centennial Symposium, Randolph-Macon Woman's College, March 26-28, 1992*, eds. Elizabeth J. Lipscombe, Frances E. Webb, and Peter Conn. Westport, Conn.: Greenwood Press, 1994.
  Shortly before her death the Chinese government refused Buck a visa despite the fact that she had devoted her whole life to "reconciling East and West winds." Haiping reviews the history of her reputation in China in trying to explain why. Most of Buck's works from the 1930's and 1940's were translated and widely read in China with critical reception ranging from positive identification of her as a special friend who wrote in the natural style of classic Chinese novels, to harsh criticism of her superficial and inaccurate portrait of Chinese life. During the Cold War period of Sino-American hostility, Buck's books were banned and several articles were published condemning her work as cultural imperialism. The current generation of Chinese young people have never heard of her.

La Farge, Ann. *Pearl Buck.* New York: Chelsea House Publishers, 1988.
  This illustrated biography, part of the American Women of Achievement series, is written for young readers. In addition to reviewing Buck's literary career, La Farge highlights her humanitarian activities culminating with the establishment of the Pearl S. Buck Foundation to provide education and support to Amerasian children in their respective homelands. This long and productive life became a model for civil rights leaders and women's rights activists of the

1960's. At the age of eighty-one, Buck was named by *Good Housekeeping* one of the most admired women in America, in third place after Rose Kennedy and Mamie Eisenhower.

Lipscombe, Elizabeth J., Frances E. Webb, and Peter Conn, eds. *The Several Worlds of Pearl S. Buck: Essays Presented at a Centennial Symposium, Randolph-Macon Woman's College, March 26-28, 1992.* Westport, Conn.: Greenwood Press, 1994.

This collection of twelve essays, including the ones by Conn, Haiping, and Thomson annotated here, is divided into three parts focusing on Buck's life and relationship with China, her humanitarian activities, and her literary career. Several of the essays discuss *Of Men and Women* (1941), a feminist critique of separate male and female economic spheres, and *My Several Worlds: A Personal Record* (1954), Buck's autobiography. There is also an extensive bibliography of primary and secondary sources on Buck and on China, an essay on the filming of *The Good Earth*, and an essay on Buck's writings about disabled children.

Stiriling, Nora. *Pearl Buck: A Woman in Conflict.* Piscataway, N.J.: New Century Publishers, 1983.

Stiriling begins her biography with a dramatic narrative of the Nanking Incident and its impact on Buck's family, which was trapped between warring factions in China's civil war. She sees Buck as a woman who constantly remade herself to win public approval. Buck's public image as a woman in total command of her life hid a fundamental insecurity and dependence on a series of men who became younger and "less worthy" as she got older. Stiriling provides a detailed description of each of these relationships and attempts to explain what each offered to Buck. She also provides general information about Buck's novels and philanthropic activities. A bibliography and photographs are included.

Thomson, James C., Jr. "Pearl S. Buck and the American Quest for China," in *The Several Worlds of Pearl S. Buck: Essays Presented at a Centennial Symposium, Randolph-Macon Woman's College, March 26-28, 1992,* eds. Elizabeth J. Lipscombe, Frances E. Webb, and Peter Conn. Westport, Conn.: Greenwood Press, 1994.

Thomson begins with a brief history of American attitudes toward China from the eighteenth century through the Tiananmen "tragedy" (1989). He then reviews Buck's experience of China, "cocooned within a foreign missionary compound" as a child, then traveling through the rural countryside with her first husband as a young woman. Thomson also recounts the controversy surrounding her Nobel Prize, the enmity of both the Chinese government and the American academic establishment toward her work, and the "grandiosity" she developed in later years. Still, he concludes, her accomplishments were extraordinary and she must be credited for helping her countless readers understand the fundamental humanity of the Chinese people.

WILLA CATHER
1873-1947

Cather was born in Gore, Virginia, the first of seven children, and later moved with her family to Red Cloud, Nebraska, a frontier town which she memorialized in her novels. After graduation from the University of Nebraska, Cather worked as a journalist and then took a job in Pittsburgh, where she lived for ten years and began writing fiction. In 1906 Cather moved to New York to join the staff of *McClure's Magazine*. She resigned from her editorial position there following its serialization of her first novel, *Alexander's Bridge*, in 1912. Over the next ten years Cather published five novels—*O Pioneers!* (1913), *The Song of the Lark* (1915), *My Ántonia* (1918), *One of Ours* (1922), and *A Lost Lady* (1923)—and received a Pulitzer Prize. Despite her growing literary reputation, Cather was becoming disillusioned with American life and suffering from poor health and depression. The next set of novels she would write—*The Professor's House* (1925), *My Mortal Enemy* (1926), *Death Comes for the Archbishop* (1927), and *Shadows on the Rock* (1931)—are more complex works which explore individual alienation in historical and religious contexts. Cather's last major projects were a complete edition of her works for Scribner's in 1937 and the novel *Sapphira and the Slave Girl* (1940).

Reissued Editions
Most of Cather's fiction is available in one or more hardback and paperback editions; there are also audiocassettes of her most popular stories.

Alexander's Bridge. New York: New American Library, 1988.

Collected Stories. New York: Random House, 1992.

Death Comes for the Archbishop. New York: Random House, 1993.

A Lost Lady. New York: Random House, 1990.

Lucy Gayheart. New York: Random House, 1976.

My Ántonia. New York: Penguin Books, 1994.

My Mortal Enemy. New York: Random House, 1990.

O Pioneers! New York: Random House, 1992.

On Writing: Critical Studies on Writing as an Art. Lincoln: University of Nebraska Press, 1988.

One of Ours. New York: Random House, 1991.

The Professor's House. New York: Random House, 1990.

Sapphira and the Slave Girl. New York: Random House, 1975.

Shadows on the Rock. New York: Random House, 1995.

The Song of the Lark. New York: New American Library, 1991.

Biography and Commentary
Arnold, Marilyn. "Two of the Lost," in *Willa Cather's Short Fiction.* Columbus: Ohio University Press, 1984.

Arnold identifies "A Wagner Matinee" and "Paul's Case" as two of Cather's best stories—the former about "human love and appreciation," the latter about the "ultimate alien" who is at home nowhere. Both stories are from *The Troll Garden,* a collection which focuses on the price to be paid for the pursuit of art or wealth.

Bloom, Harold, ed. *Modern Critical Views: Willa Cather.* New York: Chelsea House Publishers, 1985.

This collection of fifteen critical essays and appreciations written between 1942 and 1984 is followed by a chronology and bibliography. It includes the Arnold piece on two stories and the Murphy piece on the "archbishop" annotated here.

Carlin, Deborah. *Cather, Canon, and the Politics of Reading.* Amherst: University of Massachusetts Press, 1992.

Despite critical interest in Cather from scholars representing a wide diversity of reading communities, her late novels have often been ignored, perhaps because they do not seem to fit easily into any particular critical perspective. Some critics have argued that the late works depict Cather's escape into "art" as a reaction against the disorder of the modern world. Carlin argues that these novels are too complex and contradictory to be so easily understood and that they ultimately question the possibility of interpretation yielding an "ordered or fixed meaning." In her analysis of *My Mortal Enemy, Shadows on the Rock, Lucy Gayheart, Sapphira and the Slave Girl,* and the short story "Old Mrs. Harris" Carlin notes Cather's "self-reflexive revision" of conventional forms and the troubling questions she raises about race, class, power, and sexuality.

Carlin, Deborah and Janet Benton, eds. *Legacy* 9, no. 1 (Spring 1992).

This special issue on Willa Cather contains reviews of books, including those by Lee and Skaggs annotated here, profiles of Cather's friends, Louise Pound and Dorothy Canfield Fisher, and three new essays on *Sapphira and the Slave Girl, A Lost Lady,* and *Lucy Gayheart.*

Donovan, Josephine. "The Pattern of Birds and Beasts: Willa Cather and Women's Art," in *Writing the Woman Artist: Essays on Poetics, Politics, and Portraiture,* ed. Suzanne W. Jones. Philadelphia: University of Pennsylvania Press, 1991.

Donovan analyzes the impact of Sarah Orne Jewett on Cather's conception of the artist. Cather's early novels define the artist as a "vivisector" whose work demonstrates a sadistic dominance over nature. Through Jewett's influence, Cather in her later work came to see the artist as more in sympathy with her material. Donovan sees this shift as an unconscious acceptance of "women's art," the notion that daughters elaborate on the unacknowledged "everyday" arts (gardening, cooking, quilting) of their mothers. She demonstrates Jewett's influence on Cather through examination of five major novels from *O Pioneers!* to *The Professor's House.*

Flannigan, John H. "Thea Kronborg's Vocal Transvestism: Willa Cather and the 'Voz Contralto.'" *Modern Fiction Studies* 40, no. 4 (Winter 1994): 737-763.

Flannigan examines Thea's musical choices in *The Song of the Lark* in terms of her desire for "gender transformations." He also compares her performances with those of Olive Fremstad, the opera singer whom Cather used as her model. For both Thea and Olive, the contralto voice itself provided a new vocal range in which male and female were merged.

Fryer, Judith. *Felicitous Space: The Imaginative Structures of Edith Wharton and Willa Cather.* Chapel Hill: University of North Carolina Press, 1986.

Fryer analyzes Cather's novels in terms of her attempt to find a mode of artistic creation which was neither as artificial as the carefully constructed drawing rooms of Wharton and James, nor as purely spontaneous as the open-air naturalism of Dreiser and Norris. Cather's interest in construction begins with the real bridge Alexander builds, a very different structure from the piece of pottery, the quilt, fruit cave, or attic sewing room in later novels. Cather sees form as the necessary envelope, the body which contains and gives shape to desire. Ultimately, the American Southwest became "her spiritual center," a liberating space which freed her imagination as she concentrated on her inner vision and simplified her own literary edifices.

Gilbert, Sandra M., and Susan Gubar. "Lighting Out for the Territories: Willa Cather's Lost Horizons," in *No Man's Land 2: Sexchanges.* New Haven: Yale University Press, 1989.

Gilbert and Gubar focus on Cather's skepticism about conventional sex roles and her ongoing critique of erotic desire. Focusing on her two major pioneer novels, *My Antonia* and *O Pioneers!*, they show how she uses the frontier to mythologize a period in history before "the fall into gender," when women were "economically productive and socially central." Later works are less explicit about "female potency" and more concerned with the need to separate love from erotic desire and erotic desire from artistic ambition. In *The Professor's House* these tensions reach their dramatic height, demonstrating how preoccupied Cather had become with the renunciation of desire itself.

Harrell, David. *From Mesa Verde to The Professor's House.* Albuquerque: University of New Mexico Press, 1992.

Harrell sees Cather's knowledge of Mesa Verde as the major determinant of the novel's structure and meaning. In support of this thesis, he documents Cather's lifelong interest in the cliff dwellers and her visit to Mesa Verde in 1915. He then compares "Tom Outland's Story" with that of Dick Wetherill, who first discovered Mesa Verde. Blue Mesa is a "thoroughly idealized version" of Mesa Verde which allowed Cather to celebrate primitive life in contrast to the disintegrating world she saw around her. Harrell supplements this analysis with his own chronology of *The Professor's House*, photographs of Mesa Verde, and an extensive bibliography, including relevant letters and historical brochures.

Harris, Jeanne. "Aspects of Athena in Willa Cather's Short Fiction." *Studies in Short Fiction* 28, no. 2 (Spring 1991): 177-182.

Harris examines four Cather stories—"Tommy the Unsentimental" (1896), "Resurrection" (1897), "The Treasure of Far Island" (1902), and "Flavia and Her Artists" (1905)—for examples of "compelling" female figures who embody the "androgynous" physical and spiritual characteristics of the goddess Athena. These female protagonists with their "gray fearless eyes," their athletic prowess, and their identity as a "father's child" express Cather's dissatisfaction with traditional notions of femininity.

Kaye, Frances W. *Isolation and Masquerade: Willa Cather's Women.* New York: Peter Lang, 1993.

Kaye is highly critical of Cather's political vision, which she defines as racist, anti-Semitic, conservative, and elitist. Because of the seductive beauty of Cather's language and the power of her "great heroines," Kaye feels she must warn readers against identifying with characters who are "exceptional" rather than "exemplary," and who "repudiate" the concerns of the average woman. Cather's major protagonists are either women who "operate in magnificent isolation" or male characters who may reflect elements of Cather's own life experience. Kaye analyzes Cather's novels chronologically in order to demonstrate how she ultimately resolved her ambivalence about women by writing *Death Comes for the Archbishop*, a novel which highlights a loving relationship between two men, with female characters safely and sympathetically depicted in the background.

Leddy Michael. *The Professor's House* and the Professor's Houses." *Modern Fiction Studies* 38, no. 2 (Summer 1992): 444-454.
    Leddy disagrees with the usual interpretation of St. Peter's two houses as representing polar opposites of good and bad, arguing that Cather intends a more complex, even contradictory reading. St. Peter is not simply a victim of materialism in search of a refuge; his old study does not simply represent "an isolated high ground." St. Peter, in fact, complains about the inconveniences of the old house and admires some artistic features of the new; he also welcomes unexpected visitors to his study. Leddy concludes that St. Peter, like Cather, is attracted to the old out of nostalgia, not because it is absolutely better than the new.
    See also Michael Leddy, "The Professor's House: The Sense of an Ending," *Studies in the Novel* 23, no. 4 (Winter 1991): 443-451, in which the author argues that the ending of this novel is not as pessimistic as generally viewed.

Lee, Hermione. *Willa Cather: Double Lives.* New York: Pantheon Books, 1989.
    This comprehensive biography includes photographs, a bibliography of secondary sources, and a list of collections of correspondence. Lee identifies Cather as the only woman writer to have appropriated the male pioneer tradition. Her "androgynous version" of the frontier story is clearly related to her own alienation from conventional femininity, though not a simple matter of repression. Cather was critical of "female weakness and emotionalism" and dedicated to "classic heroic forms," but this does not mean, according to Lee, that her fiction encodes a covert homosexuality, as other critics have argued. Cather's fiction is filled with "complex and rich" portraits of women: immigrants, theatrical ladies, obstructive matriarchs, and groups of stoic domestic workers. These and the many "contraries" in her writing are the major focus of Lee's biography.

March, John. *A Reader's Companion to the Fiction of Willa Cather,* ed. Marilyn Arnold. Westport, Conn.: Greenwood Press, 1993.
    This monumental encyclopedia offers alphabetized references to thousands of significant characters and allusions in Cather's work. References range from an explanation of the "circle" Jim Burden sees outside his window in *My Antonia* to identification of a Swedish mineralogist as the model for the German investor in *The Professor's House*. March began collecting this information in the late 1940's; Arnold and her student assistants checked and updated it for this volume.

Meyering, Sheryl L. *A Reader's Guide to the Short Stories of Willa Cather.* New York: G. K. Hall, 1994.

This comprehensive work provides the publishing history of each of Cather's stories, followed by an identification of major sources and influences, analysis of the story's relationship to Cather's work in general, and a review of critical discussions of the story.

Murphy, John J. "Filters, Portraits, and History's Mixed Bag: *A Lost Lady* and *The Age of Innocence.*" *Twentieth Century Literature* 38, no. 4 (Winter 1992): 476-485.
Despite the apparent lack of contact between Wharton and Cather, Murphy assumes Cather must have read *The Age of Innocence* and looks for evidence of its influence on *A Lost Lady*. After identifying similarities in characters, theme, and narrative technique, he concludes that both works reflect a mood of nostalgia and both teach the complexity of history, society, and human relationships.

_____. "Willa Cather's Archbishop: A Western and Classical Perspective." *Western American Literature* 13, no. 3 (Summer 1978): 161-169.
Murphy sees Jean Marie Latour, the protagonist of *Death Comes for the Archbishop*, as a variation on the typical Western hero exemplified by Huck Finn and the Virginian, Natty Bumppo. Moreover, Latour resembles Virgil's Aeneas in his stoic acceptance of fate and his apparent lack of passion; these contribute to the "timelessness" of his character.

O'Brien, Sharon. *Willa Cather: The Emerging Voice.* New York: Oxford University Press, 1987.
O'Brien focuses on Cather's childhood, adolescence, and the early years of her career to examine what she sees as the two key issues in her life: "her struggle to resolve the culturally imposed contradictions between femininity and creativity" and the long period of artistic apprenticeship between her first short story and her first novel. O'Brien credits several feminist theorists for helping her identify certain patterns in Cather's life and work and explains her decision to discuss Cather's lesbianism as based on her reading of love letters Cather wrote to Louise Pound while a college student. O'Brien concludes that with the writing of *O Pioneers!* and *The Song of the Lark* Cather moved beyond her earlier "infatuation with male values" to an appreciation of what she had once known as a child, "the narrative power of women's voices."
See also: Sharon O'Brien, "Mothers, Daughters, and the 'Art Necessity': Willa Cather and the Creative Process," in *American Novelists Revisited: Essays in Feminist Criticism,* ed. Fritz Fleischmann. Boston: G. K. Hall, 1982.

O'Connor, Margaret Anne, ed. *Women's Studies* 11, no. 3 (1984).
This special issue on Cather includes essays by Susan J. Rosowski, Marilyn Arnold, and other Cather critics, as well as photographs of Red Cloud with captions chosen from Cather's writings. The focus of the

essays is on Cather as a woman and how gender affected her vision of the world. There is also discussion of the response her work received from the male critical establishment.

Rosowski, Susan J. *The Voyage Perilous: Willa Cather's Romanticism.* Lincoln: University of Nebraska Press, 1986.

This illustrated text has as its premise that Cather's work is best understood as "romantic" in the literary historical meaning of the term. Her major themes—love of nature, exaltation of youth and the superior individual, and a sympathetic identification with the past—are typical of nineteenth century romanticism, as is her focus on the power of imagination "to transform and give meaning to an alien or meaningless material world." Rosowski offers her own reading of each of Cather's major novels in terms of its romantic elements, and concludes that the early works celebrate the power of imagination, the middle works depict its role as a vehicle for personal salvation, and the late works explore the dark "gothic" side to life revealed through imagination.

Skaggs, Merrill Maguire. *After the World Broke in Two: The Later Novels of Willa Cather.* Charlottesville: University Press of Virginia, 1990.

Skaggs identifies 1922 as a watershed year for Cather, the beginning of a "slide toward despair." The text offers an analysis of Cather's last eight novels in the context of her personal experiences and responses to critical reviews. Skaggs sees Cather as "ferociously competitive" and "thin-skinned," as a highly self-conscious and controlling artist whose fiction contains "no accidents." With *One of Ours* Cather set out to prove she could write a "manly battle" narrative; when critics panned the novel despite its Pulitzer Prize, she responded with "frenzied activity," alternating between depression and exhilaration as she faced the many traumas which marked her life over the next twenty years.

Stuckey, William J. *Modern Fiction Studies* 36, no. 1 (Spring 1990).

This special issue includes ten biographical and critical essays and a review of recent books on Cather.

Wasserman, Loretta. *Willa Cather: A Study of the Short Fiction.* Boston: G. K. Hall, 1991.

This text is divided into three sections with a chronology and bibliography appended. The first includes background information on Cather's life and aesthetic theories, and Wasserman's interpretation of approximately fifteen of Cather's best-known stories. The second part includes excerpts from a memoir and from interviews with Cather. The third contains reprints of five essays on Cather's stories by other well-known critics.

Woodress, James. *Willa Cather: A Literary Life.* Lincoln: University of Nebraska Press, 1987.

This is a comprehensive illustrated biography with extensive notes. Woodress sees Cather as an "extraordinarily gifted" and ambitious woman with an intense passion for art. He begins his discussion of her life and work with her trip West to visit her brother in Arizona after six years as an editor at *McClure's Magazine*, a trip which proved a "watershed" for Cather. Her best novels, according to Woodress, were written in the 1920's, when she felt most alienated from American life and was able to utilize her own experiences "to weave the myths of the American past" into a "magical fabric." Woodress looks at the sources of Cather's fictions, their critical reception, and the personal and historical context in which they were written. He quotes generously from hundreds of letters, interviews and speeches, reminiscences, and Cather's own fiction and nonfiction writings.

ELLEN GLASGOW
1873-1945

Glasgow was born in Richmond, Virginia, the eighth of ten children. Her father was a stern, Calvinist businessman, her mother a gentle and frail woman who died when Glasgow was twenty. Glasgow was a voracious reader of nineteenth century novelists and intellectuals, including Charles Darwin, whose theories made a major impression on her. Glasgow's first novel, *The Descendant* (1897), was published anonymously and received a positive critical reception. This was followed by two additional novels, *Phases of an Inferior Planet* (1898) and *The Wheel of Life* (1906), which like the first deal with problems faced by a woman artist living in New York. Glasgow spent many years traveling, then returned permanently to Richmond after her father's death in 1916. Despite an intermittent romance with a well-known lawyer-politician, Glasgow's life was a lonely one, limited by deafness and an accompanying shyness. Her best novels are closely tied to her own life and her experience of the South: *Virginia* (1913), *Life and Gabriella* (1916), *Barren Ground* (1925), *The Romantic Comedians* (1926), *The Sheltered Life* (1932), and *Vein of Iron* (1935). By the time of her Pulitzer Prize in 1942 for *In This Our Life*, Glasgow was widely recognized as a major American author.

Reissued Editions
Barren Ground. San Diego, Calif.: Harcourt Brace Jovanovich, 1985.

The Descendant. Salem, N.H.: Arno Press, 1977.

Ellen Glasgow's Reasonable Doubts: A Collection of Her Writings, ed. Julius Rowan Raper. Baton Rouge: Louisiana State University Press, 1988.

The Freeman and Other Poems. New York: AMS Press, 1976.

In This Our Life. Modesto, Calif.: American Reprints Co., 1987.

The Romantic Comedians. Salem, N.H.: Arno Press, 1977.

The Sheltered Life. Charlottesville: University Press of Virginia, 1994.

Vein of Iron. San Diego, Calif.: Harcourt Brace Jovanovich, 1983.

Virginia. New York: Penguin Classics, 1989.

The Woman Within: An Autobiography. Charlottesville: University Press of Virginia, 1994.

Biography and Commentary

Anderson, Mary Castiglie. "Cultural Archetype and the Female Hero: Nature and Will in Ellen Glasgow's *Barren Ground.*" *Modern Fiction Studies* 28, no. 3 (Autumn 1982): 383-393.

Anderson contrasts Dorinda Oakley's heroic quest for self with the archetypal patterns of the traditional male quest story. In particular, she considers Dorinda's progress into "self-consciousness and self-determination," which in the male paradigm would be associated with movement away from femaleness. Glasgow resolves the apparent contradiction between the female association with nature and regeneration and the male quest to separate from nature as mother by substituting the land itself for the maternal archetype. Ultimately, Dorinda unites the Earth Goddess with the Promethean hero by bridging the culturally assumed gulf dividing man and nature and by extending her transformative power beyond "personal biological" reproduction.

Caldwell, Ellen M. "Ellen Glasgow and the Southern Agrarians." *American Literature* 56, no. 2 (May 1984): 203-213.

Until *Barren Ground,* her sixteenth novel, Glasgow's work was marked by a bitter satire of the southern aristocratic code. Beginning with this novel her work embraces traditional values and depicts characters struggling to recover a regional identity in the face of modern chaos. Though Glasgow's embrace of regionalism was tempered by irony, under the influence of Allen Tate and his colleagues at Vanderbilt University she came to respect the Agrarian group's belief that life, like literature, acquires "beauty and purpose" only when it is "governed by forms preserved from the past."

Chandler, Marilyn R. "Healing the Woman Within: Therapeutic Aspects of Ellen Glasgow's Autobiography," in *Located Lives: Place and Idea in Southern Autobiography*, ed. J. Bill Berry. Athens: University of Georgia Press, 1990.

Chandler notes that Glasgow's autobiography is the only work she did not actively seek to publish, leaving it to the executors of her estate to decide whether or not it should be shared with the public. It is, in effect, a particularly revealing document filled with images of imprisonment and sensational descriptions of Glasgow's emotional life in terms of its terrors, tortures, and anguish. Glasgow saw her "self" as a "locus of conflict" between her inner and outer worlds and her inner and outer voices. The chapters alternate between "intensely personal" private moments and "oddly sanguine" accounts of public events. Chandler believes that the detailing of her most constant afflictions must have provided Glasgow with a form of release from the masks of irony and gaiety she assumed in public.

Holman, C. Hugh. "'Time . . . The Sheath Enfolding Experience': The Past as a Way of Life," in *The Immoderate Past: The Southern Writer and History*. Athens: University of Georgia Press, 1977.
    Holman sees *Battleground* (1902), the most "strictly historical" of Glasgow's novels, as typical of her lifelong portrayal of Virginia's aristocratic life before and after the Civil War. Don Montjoy, the novel's protagonist, represents the best and worst of southern traditions: the charm and grace as well as the violence and dishonesty. In the end, he is left with few illusions but manages to face the drab future with fortitude and stoicism. Though *Battleground* is primarily a novel of manners, it is based on solid historical research; Glasgow pored over diaries, letters, and journalistic accounts of the war to substantiate family legends and personal experience.

Jones, Anne Goodwyn. "Ellen Glasgow: The Perfect Mould," in *Tomorrow Is Another Day: The Woman Writer in the South, 1859-1936*. Baton Rouge: Louisiana State University Press, 1981.
    Jones begins by reviewing Glasgow's family history, her autobiography, and her nonfiction writings to establish her attitudes about the South, feminism, and her own art. She then focuses on two novels to demonstrate the tension in Glasgow's fiction between romanticism and realism. According to Jones, in *Virginia* Glasgow set out "to define and embalm the southern lady of the 1880's," but ended up almost "enshrining her." *Life and Gabriella* does the opposite; it dissects the southern gentleman and creates a "new woman" who, despite her energy and self-reliance, ends up capitulating to a superior man. Jones ends her essay with a discussion of Glasgow's friendship with Marjorie Kinnan Rawlings during the last years of her life.

Rainwater, Catherine. "Narration as Pragmatism in Ellen Glasgow's *Barren Ground*." *American Literature* 63, no. 4 (December 1991): 664-682.
    Rainwater offers a close reading of the novel for evidence of Glasgow's "extensive and creative thought" about the implications of pragmatism. In general, *Barren Ground* demonstrates Glasgow's belief that skepticism is the key to tolerance. Its protagonist, Dorinda Oakley, is an amateur philosopher who recognizes contradictions and tries to think clearly. For example, she notes that the railroad brings freedom,

but also exercises control over human life. The narrative is itself designed to encourage active reader participation in the search for meaning and to test readers' preconceived ideas.

Raper, Julius Rowan. *From the Sunken Garden: The Fiction of Ellen Glasgow, 1916-1945.* Baton Rouge: Louisiana State University Press, 1980.

This is a book-length study of Ellen Glasgow's major novels, supplemented by a bibliography. It is based on the premise that the fiction Glasgow wrote from 1916 on is more "intensely psychological" than her earlier work, which relied on a kind of "surface realism" and therefore failed to get at the emotional truth of characters. In his analysis of ten novels and several short stories, Raper traces the progression in Glasgow's characterizations which, he believes, reach their climax in *The Sheltered Life.* This novel, Glasgow's "most intense and beautiful," reveals the dangers inherent in "evasive idealism" and the "phantasies" characters project upon others. Though Glasgow was unable fully to control her characters, perhaps because she was "not on intimate terms with her own demons," readers continue to find enormous psychological appeal in the "phantasy"-filled buried life of her major protagonists, Raper concludes.

See also: Julius Rowan Raper. "Once More to the Mirror: Glasgow's Technique in *The Sheltered Life* and Reader-Response Criticism, " in *Modern American Fiction*, ed. Thomas Daniel Young. Baton Rouge: Louisiana State University Press, 1989.

Scura, Dorothy M., ed. *New Perspectives on Ellen Glasgow.* Knoxville: University of Tennessee Press, 1995.

This collection of fifteen essays includes the text of a newly discovered short story, "Ideals," and of Glasgow's previously unpublished letters to friend and fellow writer Louise Chandler Moulton.

Seidel, Kathryn Lee. "Culture and Personality: Ellen Glasgow's Belles," in *The Southern Belle in the American Novel.* Tampa: University of South Florida Press, 1985.

In Glasgow's early fiction, written in the first two decades of her career, characters are depicted as victims of society; in her later fiction they "choose" to suffer and are all the more miserable given their complicity in their own fate. Seidel sees the "belles" of Glasgow's mature fiction as obsessed by beauty and fantasy, with a neurotic need for love. The masochism exhibited by these women follows the paradigm of the neurotic personality established by the psychoanalyst Karen Horney, who argued that it was brought on by the lack of outlets for women's self-expression in patriarchal cultures. According to Seidel, the southern belles of Glasgow's last few novels are either "pathetic anachronisms" or narcissistic seekers after love and pleasure, who can avoid suffering only by a total rejection of sexuality. The only "admirable women" in these works are drawn from the middle and lower classes.

Thiebaux, Ellen. *Ellen Glasgow.* New York: Frederick Ungar, 1982.
This text includes a biographical essay, a chronology and bibliography, discussion of approximately twenty novels, plus a chapter on Glasgow's short stories and poetry. Thiebaux identifies Glasgow as the "first writer of the modern South," to which she helped give literary definition. Her constant subject is the social history of Virginia with its decaying agrarian aristocracy. Glasgow's tone ranges from "delicate" to "'tragic" irony; her works are populated by upper-class women and "doughty" folk heroines. Thiebaux concludes that among Glasgow's work are six novels of enduring value: *The Deliverance* (1904), *The Miller of Old Church* (1911), *Virginia, Barren Ground, The Romantic Comedians,* and *The Sheltered Life.*

Wagner-Martin, Linda. *Ellen Glasgow: Beyond Convention.* Austin: University of Texas Press, 1982.
Wagner's biography focuses on the relationship between Glasgow's life and her best work. She sees Glasgow as a "chronicler" of American women's lives whose portraits convey the complexity of the "female heart and mind" in women who represent a wide variety of life experiences. Glasgow was herself a frail woman who suffered from deafness and an increasing sense of alienation. "Cautiously defiant," Glasgow produced her best work late in her career, when she dropped an "imitative masculine voice" and began to focus more on female characters. Wagner discusses each of Glasgow's major works with special attention to *Vein of Iron,* her "richest" and most universal fiction. The text is supplemented by a bibliography of primary and secondary sources.

Winniford, Lee. "Suppressing the Masculine Metanarrative: The Uncaging of Glasgow's *Barren Ground.*" *Journal of Narrative Technique* 24, no. 2 (Spring 1994): 141-152.
Winniford analyzes the narrative structure of *Barren Ground* for evidence of ways in which the novel subverts traditional fairy tale and marriage plots. Though the novel seems linear, it actually moves forward and backward in a "layering effect." The three-part symphony structure of statement, departure, and return which the novel seems to follow is also subverted through the apparent omissions and contradictions other critics have assumed were accidental. Dorinda's failure to marry the prince, as well as her inability to synthesize the poles of her divided self, is paralleled by the novel's own struggle to define a structure for itself apart from patriarchal norms.

JOSEPHINE HERBST
1892-1969
Herbst was born in Sioux City, Iowa, the third of four daughters.

She completed college at the University of California, Berkeley, after years spent supporting herself with clerical positions. In 1919 Herbst moved to New York City, where she became part of radical literary and political circles. In 1922 she went to Berlin and then to Paris, where she met John Herrmann, whom she later married. They bought a farmhouse in Erwinna, Pennsylvania, where Herbst was to do all her writing, beginning with her first published novel, *Nothing Is Sacred* (1928). The first volume of her trilogy, *Pity Is Not Enough*, followed in 1933. With the next two volumes, *The Executioner Waits* (1934) and *Rope of Gold* (1939), Herbst achieved recognition as the literary peer of her personal friends, Katherine Anne Porter, Ernest Hemingway, and John Dos Passos. Herbst was close to many members of the Communist Party but never joined herself, and her criticism of her husband's radical political activities contributed to the breakup of their marriage. The 1940's were lonely and difficult years for Herbst, especially after she was fired from a government job for her political activities, though she did write two novels: *Satan's Sergeants* (1941) and *Somewhere the Tempest Fell* (1947). In the 1950's her house again became a gathering place for writers as she worked on a variety of projects, including her memoirs and an appreciation of two eighteenth century botanists, *New Green World* (1954).

Reissued Editions
The Executioner Waits. New York: AMS Press, 1977.

Nothing Is Sacred. Salem, N.H.: Arno Press, 1977.

Rope of Gold: A Novel of the 1930's. Old Westbury, N.Y.: Feminist Press, 1984.

The Starched Blue Sky of Spain and Other Memoirs. New York: HarperCollins, 1991.

Biography and Commentary
Bevilacqua, Winifred Farrant. *Josephine Herbst.* Boston: G. K. Hall, 1986.
   This volume in Twayne's United States Authors series includes a chronology, bibliography, biographical essay, and analysis of Herbst's major novels. It also includes chapters on her memoirs and journalism and on her narrative technique. Bevilacqua agrees with Elinor Langer's assessment of Herbst's trilogy as one of the most important studies of American history from the 1860's to the 1930's and compares it favorably to the work of Dos Passos, Steinbeck, and Hemingway. All of Herbst's work—novels, stories, essays, biography, and memoirs— provides a historical record as perceived by a "sensitive and intelligent observer" of modern society and human consciousness.

Kramer, Hilton. "Who Was Josephine Herbst?" *The New Criterion* 3, no. 1 (September 1984): 1-14.

Kramer disapproves of what he identifies as a feminist resurrection of Herbst, whom he sees as a "failed woman" and a "failed writer," though he admits that many young women are moved by her novels in a way he never was. As a "friend" of Herbst and executor of her estate, he also admits to his own bias in evaluating her life and career. In general, he approves of Langer's biography (see below), which he praises for its "meticulous" and honest description of Herbst's grim and unpleasant life. However, he believes that Langer, like most other pro-Herbst critics, glosses over the unpleasant truth about her relationship to Stalinism. According to Kramer, Herbst publicly "swallowed" revelations about the purges and trials in Russia out of loyalty to the "left" and to her husband; this duplicity began a pattern of personal "ruthlessness and brute callousness" for which she has been justly criticized.

Langer, Elinor. *Josephine Herbst: The Story She Could Never Tell.* Boston: Little, Brown, 1983.

This illustrated biography makes extensive use of Herbst's own letters, her published and unpublished memoirs, and her notebooks. Because Herbst was a "reliable observer," the "primary archive" speaks for itself, according to Langer. Langer sees Herbst as a "substantial writer" whose work as a leftist and feminist was almost totally ignored by the literary academic establishment, despite the fact that many of its most distinguished members considered themselves her friends. The biography describes Herbst's early education and later introduction to radicalism at Berkeley, her first love affair, her marriage to John Herrmann, her friendships with her sister Helen, Katherine Anne Porter, and Jean Garrigue, her political trips to Russia and Spain, and her investigation by the F.B.I. It also traces the progression of her career from writing for little magazines in the 1920's to international quarterlies in the 1950's and 1960's. Langer concludes by focusing on Herbst's reading of Doris Lessing's *The Golden Notebook* (1962), the autobiographical novel Herbst would have liked to write, which is in many ways "the story of her life."

Rideout, Walter B. "Forgotten Images of the Thirties: Josephine Herbst." *The Literary Review* 27, no. 1 (Fall 1983): 28-36.

This biographical essay focuses on Herbst's trilogy and its relationship to her life, especially to her mother. Rideout briefly summarizes the content of each of the novels and concludes that they not only describe the realities of oppression but also teach the importance of compassion, and show how the history of an individual, a family, and a nation helps to shape the future. Herbst's radicalism, according to Rideout, was "as much an affair of the heart as of the head."

EDITH SUMMERS KELLEY
1884-1956

Kelley was born and raised in Ontario, Canada, then moved to New York City at the age of nineteen. In 1906 she took a position as secretary to Upton Sinclair at his socialist commune. At the commune she became a close friend of Sinclair Lewis and Alan Updegraff, the latter of whom she married. She had two children, then divorced Updegraff to live with Claude Fred Kelley. Despite never marrying him officially, she took his name and traveled west with him in pursuit of a variety of jobs, including tenant tobacco farming in Kentucky and alfalfa and chicken ranching in California. Her two novels, *Weeds* (1923) and *The Devil's Hand* (1974), published posthumously, both deal with her own experiences of working-class poverty and frustrated artistic ambitions.

Reissued Edition
Weeds. Old Westbury, N.Y.: Feminist Press, 1982.

Biography and Commentary
Goodman, Charlotte. "Introduction to Edith Summers Kelley's 'The Old House.'" *Women's Studies* 10, no. 1 (1983): 63-78.

In her introduction to the text, which is printed in this issue, Goodman establishes the significance of the story for modern readers. "The Old House" focuses on the feelings of isolation and entrapment experienced by a female portrait painter following her marriage and move to the country. Despite a marriage contract, a kind of prenuptial agreement which both husband and wife sign, the wife finds herself doing more and more of the household chores with less and less time for her own work.

_____. "Widening Perspectives, Narrowing Possibilities: The Trapped Woman in Edith Summers Kelley's *Weeds*," in *Regionalism and the Female Imagination*, ed. Emily Toth. New York: Human Sciences Press, 1985.

Goodman begins with basic biographical information about Kelley's life and career and then summarizes the plot and themes of her major novel. Goodman sees the central issue in Kelley's work as "the fate of the sensitive woman whose spirit rebels against the strictures imposed by biological, social, and economic factors." *Weeds* adds to the literary portraits of the working class in the novels of Steinbeck and Dreiser through its "compassionate presentation of the stresses of farm life" and its revelation of the "inequities" which prevent women from reaching their full potential.

Lootens, Barbara. "A Struggle for Survival: Edith Summers Kelley's *Weeds*." *Women's Studies* 13, nos. 1-2 (1986): 103-113.

Despite the novel's lack of popularity in the 1920's, Lootens believes it deserves a larger readership today because of the "compassion and understanding" with which it speaks to women whose own lives are circumscribed by poverty, biology, and tradition. In Lootens's analysis, the novel's protagonist, Judy Blackford, is a "classic tragic hero" who rebels more and more passionately yet futilely against her fate. Like many classicists, Kelley effectively uses images of light and dark to create a symbolic correspondence between the natural world and the protagonist's spiritual condition. And though the novel is "painful" in its unsentimental portrayal of Blackford's life, it has important insights to offer about womanhood and the values of dignity and self-respect.

KATHERINE ANNE PORTER
1890-1980

Porter was born in Indian Creek, Texas, one of five children who were raised by their father and grandmother following their mother's death when Porter was less than two years old. Porter was educated at convent schools, ran away to get married at the age of sixteen, got divorced three years later, and went to Chicago to work as a journalist. She had two additional brief marriages and traveled extensively throughout her life in Europe and Mexico, where she became involved in the politics of the Mexican Revolution. Porter's first volume of short stories, *Flowering Judas*, was published in 1930. It was followed by *Noon Wine* (1937), *Pale Horse, Pale Rider* (1939), and *The Leaning Tower and Other Stories* (1944). Porter supported herself as a reporter, writer of screenplays, translator, lecturer, and writer-in-residence. She also received several fellowships and grants based on her growing reputation as a superb stylist, which culminated in a National Book Award and Pulitzer Prize for her *Collected Stories* (1965). *Ship of Fools* (1962), Porter's one novel, was a great commercial success, though it did not receive the same critical acclaim as her stories.

Reissued Editions
The Collected Essays and Occasional Writings of Katherine Anne Porter. New York: Houghton Mifflin, 1990.

The Collected Stories of Katherine Anne Porter. New York: Harcourt Brace Jovanovich, 1979.

Flowering Judas and Other Stories. New York: Harcourt Brace Jovanovich, 1990.

Pale Horse, Pale Rider: Three Short Novels. New York: Harcourt Brace Jovanovich, 1990.

Ship of Fools. New York: Little, Brown, 1984.

Biography and Commentary
Bloom, Harold, ed. *Modern Critical Views: Katherine Anne Porter*. New York: Chelsea House, 1986.

This is a collection of twelve reprints of essays and book chapters written between 1969 and 1983, including well-known pieces by Robert Penn Warren and Eudora Welty, as well as excerpts and reprints of studies by Givner, Jorgensen, Moddelmog, and DeMouy annotated here.

Cheatham, George. "Katherine Anne Porter's Enacted Fables." *Mississippi Quarterly* 46, no. 1 (Winter 1992-1993): 121-127.

This essay/review uses the occasion of two publications—Givner's biography of Porter (see below) and Unrue's collection of Porter's book reviews—to insist on the need for further study of Porter's life and modernist aesthetic. Cheatham begins by looking at two stories, "The Grave" and "Rope," to demonstrate the "pseudo-objectivity" of Porter's narrative technique. He ends by analyzing passages from the false testimony she gave to the F.B.I. against her "friend" Josephine Herbst. Though Cheatham agrees with Givner's psychological explanation for her duplicity, he also sees the testimony as typical of Porter's fiction in its modernist merging of narration and character. Porter wanted both to rewrite life and to create true art; in this case her fiction had real-life consequences with the potential of destroying Herbst's life.

DeMouy, Jane Krause. *Katherine Anne Porter's Women: The Eye of Her Fiction*. Austin: University of Texas Press, 1983.

This text contains a chronology of Porter's fiction, a bibliography, and analysis of her major fiction. DeMouy believes that Porter wrote out of her own psychology as a woman and that her stories are best classified in terms of their protagonists' experience of the "interior and exterior" aspects of their own femininity. Early Porter stories (1922-1929) describe women in conflict with themselves or society. With "The Jilting of Granny Weatherall" (1929) Porter's stories become more psychologically profound in their depiction of this conflict and in their understanding of the complexity of the unconscious mind. Later stories (1935-1942) see love as impossible with characters who oppose marriage and traditional domestic roles. *Ship of Fools* (1962) universalizes the conflict between love and independence through characters who represent every possible variation on the theme.

Givner, Joan. *Katherine Anne Porter: A Life*. New York: Simon and Schuster, 1982.

This is a comprehensive literary biography complemented by photographs and extensive source notes. Givner sees Porter as a "vivid personality" who tried to transform her personal history so her life might appear "as elegant and structured" as her short stories. The "truth" was particularly difficult to unearth given Porter's careful editing of information about her life; still, Givner's research reveals a more sympathetic woman than the arrogant public persona Porter pretended to be. Givner also marvels at the "external panorama" of

Porter's life. She was, in fact, a witness to many of the twentieth century's major historical events; she was in Berlin during Hitler's rise to power, in Mexico City during the Obregón revolution, and at the age of eighty-two at Cape Canaveral for the moon shot.

Gretlund, Jan Nordby. "Katherine Anne Porter and the South: A Corrective." *Mississippi Quarterly* 34, no. 4 (Fall 1981): 435-444.
Despite the lack of reliable evidence about the first thirty years of Porter's life, it is known that she was brought up in accordance with the "best" of southern codes. Gretlund argues that critics who do not understand Porter's emotional involvement with the South will inevitably misread her work; she offers examples of such misreading to prove her point. Gretlund sees Porter's love for the South reflected in all of her work, even in stories not directly about it.

Hendrick, Willene, and George Hendrick. *Katherine Anne Porter.* Boston: G. K. Hall, 1988.
This is an updated edition of a 1965 volume in Twayne's United States Authors series which includes a chronology, bibliography, biographical essay, and analysis of Porter's major works. Three chapters are devoted to Porter's fiction: her Mexican stories, her fictionalized autobiographies, and those stories with southwestern, German, and Irish settings. A fourth chapter covers nonfiction and her novel, *Ship of Fools*, with a sampling of the mixed critical reviews it received. The Hendricks see Porter as a "conscious artist" whose stories demonstrate a consistent mastery of narrative technique. Her major themes concern cultural displacement, unhappy marriages, and human suffering and disappointment. Despite her own difficult and chaotic life, Porter "persevered" and produced a "significant body of literary works" with "timeless" appeal.

Hilt, Kathryn, and Ruth M. Alvarez. *Katherine Anne Porter: An Annotated Bibliography.* New York: Garland, 1990.
This bibliography contains a comprehensive list of primary sources, including Porter's translations and journalism, and secondary sources divided into four categories: general criticism and biography, criticism of individual stories and books, book reviews, and dissertations. There are several hundred annotations of articles, book chapters, and full-length studies of Porter's fiction with more than twenty of her best-known stories represented in the section on individual works.

Jorgensen, Bruce W. "'The Other Side of Silence': Katherine Anne Porter's 'He' as Tragedy." *Modern Fiction Studies* 28, no. 3 (Autumn 1982): 395-404.
Jorgensen begins by summarizing responses to the story by both critics and his own students, most of whom he sees as "excessive" in their pity or their condemnation of Mrs. Whipple, Porter's protagonist. The story asks readers, according to Jorgensen, to make a balanced

judgment of the "unadmitted guilt and hostility" as well as the natural motherly love Mrs. Whipple seems to express for her retarded son. In the end, the story achieves a truly tragic "catharsis" as Mrs. Whipple is finally able to hear "the other side of her son's inarticulate silence."

Lavers, Norman. "'Flowering Judas' and the Failure of *Amour Courtois*." *Studies in Short Fiction* 28, no. 1 (Winter 1991): 77-82.

Lavers summarizes an earlier interpretation of the story as a religious allegory involving secular, erotic, and religious forms of love. Though he agrees with this interpretation, he argues that it overlooks the centrality of courtly love to the story's symbolic patterns. His "correction" provides a brief history of the courtly love tradition and analysis of Laura's role, in keeping with her Petrarchan namesake, as a link between the "fleshly" and the "spiritual."

Machann, Clinton, and William Bedford Clark, eds. *Katherine Anne Porter and Texas: An Uneasy Relationship.* College Station: Texas A&M University Press, 1990.

This illustrated volume includes essays which grew out of a 1988 symposium at Texas A&M and a few pieces (see the Stout annotation below) written expressly for it. The introduction documents the history of the "feud" between Porter and her home state; there are also personal recollections, critical discussions of Porter's Texas stories, and a bibliographic essay on Texas-related primary and secondary sources.

Moddelmog, Debra A. "Narrative Irony and Hidden Motivations in Katherine Anne Porter's 'He.'" *Modern Fiction Studies* 28, no. 3 (Autumn 1982): 405-413.

Moddelmog sees this story as a brilliantly ironic depiction of hypocrisy. She argues that many critics have been misled by Mrs. Whipple's self-serving rationalizations and have taken her to be the "weak but well-meaning mother of a retarded child," rather than a vain and self-deceived woman. The key to Moddelmog's analysis is Porter's use of both direct quotation and indirect third-person narration to reveal the psychology behind Mrs. Whipple's sentiments.

Stout, Janis P. "Estranging Texas: Porter and the Distance from Home," in *Katherine Anne Porter and Texas: An Uneasy Relationship*, eds. Clinton Machann and William Bedford Clark. College Station: Texas A&M University Press, 1990.

Stout believes that Porter's best work is set in Mexico or in a place that is and is not Texas. There are two reasons why readers do not identify her work as about Texas, even in stories that are most directly about her Texas childhood. First, she writes of Texas in its southern rather than its more common western aspect. Second, she tends to distance herself from "home" to the point of falsifying personal recollections in stories that seem to be autobiographical. Porter herself wanted to escape from her past yet yearned for its security. This ambivalence, with its mix of nostalgia and resistance to the past, is the source of Porter's "detached fictive voice," Stout concludes.

_____. *Katherine Anne Porter: A Sense of the Times.* Charlottesville: University Press of Virginia, 1995.
    This comprehensive biography makes extensive use of Porter's lifelong correspondence to get at the profound conflicts in her sense of regional, class, and gender identity. Stout also traces Porter's shifting political allegiances, including both her "leftism" in the 1920's and 1930's and her later attraction to the "rightist" radicalism of the southern Agrarians, who insisted on the value of tradition and stability. Stout sees Porter as a woman driven by many demons, whose one unfailing commitment was her dedication to art. Ultimately, her life and her work embodied the contradictions of twentieth century modernism; however, unlike other modernists, her stories continue to be read and loved because of their particular "beauty."

Unrue, Darlene Harbour. "Katherine Anne Porter's Politics and Another Reading of 'Theft.'" *Studies in Short Fiction* 30, no. 2 (Spring 1993): 119-126.
    Unrue traces Porter's earliest political activities as a feminist and a socialist to her later involvement with the Mexican Revolution and the protest in support of Sacco and Vanzetti. Although Porter vehemently insisted on the separation of art and politics, many of her works contain political themes and reflect her knowledge of political theory. "Theft," for example, depicts the spiritual vacuum created by self-indulgent materialism, with each of its characters related to the protagonist through money.

_____. *Understanding Katherine Anne Porter.* Columbia: University of South Carolina Press, 1988.
    This volume in the series Understanding Contemporary American Literature includes a bibliography, chapters on *Ship of Fools* and Porter's nonfiction, and an analysis of her major stories grouped by settings: Mexico, the old South, the rural Southwest, New England and Greenwich Village, and wartime Europe. For each story she discusses, Unrue provides a plot summary, the original place of publication, particular connections with Porter's own life, and a brief analysis of structure, imagery, narrative technique, and theme. The text begins with an overview of Porter's literary career, leading to the conclusion that Porter's style grows out of her "quest for truth" and is marked by "classical humanism" and a careful attention to verisimilitude.

Walsh, Thomas F. "Xochitl: Katherine Anne Porter's Changing Goddess." *American Literature* 52, no. 2 (May 1980): 183-193.
    Walsh sees Porter's sketch of a happy primitive world in "The Children of Xochitl" and her depiction of "brutalizing peonage" in the story "Hacienda" as representative of the poles of her Mexican period,

1920-1931. The transformation of Xochitl from goddess of life to goddess of death followed Porter's own disillusionment with the Mexican Revolution and offers a key to the development of Edenic images in her fiction. As examples, Walsh cites the shattered dream of Edenic happiness in *Pale Horse, Pale Rider* and the reduction of Eden to a "wistful metaphor" in *Ship of Fools.*

Warren, Robert Penn, ed. *Katherine Anne Porter: A Collection of Critical Essays.* Englewood Cliffs, N.J.: Prentice-Hall, 1979.
This collection includes essays by Warren, Cleanth Brooks, Eudora Welty, V. S. Pritchett, Edmund Wilson, and Mark Schorer.

MARJORIE KINNAN RAWLINGS
1896-1953
Rawlings was born in Washington, D.C., the only daughter and older child of a U.S. patent examiner. She graduated Phi Beta Kappa with a major in English from the University of Wisconsin, and began a career as a journalist. From 1928 to 1947 she farmed and wrote from an orange grove she and her husband Charles Rawlings had bought in Hawthorn, Florida, near the Cracker families of Cross Creek that she would immortalize in her novels. Her first short collection of character sketches, "Cracker Chidlings: Real Tales from the Florida Interior" (1930), was published in *Scribner's.* Rawlings's career as a writer took off in 1933 with her first prize in the O. Henry contest for the story "Gal Young Un" and a Book-of-the-Month Club selection for her first novel, *South Moon Under* (1933). Rawlings is best known today for *The Yearling* (1938) which received a Pulitzer Prize and was made into an Academy Award-winning film. It is a classic story of an orphan boy, a character she also featured in her stories "A Mother in Manville" (1936) and "Mountain Prelude" (1947). In 1941 Rawlings married Norton Sanford Baskin following her divorce from her first husband. In 1942 Rawlings published *Cross Creek,* a chronicle of her years in Florida known for its lively portraits of the black women who were her neighbors. Then, in 1947, she purchased an old farmhouse in rural New York which became her summer home and the fictional locale of future works, including *The Sojourner* (1953). When Rawlings died she was working on a biography of Ellen Glasgow.

Reissued Editions
Cross Creek. New York: Collier Books, 1987.

The Marjorie Rawlings Reader, ed. Julia Scribner Bigham. Jacksonville, Fla.: San Marco Bookstore, 1988.

Short Stories by Marjorie Kinnan Rawlings, ed. Roger L. Tarr. Gainesville: University Press of Florida, 1994.

The Yearling. New York: Collier Books, 1988.

Biography and Commentary
Preu, Dana McKinnon. "A Woman of the South: Mattie Syles of *Gal Young Un.*" *The Southern Quarterly* 22, no. 4 (Summer 1984): 71-84.
   Preu, the actress who played Mattie, offers her explanation for the critical success of this 1979 film adaptation of Rawlings's 1932 O'Henry Award-winning story. Preu and director Victor Nuñez were able to convey the "essential humanity" of this lonely, middle-aged widow by sticking to the story's clear plot-line and in-depth characterization, and by avoiding the temptation to glamorize, stereotype, or sentimentalize Mattie. Ultimately, the film demonstrated the relevance of the original story fifty years after its publication.

Schmidt, Susan. "Finding a Home: Rawlings's *Cross Creek.*" *The Southern Literary Journal* 26, no. 2 (Spring 1994): 48-57.
   Schmidt sees *Cross Creek* as a book of literature, not just as a collection of nonfiction essays, which deserves serious critical attention. Her own analysis of these essays establishes their relationship to Rawlings's life and her other work. Schmidt highlights Rawlings's attempt to capture the spirit of a particular place and people and to portray a sense of her "struggle and triumph to earn a living and find a home on her citrus grove in Florida."

Silverthorne, Elizabeth. *Marjorie Kinnan Rawlings: Sojourner at Cross Creek.* Woodstock, N.Y.: The Overlook Press, 1988.
   This illustrated biography is based on the author's research in the Rawlings archives and discussions with her widower. Silverthorne discusses Rawlings's childhood, her struggles as a young journalist in New York, her literary friendships, and her discovery and love of the Florida woods and swamps—a frontier world she felt compelled to capture on paper before it disappeared. Silverthorne portrays an independent, vigorous, and lively woman who delighted in wild and stormy weather and the rich sensual texture of nature.

Stephenson, William. "Fawn Bites Lion: Or, How MGM Tried to Film *The Yearling* in Florida." *The Southern Quarterly* 19, nos. 3-4 (Spring-Summer 1981): 229-239.
   Metro-Goldwyn-Mayer bought the film rights to *The Yearling* in 1938; however, it took seven years and several sets of actors and directors before the film was finally completed. Stephenson sees the decision to film on location in Florida as the source of the major problems. He details the obstacles the studio faced in the search for the boy to play Jody, the creation of "authentic" outdoor sets, the problems with animals and local Floridians, and the loss of Spencer Tracy as the original father. The film went on to win three Academy Awards, but first the studio had to be taught a few lessons by Mother Nature, Stephenson concludes.

MARY ROBERTS RINEHART
1876-1958

Rinehart, the older of two daughters, was born and raised in Allegheny, Pennsylvania. She married a young doctor in 1896, the year of her graduation from nursing school, and had three sons in the next five years. In 1903, Rinehart decided to help out with family finances by writing and within the year had sold forty-five stories. With the publication of *The Circular Staircase* (1908), one of her first full-length mysteries, she achieved preeminence in a genre she was said to have founded, a fusion of romance and comedy with a detective story. Rinehart wrote an additional sixty books, served as a European correspondent during World War I, and became involved in several social causes following the war while living in Washington, D.C., and spending summers on a Wyoming ranch. She became one of America's most popular writers, with eleven books on the top-ten best-seller list between 1910 and 1940. *The Bat* (1920), her most successful drama, toured the country with six road companies and was filmed for television and for three different film versions. *My Story*, Rinehart's autobiography, was published in 1931.

Reissued Editions
Note: In 1995 there were forty-five editions of Rinehart mysteries as well as several audiocassettes available; a few of the most popular are listed here. Zebra Books, a division of Kensington Publishing Corporation, has current reprints of almost all of Rinehart's work.

The Circular Staircase. Cutchogue, N.Y.: Lightyear Press, 1984. New York: Zebra Books, 1991.

The Frightened Wife and Other Murder Stories. New York: Zebra Books, 1988. Thorndike, Maine: Thorndike Press, 1993.

The Man in Lower Ten. New York: Zebra Books, 1990. Thorndike, Maine: Thorndike Press, 1992.

The Wall. New York: Zebra Books, 1989.

The Window at the White Cat. New York: Zebra Books, 1990.

Biography and Criticism
Cohn, Jan. *Improbable Fiction: The Life of Mary Roberts Rinehart*. Pittsburgh: University of Pittsburgh Press, 1980.

This illustrated biography with a bibliography appended is partially based on the discovery of an unpublished diary written for her children at the end of Rinehart's life. Cohn finds these hundred pages to be truer than the official autobiography, *My Story*, which simply affirmed the Rinehart myth that she wrote only because of financial necessity and chance opportunities. Cohn provides evidence that Rinehart enjoyed her fame and riches, that even into her eighties she radiated energy, vitality, and power despite her presumed adherence to nineteenth century domestic mores. Cohn traces Rinehart's progress from a housewife and mother who scribbled stories in her spare time to her growing celebrity following the popular success of *The Circular Staircase* in 1908 and especially of her war articles for *The Saturday Evening Post*, based on firsthand accounts of the Belgian, French, and English fronts and hospitals. Rinheart's life represents a progression from genteel poverty to "tycoon-hood" that is reminiscent of Horatio Alger, Cohn concludes.

_____. "Mary Roberts Rinehart," in *Ten Women of Mystery*, ed. Earl F. Bargainnier. Bowling Green, Ohio: Bowling Green State University Popular Press, 1981.
     This essay includes photographs, a chronology, a bibliography, and diagrams of Rinehart's most complex character configurations, contrasting surface and "buried" stories. Cohn divides Rinehart's career into four periods and offers a brief analysis of representative works from each. Rinehart's three early mysteries (1906-1908) were "astonishing" blends of mystery, romance, and humor written in a few weeks with little revision. By 1913 her novels had become more sophisticated in their psychological portraits of hidden motives and repressed emotions, but Rinehart still considered the writing of mysteries a "sideline" to her real work as a writer of "serious" fiction and drama. Rinehart's best mysteries were published in the 1930's and marked by cross-class marriages between ruthless young women and aristocratic men. These were followed by the "flawed" works of the post World War II period. Cohn concludes that Rinehart's work defies classification, belonging to neither the American school of tough-guy detectives nor the British one of intellectual puzzles.

Dance, James C. "Spinsters in Jeopardy." *The Armchair Detective* 22, no. 1 (Winter 1989): 28-37.
     Dance notes that Rinehart's spinster heroines are usually cast in the role of "involved observer" or assistant to the principal detective; they are almost never major sleuths themselves. As a result of being placed in dangerous situations, these heroines are forced to stretch their powers of intuition and often end up more perceptive and liberated than they had been before. Early Rinehart heroines were often wealthy dowagers; later ones were younger and less well-to-do. Though Rinehart's detective stories have not dated too badly, much of their appeal depends on an old-fashioned spinster acting out of character, a role which late twentieth century readers and moviegoers may find harder to accept.

MacLeod, Charlotte. *Had She But Known: A Biography of Mary Roberts Rinehart.* New York: Warner Books, 1994.
     Though this biography does not contain documentation, MacLeod, a mystery writer herself, acknowledges her debt to the Cohn work above. MacLeod sees Rinehart's life as filled with contradictions and

anomalies. She was torn between a desire for middle-class respect and a life of adventure; she campaigned against social ills and for the rights of Native Americans, and also enjoyed playing the socialite as she dined in silks and diamonds at the White House; at first she wrote to cover household expenses, later to support her own reckless spending. Rinehart's marriage was itself an ongoing struggle between power and devotion. For fifty years Rinehart was America's best-known, best-loved, and best-paid writer, yet she was almost completely forgotten twenty years after her death.

Maio, Kathleen L. "Had-I-But-Known: The Marriage of Gothic Terror and Detection," in *The Female Gothic*, ed. Juliann E. Fleenor. Montreal: Eden Press, 1983.
　　In this essay, Maio identifies the major writers of HIBK (Had-I-But-Known) mysteries, which differ from traditional detective stories because of their complicated subplots and emotional cross-currents, and their focus on a woman telling her own story. In HIBK, "there is no sense of security—no sense that a heroic male figure has things under control." Maio calls Rinehart the "mother" of HIBK and *The Circular Staircase* its "cornerstone," a novel she wrote as a "semi-satire" on the pompousness of traditional crime stories. HIBK has been condemned as unrealistic and romanticized; Maio believes, however, that its focus on nightmares and obsessive rethinking the past is far truer to the typical human response to threats of violence than stories of "dapper detectives" who disappear from the characters' lives as soon as their mysteries are solved.

MARI SANDOZ
1896-1966
　　Sandoz, the eldest of six children, was born on a homestead in northwestern Nebraska, where she grew up listening to the storytelling of visiting Native Americans, trappers, traders, and settlers. At the age of sixteen she began a sporadic career as a country schoolteacher. She married at the age of seventeen, divorced her husband five years later, and moved to Lincoln, where she began studies at the University of Nebraska. Sandoz's first short stories were published under her married name, Marie Macumber. Her big breakthrough came with the publication of *Old Jules* (1935), a portrait of her brilliant, eccentric, and sometimes brutal father, which won the Atlantic Press Non-Fiction Contest and was featured by the Book-of-the-Month Club. From then on, Sandoz was able to support herself through her writing and an occasional stint as a writing workshop instructor. *Old Jules* was followed by *Crazy Horse* (1942), *Cheyenne Autumn* (1953), *The Buffalo Hunters* (1954), *The Cattlemen* (1958), and *The Beaver Men* (1964), Sandoz's narrative series on the Great Plains which became well-known for its vivid mix of fiction and history. Her other works included *Slogum House* (1937) and *Capital City* (1939), novels about ruthless antilabor Fascists; two children's books about Indians, *The Horsecatcher* (1957) and *The*

Story Catcher (1963); and a sketch of the Indians she had known as a child, *These Were the Sioux* (1961).

Reissued Editions
Note: Many of Sandoz's books have been reissued by the University of Nebraska Press since the 1970's, including the following:

Capital City. Lincoln: University of Nebraska Press, 1982.

Cheyenne Autumn. Lincoln: University of Nebraska Press, 1992.

Crazy Horse. Lincoln: University of Nebraska Press, 1992.

The Horsecatcher. Lincoln: University of Nebraska Press, 1986.

Hostiles and Friendlies: Selected Short Writings. Lincoln: University of Nebraska Press, 1992.

Old Jules. Lincoln: University of Nebraska Press, 1985.

These Were the Sioux. Lincoln: University of Nebraska Press, 1985.

Biography and Criticism
Downey, Betsy. "Battered Pioneers: Jules Sandoz and the Physical Abuse of the American Frontier." *Great Plains Quarterly* 12, no. 1 (Winter 1992): 31-49.
　　Downey argues that Jules Sandoz's violence toward his family was typical of frontier family life in the late nineteenth century.
　　See also Betsy Downey, "Battered Pioneers: The Problem of Male Violence Against Women as Seen Through Mari Sandoz's *Old Jules*," in *Old West-New West: Centennial Essays*, ed. Barbara Howard Meldrum, Moscow: University of Idaho Press, 1993.

Graulich, Melodie. "Every Husband's Right: Sex Roles in Mari Sandoz's *Old Jules*." *Western American Literature* 18, no. 1 (1983): 3-20.
　　Graulich examines Sandoz's ambivalence about her parents—the degree to which she identified with her mother while, at the same time, desiring her father's freedom and self-confidence. As one of the few writers to explore the institution of marriage in the pioneer West, Sandoz shows how western women were often the victims of the frontier's celebrated freedom and how that same freedom liberated the violent, restless, and egotistical dark side of men. *Old Jules*, according to Graulich, is a "catalogue of male-caused tragedies in women's lives." It is a depressing book for women readers, but an especially important one for what it reveals about the difficulties of writing as a woman while aspiring to the independence and active life of a man.

See also: Melody Graulich, "Violence Against Women in Literature of the Western Family," *Frontiers* 7, no. 3 (1984): 14-20.

Mattern, Claire. "Rebels, Aliens, Outsiders, and the Nonconformist in the Writing of Mari Sandoz." *CEA Critic* 49, nos. 2-4 (Winter 1986-Summer 1987): 102-113.
This is a very sympathetic biographical essay which relates Sandoz's major works to the history of her life. Mattern sees Sandoz as a passionate woman who had experienced the "inferno" and was later healed by her profound relationship with the earth.

Rippey, Barbara. "Toward a New Paradigm: Mari Sandoz's Study of Red and White Myth in *Cheyenne Autumn*," in *Women and Western American Literature*, eds. Helen Winter Stauffer and Susan J. Rosowski. Troy, N.Y.: Whitston, 1982.
Rippey discusses Sandoz's presentation of Indian myth as an expression of Indian tradition and culture, and white myth as the justification for the white invasion and violation of Indian culture. She also discusses *Old Jules*, Sandoz's biography of her father, and *Crazy Horse*, her biography of the Oglala chief. Sandoz is best remembered, according to Rippey, for her "brutally realistic depictions of frontier violence and lawlessness."

Stauffer, Helen Winter. *Mari Sandoz: Story Catcher of the Plains*. Lincoln: University of Nebraska Press, 1982.
This is a comprehensive illustrated biography with complete listings of Sandoz's published and unpublished works and bibliographies of archival materials, media references, and secondary sources. Stauffer considers the influence of Sandoz's harsh frontier childhood on her life and work and highlights her relationships with friends, literary colleagues, and publishers. Her chronological examination of Sandoz's major works emphasizes her painstaking method of writing and research as well as her primary motivations—her empathy with Native Americans and her desire to correct myths about the West. Sandoz deserves consideration as a first-rate writer who was able to appreciate the importance both of accurate historical information and of graceful literary detail.
See also Stauffer's abbreviated version of this biography: *Mari Sandoz*. Boise, Idaho: Bosie State University Press, 1984.

Villiger, Laura R. *Mari Sandoz: A Study in Post-Colonial Discourse*. New York: Peter Lang, 1994.
Lang looks at Sandoz's major works in the context of multiculturalism and postcolonial theories.

EDITH WHARTON
1862-1937

Wharton was born to a wealthy "old New York" family and raised to live the privileged life of an aristocratic young woman. In 1885, at the age of twenty-three, she married Edward Wharton, a socially prominent Bostonian, and began a conventional high society existence, traveling back and forth to Europe. The childless marriage was clearly not a happy one, and though the couple did not divorce until 1913, Wharton devoted more and more of her time to her writing and eventually established her own residence in Paris. Her first published fiction was the short story, "Mrs. Manstey's View" (1891); her first published book was *The Decoration of Houses* (1897), which she wrote in collaboration with a Boston architect. In 1899 Wharton published two collections of short stories; her first novel, *The Valley of Decision,* was published in 1902 and followed in 1905 by *The House of Mirth,* the best-seller which made Wharton famous. In the next years, Wharton continued to write stories, travelogues, and novels, including *Ethan Frome* (1911), *The Reef* (1912), *The Custom of the Country* (1913), and *Summer* (1917). Wharton was an ardent Francophile; she lobbied for American participation in World War I and received the Legion of Honor from the French government in recognition of her charitable work with refugees. *The Age of Innocence* (1920), for which she received the Pulitzer Prize, was written in the wake of the War and the deaths of many close friends. Other late novels included *The Glimpses of the Moon* (1922), *The Mother's Recompense* (1925), *Twilight Sleep* (1927), and *Hudson River Bracketed* (1929). Wharton's autobiography, *A Backward Glance* (1934), offered a carefully edited version of her life which has been substantially corrected by biographical studies made possible with the opening of the Yale University collection of her papers in 1968 (see Lewis and Wolff below). Wharton was still traveling through Europe and working on a final novel, *The Buccaneers,* in the last year of her life.

Reissued Editions
Note: In 1995 there were sixty-eight editions of Wharton works as well as many audiocassettes available. R. W. B. Lewis has collected all of Wharton's published short stories in two volumes (New York: Scribner's, 1987) and there were at least five reissues of *Ethan Frome* and seven of *The House of Mirth* published between 1987 and 1995, including a Norton Critical Edition of each. Listed below are a dozen of the most recent paperback editions of Wharton's best-known novels and short stories.

The Age of Innocence. New York: Collier Books, 1992.

The Buccaneers (completed by Marion Mainwaring). New York: Penguin Books, 1993.

The Custom of the Country. New York: Alfred A. Knopf, 1994.

The Edith Wharton Reader. New York: Collier Books, 1989.

Ethan Frome. New York: Signet Books, 1992.

The Glimpses of the Moon. New York: Collier Books, 1994.

The Ghost Stories of Edith Wharton. New York: Scribner's, 1985.

The House of Mirth. New York: Alfred A. Knopf, 1991.

Old New York: Four Novellas. New York: Scribner's, 1995.

Roman Fever and Other Stories. New York: Collier Books, 1993.

Selected Short Stories. New York: Scribner's, 1991.

A Son at the Front. DeKalb: Northern Illinois University Press, 1995.

Summer. New York: Signet Books, 1993.

Biography and Criticism
Note: Since the publication of Lewis's biography in 1975 and Wolff's in 1977, there have been hundreds of studies of Wharton's life and work. Two comprehensive bibliographies were published in 1990— Stephen Garrison's *Edith Wharton: A Descriptive Bibliography*, University of Pittsburgh Press, covers all primary materials; Kristin Lauer's and Margaret Murray's *Edith Wharton: An Annotated Secondary Bibliography*, Garland Publishing, contains 1200 items from 1897 to 1987. The articles and books referenced here represent a sampling of the best-known and most frequently cited, with some attempt to indicate the variety of criticism Wharton's work has spawned.

Ammons, Elizabeth. "Cool Diana and the Blood-Red Muse: Edith Wharton on Innocence and Art," in *American Novelists Revisited: Essays in Feminist Criticism*, ed. Fritz Fleischmann. Boston: G. K. Hall, 1982.
  Ammons sees May Welland as Wharton's response to Henry James's infatuation with the American girl. May is Isabel Archer stripped of the illusion of freedom; she is the real victim of America's obsession with innocence, a Diana who is both "ancient and artificial." Ellen Olenska is everything May is not, an artist whose medium is life itself. This woman of intellect and artistic disposition is such a threat to old New York society that she must be expelled. Ironically, this same society pays to see unconventional women masquerade as ingenues like May in opera and popular drama, of which Wharton provides several "real"

examples. Ammons identifies *Age of Innocence* as the pinnacle of Wharton's career.

_____. *Edith Wharton's Argument with America*. Athens: The University of Georgia Press, 1980.

Ammons examines most of Wharton's major fiction in terms of its ever more sophisticated critique of "the woman question." She begins by establishing the pervasiveness of women's issues in the 1890's with a description of the Woman's Building at the 1893 Chicago World's Fair and the many stories by and about women in *Scribner's* and *Century*, the two magazines that first published Wharton's work. Unlike most of her contemporaries, Wharton focused on the "pain of being a woman" rather than on the wonderful new opportunities for women. Ammons rates *The Custom of the Country*, a superb satire of American marriages as businesses, as Wharton's best novel. She concludes with a discussion of Wharton's last novels, *Hudson River Bracketed* and *The Gods Arrive*, which she finds surprising in their mystic concern with matriarchy; the mythological Mothers have replaced the Furies, which dominated much of the rest of her work.

Bendixen, Alfred, and Annette Zilversmit, eds. *Edith Wharton: New Critical Essays*. New York: Garland Publishing, 1992.

A collection of eighteen essays which cover much of Wharton's fiction. Many of these are based on scholarly papers presented at conferences sponsored by the Edith Wharton Society since its founding in 1984. Also included are studies of the major novels by Showalter, Wolff, Fryer, and Ammons, which have appeared in other journals and books, plus McDowell's analysis of the ghost stories which is referenced here.

Benstock, Shari. *No Gifts from Chance: A Biography of Edith Wharton*. New York: Scribner's, 1994.

This comprehensive biography, with photographs and source notes which include references to sixty-three individuals, is based on a "new" reading of the Yale papers. Benstock disagrees with earlier assessments of Wharton's nervous disorders and argues that she may never have suffered the severe nervous breakdown and subsequent rest cure which is part of the current Wharton mythology. She sees Wharton as an ambitious and self-determined woman who "fashioned life to her own desires." In addition to providing personal and historical context to Wharton's career, Benstock quotes frequently from her poetry and summarizes briefly the plot of each of her major stories and novels. Benstock concludes that Wharton's writing fluctuated between social satire and forays into psychological and parapsychological worlds.

Bloom, Harold, ed. *Modern Critical Views: Edith Wharton*. New York: Chelsea House Publishers, 1986.

This collection includes ten essays written between 1968 and 1986 which discuss seven of her novels and her ghost stories. It also includes R. W. B. Lewis's introduction to Wharton's collected short stories and the Dimock and Showalter articles referenced here.

Dimock, Wai-chee. "Debasing Exchange: Edith Wharton's *The House of Mirth.*" *PMLA* 100, no. 5 (October 1985): 783-792.

Dimock demonstrates how the language of the marketplace dominates much of the novel and analyzes the actions of the major characters in terms of the principles of exchange. Selden, for example, enjoys observing Lily because such spectatorship "costs him nothing" and allows him to enjoy her beauty without having to pay for it. As for Lily, Dimock sees her as the only character who ends up paying "scrupulously" for everything she gets and, "ironically," being defeated by her insistence on playing by economic rules everyone else routinely breaks. Her final act of generosity—destroying her "last asset," Bertha's letters to Selden—is typical of her tendency to spend "more than she could afford" and proves ultimately meaningless in such a world.

Ehrlich, Gloria. *The Sexual Education of Edith Wharton*. Berkeley: University of California Press, 1992.

Ehrlich sees Wharton as an "ardent and imaginative" woman whose emotional development was "derailed" by "flaws" in her relationship with her mother. The victim of intense forms of neurasthenia, Wharton used her creativity and intellect, especially in her late novels, to create the "inner mother" she craved. Ehrlich traces the relationship between her art and her life with special attention to the significance of her "belated sexual awakening" in a mid-life affair, and the way in which her circle of male friends functioned as a substitute "composite husband."

Fedorko, Kathy A. "Edith Wharton's Haunted Fiction: 'The Lady Maid's Bell' and *The House of Mirth*," in *Haunting the House of Fiction*, eds. Lynette Carpenter and Wendy K. Kolmar. Knoxville: University of Tennessee Press, 1991.

Fedorko compares these two works, both written shortly after Wharton's nervous breakdown, to demonstrate her use of the gothic to "enact" a "psychic drama of repressed female language and eroticism that was part of her own experience." Alice Hartley, the narrator of "The Lady Maid's Bell," encounters "cruelty, suppression, and gloom" inside a haunted house and marriage. Lily, the protagonist of *The House of Mirth*, is "haunted" in a metaphoric sense by "loneliness, deceit, and sexual manipulation." Both have "dark doubles" (Emma and Bertha) who represent sexual knowledge; both confront sexual secrets (in Lily's case the love letters she ultimately burns); both suffer because of their inability to speak and be heard.

Fryer, Judith. *Felicitous Space: The Imaginative Structures of Edith Wharton and Willa Cather.* Chapel Hill: University of North Carolina Press, 1986.

Fryer offers a complex and free-ranging discussion of Wharton's life and major works, including *The Decoration of Houses, Italian Villas and Their Gardens,* and her autobiography, *A Backward Glance,* loosely organized around tensions between private and public spaces, functionality and ornamentation, and harmony and disorder. Fryer sees Wharton's fiction as rich with insights about the connections between human spaces and human relationships. Lily, for example, lacks roots and a house to call her own, and Undine represents forces which threaten the civilized structures necessary to the creation of community within a city. When Wharton designed her own house, The Mount, she made sure its passageways would control human interaction and that each room would function as a self-contained protective enclosure. Similarly, her gardening and writing allowed Wharton to divide her life into carefully delineated spaces—inside and outside, private and public—which prevented the unfettered growth of any natural force which might threaten the harmonious symmetry of her carefully constructed self.

Gilbert, Sandra M., and Susan Gubar. "Angel of Devastation: Edith Wharton and the Arts of the Enslaved," in *No Man's Land 2: Sexchanges.* New Haven: Yale University Press, 1989.

The authors see Wharton, not as a misogynist, as was sometimes supposed, but as a woman who "loathed" the socialization of "ladies" as "ornamental, exploitative, and inarticulate" sexual predators. Her fiction, when considered as a whole, may offer "the most searching—and searing—feminist analysis of the construction of 'femininity'" in America produced by any twentieth century novelist, they conclude. As a novelist, Wharton wrote from a sociological perspective and was clearly influenced by Thorstein Veblen's *The Theory of the Leisure Class* (1899), which described the modern wife as the "ceremonial consumer" of the goods her husband's wealth provided. Wharton was herself brought up to be just the kind of parasitic ornamental woman whose fate she so devastatingly dramatizes in her novels, and she suffered throughout her life as her feminine self struggled against the "intellectual tomboy" and "presumptuous" writer. Gilbert and Gubar offer their own readings of Wharton's life, major works, and strange ghost stories in light of this conflict.

Goodwyn, Janet. *Edith Wharton: Traveller in the Land of Letters.* New York: St. Martin's Press, 1990.

Goodwyn organizes her discussion of Wharton's work by topography; she considers her first novel, *The Valley of Decision,* in relation to her two books about Italy, the novels set in France in the context of related travelogues, and her American novels in light of the "sea-change" in the relationship between the United States and Europe following American entry into World War I. Goodwyn sees Wharton's skillful use of specific landscapes as the result of an artistic apprenticeship which included writing guidebooks based on meticulous observation.

Hadley, Kathy Miller. "Ironic Structure and Untold Stories in *The Age of Innocence*." *Studies in the Novel* 23, no. 2 (Summer 1991): 262-272.
   Hadley sees the "untold stories" of Ellen Olenska and May Welland as undermining Wharton's apparent telling of a conventional nineteenth century romance and *Bildungsroman* from a male point of view. What Newland Archer wants is "the ability to move between May's and Ellen's worlds without any cost to himself" and without having to give up one for the other. His quest is inevitably unfulfilled since he seeks a "dreamworld" rather than an "actual place," falsely believing that Ellen represents "the freedom of a world different from his own." Hadley shows how Wharton changed the original versions of the novel "ostensibly" to make Ellen a minor and more acceptable character but, in fact, inviting the reader to speculate about her story because of Newland's own obsession with it. Newland falsely assumes Ellen would only want to be free from one man in order to relinquish her freedom to another. Unlike the typical nineteenth century romance, Ellen's story ends in neither death nor marriage.

Inness, Sherrie A. "An Economy of Beauty: The Beauty System in Edith Wharton's 'The Looking Glass' and 'Permanent Wave.'" *Studies in Short Fiction* 30, no. 2 (Spring 1993): 135-144.
   Inness begins with an analysis of the "socially-constructed nature of beauty" which she sees as a key theme in Wharton's work as exemplified by these two stories. Wharton describes both the providers who are "empowered" by the beauty system and the victims who base their self-worth on their physical beauty. Both stories explore the impact of the beauty system on male-female relationships and the ways in which it "imprisons" women who are unable to take an objective view of "beauty technology and its claims." Wharton's "totalized approach" allows for a complex understanding of the beauty system which provides status and privilege to some women, while confining and oppressing others.

Lewis, R. W. B. *Edith Wharton.* New York: Harper & Row, 1975.
   Based on his investigation of the Wharton papers which were opened to the public in 1968 and countless other documents detailed in the biography's appendices, Lewis has written an exhaustive account of Wharton's life from birth to death. Awarded the Pulitzer Prize and recognized as the "definitive" biography of Wharton, Lewis's work provides extensive background information on each of Wharton's homes and most of her friends and traveling companions. It also includes a brief discussion of all of her major writings.

McDowell, Margaret B. "Edith Wharton's Ghost Tales Reconsidered," in *Edith Wharton: New Critical Essays*, eds. Alfred Bendixen and Annette Zilversmit. New York: Garland Publishing, 1992.

McDowell sees Wharton's early ghost stories written prior to 1916 as clearly focused on a "breach of morality" usually brought about by adultery or sexual abuse. The later stories, most of which were published in the last ten years of Wharton's life, are more psychologically complex with "less explicable" ghostly elements. It is never clear whether natural or supernatural causes are behind the malevolent forces which threaten characters' lives, and philosophical issues are left unresolved. McDowell sees this ambiguity as indicative of Wharton's "mature" art and notes the frequent warnings against turning oneself into a ghost through excessive nostalgia for the past.

Pfeiffer, Kathleen. "*Summer* and Its Critics' Discomfort." *Women's Studies* 20, no. 2 (1991): 141-152.

Pfeiffer identifies Charity Royall as the "new American heroine" because of her close association with the physical Earth and her struggle as an orphan for autonomy and recognition. Her guardian, lawyer Royall, is then the American patriarch who "embodies the old, established, and failed order." Charity's loss of virginity "parallels the rape of the land which has progressively degenerated" the country. In the end, she abandons her dreams and allows herself to be "co-opted" by the male power structure. Wharton, in expressing her "feminist anger" and disillusionment with America, demonstrates the impossibility for a woman to become a Horatio Alger by escaping the "boundaries of her birth and upbringing."

Pizer, Donald. "The Naturalism of Edith Wharton's *The House of Mirth*." *Twentieth Century Literature* 41, no. 2 (Summer 1995): 241-248.

Pizer notes that the novel is typical of naturalism in that Lily Bart is described as the victim of social conditioning, a "screw or cog" in the machine of life. The ending, however, offers two alternative forms of belief and value. Nettie Struther's ability to triumph in the face of physical and social handicaps is proof of the power of the human will. Moreover, the love between Selden and Lily, though unfulfilled in life, is proof of man's spiritual dimension and capacity for transcendence.

Price, Kenneth M., and Phyllis McBride. "'The Life Apart': Text and Contexts of Edith Wharton's Love Diary." *American Literature* 66, no. 4 (December 1994): 663-688.

Price and McBride include excerpts from eleven diary entries as evidence that the unpublished history of Wharton's affair with Morton Fullerton reflects Wharton's fictional practices and was probably written with a future audience in mind. Though most revealing as a document of self-analysis and self-creation, the diary can be read as a "conventional seduction" story. The authors also provide background on the Ronsard poem from which Wharton took her original title, *L'Ame close*, and on Fullerton himself, whose "multifaceted and open personality" proved seductive to a variety of artists, male and female.

Showalter, Elaine. "The Death of the Lady (Novelist): Wharton's *The House of Mirth*," in *Sister's Choice: Tradition and Change in American Women's Writing*. Oxford: Clarendon Press, 1991.
   Showalter sees Lily Bart at the age of twenty-nine as too old to change the patterns of her life and, therefore, locked into the role of the perfect lady. This role, like Wharton's own as the Perfect Lady Novelist, prevents her from articulating her own situation. Both Lily and Wharton seem trapped between two worlds: a "homosocial women's culture" and the "heterosexual fiction of modernism." Lily's final realization that her social status does not "exempt her from the sufferings of womanhood" marks her decline from high society to the working class. Her final hallucination of holding Nettie Struther's baby expresses her new sense of membership in a community of women. By choosing to have Lily die, Wharton, Showalter argues, finally rejects the "escapism of the lady's world" and enters the ranks of the professional writer able "to deal seriously with the sexual relationships of men and women in a modern society."

Singley, Carol J. *Edith Wharton: Matters of Mind and Spirit*. New York: Cambridge University Press, 1995.
   This intellectual biography looks at the philosophy, theology, and metaphysics that provided the foundation for Wharton's fiction. *Ethan Frome*, for example, is considered as a critique of Calvinism, *Summer* in terms of Emersonian transcendentalism, and *The Age of Innocence* as an expression of Puritan Hellenism. In order to situate Wharton firmly in the intellectual environment of her times, Singley discusses the books Wharton read, the writers with whom she corresponded, and the particular theories that excited her.

Tinter, Adeline R. "Mothers, Daughters, and Incest in the Late Novels of Edith Wharton," in *The Lost Tradition: Mothers and Daughters in Literature*, eds. Cathy N. Davidson and E. M. Broner. New York: Frederick Ungar, 1980.
   Tinter looks at three novels she calls Wharton's "Sophoclean trilogy"—*The Old Maid* (1924), *The Mother's Recompense* (1925), and *Twilight's Sleep* (1927)—in the context of Wharton's relationships with her own mother and father. These novels are narrated from the mother's point of view, despite the fact that Wharton herself was never a mother. They depict an archetypal struggle between mother and daughter which conceals a struggle for the father with incestuous implications. Tinter also notes that Wharton's conflict-filled "modern" family relationships seem consciously to contradict the didactic novels of Grace Aguilar (Wharton borrowed one of her titles from Aguilar's

1864 novel, *The Mother's Recompense*), which advise mothers to keep actively involved in and in control of their daughters' activities.

Wagner-Martin, Linda. *The House of Mirth: A Novel of Admonition.* Boston: G. K. Hall, 1990.

This short book provides a straightforward analysis of the novel in terms of narration, major characters, and structure. It also provides background on the novel's sources and critical reception, and includes a chronology and brief annotated bibliography.

Waid, Candace. *Edith Wharton's Letters from the Underground: Fictions of Women and Writing.* Chapel Hill: University of North Carolina Press, 1991.

Waid analyzes Wharton's works in terms of recurring "failed artists, unfinished texts, and anxieties about silence, inarticulateness, and suffocation." She sees these themes, as well as Wharton's references to Persephone, as evidence of Wharton's preoccupation with the problems of the female artist. Moreover, Waid believes that Wharton's fascination with depths and interiors is part of her reaction against what she perceived to be the superficiality of the "scribbling" women writers of sentimental fiction. For women to achieve the greatness of the best realistic art, they would have to risk leaving the security of the surface and cross into the perilous depths.

White, Barbara A. *Edith Wharton: A Study of the Short Fiction.* New York: Twayne Publishers, 1991.

White provides a comprehensive study of Wharton's 85 short stories, including analysis of major themes, narrative technique, critical merit, and connections to the author's life and theories on art. Though sometimes considered cold and artificial, Wharton's stories should be appreciated for their complex treatment of point of view and the doubleness of human experience. White traces the gender shift in Wharton's narrators: the early stories have an equal mix of male and female "reflectors," the middle stories rely almost exclusively on male points of view, and the later stories often use female narrators from the lower or servant class. White also classifies Wharton's work by theme: artist stories, father-daughter stories, marriage-divorce stories, and ghost stories. Of particular interest to White are stories about "frozen silences" and buried secrets, which she sees as coded tales of incest.

Wolff, Cynthia Griffin. *A Feast of Words: The Triumph of Edith Wharton.* Reading, Mass.: Addison-Wesley, 1994.

Wolff's biography is considered the definitive psychological study of Wharton's life and work. She traces the route Wharton took from an unhappy childhood to a career as a successful writer, a "laborious journey" made excruciatingly painful by Wharton's desire both to be "feminine" in Victorian terms and to use her talents and her energies to achieve independence. Wharton's work explores many of the problems she faced in life: the pain of isolation, the complexity of mother-daughter relationships, the paradoxes inherent in female sexuality. In the process of transforming her private experiences into fiction Wharton triumphed over her own illness and became, in Wolff's estimation, one of the half dozen greatest novelists in American literary history.

Note: This is an updated version of Wolff's 1977 work published by Oxford University Press. It includes reprints of two essays—"Cold Ethan and 'Hot Ethan,'" (see below) and "Lily Bart and Masquerade," originally published in *Wretched Exotic: Essays on Edith Wharton in Europe*, eds. Katherine Joslyn and Alan Price. New York: Peter Lang Press, 1993.

——————. "Cold Ethan and 'Hot Ethan.'" *College Literature* 14, no. 3 (Fall 1987): 230-245.

Wolff reads *Summer* as "an almost literal inversion" of *Ethan Frome,* as a tale of "passion and self-assertion," rather than of "passivity and dependency." Comparing the two in light of Wharton's own experience as a woman tied to a "ghost of a husband," a woman who belatedly discovers passion outside of marriage, can help readers understand the lessons life had taught Wharton. Though *Ethan Frome* leaves the reader wondering about the reasons for the protagonist's entrapment, *Summer* makes it clear that Wharton believes men and women are to some degree responsible for their own fates. We may be limited by the society in which we live and the choices we make, but we need not be immobilized by them.

LAURA INGALLS WILDER
1867-1957

Wilder was born in the Wisconsin woods and moved with her family throughout the Midwest in search of a better life. They finally settled in De Smet, South Dakota, where Wilder met and married her husband. The couple bought a farm in Missouri where Wilder raised chickens and began to write articles for the local papers. It was her daughter, Rose Wilder Lane, who encouraged Laura to write about her early life. In 1930 at the age of sixty-three, she began the first of the seven Little House books: *Little House in the Big Woods* (1932), *Little House on the Prairie* (1935), *On the Banks of Plum Creek* (1937), *By the Shores of Silver Lake* (1939), *The Long Winter* (1940), *Little Town on the Prairie* (1941), and *These Happy Golden Years* (1943). She also wrote *Farmer Boy* (1933), based on her husband's childhood. A collection of her letters to her husband and a journal she kept during their trip to Missouri, as well as a fictionalization of their early years together, were published posthumously.

Reissued Editions

Note: All of the Little House books, as well as the posthumous *The First Four Years* and *On the Way Home*, are frequently reissued. In the 1990's HarperCollins published several new adaptations of Wilder's books, including *Dance at Grandpa's, Going to Town,* and *Holiday Stories,* in addition to the seven original Little House books. There are video adaptations of the books and the television series as well as Laura Ingalls Wilder family collections and cookbooks. Other publishers of Wilder's work include Harper & Row, Houghton Mifflin, Puffin Books, Cornerstone Books, and Scholastic Books. Finally, there is *A Little House Sampler,* which was brought out by the University of Nebraska Press in 1988.

Biography and Commentary
Erisman, Fred. *"Farmer Boy*: The Forgotten 'Little House' Book." *Western American Literature* 28, no. 2 (Summer 1993): 123-130.
Erisman sees *Farmer Boy* as a key volume in the Little House series because it demonstrates the significance of farmers to the development of the West. Farmers like the Wilder family knew how to domesticate nature and brought law, education, religion, and commerce to the wilderness. They were more "socially assimilated" and "economically aware" than the westward-looking Ingallses. Successful development of the frontier depended on a synthesis of the characteristics represented by the two families.

Fellman, Anita Clair. "Laura Ingalls Wilder and Rose Wilder Lane: The Politics of a Mother-Daughter Relationship." *Signs* 15, no. 3 (Spring 1990): 535-561.
Fellman traces the history of the "intense and troubled relationship" between mother and daughter, especially during the Depression years, when Lane, a struggling writer, moved back in with her aging parents. She blames both women's persistent belief in "solitary" individualism rather than a more "collective" notion of society as part of their problem in achieving the kind of "nurturance" from each other that they both craved. Despite her anger when her mother asked her to leave the family farm, Lane continued to play a "parental" role in assisting her mother with her writing. Ironically, though Lane, a prolific journalist and best-selling novelist, was far better known than her mother in their lifetimes, today her work has been almost entirely forgotten.

Frey, Charles. "Laura and Pa: Family and Landscape in *Little House on the Prairie." Children's Literature Association Quarterly* 12, no. 3 (Fall 1987): 125-128.
Frey focuses, in particular, on the "tensions" in Laura's relationship with her father and Wilder's use of a narrative perspective which projects both a child's and an adult's sensibility. For example, the female child's desire for comfort and security is downplayed in the adult narration of a journey filled with danger and discomfort which was undertaken simply because Pa wanted to move on. At first, Laura and her sister appear "somewhat passive and doll-like" in keeping with the patriarchal division of their family life; as the novel progresses,

Laura develops a complex personality unrestricted by the traditional roles of either her father or mother.

Gilead, Sarah. "Emigrant Selves: Narrative Strategies in Three Women's Autobiographies." *Criticism* 30, no. 1 (Winter 1988): 43-62.
    Gilead compares the autobiographical work of three writers—Isak Dinesen's *Out of Africa* (1965), Maxine Hong Kingston's *The Woman Warrior* (1976), and Wilder's Little House series—in order to demonstrate that they combine the typical pioneer or immigrant story with the typical woman's story about the "quest for selfhood," both of which share similar themes and narrative plots. In particular, Gilead notes the play between wilderness and civilization, and between openness and enclosure in these works. The early Little House books show Laura often alone in nature as a pleasure-seeking, amoral, and androgynous child. Later, as she progresses toward acceptance of social structures, she feels guilty about self-indulgence and aware of the necessity of work. Changes in her clothing are often used as a metaphor for the "binding of the self" which accompanies this progression.

Holtz, William. "Closing the Circle: The American Optimism of Laura Ingalls Wilder." *Great Plains Quarterly* 4, no. 2 (Spring 1984): 79-90.
    Holtz finds Wilder's insistence on the myth of the frontier as a new promised land increasingly problematic in the later books of the Little House series. Such optimism fails to acknowledge the impossibility of true self-sufficiency on prairie farms at the mercy of extreme weather and distant markets. It also fails to encompass the darker tragedy implicit in the father's "disappointed dreams," the mother's and sister's "bleak and impoverished later years," and Wilder's own experience of failure. Wilder's imagination could only take her so far into the darkness of reality; it could describe the difficulty and struggle of the family's life, but not its defeats; it could take Laura to the "verge of maturity," but not allow her to enter it. Ultimately, the Little House books cannot and do not modify their romantic view in light of the unsettling realities of a complex world.

Miller, John E. *Laura Ingalls Wilder's Little Town: Where History and Literature Meet.* Lawrence: University Press of Kansas, 1994.
    Miller, in this illustrated text, uses Wilder's last five novels, including the posthumous *The First Four Years*, an "adult" novel based on her first years of marriage, as a case study of the relationship between fiction and history. Wilder's readers assumed that the works were historical and social historians have, if fact, found them useful because of the careful detail Wilder provided about home furnishings, work habits, clothing styles, farm economics, methods of travel, religious practices, education, entertainment, even town layout. Also of interest are Wilder's omissions—she did not write about politics, ethnic divisions, or the exploitation of railroad workers. Her own respect for the simple life lived close to nature, her optimism and love of beauty,

the influence of her daughter as editor, and the storytelling conventions she observed, especially the use of a "girlish point of view," all limited the historical scope of the novels. Still, Miller concludes they are of value as a supplement to and humanization of traditional history.

Mowder, Louise. "Domestication of Desire: Gender, Language, and Landscape in the Little House Books." *Children's Literature Association Quarterly* 17, no. 1 (Spring 1992): 15-19.

The Little House books, as interpreted by Mowder, dramatize two parallel processes—the domestication of the frontier by mothers creating homes out of wilderness, and the enculturation of the female child from free-spirited and vocal to well-behaved and silent. This progression is symbolized by the "china shepherdess" and the Indian, the "primary totems" within the series, which correspond to the two sisters—the blond and feminine Mary, the brown and barefoot Laura. As the Indians and wolves must be driven out so that houses may be built with shelves to display the china shepherdess, there is a corresponding loss of the frontier's freedom and spontaneity. Laura tries, but is ultimately unable to resist her own transformation into a lady. Sadly, she can only make herself heard by recalling the childish desires long since repressed.

Romines, Ann. "*The Long Winter*: An Introduction to Western Womanhood." *Great Plains Quarterly* 10, no. 1 (Winter 1990): 36-47.

Romines offers a "feminist reading" of *The Long Winter*, the central and perhaps the "best" novel in the Little House series. The previous novel, *By the Shores of Silver Lake*, is dominated by "linear male aspirations," with Pa making the family move five times in one year. In contrast, *The Long Winter* is dominated by women's work, with mother and daughters forced to stay inside the house during the seven months of terrible stormy weather. Laura's previous admiration for her father and his adventures here transfers to her mother, whose competence and ingenuity keep the family fed and entertained. Despite her love of the great outdoors and her antipathy for needlework and other female tasks in confined spaces, Laura praises the beautiful shawl her mother has woven, which was so like her, "soft and yet firm and well-wearing." This shawl, which the mother presents as their shared heritage, is the symbol of women's culture, according to Romines, and represents the "cyclical household rhythms" which stand in counterpoint to the chaos outside the harmony of the home.

Spaeth, Janet. *Laura Ingalls Wilder*. Boston: G. K. Hall, 1987.

This volume in Twayne's United States Authors series includes a chronology, bibliography, a biographical essay, and discussion of each of the Little House books. Spaeth sees Wilder's novels as offering a "supplement" to traditional history textbooks by focusing on the girls and women who participated in the pioneer movement westward following the Homestead Act of 1862. In addition to their historical accuracy, the books have been praised for their honest portrayals of an

American family and of the child's point of view. Spaeth analyzes their basic literary characteristics, Wilder's artistic concerns and the active role of her daughter in guiding Wilder's career. She also considers the relationship between the books and Wilder's own life, and between the television series and the books.

Susina, Jan. "The Voices of the Prairie: The Use of Music in Laura Ingalls Wilder's *Little House on the Prairie.*" *The Lion and the Unicorn* 16, no. 2 (1992): 158-166.
Susina sees this novel as literally "saturated" with music which symbolically links the settlers with nature. Pa and his "ubiquitous fiddle" is the major musical "voice," but there are also the song of the wolves and the lullabies of cowboys which represent the "raw power" associated with the prairie. Throughout the novel, Pa becomes a kind of frontier Orpheus who can call the stars into song and bring human and animal together "in harmony."

ANZIA YEZIERSKA
1883-1970
Yezierska, one of ten children, was born in Ploch, a Polish town in Russia; the family emigrated to New York's lower East Side in 1893. Her strongly patriarchal father was a Talmudic scholar who depended on his wife and children for the family support. Yezierska left home to learn English after watching her older sisters married against their wishes to other immigrant men. She herself married twice. The first marriage ended quickly in an annulment; the second was to her husband's best friend, with whom she had a daughter. After three years Yezierska asked for a divorce and gave up custody of her child. A brief but intense affair with the educator John Dewey helped inspire Yezierska to take up writing with the aim of mediating between her immigrant past and mainstream American culture. Her early fiction won quick acclaim and her collection, *Hungry Hearts* (1920), ten stories of lower East Side life, was purchased by the Hollywood producer Samuel Goldwyn for ten thousand dollars. Five books followed: *Salome of the Tenements* (1922), Yezierska's first novel; *Children of Loneliness* (1923), a collection of nine stories; *Bread Givers* (1925), an autobiographical novel; *Arrogant Beggar* (1927) and *All I Could Never Be* (1932), her last two novels. Despite her earlier success, Yezierska had difficulties finding publishers for these works and lived in relative obscurity and poverty until the 1950's, when she published a somewhat fictionalized autobiography, *Red Ribbon on a White Horse* (1950). She spent her last years writing articles and stories about the plight of the elderly.

Reissued Editions
Bread Givers. New York: G. Braziller, 1975.

How I Found America: Collected Stories of Anzia Yezierska. New York: Persea, 1991.

Hungry Hearts and Other Stories. New York: Persea, 1995.

The Open Cage: An Anzia Yezierska Collection. New York: Persea, 1979.

Red Ribbon on a White Horse. New York: Persea, 1987.

Salome of the Tenements. Champaign: University of Illinois Press, 1995.

Biography and Commentary
Dearborn, Mary V. "Anzia Yezierska and the Making of an Ethnic American Self," in *The Invention of Ethnicity*, ed. Werner Sollors. New York: Oxford University Press, 1989.

Dearborn sees Yezierska's life as a case study of "the invention of ethnicity in American culture." Though the "sweatshop Cinderella" was a character created by Sam Goldwyn's publicity machine, Yezierska herself contributed to the myth by neatly erasing twenty years of her life so it would appear she had gone straight from the ghetto to Hollywood. Eventually she fled Hollywood, but the Cinderella myth endured even as her literary reputation declined. The same ethnic traits for which she was once praised later resulted in her work being dismissed as overly emotional and intense. Yezierska clearly suffered as her glorified ethnicity backfired, while she continued to feel alienated from her parents and her ghetto past.

Henriksen, Louise Levitas. *Anzia Yezierska: A Writer's Life.* New Brunswick, N.J.: Rutgers University Press, 1988.

This illustrated biography by Yezierska's daughter includes photographs, newspaper clippings, and extensive quotations from Yezierska's letters. Henriksen credits Mary Dearborn, Carol Schoen, and other feminist scholars with sparking her interest in her mother's life and providing her with correspondence they had unearthed. Jo Ann Boydston, a John Dewey scholar, aided her in the research and writing of the book.

Kamel, Rose. "'Anzia Yezierska, Get Out of Your Own Way': Selfhood and Otherness in the Autobiographical Fiction of Anzia Yezierska." *Studies in American Jewish Literature* 3 (1983): 40-50.

Kamel looks at three works in particular: *Red Ribbon on a White Horse*, the memoir of Yezierska's youth written at the end of her life; *Hungry Hearts*, Yezierska's early melodrama, which was made into a film; and "Dreams and Dollars" in *Children of Loneliness*, the fictionalization of her Hollywood experience, which illustrates her inability to come to terms with the movie-set version of her life. Kamel connects Yezierska's family and friends to the "firmly earthbound mother figures" and the platonic Protestant father figures which populate her fiction. She concludes that Yezierska was never able to distance herself enough from her life to develop her true talent.

Lem, Ellyn. "A Voice out of the Fishbowl: Yezierska's Argument for Seeing the Slum from Within." *CEA Critic* 58, no. 1 (Fall 1995): 66-73.

In the 1890's, many American social reformers and writers wrote about life in the slums without realizing that they might be distorting the experiences of the people they had observed. Lem compares the work of Stephen Crane, Joseph Riis, and others who purport to "understand" the lives of poor immigrants with that of Yezierska, who writes from firsthand experience. One of her late novels, *The Arrogant Beggar*, specifically addresses the "mistrust" which has developed between social workers and the poor. Lem argues that Yezierska's work is significant because of its "continual dramatization" of the gap between the goals of ghetto inhabitants and the misguided notions of those who seek to assist these "aliens."

Levin, Tobe. "How to Eat Without Eating: Anzia Yezierska's Hunger," in *Cooking by the Book: Food in Literature and Culture*, ed. Mary Anne Schofield. Bowling Green, Ohio: Bowling Green State University Popular Press, 1989.

Yezierska dramatizes intergenerational conflict with food and often equates assimilation with American eating practices. The titles of her novels and stories reveal her obsession with food. Levin focuses on several examples: "Fat of the Land" portrays a woman unable to conform to the stereotype of the American lady partly because she continues to crave herring and onions even after achieving prosperity; *Children of Loneliness* ends in a restaurant where the second-generation daughter expresses her repugnance toward her parents' table manners; "Hunger," *Bread and Wine in the Wilderness*, and *My Own People* are filled with images of food and scenes of eating.

See also: Ellen Golub. "Eat Your Heart Out: the Fiction of Anzia Yezierska." *Studies in American Jewish Literature* 3 (1983): 40-50.

Oates, Joyce Carol. "Imaginary Cities: America," in *Literature and the Urban Experience*, eds. Michael C. Jaye and Ann Chalmers Watts. New Brunswick, N.J.: Rutgers University Press, 1981.

Oates sees Yezierska as one of a group of writers, including Stephen Crane, Upton Sinclair, and Theodore Dreiser, who depict the "City" as a place where people die as a result of human cruelty and unspeakable slum conditions. Though less well-known than her male contemporaries, Yezierska is a "more realistic portrayer" of the realities of slum life, which she describes from personal experience. Unlike Crane and Dreiser, she accepts the concept of Americanization yet also understands the price one pays for assimilation. Yezierska's work, though "shamelessly melodramatic" and lacking in the ambiguities that "enrich" serious literature, is thoroughly convincing and honest, particularly in its portrayal of its women protagonists, Oates concludes.

Schoen, Carol B. *Anzia Yezierska*. Boston: G. K. Hall, 1982.
This volume in Twayne's United States Authors series includes a chronology and bibliography, a biographical essay, and analysis of Yezierska's five full-length works and two volumes of short pieces. Schoen places Yezierska's life and work in the context of the East European Jewish immigrant experience and attempts to clarify the difference between the "I" who narrates the stories and the author's own life. For each story and novel she discusses, Schoen provides a summary of the basic plot and the work's critical reception, as well as her own reading. Schoen praises Yezierska's skill in creating scenes and characters but faults her for letting her "moral indignation" and "prophetic zeal" lead to "dishonest endings."

Wexler, Laura. "Looking at Yezierska," in *Women of the Word: Jewish Women and Jewish Writing*, ed. Judith R. Baskin. Detroit: Wayne State University Press, 1994.
In this biographical essay, Wexler argues for a new reading of Yezierska's work, especially her major novel, *Bread Givers*, which would emphasize the author's role as a "literary witness" to "gender, race, ethnic, and class conflicts of the past." Though Yezierska herself contributed to the sentimental reading of her work as "local color" writing produced by a "primitive voice from the ghetto," such a reading may miss the complexity of the world she describes and the occasional irony in the depiction of her heroines. Wexler concludes that critics need to replace the "insouciant myths" of immigrant life with the "denser image" of family discord and bitter realities.

Wilentz, Gary. "Cultural Mediation and the Immigrant's Daughter: Anzia Yezierska's *Bread Givers*." *MELUS* 17, no. 3 (Fall 1991-1992): 33-41.
Wilentz analyzes the novel in terms of its protagonist's attempt to mediate between her Jewish roots and her new national identity. This "double bind" is further complicated by gender considerations dramatized in her stormy relationship with her father. Though the novel seems to have a happy ending in which familial and cultural reconciliation is achieved, the melancholy tone undermines such a conclusion. Moreover, the last paragraph, in leaving unresolved the issue of the father coming to live with the young couple, "unravels" the presumably "neatly tied ends" of this final chapter.

Chapter 3
POETS, DRAMATISTS, AND EXPERIMENTAL WRITERS

Some scholars would argue that a tradition of American women's poetry begins only in the 1960's, or perhaps with the first complete collection of Emily Dickinson's poetry in 1955, approximately one hundred years after she wrote her first poem. There was no highly respected and well-known female poet in America in the late nineteenth century, no Elizabeth Barrett Browning or Christina Rossetti, though earlier in the century there were women like Lydia Sigourney who achieved extraordinary popularity. Because of the ongoing professionalization of literature and because poetry came to be considered the most sacred and intellectual (hence male) of literary genres, women found it increasingly difficult to be taken seriously as poets. Moreover, the nineteenth century separation of male and female activity into distinct spheres, each with its own culture, meant that the writing of lyric poetry with "universal" and transcendent meaning belonged to a male elite who merited the support of patrons, whereas the writing of popular and often sentimental fiction could be seen as an appropriate occupation for women who "had" to work. Not surprisingly, then, Emily Dickinson made little effort to publish her work; rather, she preserved many of her seventeen hundred poems in carefully bound booklets as if she understood they needed to wait for future generations to be appreciated.

It took the modernist and feminist movements of the early twentieth century to produce the first real generation of American women poets, including Amy Lowell, H. D. (Hilda Doolittle), Louise Bogan, Marianne Moore, and Gertrude Stein. Aided by the bohemian freedoms of Paris and Greenwich Village and the presumed objectivity of experimental artistic forms, these women found their work supported and encouraged. Moreover, several played leadership roles in the literary life of their times: H. D. and Moore edited two of the most influential literary journals, *Poetry* and *The Dial*; Lowell introduced the French Symbolists to American readers; Bogan was poetry editor of *The New Yorker* for over forty years; and Stein entertained the avant-garde in her famous salon. Three female poets of this period—Lowell, Moore, and Edna St. Vincent Millay—received Pulitzer Prizes. Despite the real success of women poets in the 1920's and 1930's, most critics focused almost exclusively on the formalist characteristics of their work. It has only been since the 1960's that feminist scholars have revisited this poetry to search for its hidden messages and to try to understand the social and personal context out of which they emerged.

Throughout the twentieth century the female modernist poets have continued to receive more positive critical attention than those women who relied on traditional forms and conventional language. Millay—the most popular American poet of the 1920's—was considered "old fashioned" early in her career, as was Elinor Wylie, who followed her in the writing of sonnets about love. Female poets writing outside mainstream American culture also found it difficult to be taken seriously. The female poets of the Harlem Renaissance, for example, never received the attention of their male counterparts. Other ethnic poets have been relegated to the margins of literary history, including Emma Lazarus (1849-1887), the Jewish writer the final lines of whose poem "The New Colossus" (1883) are immortalized on the Statue of Liberty.

The early twentieth century also saw the beginnings of feminist drama. Despite the fact that acting was always a possible way for women to earn a living, any career associated with the theater was considered suspect throughout the nineteenth century. Many female poets wrote occasional plays to be performed in intimate settings, but few considered the commercial theater an appropriate outlet for their artistic impulses. The rise of regional art and experimental theaters throughout the country, which coincided with the emerging bohemian spirit of Greenwich Village in the 1920's, created opportunites for women to attempt writing drama for the stage. The Provincetown Players, the most famous of the "little" theaters for giving Eugene O'Neill his start, also offered opportunities to women writers, including Djuna Barnes, Edna St. Vincent Millay, and Susan Glaspell—one of the theater's founders and major contributors. The most successful woman playwright of the first half of the twentieth century was Rachel Crothers, the first woman to write for Broadway, who produced more than two dozen plays for such stars as Tallulah Bankhead, Katherine Cornell, and Gertrude Lawrence. Crothers not only directed her own plays, she also designed the sets and took charge of casting. Other signficant playwrights of the period whose work can be found in new anthologies include Zona Gale, Zoe Akins, and the novelist/screenwriter Edna Ferber. In general, however, there are fewer critical studies of women playwrights than of women poets. Those writers who have attracted the most serious critical attention, Crothers and Glaspell in particular, produced works with potentially feminist messages considered relevant to late twentieth century audiences.

Despite the canonization of certain types of female writers to the possible exclusion of others, feminist literary historians continue to search for "lost" poets and dramatists and to reconsider the reputations of those who have been overlooked or devalued. Djuna Barnes, included here because her innovative prose, like that of Gertrude Stein, was considered a form of poetry, was "rediscovered" only in the 1990's. Other poets who were well known in their day—the Marxist poet Genevieve Taggard, the African American poet Anne Spencer, and the Native American poet Emily Pauline Johnson, for example—have begun to experience revivals, though there is not yet enough secondary material available on them to justify inclusion in a bibliography. Since 1975 there have been many fine studies of American women's poetry and several new anthologies, including ones dedicated to nineteenth century women's poetry, twentieth century women's poetry, and poetry by black American women. Most feminist and literary journals, *Women's Studies* and *Twentieth Century Literature* in particular, regularly include articles on female poets; and major reference works, for example *The Columbia History of American Poetry,* edited by Jay Parini, now regularly include essays on Dickinson and on the female modernist and experimental poets of the early twentieth century.

GENERAL STUDIES
Barlow, Judith E., ed. *Plays by American Women: The Early Years.* New York: Avon Books, 1981.
    This volume includes an introduction, a selected bibliography, and the full texts of five plays from Anna Cora Mowatt's *Fashion* (1845), a comedy written by a well-known actress, to Sophie Treadwell's *Machinal* (1928). Also included are Rachel Crothers's *A Man's World* (1909), Susan Glaspell's *Trifles* (1916), and Zona Gale's *Miss Lulu Bett* (1920).

Berg, Temma F., ed. *Engendering the Word: Feminist Essays in Psychosexual Poetics.* Urbana: University of Illinois Press, 1989.
    This collection focuses on the relationship between language and sexual identity and includes several essays on the work of H. D., Marianne Moore, and Emily Dickinson.

Chinoy, Helen Krich, and Linda Walsh Jenkins, eds. *Women in American Theater.* New York: Theater Communications Group, 1981 and 1987.
    This comprehensive text includes essays on women as actresses, women playwrights, and theatrical stereotypes of women. Appended are lists of theater awards received by women, conferences and festivals, feminist theaters, secondary works, film and video resources, and a compilation of women playwrights and their plays. There are essays on Rachel Crothers, Gertrude Stein, and Susan Glaspell, and an introductory essay on the history of American women in the theater.

Dickie, Margaret. "Women Poets and the Emergence of Modernism," in *The Columbia History of American Poetry.* New York: Columbia University Press, 1993.
    Dickie sees Gertrude Stein, H. D., and Marianne Moore as among "the most tenacious and experimental writers of their day." Nonetheless, their contributions to Modernism have been neglected, perhaps because their male contemporaries praised them for the ways in which their work resembled their own, rather than for the unique properties of their poetry. Dickie offers her reading of their literary careers, noting the

importance of the female body to their poetry and their frequent use of metaphors related to childbirth and maternity. She concludes that all three were far ahead of their times given their concern to establish a poetics based on their own experience as women.

See also: Margaret Dickie and Thomas Travisano, eds., *Gendered Modernisms: American Women Poets and Their Readers*. Philadelphia: University of Pennsylvania Press, 1996. This includes essays on H. D., Millay, Moore, and others.

Dodd, Elizabeth. *The Veiled Mirror and the Woman Poet*. Columbia: University of Missouri Press, 1992.

Dodd defines a new genre, "personal classicism," which she sees as typical of women poets from Emily Dickinson to Sylvia Plath and Sharon Olds. This genre combines romantic individualism and lyricism with classic formal and tonal control. Women writing about their own emotions and feelings may feel compelled to mask their most personal voice because they may want to dissociate themselves from the overly sentimental work of so-called "poetesses" and because they have been taught that only the private lives of men can be considered "universal." To develop further her theory, Dodd focuses on the work of four poets—H. D., Louise Bogan, Elizabeth Bishop, and Louise Gluck.

Drake, William. *The First Wave: Women Poets in America, 1915-1945*. New York: Macmillan, 1987.

Drake explores the "dynamics" behind this "surge of women's creativity" through examination of the interrelationships that both "nourished" and "obstructed" the careers of twenty-six of the best-known poets. For example, he considers Louise Bogan's, Marianne Moore's, and Edna St. Vincent Millay's relationships with their mothers; Elinor Wylie's and Millay's relationships with their husbands; and the friendships between pairs of poets—Marianne Moore and Lola Ridge, Louise Bogan and Marianne Moore. He also includes a chapter on the particular problems faced by black poets of this period. Appendixes include a chronology and a listing of publications and anthologies where each poet's work can be found.

France, Rachel, ed. *A Century of Plays by American Women*. New York: Richards Rosen Press, 1979.

This is a collection of scenes from twenty-three plays written between 1900 and 1974, including works by Rachel Crothers, Susan Glaspell, Gertrude Stein, Djuna Barnes, Edna Ferber, and Georgia Douglas Johnson. The volume contains brief biographies of each playwright and a chronological listing of twentieth century plays by women. In her introduction, France discusses women's roles in the Provincetown Players, the Negro Players, and other "little theaters." She notes that the names of women first appear in lists of "best plays" in the 1890's and concludes that there is a longer and more consistent tradition of American women writing for the stage than has generally been acknowledged.

Friedman, Sharon. "Feminism as Theme in Twentieth Century American Women's Drama." *American Studies* 25, no. 1 (Spring 1984): 69-89.
    Friedman considers the work of four women who wrote plays between 1916 and 1960: Susan Glaspell, Rachel Crothers, Lillian Hellman, and Lorraine Hansberry. She provides background information on each and analyzes the kinds of statements each made about women's roles. Though Hellman is the least focused on women's issues, all four portray women responding to their status as women and their desire for social freedom. Friedman also notes that few women prior to the twentieth century received financial backing to produce their plays unless they had friends or family with theater connections.

Gilbert, Sandra M., and Susan Gubar, eds. *Shakespeare's Sisters: Feminist Essays on Women Poets*. Bloomington: Indiana University Press, 1979.
    Sections II and III of this collection focus on nineteenth- and early twentieth century American and British poets, including Emily Dickinson, H. D., Marianne Moore, and Edna St. Vincent Millay; the essay by Gloria T. Hull on African American women poets referenced here is included. There is also a bibliography listing studies of individual poets. The "purpose" of the anthology, according to its editors, is to analyze the achievement of representative writers within a social context which made it extremely difficult for them as women to be taken seriously as writers of poetry.

Gould, Jean. *American Women Poets: Pioneers of Modern Poetry*. New York: Dodd Mead & Company, 1980.
    Gould offers biographical studies of ten poets born in the nineteenth century: Emily Dickinson, Amy Lowell, Gertrude Stein, Sara Teasdale, Elinor Wylie, H. D., Marianne Moore, Edna St. Vincent Millay, Louise Bogan, and Babette Deutsch. Each biography includes basic information about the poet's life and writings as well as her influence on the evolution of modern poetry and the particular struggles she faced as a woman in obtaining recognition for her work. A bibliography of primary and secondary sources is also included.

Hanscombe, Gillian, and Virginia L. Smyers. *Writing for Their Lives: The Modernist Women 1910-1940*. Boston: Northeastern University Press, 1988.
    Hanscombe and Smyers identify fourteen British and American women, including H. D., Marianne Moore, Amy Lowell, Gertrude Stein, and Djuna Barnes, who formed a kind of informal network which provided them with the financial and literary support they needed to write. They lived as they wrote, abandoning both literary and social conventions, some more covertly than others. Hanscombe and Smyers

review the lives and literary careers of these women, focusing on how their literary experimentation translated into complex and unusual relationships both homosexual and heterosexual. Even the decision to remain "unattached" had potentially subversive implications given society's assumption that women's destiny was to marry and have children. The text is filled with interesting tidbits about the unusual lives led by these women; it also contains photographs and a bibliography of individual writers' publications and of critical sources.

Honey, Maureen. "Survival and Song: Women Poets of the Harlem Renaissance." *Women's Studies* 16, nos. 3-4 (1989): 293-315.

Though poetry written by black women during the 1920's is considered "anachronistic" by the literary establishment, Honey believes it merits attention for its anticipation of contemporary issues. Poetry was, in fact, the genre of choice for readers and writers in the 1920's. Moreover, despite reliance on traditional lyrical and pastoral forms, poems by black women reveal "rebellious messages" which can be understood if they are read in the "context" of a female literary tradition. Honey reviews the previous discussions of this poetry and offers her own analysis of its major themes, in particular, the struggle to find images that reflected black female identity in a culture that glorified whiteness.

Howe, Florence, ed. *No More Masks: An Anthology of Twentieth Century American Women Poets.* New York: HarperCollins, 1993.

This anthology is divided into three generations, the first of which covers poets born between 1870 and 1920, and includes several poems by each of the women mentioned here with the exception of Emily Dickinson. In her introduction Howe explains that there were two informal groups of women poets in the early 1900's—one white and one black—who "knew little of each other." Few of the black poets were able to print volumes of their work, though individual poems were known through publication in African American literary journals of the time. Howe includes in her anthology poems by Anne Spencer and Alice Dunbar-Nelson, the wife of Paul Lawrence Dunbar. For the first pioneering generation of women, both black and white, writing poetry meant doing something "queer" in the face of a hostile and disapproving society.

Hull, Gloria T. "Afro-American Women Poets: A Bio-Critical Survey," in *Shakespeare's Sisters: Feminist Essays on Women Poets*, eds. Sandra M. Gilbert and Susan Gubar. Bloomington: Indiana University Press, 1979.

Hull argues that black women poets gave birth to their own "Anglo-African" tradition rather than simply accepting Western ideas and conventions. After discussing Phillis Wheatley's life and poetry, Hull turns to Frances Harper, the "key" female poet of the nineteenth century (see chapter 5), and discusses her early anti-slavery poetry and last volume of poems, *Sketches of a Southern Life* (1872). There were no more "queens" on the poetry throne until Margaret Walker and Gwendolyn Brooks began publishing in the 1940's and 1950's (they are not included in this bibliography since most of their work was completed after 1948), but there were at least seven women who were active in the Harlem Renaissance. Georgia Douglas Johnson published three volumes of poems between 1918 and 1938, Anne Spencer—a less prolific but more "arresting" poet—wrote quite dramatic and experimental poetry, and Helene Johnson dealt most explicitly with "racial protest" themes. The other four—Angelina Grimké, Jessie Fauset (primarily a novelist, see chapter 5), Effie Newsome, and Gwendolyn Bennett—published very little and have been relegated to "footnotes and appendixes."

Larsen, Jeanne. "Lowell, Teasdale, Wylie, Millay, and Bogan," in *The Columbia History of American Poetry.* New York: Columbia University Press, 1993.

   Larsen identifies a tradition of female lyricism which encompasses the work of these five poets. Passionate, sensual poetry marked by "musicality" and graceful form as written by Sara Teasdale, Elinor Wylie, and Edna St. Vincent Millay, in particular, was extraordinarily popular in the 1920's yet fell into disfavor by mid-century. Amy Lowell, Louise Bogan, and many other women poets have also been neglected but are now being rediscovered as part of a general reassessment of the "golden years" of American poetry. Larsen offers her own reading of the five poets based on new information in biographies and critical studies.

Ostriker, Alicia. "I'm Nobody: Women's Poetry, 1650-1960," in *Stealing the Language: The Emergence of Women's Poetry in America.* Boston: Beacon Press, 1986.

   In this chapter Ostriker names Dickinson "America's first radically experimental poet" and the first "woman poet" to use coded, duplicitous language to parody "the dominance of masculinity and rationality in culture." She then identifies three groups of women poets in the following generation: lyricists such as Sara Teasdale, Edna St. Vincent Millay, and Louise Bogan; modernist intellectuals such as Gertrude Stein, Amy Lowell, Marianne Moore, and H. D.; and those writers, less well-known today, who wrote poetry of social conscience dealing with working-class and humanitarian issues. These poets constitute the "past" behind the "extraordinary tide" of women's poetry which Ostriker sees beginning in 1960 and which is the subject of the rest of her book.

Schuleter, June, ed. *Modern American Drama: The Female Canon.* Cranbury, N.J.: Associated University Presses, 1990.

   This collection of twenty-two essays examines a wide range of women playwrights from feminist perspectives. Many of the essays focus on the themes of rejection and rebellion in the work of writers such as Rachel Crothers, Susan Glaspell, Djuna Barnes, Lillian Hellman, and Gertrude Stein. Several discuss contemporary African American playwrights. The introduction offers Schuleter's explanation of the volume's central paradox—the construction of new canons in the face of the "deconstruction" of old ones.

Shafer, Yvonne B. *American Women Playwrights, 1900-1950*. New York: Peter Lang, 1995.

This comprehensive reference includes short biographical essays on thirty-five women playwrights, a listing of their honors, awards, and runs on Broadway, and an extensive bibliography. All of the writers referenced in this bibliography who wrote plays, whether primarily poets, novelists, or dramatists, are covered.

Stetson, Erlene, ed. *Black Sister: Poetry by Black American Women, 1746-1980*. Bloomington: Indiana University Press, 1981.

This is a comprehensive anthology with selections by fifty-eight writers, divided into two sections— "Eighteenth and Nineteenth Century Poets" and "Twentieth Century Poets"—followed by a bibliography of anthologies, criticism, and primary sources organized by poet. There is an introduction to each section highlighting the contributions of a small group of the most significant poets and a general introduction which identifies the general themes and poetic techniques common to African American women poets. Stetson argues that black women writers have had to contend with two large issues in their poetry—how to assert their identity in a world that does not acknowledge their existence, and how to balance their rage in order to express the full range of human emotions.

Walker, Cheryl. *Masks, Outrageous and Austere: Culture, Psyche, and Persona in Modern Women Poets*. Bloomington: Indiana University Press, 1991.

This text, in a sense a sequel to *The Nightingale's Burden* (see entry below), focuses on six women—Amy Lowell, Sara Teasdale, Elinor Wylie, H. D., Edna St. Vincent Millay, and Louise Bogan—who represent the "full flowering" of the nightingale tradition. Walker offers a separate essay on each in which she defines the kind of persona the poets used, then analyzes related psychic factors in their lives. She also looks at the larger cultural context in order to demonstrate how each poet's work can be read for its revelations about the world in which she lived and the ways in which she mediated its race, class, and gender conventions.

_____. *The Nightingale's Burden: Women Poets and American Culture before 1900*. Bloomington: Indiana University Press, 1982.

Walker's "project" is to identify the historical and cultural factors which have led women to write certain kinds of poems such as "the sensibility poem, the free bird poem, the sanctuary poem, and the poem of secret sorrow." Because they lack the "authority" of their male counterparts, female poets have often written obliquely and in "cramped forms." In order to "hear" what they have to say, it is necessary to reconstruct the context in which they wrote. Walker concentrates primarily on the nineteenth century and concludes that there is a particular intensity to the work of Dickinson and other female poets which allows the reader to feel a "vibrant surge of personality," an inner voice lacking in the work of their male counterparts.

_____, ed. *American Women Poets of the Nineteenth Century.* New Brunswick, N.J.: Rutgers University Press, 1995.
      This anthology includes a wide variety of poetry written between 1820 and 1920, much of it for the popular press; Emily Dickinson is not represented. Walker's introduction establishes the historical and cultural context in which this poetry was produced, the critical reception it found in its own time and in later periods, and her own evaluation of the relative talent of representative women writers. Brief biographical essays and bibliographies precede each set of selections.

Watts, Emily Stipes. *The Poetry of American Women from 1632 to 1945.* Austin: University of Texas Press, 1977.
      The last two chapters of Watts's book, "1850-1950: Refinement and Achievement" and "1900-1945: A Rose Is a Rose with Thorns," offer a literary history of the period, which considers women's contributions to both the content and style of American poetry. Watts sees 1850 as a turning point marked by several major developments: the commercial success of frontier poets, the appearance of poetry by black and Jewish women, and the probable writing of Emily Dickinson's first poem. The final years of the nineteenth century and the first decade of the twentieth were particularly important for women poets who wrote about universal rather than strictly American themes and who began to experiment with poetic structure. Watts focuses on such major figures as Emily Dickinson, H. D., Amy Lowell, Marianne Moore, Gertrude Stein, and Edna St. Vincent Millay, as well as many other less well-known poets.

DJUNA BARNES
1892-1982
      Barnes was born in New York, the child of eccentric, bohemian parents. As a young woman she moved to Greenwich Village to pursue a career as a free-lance artist and journalist. In 1915 she published *The Book of Repulsive Women*, a small collection of poems and drawings which helped establish her own eccentric reputation, cultivated through her flamboyant dress and lifestyle. Barnes moved to Paris in the 1920's and traveled in the circle of expatriate writers there. Her first experimental novel, *Ryder* (1928), was soon followed by *The Ladies*

Almanack (1929), a humorous celebration of the "lesbian ladies" of Paris. Later, living outside London under the patronage of Peggy Guggenheim, who would help support her throughout her life, Barnes wrote her most famous work, *Nightwood* (1936), which quickly attracted critical attention thanks to an introduction by T. S. Eliot, and received praise as a masterpiece of black humor and literary modernism. Barnes returned to New York because of the war. For the last forty years of her life she lived a celibate and healthy life in quasi-retirement, writing very little with the exception of her verse drama, *The Antiphon*, first performed in 1958.

Reissued Editions
At the Roots of the Stars: The Short Plays. Los Angeles: Sun and Moon Press, 1995.

The Book of Repulsive Women. Los Angeles: Sun and Moon Press, 1994.

Ladies Almanack. New York: New York University Press, 1992.

Nightwood: The Original Version and Related Drafts. Normal, Ill.: Dalkey Archives Press, 1995.

Ryder. Normal, Ill.: Dalkey Archives Press, 1990.

Smoke and Other Early Stories. Los Angeles: Sun and Moon Press, 1988.

Biography and Commentary
Benstock, Shari. "Djuna Barnes," in *Women of the Left Bank: Paris, 1900-1940*. Austin: University of Texas Press, 1986.
    Benstock attempts to counter the "myth" of the eccentric, expatriate writer with analysis of Barnes's major works in the context of her participation in a "community of serious women writers in Paris." She sees Barnes as the most important writer of this community and interprets her work as a "critique of woman's place in Western society." After her return to New York, she began to take care of herself, not out of "eccentricity," Benstock writes, but perhaps because her famously beautiful body "was no longer on display and no longer vulnerable to sexual involvement."

Broe, Mary Lynn, ed. *Silence and Power: A Reevaluation of Djuna Barnes*. Carbondale: Southern Illinois University Press, 1991.
    This collection includes a bibliography, photographs, reminiscences, excerpts from reviews and letters, and eighteen new essays which reconsider Barnes's work in light of feminist theory. The full range of her work, from her earliest poems and journalism to her late play, *The Antiphon*, is discussed with special attention to *Ryder, The Ladies*

Almanack, and *Nightwood.* Throughout these essays Barnes is viewed as "interrogating conventional gender dichotomies" and flouting every possible taboo.

Field, Andrew. *DJUNA: The Formidable Miss Barnes.* Austin: University of Texas Press, 1983.
    Field's study of Barnes's life and work is considered the definitive biography. The text is supplemented by photographs, samples of Barnes's drawings and poems, and an extensive bibliography of primary and secondary sources. Field begins by highlighting the key points of Barnes's career from her work as a young journalist to the publication of *The Antiphon* after twenty years of silence. He then reviews her personal history which he considers dominated by the single fact of her hatred for her father. The rest of the biography fills in details about her personal relationships and the life she led in Greenwich Village, Paris, and London. Field sees Barnes as a writer of the grotesque in the tradition of Rabelais and Chaucer rather than of the modernists with whom she is usually compared. Her "unique artistic voice," because so unusual, has resulted in her work being "put to the side," revered rather than read.

Fuchs, Miriam. "Djuna Barnes and T. S. Eliot: Authority, Resistance, and Acquiescence." *Tulsa Studies in Women's Literature* 12, no. 2 (Fall 1993): 289-313.
    Fuchs analyzes three decades of correspondence for evidence of Eliot's influence on Barnes and the nature of their personal and professional relationship. Because of their friendship, they were both "cordially dishonest" with each other. Moreover, Eliot as editor pursued his own agenda and made it difficult for Barnes to disagree with his revisions. Though the relationship was initially helpful to Barnes's career, it ultimately hampered her progress and led her to alter her work against her own better judgment.

Gerstenberger, Donna. "The Radical Narrative of Djuna Barnes's *Nightwood,*" in *Women's Experimental Fiction,* eds. Ellen G. Friedman and Miriam Fuchs. Princeton, N.J.: Princeton University Press, 1989.
    Gerstenberger believes that Barnes has not received enough recognition for the "radical" narrative form of *Nightwood.* Most critics have focused on its subject matter—a civilization in decay as also described by T. S. Eliot in *The Wasteland.* Barnes's text puts in question all "conventional" readings of experience based on dualistic Western logic and undermines Western faith in the coherence of history. The novel, in fact, begins with a "mock-creation" story that makes fun of narration itself.

Herring, Phillip. *DJUNA: The Life and Work of Djuna Barnes.* New York: Viking, 1995.
    This illustrated biography focuses on Barnes's friends and

acquaintances, including T. S. Eliot's second wife, Valerie, and the raconteur and abortionist Daniel A. Mahoney, whose stories gave Barnes ideas for Dr. O'Connor's horrifying monologues in *Nightwood*. Herring sees Barnes as neither so poor nor so misanthropic as is generally believed, though he confirms stories about her cruelty to those who helped support her. Her life was fully as weird as her fiction; her wit was legendary; her admirers included some of the century's most famous writers.

Kaivola, Karne. "Djuna Barnes and the Politics of the Night," in *All Contraries Confounded: The Lyrical Fiction of Virginia Woolf, Djuna Barnes, and Marguerite Duras*. Iowa City: University of Iowa Press, 1991.
     Kaivola sees Barnes's work as filled with a doubleness and ambivalence which marks the "the boundaries between what is socially sanctioned and what is forbidden." Barnes's characters lead marginal lives outside the dominant culture, yet "internalize its norms" so that they end up "in collusion" with the sources of their own victimization. *Nightwood* is a particularly disturbing text precisely because of the way it subverts our expectations about the structure of society and human sexuality. Nonetheless, the history of the novel's publication, including extensive editing by T. S. Eliot, reveals the societal constraints to which the work was subjected despite the apparent freedom with which Barnes wrote.

Kannenstine, Louis F. *The Art of Djuna Barnes: Duality and Damnation*. New York: New York University Press, 1977.
     Kannenstine offers a comprehensive study of Barnes's work, including her early journalism and plays, her short stories, and her poetry, to establish her importance not just as the author of *Nightwood*, but as a major figure in American literature. He sees "ambiguity" as central to Barnes's vision of the instability of human existence in the face of a confusing world. The work is marked by a "modern sense of despair" and a "mordant wit"; at its best it achieves a distinctive "architectonic" quality.

Marcus, Jane. "Laughing at Leviticus: *Nightwood* as Woman's Circus Epic," in *Silence and Power: A Reevaluation of Djuna Barnes,* Mary Lynn Broe, ed. Carbondale: Southern Illinois University Press, 1991.
     Marcus sees *Nightwood* as a "Rabelaisian comic epic" which satirizes Freudian psychoanalysis and, at the same time, warns of the dangers of Fascism. The novel's large cast of characters—Jews, homosexuals, lesbians, transvestites, gypsies, blacks, and circus performers—represents precisely those groups defined as abnormal by the Nazis and condemned to dehumanization and death. This political vision is conveyed in a rich and wonderfully bawdy language filled with puns and an extraordinary range of literary and historical allusions.

Plumb, Cheryl J. *Fancy's Craft: Art and Identity in the Early Works of Djuna Barnes*. London, Associated University Presses, 1986.
Plumb looks at Barnes's early work as a deliberate rebellion against naturalism and places it in the context of early twentieth century symbolism. She focuses on both the experimental, avant-garde literary characteristics and the thematic attack on middle-class conventions. Barnes was interested in what motivates individuals in their quest for moral values; despite her cynicism, she saw the individual as capable of moral choice.

Rieke, Alison "Two Women: The Transformations," in *Faith of a (Woman) Writer*, eds. Alice Kessler-Harris and William McBrien. Westport, Conn.: Greenwood Press, 1988.
Rieke sees *Nightwood*, despite its radical style, as a direct descendent of such nineteenth century novels as Henry James's *The Bostonians* and Nathaniel Hawthorne's *The Blithedale Romance*. All three works share "paired New England heroines" who represent polar opposites in terms of stereotypic female characteristics. The childlike woman is then the object of desire for a male and female who compete for control of her; she is a passive victim whose sense of worth depends on others' desire for her.

Scott, James B. *Djuna Barnes*. Boston: Twayne Publishers, 1976.
Scott offers a comprehensive study of Barnes's life and literature, which he places in the context of the "lost generation" of expatriate American writers of the 1920's and 1930's. He sees her work as dominated by a despairing sense of "mankind's essential isolation" expressed in a naturalistic vision. Her constant experimentation with form and style is a reflection of the mood of the post-World War I period and the "highly charged" Parisian environment she enjoyed under the influence of friends such as T. S. Eliot and James Joyce.

LOUISE BOGAN
1897-1970
Louise Bogan, born in Maine, had an unstable and difficult childhood as the second child of parents whose stormy relationship often resulted in separation. She began writing poetry at the age of fourteen while a student at Boston Girls' Latin School. She attended Boston University for a year, then married an army officer who died shortly after the birth of their daughter. A second marriage to a fellow poet ended in divorce. Bogan's early published poems were widely praised and soon collected in her first book, *Body of This Death* (1923). This was followed by *Dark Summer* (1929), *Sleeping Fury* (1937), *Poems and New Poems* (1941), *Collected Poems, 1923-1953* (1954), and *The Blue Estuaries: Poems, 1923-1968* (1968). Bogan's poetry is characterized by its controlled formalist style, which provides an austere framework for lyric poems based on highly personal and painful experiences. Bogan was also known as a distinguished critic

who served as poetry editor for *The New Yorker* for almost forty years. Among the many honors she received for her poetry were the Bollingen Prize (1955) and recognition as one of five "distinguished senior American writers" from the National Endowment for the Arts (1967); she held the Library of Congress Chair of Poetry from 1945 to 1946.

Reissued Editions
The Blue Estuaries: Poems, 1923-1968. New York: Ecco Press, 1977.

Biography and Commentary
Bowles, Gloria. *Louise Bogan's Aesthetic of Limitation.* Bloomington: Indiana University Press, 1987.

Bowles identifies Bogan as a major modernist poet who used formalist aesthetic techniques to control female emotion. In effect, her continual process of self-editing resulted in self-silencing. Bowles argues that Bogan's quest for perfection was fueled by her desire to dissociate herself from other women poets and to maintain her precarious psychological balance. Her best work is marked by a complex ambivalence about women and about differing male and female literary traditions. Bowles's discussion begins by focusing on this ambivalence and then offers a detailed feminist analysis of Bogan's major poems.

Collins, Martha. *Critical Essays on Louise Bogan.* Boston: G. K. Hall, 1984.

This collection includes reviews and articles dating from 1925 to 1984, with five new essays by Deborah Pope, Ruth Limmer, Diane Wood Middlebrook, Carol Moldaw, and Sandra Cookson written expressly for the volume. Collins's introduction offers a summary of Bogan's career in light of the critical reception her poetry received. Considered a poet's poet, Bogan has never been widely read or reviewed. However, the women's movement has generated new interest in her life and work which, according to Collins, are best appreciated with a "fusion of intellectual, emotional, and aural attention."

DeShazer, Mary. "'My Scourge, My Sister': Louise Bogan's Muse," in *Coming to Light: American Women Poets in the Twentieth Century,* eds. Diane Wood Middlebrook and Marilyn Yalom. Ann Arbor: University of Michigan Press, 1985.

DeShazer analyzes Bogan's creation of "powerful female personae" who are both sources of inspiration and metaphors for the ambivalence she feels about her own creativity. Like Cassandra, Bogan sees herself as "empowered with song but ignored by all." The female figures she invokes are both "demonic and sustaining," "solitary and strong," "silent and vocal." Without the presence of "external others" who serve most male poets as muse, the female poet must become her own muse, which often means creation of a monstrous alternate self.

Dodd, Elizabeth. "The Knife of the Perfectionist Attitude," in *The Veiled Mirror and the Woman Poet.* Columbia: University of Missouri Press, 1992.

Dodd sees Bogan as a "modernist" who used imagery to express emotion without the addition of a personal "authorial" voice. Though Bogan believed that personal feelings should be the basis of lyric poetry, she used a variety of techniques to distance herself from her poetry, including male speakers and subjects. Dodd argues that Bogan's hatred of confessional poetry led her to suppress some of her most revealing poems which might have been among her best work.

Frank, Elizabeth. *Louise Bogan: A Portrait.* New York: Alfred A. Knopf, 1985.

This comprehensive biography, based on Bogan's memoirs, letters, and writings, interweaves the poetry and the events of her life. Frank sees Bogan as a complex individual—the difficult, jealous wife and the tender and gifted poet who nurtured the careers of many young writers while poetry critic for *The New Yorker.* Frank quotes extensively from Bogan's poetry; the book includes notes for those quotations, photographs of family and friends, and a bibliography of Bogan's work.

Peterson, Douglas L. "The Poetry of Louise Bogan." *The Southern Review* 19, no. 2 (Winter 1983): 73-87.

Peterson offers an appreciative reading of Bogan's poetry in terms of her stoicism. He argues that her work has not received the recognition it deserves because she remained a formalist when poetic experimentation was the norm. Her rejection of freer forms was part of a self-imposed discipline of "withdrawal, denial, and indifference," her impossible attempt to find an escape from the painful realities of her life. Her best poetry, according to Peterson, is preoccupied with time and mortality, beautifully and "cleanly" expressed with the "measured regularity" of traditional meters.

Ridgeway, Jacqueline. *Louise Bogan.* Boston: G. K. Hall, 1984.

Ridgeway sees Bogan's commitment to highly formal poetry as a "ritualistic" way of dealing with complexities that are beyond rational comprehension. This insight is then the basis of her explication of Bogan's work, which she traces from the early poems through the publication of her final collection, *The Blue Estuaries*, covering a lifetime of work. Ridgeway also discusses Bogan's short stories, her relationship with the metaphysical tradition, and her critical reception. The book includes a chronology and a bibliography of primary and secondary sources.

RACHEL CROTHERS
1870-1958

Crothers was born and raised in central Illinois, the youngest of four surviving children. Both of Crothers's parents were physicians; her mother began her medical studies when Rachel was a child. Crothers formed a dramatic club in her high school and later attended the New England School of Dramatic Instruction in Boston. In her mid-twenties she went to New York hoping to find a career as an actress. After completing a term at the Stanhope-Wheatcroft School of Acting, she was hired as a teacher and director of the one-act plays the school produced to showcase the talents of its students. She was also able to write and produce her own one-act plays, a useful apprenticeship for her first professionally produced full-length play, *The Three of Us* (1906). Six plays followed in the next ten years dealing with social problems such as prostitution, conflicts between marriage and career, and the moral responsibilities of women. Crothers's later plays with their sentimental mix of comedy and romance were far greater commercial successes, including *Old Lady 31* (1916), *A Little Journey* (1918), and *39 East* (1919). In the 1920's and 1930's, the third phase of her career, Crothers wrote witty comedies of manners focused on women who longed for liberated lifestyles and ended up living traditional lives. Crothers also continued to write about double standards for male and female sexual behavior in plays such as *When Ladies Meet* (1932), which won the Dramatist Guild's Megrue Prize for best comedy of the 1932 season. *Susa and God* (1937), Crothers's last play, won the Theater Club's gold cup and was made into a 1940 movie starring Joan Crawford. In addition to her thirty-year career in the theater, Crothers ran major relief organizations during two world wars and the Depression.

Reissued Editions
Note: Though Crothers's plays have not been reissued in other than occasional acting editions, they are included in the Barlow and France anthologies annotated at the beginning of this chapter.

Biography and Criticism
Abramson, Doris. "Rachel Crothers: Broadway Feminist," in *Modern American Drama: The Female Canon*, ed. June Schuleter. New York: Associated University Presses, 1990.

   Crothers managed to have a highly successful career and still "tuck" women-centered questions into social comedies. Abramson reviews the critical reception of each of Crothers's major plays, calling *A Man's World* her "bravest" and perhaps her "best" work. This 1910 play as well as *He and She* (1911) are the two most likely Crothers dramas to be included in a twentieth century feminist canon, Abramson concludes.

Clark, Larry D. "Female Characters on the New York Stage in the Year of Suffrage: Enter Advocacy, Quietly, Stage Left." *Theater History Studies* 7 (1987): 51-60.

   Clark identifies Crothers's *He and She* and John Ervine's *Jane Clegg* as the only two New York plays of 1920 to provide complex portraits of women which evaded prevailing stereotypes.

Gottlieb, Lois. "Looking to Women: Rachel Crothers and the Feminist Heroine," in *Women in American Theater*, eds. Helen Krich Chinoy and Linda Walsh Jenkins. New York: Theater Communications Group, 1987.
   Gottlieb traces the development of Crothers's feminism throughout her career. She credits her with creation of an important female type—the woman who looks to other women for help and affirmation. This type reflected the most positive stage of the women's movement, according to Gottlieb's intepretation, when "sex solidarity" was put to work to aid the evolution of all women. Later Crothers plays portray feminists as comic figures struggling to maintain their equilibrium in the heady postwar years without the mutual support previous generations had enjoyed.
   See also: Gottlieb's full-length study of Crothers's life and work in Twayne's United States Authors series, Boston: G. K. Hall, 1979. This text includes a bibliography, chronology, and analysis of each of Crothers's published plays.

Shafer, Yvonne B. "The Liberated Woman in American Plays of the Past." *Players Magazine* 49 (Spring 1974): 95-100.
   Shafer identifies *A Man's World* (1910) as the first "feminist" play and the one which established Crothers as the "chief spokesman for women in the theater." She notes that many of Crothers's plays deal with the problem of the double standard, some seriously, some comically, and that her pessimistic appraisal of the difficulties faced by career women probably reflects her own experience. Shafer concludes that Crothers "excelled" as an actress, playwright, and director, and that both her life and her work contributed to the evolution of women's rights.

Sutherland, Cynthia. "American Women Playwrights as Mediators of the 'Woman Problem.'" *Modern Drama* 21 (September 1978): 319-336.
   Sutherland sees Crothers as belonging to a group of writers born in the 1870's, including Zona Gale, Zoe Akins, and Susan Glaspell, who chronicled the "increasingly noticeable effects of free love, trial marriage, the 'double standard,' career, divorce, and war on women's lives." She traces the development of Crothers's attitudes about feminism, noting her ambivalence in the 1920's and her final alienation from feminist causes in her last plays.

EMILY DICKINSON
1830-1886
   Emily Dickinson, the "Belle of Amherst," has become as famous for her presumed eccentric lifestyle has for her highly innovative and unorthodox poetry. The granddaughter of one of the founders of Amherst College and the daughter of a prominent Massachusetts judge and congressman, Dickinson as an adult led a reclusive life, rarely venturing beyond her parents' house and garden, always dressed in

white. Sitting at a small table in her corner bedroom, she wrote more than seventeen hundred poems, half of which were bound together into booklets with darning thread, then left to be discovered and read following her death. The first of these were published in 1890 with much of their unique punctuation and typography "corrected." An authoritative, three-volume edition of her work, including poems found in letters to friends, was originally published in 1955. Much of Dickinson's verse is written in enigmatic and often witty four-line stanzas marked by discordant rhymes and word usages which subvert traditional meanings. She writes of love, nature, death, and religion; of daisies, snakes, gnats, roses and spiders; of kings and queens, conquerors, goblins, madonnas and wives, creating a symbolic universe which must be deciphered to be fully understood.

Reissued Editions
Note: Dickinson's work is widely anthologized; *The Poems of Emily Dickinson* (1955) and *The Complete Poems of Emily Dickinson*, 3 vols. (1960), both edited by Thomas H. Johnson are published by Harvard University Press. Collections of selected poems have been published by G. Braziller (1989), Dover Publishers (1990), Courage Books (1991), Knopf (1993), and St. Martin's Press (1993).

Biography and Commentary
Barker, Wendy. *Lunacy of Light: Emily Dickinson and the Experience of Metaphor*. Carbondale: Southern Illinois University Press, 1987.
   Barker sees the metaphoric use of light as a key to many of Dickinson's least understood poems. References to light appear more than one thousand times in Dickinson's work, more often than any other metaphor. Like many other women writers, Dickinson subverts the traditional association of the sun with goodness and order, and of darkness with evil and chaos. In her poetry, it is darkness which provides a quiet refuge while the sun may "dazzle" but then "burn" those who turn to it. Artistic triumph occurs for Dickinson when "kindlier" lights reduce the "male sun's destructive power."

Bennett, Paula. *Emily Dickinson: Woman Poet*. Iowa City: University of Iowa Press, 1990.
   Bennett places Dickinson within a female literary tradition. She notes that Dickinson lived within a circle of women on whom she relied for emotional support and that she wrote from the heart about traditional female topics, though instead of providing "bromides" about nature and eternity, her poetry reflected her own anxieties and doubt. Bennett also compares Dickinson with her male contemporaries and concludes that her ambiguous and fragmentary style expresses her rebellion against the law and order of patriarchal society.
   See also: *My Life a Loaded Gun: Female Creativity and Feminist Poetics*, Boston: Beacon Press, 1986; here Paula Bennett discusses the poetry of Dickinson, Sylvia Plath, and Adrienne Rich in terms of the

issues of "self-redefinition and self-empowerment" which "My Life had stood—a Loaded Gun" brilliantly established as central to women's art.

Buckingham, Willis J., ed. *Emily Dickinson's Reception in the 1890's: A Documentary History*. Pittsburgh: University of Pittsburgh Press, 1989.
      This is a comprehensive collection of published reviews and comments from a wide variety of sources, including literary journals, daily newspapers, sorority quarterlies, and children's magazines, with an appendix of private references from diaries and letters. Buckingham's introductory overview summarizes the variety of reader responses to the first published edition of Dickinson's poetry. Most people, especially women, New Englanders, and younger critics, "delighted" in Dickinson's "originality, strangeness, and force." At the beginning and end of the decade, the poetry was considered "high brow"; in between it was considered "popular." In general, the 1890's was a receptive decade for Dickinson's unique talents, though her work was not fully understood and the "rage" for her poetry soon faded.

Doriani, Beth Maclay. *Emily Dickinson: Daughter of Prophecy*. Amherst: University of Massachusetts Press, 1996.
      This is a comprehensive critical study of all of Dickinson's poetry.

Eberwein, Jane Donahue. *Dickinson: Strategies of Limitation*. Amherst: University of Massachusetts Press, 1985.
      Eberwein interprets Dickinson's poetry as an implicitly religious quest to bridge the gap "between limitation and boundlessness." Her frequent references to "smallness," to the "soaring wren," and the "Christlike Daisy" demonstrate her belief that smallness may be a blessing, "an ironic asset in the quest of circumference," the barrier or boundary of life. Eberwein sees Dickinson's deliberate "cultivation of limitation" as an intensification of her own power which could bring her closer to the immortality she craved.

Ferlazzo, Paul J. *Critical Essays on Emily Dickinson*. Boston: G. K. Hall, 1984.
      This collection of reviews and articles dating from 1890 to 1984 includes an introductory bibliographic essay which summarizes the history of Dickinson manuscripts, biography, and criticism. The collection begins with two pieces by Thomas Wentworth Higginson; contains excerpts from book-length studies of Dickinson by Richard Chase, Brita Lindberg-Seyersted, John Cody, and Sharon Cameron; and includes two new essays written specifically for this volume—"Doing Without: Dickinson as Yankee Woman Poet," by Jean Donahue Eberwein, and "'Everyone Else Is Prose': Emily Dickinson's Lack of Community Spirit," by Barbara Antonina Clarke Mossberg.

Gelpi, Albert. "Emily Dickinson and the Deerslayer: The Dilemma of the Woman Poet in America," in *Shakespeare's Sisters: Feminist Essays on Women Poets,* eds. Sandra M. Gilbert and Susan Gubar. Bloomington: Indiana University Press, 1979.

Gelpi reads "My Life had stood—a Loaded Gun" as a key to the psychological "dilemma" facing Dickinson and other women writers in "patriarchal America." In this reading, the unnamed "master" in the poem functions, not as a lover, but rather as a Jungian "animus" representing the male aspect of the female psyche with which the poet identifies in her quest for power. In particular, Dickinson casts her animus as James Fenimore Cooper's "woodsman," America's frontier hero, and then presents the terrible choice: whether to side with the "deerslayer" or the slaughtered "doe." Other poems of Dickinson's are not so filled with anguish but rather celebrate womanhood and the assimilation of the animus into a fully integrated self.

Gilbert, Sandra M., and Susan Gubar. "A Woman—White: Emily Dickinson's Yarn of Pearl," in *The Madwoman in the Attic: The Woman Writer and the Nineteenth Century Literary Imagination.* New Haven: Yale University Press, 1979.

Gilbert and Gubar see Dickinson's child-like, non-assertive, "I'm Nobody! Who are you?" persona as the conscious "impersonation of a madwoman" on the part of a "helpless agoraphobic, trapped in a room in her father's house." Despite the apparent renunciation of a life of her own, the trenchant irony of her poems operates like a "steel blade," subverting the very image she worked so hard to project. And though the "child mask" was to some degree freeing in that it allowed her to play with the "toys" of her imagination, it ultimately became "crippling" and addictive, forcing her to live in a prison of her own creation. All of Dickinson's metaphors, as analyzed by Gilbert and Gubar, are highly ironic and ambiguous, most particularly her use of the color "white" as symbol of virginity as well as death, the bride as well as the ghost. They use their analysis of her poetry in comparison to the work of Catherine Rossetti, Elizabeth Barrett Browning, and the Brontës to establish the psychic entrapment experienced by women who dared to write lyric poetry, the most self-assertive of literary forms.

Hockersmith, Thomas E. "'Into Degreeless Noon': Time, Consciousness, and Oblivion in Emily Dickinson." *American Transcendental Quarterly* 3, no. 3 (September 1989): 277-295.

Hockersmith analyzes poems that deal with relationships between life and death, time and consciousness, and immortality and eternity. Many of these express "uncertainty" about the essence of life itself, rather than true cynicism. Some poems describe death as oblivion; others depict art as the only source of salvation. Dickinson saw man as ultimately "insignificant," hoping for eternal perfection in the face of an indifferent universe.

Homans, Margaret. "Emily Dickinson," in *Women Writers and Poetic Identity*. Princeton, N.J.: Princeton University Press, 1989.

Homans sees Dickinson as a poet who identified with other women writers and one whose "unique power" comes in part from the way she understood her own femininity. At first, she saw her mind's own workings as "feminine," much of the external world as "masculine," and herself as Eve, "the mother of irony," the first to understand that words are not necessarily synonymous with what they name. Moreover, she had the lucidity to note that Mother Nature was itself a "fiction" which attempted to name that which is "unnameable." Dickinson's greatest "originality," according to Homans, came in later poems where she broke out of gender dualities and showed the self as a "balance of two parts that are neither different nor the same." In effect, she freed herself from all forms of sexual determinism and claimed the power of language as her own.

Juhasz, Suzanne. *Feminist Critics Read Emily Dickinson*. Bloomington: Indiana University Press, 1983.

This is a collection of eight new essays, most by critics who have written extensively about Dickinson elsewhere, including Sandra M. Gilbert, Margaret Homans, Joanne Feit Diehl, Barbara Antonina Clarke Mossberg, and Karl Keller. The volume provides a bibliography, an index of poems cited, and an introduction by Juhasz which contrasts major examples of feminist and non-feminist Dickinson criticism. Juhasz argues that traditional criticism has had trouble believing that Dickinson is who she says she is, whereas feminist critics try to understand her in terms of her own sense of self; if she tells lies about herself, these are themselves part of who she is and what she has to say.

Juhasz, Suzanne, and Cristianne Miller, eds. *Women's Studies* 16, nos. 1-2 (1989).

This special issue of *Women's Studies* contains the proceedings of a 1986 conference on Dickinson at the Claremont Colleges. It includes summaries of six workshops and two plenary sessions. Each workshop was led by two to three scholars and dedicated to a single Dickinson poem: "A solemn thing—it was—I said" (271), "He fumbles at your Soul" (315), "The—name of it—is Autumn" (656), "My Life had stood—a Loaded Gun" (754), "The farthest Thunder that I heard" (1581), and "A Word made Flesh is seldom" (1651). The plenary sessions offered general discussions of Dickinson's life and work.

Keller, Karl. *The Only Kangaroo Among the Beauty: Emily Dickinson and America*. Baltimore: Johns Hopkins University Press, 1979.

Keller sees Dickinson as a "post-Puritan woman" whose gender must be considered in analyzing her poetry because being a woman was clearly an "issue" for her. He discusses her work and life in the context of other women writers of her day and in contrast to male writers such as Emerson and Whitman. Because of Dickinson's important place in

American literary history, Keller concludes that she must be considered an "indigenous" writer rather than an "anomaly." Much of his analysis focuses on Dickinson's "wit" as "viscerally wrung" from everyday life and her "radical" use of her Puritan heritage to justify the creation of a private space in which she was free to create.

McKinstry, S. Janet. "'How Lovely Are the Wiles of Words!'—or, 'Subjects Hinder Talk': The Letters of Emily Dickinson," in *Engendering the Word: Feminist Essays in Psychosexual Poetics*, ed. Temma F. Berg. Urbana: University of Illinois Press, 1989.

McKinstry argues for a reading of Dickinson's letters as "something between autobiography and poetry." She looks at examples of letters to family and friends, letters to her literary "preceptor, Thomas Higginson, and the three so-called Master letters without any address indicated. All of these letters show Dickinson playing with language and sharpening her "linguistic tools." They also reveal her power to "transform herself into a text," in effect, to create artificial roles for herself such as the dependent child which she uses in her letters to Higginson, the "literary father" and "language doctor" whose medicine she needs. Ultimately, Dickinson's "disguises"—child, flower, nature, lover—conceal her powerful irony and the "masterful" speaking voice of her best poetry.

Martin, Wendy. "Emily Dickinson: 'A Woman—white—to be,'" in *An American Triptych: Anne Bradstreet, Emily Dickinson, Adrienne Rich*. Chapel Hill: University of North Carolina Press, 1984.

Martin sees Dickinson as a model of "eccentricity and isolation" for women poets. As a rebellious adolescent, she vowed to listen to her own voice against the dictates of the adult world; as a young woman, she wrestled with her own anxieties and fears of being judged impious and disobedient. Her white dresses both mocked the Victorian ideal of angelic femininity and announced her "white election" to the priesthood of poetry. Martin analyzes Dickinson's poetry for evidence of the way she subverted nineteenth century definitions of "true womanhood" while at the same time taking advantage of her isolation in a domestic sphere.

Mossberg, Barbara Antonina Clarke. *Emily Dickinson: When a Writer Is a Daughter*. Bloomington: Indiana University Press, 1982.

Mossberg sees Dickinson as a very "human" poet in contrast to the saint-like myth created about her. Her poetry is filled with complaints about her mother, housework, Christian values, and her own alienation. The very uniqueness of her poetic style makes readers look to her life for explanations, yet what is known about her life does not necessarily answer the questions raised about her poetry. Mossberg suggests that it may be illuminating to consider Dickinson's relationship to her parents and to her mother, in particular, while keeping in mind that her poetry may be telling us how she wants to perceive them, not what kind of parents they really were. In effect, Dickinson has created a "daughter construct" which she used both to rebel against traditional female roles and to establish her own calculated identity as a perpetual child who never left home.

Rich, Adrienne. "Vesuvius at Home: The Power of Emily Dickinson," in *Shakespeare's Sisters: Feminist Essays on Women Poets*, eds. Sandra M. Gilbert and Susan Gubar. Bloomington: Indiana University Press, 1979.
    Rich offers a very personal account of her reading of Dickinson and her attempt to "enter her mind." She looks at poems which describe the poet's relationship to her own creative energy, poems which trace the development from child to woman, and poems which explore states of psychic extremity. Rich sees Dickinson as a woman who chose to lead the life she did, who was capable of great pride and self-confirmation, and who was able to live outside the guidelines of the major orthodoxies of her time.

Runzo, Sandra. "Dickinson, Performance, and the Homoerotic Lyric." *American Literature* 68, no. 2 (June 1996): 347-363.
    Runzo notes the many personae in Dickinson's poems—bride, boy, corpse, gun, and countless others—which add up to one "monumental self-portrait" and serve to "destabilize" gender and sexuality. Poem 313, in particular, epitomizes Dickinson's reliance on hyperbole, secrecy, and the idiom of Christianity to suggest a persona on the "brink of disclosure."

Wardrop, Daneen. "Emily Dickinson's Gothic Wedding." *American Transcendental Quarterly* 10, no. 2 (June 1996): 91-110.
    Wardrop examines Dickinson's imagery in poems which deal with love, marriage, and sex, and with brides and absent bridegrooms. She notes that these poems resemble gothic novels in their depiction of "dowerless" girls searching for their "feminine treasure troves" and of the "romantic elements of wedlock gone awry." Though Dickinson's brides never find a "loving husband," they do discover "hope chests" of written words which hold promise for an "endowed" creative life.

Wolff, Cynthia Griffin. "Emily Dickinson," in *The Columbia History of American Poetry*, ed. Jay Parini. New York: Columbia University Press, 1993.
    Since Dickinson left very little information about herself or her poems, it is up to the reader to construct his or her own conception of the "author-function," the voice that we hear speaking. Wolff offers her own thirteen-point set of assumptions as to the identity of the poet; for example—that she was highly intelligent and witty, that she was proud and ambitious, that she perceived with "ruthless clarity" male dominance of the political and literary worlds, that the severe eye-trouble from which she suffered contributed to her home-boundedness, that she writes about the human condition in general, not about a

particular series of personal crises. These assumptions then form the basis of Wolff's analysis of Dickinson's poetry, a poetry which she sees as indeed "cryptic" but also marked by an extraordinary "aesthetic power."

SUSAN GLASPELL
1876-1948

Glaspell was born and raised in Davenport, Iowa. After graduating from Drake University, she worked as a reporter for the *Des Moines News* and began to publish short stories in literary magazines. In 1913, Glaspell married George Cram Cook, a well-known socialist, and moved with him to Cape Cod, where they joined Eugene O'Neill in founding the Provincetown Players. This experimental "little theater" soon became known for its innovative productions and its support of young writers such as Djuna Barnes, Edna Ferber, and Edna St. Vincent Millay. Glaspell wrote eleven plays for the theater, compared to O'Neill's fourteen. Following Cook's death while he and Glaspell were living in Greece, she married Norman Matson and returned to Cape Cod. In 1927 she published a biography of Cook and in 1928 she collaborated with Matson on the play *The Comic Artist*. Her last play, *Alison's House*, which won the 1931 Pulitzer Prize for drama, tells the story of a thinly disguised Emily Dickinson. Following the dissolution of her marriage, Glaspell again began writing fiction set in the Midwest of her childhood and youth. She published five novels in the last fifteen years of her life, but is best known today as one of the founders of modern American drama and as the author of *Trifles*, the 1916 play which has become a feminist classic.

Reissued Editions
Plays by Susan Glaspell, ed. C. W. E. Bigsby. Cambridge: Cambridge University Press, 1987.

Biography and Criticism
Alkalay-Gut, Karen. "Jury of Her Peers: The Importance of Trifles." *Studies in Short Fiction* 21, no. 1 (Winter 1984): 1-9.
    Alkalay-Gut suggests that the best way to understand both the play and the story is through the same type of close attention to small details demonstrated by the women who analyze the murder scene.

Ben-Zvi, Linda. "Susan Glaspell's Contributions to Contemporary Women Playwrights," in *Feminine Focus: The New Women Playwrights,* ed. Enoch Brater. New York: Oxford University Press, 1989.
    Glaspell was one of the first writers to write truly women-centered drama in which female protagonists spoke their own langauge and the settings and structures of the plays reflected female experience. Ben-Zvi offers her own analysis of Glaspell's major plays, including the *Inheritors*, which courageously condemned the deportation of aliens and

strikebreakers and the abridgment of freedom of speech during World War I. Her work stands as an example of someone who "dared to give dramatic shape to the struggles of women" and who risked censure and worse in taking a stand against an oppressive society.

See also Linda Ben-Zvi's discussion of the murder case on which *Trifles* is based in "'Murder, She Wrote': The Genesis of Susan Glaspell's *Trifles.*" *Theater Journal* 44, no. 2 (May 1992): 141-162.

Carpentier, Martha C. "Susan Glaspell's Fiction: *Fidelity* as American Romance." *Twentieth Century Literature* 40, no. 1 (Spring 1994): 92-113.

Carpentier argues that Glaspell's fiction deserves the same attention as her drama. She sees this novel as providing an important exposé of how romantic individualism usurps the positive value of community, especially for women.

Dymkowski, Christine. "On the Edge: The Plays of Susan Glaspell." *Modern Drama* 31, no. 1 (March 1988): 91-105.

Dymbowski sees Glaspell as a central figure in the history of twentieth century American drama whose plays depict the paradoxical nature of women's social roles. Glaspell's characters seek to push life to its limits and explore "unchartered possibilities." Because they are marginalized by society, they have the power to shape it anew. Dymkowski examines the relationship between Glaspell's theatrical methods and these themes in several of her plays, including *The Outside, The Verge, Woman's Honor,* and *Trifles.*

Hedges, Elaine. "Small Things Reconsidered: Susan Glaspell's 'A Jury of Her Peers.'" *Women's Studies* 12, no. 1 (1986): 89-110.

Hedges summarizes some of the discussion of the story generated by feminist critics in the 1970's and then offers her own interpretation. Key to an understanding of the story, according to Hedges, is knowledge of what rural women's lives were like in the late nineteenth and early twentieth centuries and the degree to which the "cult of domesticity" had become a trap. The log cabin quilt on which Minnie, Glaspell's protagonist, works comes to symbolize "both the hardships and heroisms of pioneer life." The broken stove at the kitchen's center defines the failed attempt to create a welcoming home out of the wilderness.

Makowsky, Veronica. *Susan Glaspell's Century of American Women: A Critical Interpretation of Her Work.* New York: Oxford University Press, 1983.

Makowsky discusses Glaspell's career as both ahead of and behind the times. She was raised according to the ideals of the cult of domesticity, but began her career in the era of the new woman. Makowsky traces the use of maternal metaphors in Glaspell's work; she sees Glaspell's life, especially her two marriages in which she mothered weaker men, as representative of the realities of life for American women in the early twentieth century.

Mustazza, Leonard. "Generic Translation and Thematic Shift in Susan Glaspell's 'Trifles' and 'A Jury of Her Peers.'" *Studies in Short Fiction* 26, no. 4 (Fall 1989): 489-496.

Mustazza argues that there are important distinctions between the play and story beyond the change in title. He compares the two to demonstrate Glaspell's growing interest in women's "self-injurious acquiescence" in the roles men have established for them. Though both focus on the difference between male and female concepts of justice, the story, by focusing on the "separateness of women," becomes a more disturbing and interesting work than the drama on which it is based.

Ozieblo, Barbara. "Rebellion and Rejection: The Plays of Susan Glaspell," in *Modern American Drama: The Female Canon*, ed. June Schuleter. New York: Associated University Presses, 1990.

Ozieblo argues that Glaspell's reviewers dismissed her plays as "nonsense" because they saw her female characters as a threat to "patriarchal authority." She sees *The Verge* (1921) as Glaspell's "most provocative play" in its depiction of "humankind" as imprisoned by established norms and conventions. All of Glaspell's protagonists, as analyzed by Ozieblo, are rebels who transgress society's laws knowing full well the consequences they will inevitably face.

Papke, Mary E. *Susan Glaspell: A Research and Production Sourcebook*. Westport, Conn.: Greenwood Press, 1993.

This text contains a complete bibliography of Glaspell's works, including archival material; plot summaries, production histories, and review summaries of the plays; and an annotated bibliography of secondary sources.

Waterman, Arthur E. "Susan Glaspell." *American Literary Realism* 4, no. 2 (Spring 1971): 183-191.

This biographical essay includes a reception study, a primary bibliography, and a listing of critical works on Glaspell.

HILDA DOOLITTLE (H. D.)
1886-1961

H. D. was born in Bethlehem, Pennsylvania, to an academic family whose ancestors had been founders of the Moravian faith. While at Bryn Mawr she was briefly engaged to Ezra Pound, who remained an important mentor to her throughout her life. It was Pound who submitted Doolittle's first poems for publication, signing them "H. D., Imagiste." H. D. lived most of her adult life in London. In 1913 she married the British poet Richard Aldington, from whom she was separated a few years later and eventually divorced. During the war she took over his editorship of *The Egoist*, a journal for Imagist writers, while continuing to write her own poetry. She also began her friendship with Winifred Ellerman, who wrote under the pseudonym Bryher. The two women traveled extensively together following the birth of H. D.'s daughter, Perdita. H. D.'s reputation as a leader of the Imagist movement had been firmly established with the publication of her *Collected Poems* in 1925, followed by *Red Roses for Bronze* in 1931. In 1933 and 1934 she underwent psychoanalysis with Sigmund Freud, a process she described in *Tribute to Freud* (1956) as one of the most rewarding experiences in her life. Her later work moved away from Imagism and attempted to create a female mythology primarily based on classical sources. H. D.'s total oeuvre includes thirteen volumes of poetry as well as essays, translations, dramas, and five novels.

Biography and Commentary
Benstock, Shari. "H. D. and Bryher: En Passant," in *Women of the Left Bank*. Austin: University of Texas Press, 1986.

Benstock sees H. D.'s work as marked by doubleness, in particular, an oscillation between heterosexuality and homosexuality, which reflects her confusion about her own sexual identity. Ultimately, she was unable to choose between the "heterosexual world of modernism" represented by Pound and her husband and the homosexual world of Bryher. Benstock reviews key stages in her life, including her choice of London over Paris, and her major writings, especially *Hermione* and *Helen in Egypt*, for evidence of this ambivalence. H. D., according to Benstock, was not interested in resolving conflicts; her "lived experiences" as a woman allowed her to see the limits of "Imagism," which attempted to erase emotion, and encouraged her to highlight the interplay between "oppositional elements" which inform and define each other.

Dodd, Elizabeth. "H. D., Classiciste: The Imagist Approach to Personal Classicism," in *The Veiled Mirror and the Woman Poet*. Columbia: University of Missouri Press, 1992.

Dodd sees H. D.'s use of Greek mythology and drama as a "screen" which veils her art and provides her with a mask to hide behind. While the "mythmaking" of male writers was an attempt to reimpose "masculinist, patriarchal" standards, H. D.'s "revisionist" myths served her own female point of view. She was particularly interested in Euripides, whose plays she translated, because of his complex women characters and what she perceived as his "feminine" spirit. Many of the Greek stories she translated or reinvented have for main characters intellectuals who struggle to maintain their own identity against the domination of the men they love. Dodd suggests that this is, in effect, the story of H. D.'s own life. Close examination of H. D.'s "editing choices" further reveals the degree to which she increased the power of classical allusion in order to diffuse the personal emotion.

DuPlessis, Rachel Blau, and Susan Stanford Friedman. "'Woman Is Perfect': H. D.'s Debate with Freud." *Feminist Studies* 7, no. 3 (Fall 1981): 417-430.
DuPlessis and Friedman present "The Master," a poem that H. D. had refused to publish for fear it would "spoil" the results of her analysis, as evidence of the anger H. D. felt at Freud's "tyranny" and "misogyny," as well as at his scorn for religious feelings. Though the poem, like H. D.'s famous "Tribute to Freud," presents the doctor as an oracle of wisdom and "blameless physician," it also confronts Freud's image of the almost perfect goddess who only lacks a spear. H. D. offers in response her own perfect woman, powerful and complete in herself; it is an image that celebrates female sexuality and the "tabooed eroticism" between women that Freud warned against.

Edmunds, Susan. *Out of Line: History, Psychoanalysis & Montage in H. D.'s Long Poems.* Stanford, Calif.: Stanford University Press, 1994.
Edmunds sees H. D. as a woman with two bodies—the first belongs to the perfect dancer and innocent child, the second is marked by pain and dark plots. In analyzing the interplay between these polarities in *Trilogy, Helen in Egypt,* and *Hermetic Definition,* Edmunds draws upon a wide range of contemporary critical debates that concern the psychoanalysis of children, film aesthetics, and post-colonialism, in particular. She also emphasizes the historical context of the works as a challenge to previous feminist and psychoanalytic readings. The text includes extensive notes and a listing of works cited.

Friedman, Susan Stanford. *Penelope's Web: Gender, Modernity, and H. D.'s Fiction.* Cambridge: Cambridge University Press, 1990.
Friedman offers a comprehensive reading of H. D.'s prose, both published and unpublished, in order to demonstrate the "special and complex role" it played in the development of her sense of herself as a "woman in the modern world." Unlike her tightly contained poetry, the prose is highly personal and excessive; it is filled with fragments, discontinuities, mixed genres and a feminine "fluidity." The poetry aimed for the universal and mythic, the prose for the autobiographical and historical moment. Friedman believes that the writing of the prose enabled the poet to become more personal and narrative and ultimately to write such "hybrid" texts as *Helen in Egypt.* Friedman's study includes an extensive bibliography, a chronology which includes dates of composition and publication, and a small selection of drafts and photographs.

——————. *Psyche Reborn: The Emergence of H. D.* Bloomington: Indiana University Press, 1981.
Friedman attempts to free H. D. from the "cages" of Imagism and of misogynist psychoanalytic criticism and to show how she was able to develop her own unique poetic voice. The biography is divided into two major divisions: the first examines H. D.'s relationship with Freud,

the second her interest in occult and esoteric mysticism. Friedman shows how H. D. was able to see beyond Freud's theories about women and about her particular problems and how she used the "guiding spirit of Kabbalah" in a poetic search for transcendence. This interpretation is supported through detailed examination of journals, letters, and manuscripts, and placed in the context of an intellectual history of the early twentieth century.

Friedman, Susan Stanford, and Rachel Blau DuPlessis, eds. *H. D. Centennial Issue. Contemporary Literature* 27, no. 4 (Winter 1986).
     This journal includes an unpublished tribute to H. D. by Ezra Pound, four chapters of her first novel, *Paint It Today* (1921), and five new essays, including the one by Ostriker referenced here. Three of the essays focus on specific poems—"Sea Garden," "Palimpsest," and "Hedylus."

Gelpi, Albert. "Helen in Egypt," in *Coming to Light: American Women Poets in the Twentieth Century,* eds. Diane Wood Middlebrook and Marilyn Yalom. Ann Arbor: University of Michigan Press, 1985.
     Gelpi sees *Helen in Egypt* "as the most ambitious and successful long poem" written by an American or British female poet, and one which transforms the "male war epic" into a "woman's love lyric." Gelpi offers his own reading of the poem, explaining the biographical sources for particular figures—for example, Freud as the "paternal authority" behind her portrait of the wise Theseus. Ultimately, the marriage of Helen and Achilles represents H. D's own "rebirth" as wife, mother, daughter—a complete feminine archetype.

Gubar, Susan. "The Echoing Spell of H. D.'s *Trilogy,*" in *Shakespeare's Sisters: Feminist Essays on Women Poets,* eds. Sandra M. Gilbert and Susan Gubar. Bloomington: Indiana University Press, 1979.
     Gubar uses the symbolism of the *Trilogy* (1946) to demonstrate how H. D. progressed from dependency on Freud and his patriarchal theories of what was wrong with her to a radical vision of female divinity and prophetic powers. In the first volume the mollusk, with its defensive survival techniques for a hostile world, its magical ability to transform living substance into both pearl and shell, and its womb-like characteristics, functions as a metaphor for the craft of the female poet. By the third volume H. D. moves beyond animals to the creation of human characters, identifying with Kaspar the Magian and Mary Magdala as she retells the Christ story from the perspective of two "aliens." Initially written in search of the meaning of World War II, the *Trilogy* ultimately dramatizes "the cyclical renewal of life," moving backwards in time to an "androgynous center," a "prelapsarian time of woman-worship."

Guest, Barbara. *Herself Defined: The Poet H. D. and Her World.* Garden City, N.Y.: Doubleday, 1984.
This biography is based primarily on personal recollections and private correspondence between H. D. and many of her friends and acquaintances. It is filled with personal details about the rooms H. D. inhabited, the dresses she wore, the way she managed her finances. Guest sees H. D. as an eccentric and unhappy woman. Much of the biography dwells on her forty-year relationship with Winifred Bryher, whose life is itself a major focus of the work. A few photographs are included, as well as lists of H. D.'s publications, secondary sources, and unpublished documents.

Hallenberg, Donna. "Abortion, Identity Formation, and the Expatriate Woman Writer: H. D. and Kay Boyle in the Twenties." *Twentieth Century Literature* 40, no. 4 (Winter 1994): 499-517.
Both women were "expatriated, bereaved, and separated from their families" during their early careers. Both regressed emotionally during crises brought about by difficult pregnancies. H. D., in particular, suffered from a deep-rooted anxiety about womanhood intensified by the death of her first child, the difficult circumstances surrounding the birth of her daughter, and her decision to terminate a third pregnancy. Hallenberg looks at H. D.'s early fictionalized autobiographies for evidence of the way in which she dealt with the conflict between motherhood and authorship and her other psychic needs.

Ostriker, Alicia. "What Do Women (Poets) Want? H. D. and Marianne Moore as Poetic Ancestresses." *Contemporary Literature* 27, no. 4 (Winter 1986).
Ostriker believes that H. D. and Marianne Moore can provide poets today with the strong mother figures they seek. Both offer models of excellence and subversion. Moore's poetry is secular and concrete, H. D.'s preoccupied with the sacred, mythic, and occult. H. D's imagery is marked with creative female enclosures, Moore's with "profoundly gendered" armored animals. Both defy authority and offer a visionary alternative to patriarchal culture.

Robinson, Janice S. *H. D.: The Life and Work of an American Poet.* Boston: Houghton Mifflin, 1982.
Robinson's biography focuses primarily on her reading of H. D.'s poetry, fiction, and letters, including autobiographical writings which appear here for the first time. Robinson looks to these documents for insights into H. D.'s most problematic relationships and concludes, for example, that her friendship with Ezra Pound remained a "remarkable" one throughout their lives and that she transferred her feelings for D. H. Lawrence to Sigmund Freud while under analysis. The book includes extensive quotations, photographs, a chronology, and a bibliography of primary and secondary sources.

Smith, Paul. "Wounded Woman: H. D.'s Post-Imagist Writing," in *Pound Revised*. London: Croom Helm, Ltd., 1983.
Smith looks at H. D.'s memoir of Ezra Pound, *End to Torment* (1958), and her post-Imagist poetry, particularly *Helen in Egypt* (1961), for evidence of her ongoing struggle to move beyond her mentor's powerful and constricting influence. He also considers the impact of Freud on her understanding of her female identity and of her connection to classical Greek culture. *Helen in Egypt*, which Smith sees as "preeminent" among H. D.'s poems, works through these issues as a drama "of female accession to a symbolic realm" which celebrates the female unconscious in its "resistance to patriarchal structures."

Wagner-Martin, Linda W. "H. D.'s Fiction: Convolutions to Clarity," in *Breaking the Sequence: Women's Experimental Fiction*," eds. Ellen G. Friedman and Miriam Fuchs. Princeton, N.J.: Princeton University Press, 1989.
Despite H. D.'s presumed debt to Ezra Pound and Imagism, she was always intent on finding her own voice and never a follower of trends, according to Wagner-Martin. Her friends were the avant-garde of Europe and her prose resembled the most experimental work of so-called "automatic writing." H. D. believed in "organic" form which would draw heavily on the subconscious. The result was often a "cinematic" combination of myth and the inconsequential happenings of daily life.

LILLIAN HELLMAN
1905-1984

Hellman, an only child, was born in New Orleans and raised in New York City, where she attended New York University and Columbia. In 1925 she married Arthur Kober, a writer for *The New Yorker*, who helped Hellman get jobs as a script reader. When the couple moved to Hollywood before divorcing in 1932, Hellman continued reviewing books for potential films and became friendly with several writers and actors, including Dashiell Hammett, with whom she maintained a lifelong intimate relationship. With Hammett's encouragement Hellman wrote her first popular play, *The Children's Hour* (1934), based on a true story he recommended as its plot. Following the play's critical success and long run on Broadway, Hellman was hired by Samuel Goldwyn to write screenplays. During the 1930's she also helped found the Screen Writers Guild and became involved in leftist politics. Hellman's third play, *The Little Foxes* (1939), now considered a classic of the American theater, marked the high point of her career. Hellman's final plays, including *Toys in the Attic* (1960), mark a transition in her writing toward her three volumes of memoirs: *An Unfinished Woman* (1969), *Pentimento* (1972), and *Scoundrel Time* (1976). The account of her childhood friend, Julia, in the second volume was turned into a movie highlighting Hellman's role in Julia's heroic anti-Fascist activities. The immediate success of these books and the film turned to controversy with accusations by Mary McCarthy that they were based on self-aggrandizing lies. A lawsuit against McCarthy for libel was still pending when Hellman died.

Reissued Editions
Note: There are video- and audiocassettes of many of Hellman's plays and a few acting editions available. Six of her best-known plays, including *The Children's Hour* and *The Little Foxes*, have been collected in a Random House edition originally published in 1979.

Biography and Commentary
Gillin, Edward. "'Julia' and Julia's Son." *Modern Language Studies* 19, no. 2 (Spring 1989): 3-11.
   Gillin hypothesizes that Hellman may have been influenced by Thomas Wolfe, who, in "I Have a Thing to Tell You," his 1937 semi-autobiographical short story, also described an American writer undergoing an ethical crisis aboard a train in prewar Nazi Germany. Wolfe's story resembles Hellman's memoir precisely in those places where she has been accused of describing impossibilities. Though Wolfe makes no claim for the "truth" of his story, Gillin believes it is based on an actual experience, whereas Hellman's tale, though presumably autobiographical, is not.

Goodman, Charlotte. "The Fox's Cubs: Lillian Hellman, Arthur Miller, and Tennessee Williams," in *Modern American Drama: The Female Canon*, ed. June Schuleter. New York: Associated University Presses, 1990.
   Goodman argues that *The Little Foxes*, itself clearly influenced by the plays of Ibsen and Chekhov, had a greater influence on Miller and Williams than is generally acknowledged. She establishes parallels between the characters of the three playwrights, noting that Amanda Wingfield in *A Glass Menagerie* (1945) and Blanche Dubois in *A Streetcar Named Desire* (1947) have obvious similarities with the fragile and alcoholic Birdie of *Foxes*. Hellman also predated Williams in her use of the South as a rich dramatic setting. Neither male playwright credited Hellman with positively influencing his work; both may have suffered from anxiety over her success in areas they wanted to claim for their own.

Kramer, Hilton. "The Life and Death of Lillian Hellman." *The New Criterion* 3, no. 2 (October 1984): 1-6.
   Kramer notes that many of Hellman's obituaries, while praising her plays, either ignore or skirt over the unfortunate facts of her life and politics. He, on the contrary, offers no kind words on her death and calls *Scoundrel Time* one of the "most poisonous and dishonest testaments ever written by an American author."

Lyons, Bonnie. "Lillian Hellman: The First Jewish Nun on Prytania Street," in *From Hester Street to Hollywood: The Jewish-American*

Stage and Screen, ed. Sarah Blacher Cohen. Bloomington: Indiana University Press, 1983.
Lyons notes that there are no Jewish characters and no real discussion of Judaism in Hellman's memoirs or plays, even those set in World War II. Moreover, the Hellman worldview, with its emphasis on individual courage, is closer to Hemingway than to the doubt, anxiety, skepticism, and irony typical of American Jewish literature. *Scoundrel Time*, the controversial third volume of Hellman's memoirs, is itself "obliquely anti-Jewish" and seems to equate Jewishness with "weakness, flabby accommodation, and personal self-seeking." Lyons finds this same "rigid moralism" in Hellman's plays, which she faults for their melodrama and didacticism, and their lack of "evocation and exploration."

Patraka, Vivian M. "Lillian Hellman's *Watch on the Rhine*: Realism, Gender, and Historical Crises." *Modern Drama* 32, no. 1 (March 1989): 128-145.
Patraka sees this play as limited by its embrace of a wartime ideology. Hellman uses realistic depictions of marriage as metaphors for political relationships between the United States and Europe. In so doing, she capitalizes on nostalgia for sexual inequality and portrays intelligent women self-consciously supporting their own subordination. *Julia*, on the other hand, foregrounds women's roles as political resisters who do not see a conflict between motherhood and active political struggle.

LAURA RIDING JACKSON
1901-1991

Laura Reichenthal was born and raised in New York City, the daughter of Jewish immigrants. A brilliant student, Laura became an intellectual companion to her socialist father. She attended Cornell University, where she met and married her first husband, divorcing him after a few years to join the Fugitive group of poets in Nashville. She officially changed her name to Riding with the publication of her first poems. In 1926 Riding moved to Europe, where she began a long relationship, both professional and personal, with the British poet, Robert Graves. For many years the two lived on the island Mallorca, where they ran a small press and Riding wrote fiction, criticism, and most of her poetry. Following a bitter break-up with Graves, Riding married Schuyler Jackson, a reviewer for *Time* magazine, who had rated her poetry as the most significant of her generation. She and Jackson moved to a small town in Florida where they spent thirty years working on a *Dictionary of Exact Meaning*, which was never completed. In addition to her poetry, Riding collaborated with Graves on a *Survey of Modernist Poetry* (1927), published one novel, *A Trojan Ending* (1937), and produced biographical sketches, *Lives of Wives* (1939). After the publication of her *Collected Poems* (1938), Riding renounced the writing of poetry as self-indulgent and artificial. For the last fifty years of her life, she was better known for her angry letters to anyone who dared discuss her poetry or her relationship with Graves than as the important philosophical poet she had been in her youth.

Reissued Editions
Fiction Selections. New York: Little, Brown & Company, 1990.

Lives of Wives. New York: Persea Books, 1994.

The Poems of Laura Riding: A New Edition of the 1938 Collection. New York: Persea Books, 1980.

Progress of Stories. New York: Dial Publishing Company, 1982.

Selected Poems in Five Sets. New York: Persea Books, 1993.

The Word Woman and Other Related Writings. New York: Persea Books, 1993.

Biography and Criticism
Adams, Barbara. *The Enemy Self: Poetry and Criticism of Laura Riding.* Ann Arbor, Mich.: UMI Research Press, 1990.
    This text is both a biography and a critical appreciation of Riding's poetry supplemented by a few photographs and a bibliography. Elaborating on the earlier essay annotated below, Adams emphasizes Riding's quest for perfection, her obsession with the meaning of words, and her struggle "to wrest pure poetic being" from the "bad" enemy self. It is a poetry which speaks for the "Puritan self-examining idealist." In addition to her analysis of many of Riding's poems, Adams includes a chapter on her literary theories and on her post-1938 writings.

_____. "Laura Riding's Poems: A Double Ripeness." *Modern Poetry Studies* 11, nos. 1-2 (1982): 188-195.
    Adams offers a glowing review of the new (1980) edition of Riding's last (1938) collection of poetry. She summarizes the layout of the collection and the relationship of each of the five sections to the poet's life. According to Adams, Riding wrote some of the most intellectually superior and penetrating visions of the self in modern poetry. Riding's search for a "unified self" led her toward a kind of "spiritual chastity" which could only be achieved through the "near-extinction" of the "flesh and blood self" who wrote the actual poems. It is, therefore, not surprising, according to Adams, that Riding ultimately renounced the writing of poetry following the publication of these poems.

Baker, Deborah. *In Extremis: The Life of Laura Riding.* New York: Grove Press, 1993.

In this comprehensive biography, Baker attempts to get as close to the "truth" as she can, a difficult undertaking given the extreme portraits of Riding produced by previous "detractors" and "defenders," and the angry rebuttals with which Riding continually attempted to "put the record straight." Baker sees Riding as a woman who tried hard to articulate conflicts between the various roles she played: poet, lover, editor, visionary, wife. Often she would literally change her name as part of an effort to articulate a new identity. Baker uses Riding's various names and key lines from her writings to organize her text, which also includes extensive source notes, a bibliography of Riding's publications, and photographs of friends and family.

Graves, Richard Percival. *Robert Graves: The Years with Laura Riding, 1926-1940*. New York: Penguin, 1990.
The author presents his own history of the Graves-Riding relationship as the second book in his three-volume biography of his uncle. At first Graves, his wife Nancy, and Riding all seemed to get along very well; they, in fact, went together to Egypt, where Graves had a faculty position. As the collaboration and the relationship between the two poets became more intense, Nancy suggested that they leave her alone so she would have more time for her own painting. The author credits Riding with rescuing Graves from an unhappy family situation and with inspiring his personal rebirth. He also sees her as a difficult and manipulative woman who controlled and tormented Graves until she finally reinvented herself once more in her marriage to Schuyler Jackson. This account of their stormy fourteen years together is supplemented by a family tree, illustrations, and source notes.

McGann, Jerome J. "Laura (Riding) Jackson and the Literal Truth." *Critical Inquiry* 18, no. 3 (Spring 1992): 454-473.
McGann analyzes Riding's decision to stop writing poetry in favor of prose in the context of current critical debates over whether or not poetry can speak the truth. Before this renunciation, Riding, like many poets, had believed that poetry was a source of revelation, as opposed to science, which was a source of knowledge. Later she came to see poetry as too sensuous and self-absorbed to be a vehicle for truth. The progression of her work away from poetry was indicative of the postmodern loss of faith in poetic genius, the privileging of the rhetorical over the symbolic, and the focus on words as words, all of which has brought the practice of poetry to a "crisis," according to McGann.

Rosenthal, M. L. "Laura Riding's Poetry: A Nice Problem." *Southern Review* 21, no. 1 (Winter 1985): 89-95.
Rosenthal finds Riding's poetry "full of promises" and "endlessly elusive." The ambiguities sometimes seem more indicative of unresolved psychological issues than of art, which Rosenthal finds typical of the later confessional poets. The best poems are less self-absorbed, with a wonderful melancholy resonance. Given the

psychological toll involved in Riding's tendency to merge the aesthetic and the personal, she may have chosen to renounce poetry at the age of thirty-seven rather than risk pushing her work to the extreme.

AMY LOWELL
1874-1925

Amy Lowell was born into a distinguished New England family, where she enjoyed a privileged if somewhat lonely childhood as the youngest sibling, with brothers and a sister sixteen, seventeen, and nineteen years her seniors. As a young woman, Lowell became friendly with the actress Ada Russell, who would become a lifelong companion, secretary and adviser. Lowell is best known as the outspoken leader of the Imagist movement who successfully challenged Ezra Pound's authority. She was the first woman to speak at the Harvard Poetry Club. Both a poet and a literary critic, Lowell received high marks for her second volume of poetry, *Sword Blades and Poppy Seed* (1914), and her study of French symbolism, *Six French Poets* (1915). She is also the author of *Tendencies in Modern American Poetry* (1917), a monumental biography of John Keats (1925), and *What's O'clock* (1925), a collection of her later poetry which was awarded the Pulitzer Prize posthumously (1926).

Reissued Editions
The Complete Poetical Works of Amy Lowell. Boston: Houghton Mifflin, 1955.

A Shard of Silence: Selected Poems of Amy Lowell. New York: Twayne Publishers, 1957.

Sword Blades and Poppy Seed. New York: AMS Press, 1981.

Tendencies in Modern American Poetry. New York: Octagon, 1971.

Biography and Commentary
Ambrose, Jane P. "Amy Lowell and the Music of Her Poetry." *New England Quarterly* 62, no. 1 (March 1989): 45-62.
    Ambrose reviews Lowell's poetry and prose for evidence of the ways in which she uses music as a source of inspiration. For example, Lowell wrote that she wanted to reproduce in poetry the "musical speech" of Stravinsky's string quartet, "Grotesques." Several of her poems are based on contemporary musical compositions, including "After Hearing a Waltz by Bartok." The character of Pierrot, taken from modern French music and poetry, also appears several times in her poetry. Though not a musician herself, Lowell was fascinated by the new music of her day and used her own words to "heighten" its meaning, Ambrose concludes.

Benvenuto, Richard. *Amy Lowell.* Boston: G. K. Hall, 1985.
    This volume in the Twayne United States Authors series includes a

chronology, a bibliography, a chapter on Lowell's life, a chapter on her critical prose, and a general discussion of her major narrative and lyric poetry. Benvenuto sees some truth in Lowell's reputation as a "fat, rich woman" who pushed people around. However, he also believes that she was a far better poet than is generally acknowledged; he calls her "an accomplished storyteller" and an "adept" word-painter whose best lyrics are filled with "subtle and resonant" imagery.

Francis, Lesley Lee. "A Decade of 'Stirring Times': Robert Frost and Amy Lowell." *New England Quarterly* 59, no. 4 (December 1986): 508-522.

Francis, who is Frost's granddaughter, offers a history of the literary and personal relationship between the two poets. Though they disagreed over poetic technique, they shared a distaste for romantic platitudes and a love of drama. Audiences who attended their poetry readings thoroughly enjoyed their "verbal sparring." Frost found Lowell's poetry too theoretical and too filled with "pyrotechnics"; she found his too reliant on traditional meter but came to understand that he wore well with time and gave him high praise in her discussions of American poetry. Francis reviews their "lively correspondence" for evidence of their attitudes about each other's work and of their growing affection for each other.

Gould, Jean. *Amy: The World of Amy Lowell and the Imagist Movement*. New York: Dodd, Mead, 1975.

This biography focuses on Lowell's daily life with detailed information about her personal habits and activities.

Heymann, C. David. *American Aristocracy: The Lives and Times of James Russell, Amy and Robert Lowell.* New York: Dodd, Mead, 1980.

Heymann sets his biography of Amy Lowell in the context of her extraordinarily privileged upbringing—her life at Sevenels, the palatial setting for her childhood and adult years; her membership in the Sewing Circle, a social club for "bored debutantes"; her summer home in the wealthy artists' colony at Dublin, New Hampshire. He considers the key stages in her artistic development—her discovery of Keats's poetry, her enthusiasm for the stage and love for Eleonora Duse, her relationship with Ezra Pound, and her lifelong friendship with Ada Dwyer. After discussing all of Lowell's major works, Heymann concludes that she never fully escaped the confining traditions and attitudes of her patrician background. At the end of her life her "imperial and reactionary opinions," epitomized by her support of Mussolini, mirrored those of her famous cousin, James Russell Lowell.

Ruihley, Glenn R. *The Thorn of a Rose: Amy Lowell Reconsidered.* Hamden, Conn.: Archon Books, 1975.

This work combines biography with a critical discussion of Lowell's major work.

Walker, Cheryl. "Women and Feminine Literary Traditions: Amy Lowell and the Androgynous Persona," in *Masks, Outrageous and Austere: Culture, Psyche, and Persona in Modern Women Poets.* Bloomington: Indiana University Press, 1991.

Lowell presented herself as both "lady" and "overweening man": her poetic personae are filled with contradictions and mixed messages, according to Walker. Early in her poetic career she expressed ambivalence about her female precursors and a desire to be accepted as "one of the boys." She was attracted to the masculine image of power, yet fearful of male insensitivity and brutality. And though she acknowledged the influence of Sappho, Barrett Browning, and Dickinson, as well as the authenticity of the new generation of women poets, she rejected the sensitive, romantic young woman she herself had been in the 1890's.

EDNA ST. VINCENT MILLAY
1892-1950

Millay was born and raised in Maine. The oldest of three daughters, she had a very close relationship with her mother and sisters throughout her life and stayed close to home until her long poem, "Renascence" (1912), brought her popular and critical attention. She was recruited by Vassar College, where she continued to write poetry and developed an interest in theater. Following graduation, she moved to Greenwich Village, where she quickly became known for her bohemian lifestyle as well as her romantic love poetry. Her first two published collections of poems were *Renascence, and Other Poems* (1917) and *A Few Figs from Thistles* (1920). She also wrote and directed a well-received pacifist play in verse, *Aria da Capo* (1920), and was awarded the Pulitzer Prize in 1922 for *The Ballad of the Harp-Weaver,* an expanded collection of *A Few Figs.* In 1923 Millay married the Dutch businessman Eugen Boissevain, who faithfully managed her career until his death in 1949. During these years, Millay wrote several more books of poetry, was highly successful on the poetry-reading circuit, became involved in the political movement to save Sacco and Vanzetti, and later wrote anti-Fascist propaganda for the Writers War Board. In the 1920's and 1930's Millay was the most popular poet in America, especially among the young.

Reissued Editions

The Ballad of the Harp Weaver (illustrated for children). New York: Philomel Books, 1991.

Collected Poems. New York: Book-of-the-Month Club, 1990. (Harper, 1975).

Collected Sonnets. Apple Valley, Minn.: Perennial Library, 1988.

Renascence and Other Poems. New York: Dover, 1991.

Selected Poems. New York: HarperCollins, 1991.

Take Up the Song. New York: HarperCollins, 1986.

Biography and Commentary
Brittin, Norman A. *Edna St. Vincent Millay.* Boston: G. K. Hall, 1982.
    This volume in the Twayne United States Authors series is a revised version of Brittin's 1967 study with an updated bibliography and chronology. It includes a biographical essay and discussion of Millay's major works.

Clark, Suzanne "The Unwarranted Discourse: Sentimental Community, Modernist Women, and the Case of Millay." *Genre* 20 (Summer 1987): 133-152.
    Clark discusses Millay's poetry and critical reception in the context of "modernist scorn" for the sentimental. Millay's work was itself devalued, according to Clark, because she wrote about love in a way that was easily understood. The modernists wanted poetry to be difficult and obscure, resulting in the alienation of the reader; Millay's work achieved a kind of "community" with the reader. This devaluation of the sentimental in favor of the "symbolic and tough" came about at a particular time in literary history; Clark reminds us that in the eighteenth century "sentimental" was, in fact, a term of approval.

Daffron, Carolyn. *Edna St. Vincent Millay.* New York: Chelsea House Publishers, 1989.
    Part of the American Women of Achievement series for young readers, this biography identifies Millay as a passionate woman who spoke out against injustice and campaigned for individual freedom. Daffron highlights the major events in Millay's life and career, beginning with the publication of "Renascence," the poem which made her an overnight celebrity, and ending with a discussion of the propaganda writing which tarnished her reputation in the years preceding her death. The volume includes a chronology, a brief bibliography, and an extensive selection of photographs.

Dash, Joan *A Life of One's Own: Three Gifted Women and the Men They Married.* New York: Paragon House, 1973, revised ed. 1988.
    Dash reviews the highlights of Millay's life and career from a psychological perspective, emphasizing her attempts to fulfill her mother's frustrated ambitions and to see herself "as the son her mother never had." Dash describes Millay's many love affairs, her abuse of alcohol, and her habit of writing in "baby talk" to her mothers and sisters even as a grown woman. According to Dash, Millay's marriage to Eugen Boissevain was based on a "precarious balance"; his feminine, self-sacrificing qualities made her continued career as a poet possible.

Frank, Elizabeth Perlmutter. "A Doll's Heart: The Girl in the Poetry of Edna St. Vincent Millay and Louise Bogan." *Twentieth Century Literature* 23, no. 2 (May 1977): 157-179.

Frank analyzes Millay's influence on Bogan primarily through her use of female personae to "invigorate" lyric speech. The "girl" who speaks in Millay's poems has many incarnations—Portia, Beatrice, Ophelia—and almost always seems to hover between "betrothal and betrayal." The persona's other characteristics include both a thirst for intense sensation and a tendency toward self-neglect. At her best, she is an "unflappable flapper," urbane and sophisticated. Though Bogan's "girl" is more bitter, she shares many of these qualities.

Freedman, Diane P., ed. *Millay at 100: A Critical Reappraisal.* Carbondale: Southern Illinois University Press, 1995.

This collection of twelve essays includes pieces by established scholars (Suzanne Clark, Cheryl Walker, Sandra M. Gilbert) whose discussions of American poetry are annotated in this bibliography as well as by graduate students and new Ph.D.'s currently working on Millay. The essays are divided into four groups: one on the various forms and genres in which Millay wrote and the paradox of her popularity in spite of her obscurity, the second on her "revisionary perspectives" on mothers and on women in love, the third and fourth on the concept of Millay's personae as "masquerades." Together these essays offer a new look at Millay's place in American literary history with special attention to her exclusion from the modernist canon.

Fried, Debra. "Andromeda Unbound: Gender and Genre in Millay's Sonnets." *Twentieth Century Literature* 32, no. 1 (Spring 1986): 1-22.

Fried offers her own explanation of why Millay chose such a "tidy" poetic form to express "unruly" feelings. Millay's sonnets, because so methodically exhaustive, represent a "poetics of burning one's candle at both ends," of using up life. Liberation for Millay was hard work and the sonnet allowed her to "reenact" her personal struggle against boundaries. This, according to Fried, is quite different from the Wordsworthian sonnet, which provides relief from too much liberty and with which Millay's work is usually compared.

Gould, Jean. "Edna St. Vincent Millay—Saint of the Modern Sonnet," in *Faith of a (Woman) Writer,* eds. Alice Kessler-Harris and William McBrien. Westport, Conn.: Greenwood Press, 1988.

Gould credits Millay with keeping the sonnet alive when it was considered "old-fashioned." Her best work is "modern in language" and "classical in form." Gould considers the influence of Arthur Davison Ficke on Millay, identifying the love sonnets inspired by him as among her best. She also discusses other men in Millay's life and their relationship with particular poems and stages in her career.

Stanbrough, Jane. "Edna St. Vincent Millay and the Language of Vulnerability," in *Shakespeare's Sisters: Feminist Essays on Women Poets,* eds. Sandra M. Gilbert and Susan Gubar. Bloomington: Indiana University Press, 1979.
  Stanbrough examines Millay's poetry for evidence of her true sense of self. She believes that Millay's reputation as a deviant young woman both at Vassar and in Greenwich Village was based on a carefully constructed public image. A close reading of her poems reveals a sense of confinement and frustration despite the apparent superficiality and childlike narrative voice. Particularly revealing are her extended narratives of women's psychological disintegration, for example, *Fatal Interview* (1931).

Thesing, William B. *Critical Essays on Edna St. Vincent Millay.* New York: G. K. Hall, 1993.
  This volume contains twenty-five book reviews, twenty-two articles and essays written from 1950 to 1980, a "fictional" interview with Millay, a supplementary bibliography, and an introduction which summarizes the history of Millay criticism, including several book-length studies. The Clark, Frank, Fried, and Stanbrough essays referenced above are reprinted in this collection.

MARIANNE MOORE
1887-1972
Marianne Moore was born in St. Louis and raised in Carlisle, Pennsylvania, where she and her family moved when her father returned to his parents' home following a nervous breakdown. Moore and her mother lived together and remained close friends throughout their lives. Moore began writing poetry while majoring in biology at Bryn Mawr. Her first book of poetry, *Poems* (1921), was published without her knowledge by H. D. and Bryher; Moore and H. D. had worked on the same literary magazine in college. While living in New York, Moore spent most of her time writing or reading at the Hudson branch of the New York Public Library, where she was offered a part-time job. In 1926 she assumed the editorship of *The Dial,* the leading literary journal of the day, which had previously awarded her a $2,000 prize in recognition of her literary merit. When *The Dial* ceased publication in 1929, Moore and her mother moved to Brooklyn, where she devoted herself full time to writing. In 1935 *Selected Poems* was published with an introduction by T. S. Eliot, and in 1951 her *Collected Poems* hit the poetry triple crown, receiving a Pulitzer Prize, the National Book Award, and the Bollingen Prize. Recognition and awards continued to come to Moore throughout the rest of her life. In addition to her poetry, she published several translations, including the *Fables of La Fontaine* (1954) and a collection of essays and reviews, *Predilections* (1955).

Reissued Editions
Note: There are also readings by Moore available on audiocassette.

The Complete Poems of Marianne Moore. New York: Viking Press, 1981, 1986, 1994.

The Complete Prose of Marianne Moore. New York: Viking Press, 1986.

Biography and Commentary
Note: There are several studies not annotated here which focus specifically on the relationship between Marianne Moore and the poet she mentored, Elizabeth Bishop (1911-1979). See, for example, Bonnie Costello, "Marianne Moore and Elizabeth Bishop: Friendship and Influence," *Twentieth Century Literature* 30, no. 1 (Spring 1984): 130-149; and Joanne Feit Diehl, *Elizabeth Bishop and Marianne Moore: The Psychodynamics of Creativity,* Princeton: Princeton University Press, 1993.

Bloom, Harold, ed. *Modern Critical Views: Marianne Moore.* New York: Chelsea House, 1987.
    This collection of eight reprinted essays published between 1965 and 1984 includes the Costello, Slatin, and Vendler pieces referenced here. A chronology and bibliography are appended.

Costello, Bonnie. "The 'Feminine' Language of Marianne Moore," in *Women and Language in Literature and Society,* eds. Sally McConnell-Ginet, Ruth Borker, and Nelly Furman. Westport, Conn.: Praeger Publishers, 1980.
    Costello interrogates the meaning of Moore's so-called feminine qualities, in particular her apparent embrace of "humility" as an important virtue. Most critics have assumed that this humility was a defense, a kind of protective armor Moore assumed. Costello sees it rather as a way of "gathering force," a holding back of energy to allow its release with greater force. She finds evidence for this interpretation in Moore's critical essays as well as her poetry. "Humility, affection, reserve," all of these familiar virtues are shown by Moore to be "dynamic and vital modes of response" which create an important connection between our perceptions and the world.

Durham, Carolyn A. "Linguistic and Sexual Engendering in Marianne Moore's Poetry," in *Engendering the Word: Feminist Essays in Psychosexual Poetics,* ed. Temma F. Berg. Urbana: University of Illinois Press, 1989.
    Durham focuses on Moore's concern with "sexual and gender identity" despite her apparent "gender-free" poetic experimentation. A close examination of Moore's imagery and language reveals her critique of "maleness" in poems such as "The Fish" and "Sojourn of the Whale," her positive depiction of female sexuality and eroticism in "A Jellyfish" and other poems, and her advocacy of male-female

"hybridization" or "crossbreeding" in "Nevertheless," "The Monkey Puzzle," and "Marriage."

Goodrich, Celeste. *Marianne Moore and Her Contemporaries*. Iowa City: University of Iowa Press, 1989.
This text has extensive notes and a selected bibliography. It documents the interactions between Moore and her most famous male colleagues—T. S. Eliot, Ezra Pound, Wallace Stevens, and William Carlos Williams.

Holley, Margaret. *The Poetry of Marianne Moore: A Study in Voice and Value*. New York: Cambridge University Press, 1987.
This analysis of Moore's poetry includes a separate biographical essay, a chronology of publications, and a bibliography.

Koppel, Andrew J., ed. *Twentieth Century Literature* 30, nos. 2-3 (Summer-Fall 1984).
This special issue on Moore includes "Reminiscences" by Arthur Gregor and fourteen other essays on her poetry and prose, including the Martin and Slatin articles referenced here.

Leavell, Linda. *Marianne Moore and the Visual Arts*. Baton Rouge: Louisiana State University Press, 1995.
This is an illustrated text with a bibliography of primary and secondary sources. Leavell sees the visual arts as more significant than literature to Moore's artistic development. The photographer Alfred Stieglitz and the artists associated with him were particularly important to Moore in their attempts to "synthesize new ideas about technology with traditional ideas about artistic expression." Her poetry does not try to adapt artistic techniques such as cubism into language; rather it addresses the same challenges posed by primitivism, collage, analytic cubism, and other "modernist" attempts to create a new aesthetic climate appropriate to the times. Leavell traces the development of Moore's poetry in the context of modernist theory and experimentation in both art and literature.

Martin, Taffy. "Portrait of a Writing Master: Beyond the Myth of Marianne Moore." *Twentieth Century Literature* 30, nos. 2-3 (Summer-Fall 1984): 192-209.
Martin reviews critical studies of Moore to show how her readers have viewed her as a "decorative oddity" rather than a powerful force, a "unicorn" rather than a "dragon." Moore may have contributed to the myth because of her desire to control her own power; her personality is, in effect, as contradictory as her poetry. Perhaps the most indicative of her odd animals is the "pangolin," who is both "heavily armored" and capable of "everlasting vigor," much like Moore herself in Martin's estimation.

See also: Taffy Martin, *Marianne Moore: Subversive Modernist,* Austin: University of Texas Press, 1986.

Miller, Cristianne. *Marianne Moore: Questions of Authority.* Cambridge, Mass.: Harvard University Press, 1995.

Miller provides a comprehensive analysis of Moore's work beginning with a structural analysis of the poetry's mix of personal and impersonal features. She also establishes its historical, biographical, and cultural contexts and considers Moore's influence on late twentieth century poets. Like her early twentieth century peers, Moore established a poetic that was "implicitly feminist," though based on multiple "non-gendered" points of view. The "authority" of her poetic voice comes, not from an assertion of poetic genius or supernatural inspiration, but from many sources of knowledge. Though not a true "revolutionary," Moore did manage to write poetry which both built upon and distinguished itself from three major traditions: the romantic sublime, the feminine sentimental, and the modernist impersonal.

Molesworth, Charles. *Marianne Moore: A Literary Life.* New York: Atheneum, 1990.

This comprehensive biography is based on extensive research meticulously documented.

Phillips, Elizabeth. *Marianne Moore.* New York: Frederick Ungar Publishing Co., 1982.

This study, part of Ungar's Modern Literature series, includes a chronology, a bibliography, a chapter on Moore's life, and detailed analysis of many of her poems. Phillips sees Moore as an idiosyncratic poet who insisted on her "divine right to be herself" and whose vision was dominated by a Christian faith in the world's splendor. Moore's interest in design and pattern, the intricate stanzas she created, show the influence of modernism and cubist painting. The topics she chose reflect her own personal enthusiasms. The result is poetry which can be "powerfully lucid" despite its apparent opacity.

Slatin, John M. "'Advancing Backward in a Circle': Moore as (Natural) Historian." *Twentieth Century Literature* 30, nos. 2-3 (Summer-Fall 1984): 273-326.

Slatin examines Moore's efforts to avoid direct imitation of those poets she most admires. For example, he considers the relationship between "Bird-Witted" and the work of Sir Francis Bacon from which Moore's poem takes its title, "Half Deity" and Keats's "Ode to Psyche," and "Virginia Britannia" and Wordsworth's "Intimations of Immortality." Moore, according to Slatin, both honors and parodies these writers; most important, she uses her unique syllabic patterns to avoid the risk of being "unoriginal."

Stapelton, Laurence. *Marianne Moore: The Poet's Advance*. Princeton: Princeton University Press, 1978.

Stapelton offers a comprehensive analysis of Moore's poetry and prose as well as a history of her literary career based on extensive study of unpublished manuscripts, notebooks, and correspondence. Moore's real breakthrough, according to Stapelton, came in 1915 with discovery by Kreymborg, editor of *Others*, who insisted that Moore come to New York. He put her in touch with Ezra Pound, T. S. Eliot, Wallace Stevens, and William Carlos Williams, with whom she formed significant literary relationships of mutual influence. All four developed new rhythmic patterns, all brought poetic diction closer to spoken language, all made use of presumably non-poetic subject matter. What distinguishes Moore's work is the "depth and energy of thought . . . often presented in humorous guise."

Vendler, Helen. "Marianne Moore," in *Part of Nature, Part of Us: Modern American Poets*. Cambridge: Harvard University Press, 1980.

Vendler provides a brief overview of Moore's life, work, and critical reception. She sees her as a satirist whose observations from childhood had "edge, sharpness, watchfulness, and wit." The poem, "Marriage," according to Vendler, unites the "pain of feeling" with the "pain of governance," and reflects both Moore's own isolation from human relationships and her satiric bent. Moore's male critics may have missed the human element in her poetry, seeing it as more fastidious and unfeeling than it really is.

Willis, Patricia C., ed. *Marianne Moore: Woman and Poet*. Orono, Maine: National Poetry Foundation, University of Maine, 1990.

This is a collection of essays which view Moore and her work from a variety of literary perspectives. It includes an annotated bibliography.

DOROTHY PARKER
1893-1967

Parker was raised in New York, the daughter of a Jewish garment manufacturer and a Scottish mother, who died when Dorothy was still a young child. She attended a Catholic convent school and then the fashionable Miss Dana's School in Morristown, New Jersey. Her first jobs were writing captions for photographs at *Vogue* and drama criticism for *Vanity Fair*. Parker's first collection of poetry, *Enough Rope* (1926), was a best-seller. By this time she had become a leader of the famed Algonquin Hotel's Round Table, a lively lunch group attended by other well-known writers, including Edna Ferber, Robert Benchley, and Harold Ross, who founded *The New Yorker* in 1925. Parker was soon helping to establish the satirical bent of this new magazine with her reviews (signed the "constant reader"), witty sketches, and stories. Other Parker verse collections—*Sunset Gun* (1928), *Death and Taxes* (1931), and *Not So Deep a Well* (1936)—were well-received and her story "Big Blonde" won the O. Henry Prize in 1930. Parker's personal life was often difficult and unhappy; she was separated, divorced, and remarried to her second husband several times during the last three decades of their lives.

Reissued Editions
The Complete Stories of Dorothy Parker. New York: Penguin, 1995.

The Poetry and Short Stories of Dorothy Parker. New York: Modern Library, 1994.

The Portable Dorothy Parker. New York: Viking Press, 1985.

Biography and Commentary
Acocella, Joan. "After the Laughs." *The New Yorker* 69 (August 16, 1993): 76-81.
   Acocella sees Parker as a writer whose personal insecurities prevented realization of her full artistic poetential.

Frewin, Leslie. *The Late Mrs. Dorothy Parker.* New York: Macmillan, 1986.
   This is an illustrated biography with a bibliography which attempts to penetrate the Parker legend and recreate Parker's complex persona. Frewin quotes extensively from the sixty friends and enemies of Parker whom she interviewed for the book. She also includes portraits of the major personalities of Parker's day—F. Scott Fitzgerald, S. J. Perelman, Robert Benchley, Lillian Hellman, Ernest Hemingway, and many others. Frewin sees Parker as a fragile woman with a fatal attraction to the wrong men. Her brittle facade and her wit were the only weapons she had against a world she saw without illusion. This mix of sadness and sophistication made her the "epitome" of the Jazz Age according to Frewin.

Kinney, Arthur F. *Dorothy Parker.* Boston: G. K. Hall, 1978.
   This volume in the Twayne United States Author series includes a chronology and bibliography. Kinney sees Parker as a more complex figure than is generally assumed, whose writing was "both a disclosure of personal fears and a concealment of them." Though her life alternated between periods of elation and depression, she was always respectful of her art and committed to the "purity of the English language." Kinney offers his reading of Parker's poetry, her fiction, and her literary criticism as well as an overview of her life. He pays special attention to what he terms the "sardonic depths" behind the amusing surfaces for which she is famous, and concludes that her special contribution to American literature is the European epigram, calling her the "best" epigrammatic poet in twentieth century America.

Meade, Marion. *Dorothy Parker. What Fresh Hell Is This?* New York: Penguin Books, 1987.

This illustrated biography relies extensively on letters and memoirs shared with the author by Parker's friends and relatives. Meade begins with Parker's participation in the famous Algonquin Hotel Round Table luncheons and ends with the bequest of her estate to Martin Luther King, Jr., and the National Association for the Advancement of Colored People (NAACP). Meade focuses on the dark, self-destructive side of Parker; she chronicles the chaos of Parker's life in which she constantly reinvented herself, diminished her own triumphs, and mercilessly denigrated her friends. Meade also provides a "deglamorized" portrait of the literary and cultural milieu of which Parker was both the product and the popularizer.

See also: Marion Meade, *Dorothy Parker*, New York: Villard Books, 1988.

Miller, Nina. "Making Love Modern: Dorothy Parker and Her Public." *American Literature* 62, no. 4 (December 1992): 763-784.

Miller analyzes Parker's poetry for evidence of a "modern" love discourse based on the sophistication and cynicism popularized by *Vanity Fair*. The conventional view of love described a "privatized world" in which the two lovers spoke only to each other, a relationship in which the woman was reduced to a "function" of the male subject's narcissism. Parker's poems satirize this world, "foreground" female eroticism, and involve the readers in noting the necessarily "flawed" nature of heterosexual relationships. The persona of the "loser-in-love" thereby gains a "social identity within a public arena." Miller also considers Parker's "spectacular" death poems in which dead bodies satirize the kind of public gaze commonly bestowed on the female "sexualized body" in the press or the street.

Toth, Emily. "A Laughter of Their Own: Women's Humor in the United States," in *Critical Essays on American Humor*, eds. William Bedford Clark and W. Craig Turner. Boston: G. K. Hall, 1984.

Toth credits Dorothy Parker, and her "withering one-liners and satirical stories, with freeing women from the need to be nice and to hide their anger. Her work leads directly to late twentieth century feminist humor, including the novels of Erica Jong and the wordplay of female cartoonists and stand-up comedians. Thanks to Parker, Toth concludes, women's humor has gone beyond mockery and parody to create a new culture which characteristically criticizes and subverts patriarchal norms in ways that are not always perceived as funny by men.

GERTRUDE STEIN
1874-1946

Stein, the youngest of seven children, was born in Allegheny, Pennsylvania, and raised in Oakland, California. A brilliant student, she studied psychology with William James at Harvard and then attended Johns Hopkins Medical School for two years. Stein lived briefly in

New York and London before joining her brother Leo in Paris at 27, rue de Fleurus, the site of her famous salon, which became a haven for expatriate American writers and a showcase for avant-garde painters. Her relationship with her brother was a difficult and complex one. In 1907 Stein met Alice B. Toklas, who became her lifelong companion and displaced her brother as the major influence in her life. Her first work, *Q. E. D.*, written in 1903 and published posthumously in 1950 as *Things as They Are,* recounts a lesbian love triangle probably based on personal experience. This was followed by *Three Lives* (1909), linguistically experimental stories about working-class women; *The Making of Americans* (1925), completed in 1911, a thousand page "novel" about family history; and a series of prose portraits of many of her famous friends published in the years 1908 to 1913. With these works, Stein established her reputation as a leader of the literary avant-garde. Stein's publications include the libretto *Four Saints in Three Acts* (1927), an opera for which Virgil Thomson composed the music, and the popular narrative of her own life, *The Autobiography of Alice B. Toklas* (1933). Despite the importance of her literary theories and experimentation and the wide range of her literary work, Stein is best known for her legendary salon and eccentric personality.

Reissued Editions
The Autobiography of Alice B. Toklas. New York: Random House, 1993.

Geography and Plays. Madison: University of Wisconsin Press, 1993.

Lectures in America. Boston: Beacon Press, 1985.

Picasso: The Complete Writings. Boston: Beacon Press, 1985.

Selected Writings. New York: Random House, 1990.

A Stein Reader. Evanston, Ill.: Northwestern University Press, 1993.
Tender Buttons: Objects, Food, Rooms. Los Angeles: Sun and Moon Press, 1988.

Three Lives. New York: Penguin, 1990.

The Yale Gertrude Stein Selections (previously unpublished writings). New Haven: Yale University Press, 1980.

Biography and Commentary
Benstock, Shari. "Gertrude Stein and Alice B. Toklas: Rue de Fleurus," in *Women of the Left Bank.* Austin: University of Texas Press, 1986.
　　Benstock considers the major relationships in Stein's life (her brother Leo, Picasso, Toklas), the significance of her life as an expatriate in Paris, and the potential connection between her interest in

"language as language" and her homosexuality. Picasso served as a supportive surrogate brother to Stein, listening to her theories and engaging in conversations that affirmed rather than belittled her ideas. Toklas moved in, Leo out, freeing Stein to develop a strong identity and to produce writing more sexual, erotic, and domestic than her previous works. Though Stein remained isolated because of the radical nature of her work, she refused to be marginalized. In struggling to escape the restrictive literary and cultural fashions of her times, according to Benstock, she truly "gave birth to the twentieth century" and became the "Mother of Us All."

Bloom, Harold, ed. *Gertrude Stein.* New York: Chelsea House, 1986.
This volume in the Modern Critical Views series contains fifteen essays, a chronology, and a bibliography.

Bloom, Lynn Z. "Gertrude Is Alice Is Everybody: Innovation and Point of View in Gertrude Stein's Autobiographies." *Twentieth Century Literature* 24, no. 1 (Spring 1978): 81-93.
Bloom sees Stein's presumed biography of another person to tell the story of her own life as a truly innovative creation. Such a device, in effect the use of a persona who happens to be real, allowed Stein to be self-congratulatory and yet to appear objective. It avoided a confessional tone and provided the detachment required for humor. Because readers identify with Toklas's "pleasant pleasured perspective," they gladly overlook Stein's obvious egotism.

Bridgman, Richard. *Gertrude Stein in Pieces.* New York: Oxford University Press, 1970.
Bridgman was the first scholar to organize Stein's work chronologically by date of composition rather than publication and to demonstrate connections between pieces in terms of literary concerns and interests. For example, he traces her references to "saints" from her early works through her libretto, *Four Saints in Three Acts,* and identifies particular patterns such as her frequent use of two persons at odds with each other. Despite such observations, he finds much of Stein's work "opaque" and argues that it is best understood as the record of "a modern consciousness in words" with all its quirks and inconsistencies.

Burns, Edward, ed. *Twentieth Century Literature* 24, no. 1 (Spring 1978).
This special issue on Stein contains a bibliography of bibliographies, general studies, and criticism of individual works. There are two essays on *The Making of Americans,* plus discussions of *Tender Buttons, Ida,* Stein's autobiographical writing, and her dramatic writing. The introduction by Burns affirms a new critical interest in Stein resulting from avant-garde performances of her work in the 1950's and 1960's.

Fifer, Elizabeth. "Is Flesh Advisable? The Interior Theater of Gertrude Stein." *Signs* 4, no. 3 (Spring 1979): 472-483.

Fifer analyzes Stein's erotic works made available by Yale University Press's edition of her unpublished writings. Fifer sees these as a secret autobiography filled with "joyfulness and humor" in the treatment of sexual themes. The poems are filled with coded metaphors and puns; even Stein's choice of verbs is witty and revealing.

Hoffman, Michael J. *Gertrude Stein*. Boston: G. K. Hall, 1976.

This volume, part of the Twayne United States Authors series, focuses on the work Stein produced between 1902 and 1913, her "most prolific and innovative period," during which she wrote *Three Lives, The Making of Americans, Tender Buttons,* and her famous "portraits." Hoffman traces Stein's progression from realism to cubism and discusses her relationship with Picasso as crucial to an understanding of the nature of her literary experimentation. Hoffman concludes that Stein was far more than a literary eccentric, that in fact she played a key role in the history of modernism. The text includes a bibliography and a chronology.

Kellner, Bruce. *A Gertrude Stein Companion: Content with the Example*. Westport, Conn.: Greenwood Press, 1988.

This comprehensive reference work provides an alphabetical listing of Stein's "friends and enemies" with basic biographical information on each and on their relationships with Stein, an alphabetical listing of her observations on everything from "grammar" to "men" ("American," "married," "young") to "roses," and an annotated bibliography of selected criticism. It also includes an annotated bibliography of Stein's publications, including content summaries and dates of publication, a series of poems about Stein, and assorted illustrations and photographs. Kellner's introduction explains "how to read" Stein. It is followed by critical discussions of her work by Marianne De Koven, Ulla Dydo, and Marjorie Perloff.

Neuman, Shirley, and Ira B. Nadel, eds. *Gertrude Stein and the Making of Literature*. Boston: Northeastern University Press, 1988.

This collection includes three previously unpublished pieces by Stein and thirteen critical essays about her, six of which are based on general discussions of Stein and postmodernism presented at literary conferences in 1984 and 1985. The essays written expressly for this collection offer detailed readings of particular pieces. According to the editors, all thirteen essays "reread" Stein in light of the literary theories of the 1970's and 1980's, including feminist criticism, semiotics, and deconstruction. These theories help to "normalize" what had seemed paradoxical in Stein, to "decode" the concealments, and to explain her use of language in non-referential ways—to look at how the words are used, not at what they presumably mean.

Souhami, Diana. *Gertrude and Alice.* London: Pandora Press, 1991.
    Souhami calls the relationship between Stein and Toklas the "paradigm" of a devoted marriage based on both conventional romantic love and a respect for mutual obligations. She reconstructs details of their forty years together from letters, memoirs, and publications describing how they met, the lifestyle they led, their salon and celebrity. Alice's role was to run the household, type manuscripts, protect Gertrude from unwelcome visitors, and generally to serve her genius. Together, they practiced "the art of enjoyable living" and managed to remain "uncompromisingly themselves."

Steiner, Wendy. *Exact Resemblance to Exact Resemblance: The Literary Portraiture of Gertrude Stein.* New Haven: Yale University Press, 1978.
    Stein's portraits offer fascinating examples of the ways in which she attempted to reconcile "lived experience with aesthetic experience" and to put into practice her literary theories. According to Steiner, Stein's training in psychology and philosophy helped her to understand the fundamental paradox of the portrait as a genre in which a subject cannot be known apart from the writer's own perceptions. Like the cubist painters, her concern was with issues of "representationality and resemblance"; Stein wanted to produce her own "idea" of a person while also getting at that person's fundamental reality. Steiner's text includes several illustrations and notes on the various cubist painters to whom she refers.

Stendhal, Renate. *Gertrude Stein in Words and Pictures.* Chapel Hill, N.C.: Algonquin Books of Chapel Hill, 1994.
    This text includes 360 photographs of Stein, Toklas, and their many famous friends and acquaintances, organized chronologically and matched with texts from Stein's work and from letters and memoirs of those who knew her. The introduction describes the woman who has become legendary for her eccentricity and obstinacy and discusses the way in which her appearance reflected the same degree of calculated style as her writing. Stendhal's objective in juxtaposing the words and images is to highlight the contradictory sides to Stein's life and work: the esoteric and the trivial, the philosophic and the erotic, the self-enhancing and self-ironic.

Stimpson, Catharine R. "The Mind, the Body, and Gertrude Stein." *Critical Inquiry* 3, no. 3 (Spring 1977): 489-506.
    Stimpson looks at the strategies Stein used to cope with her "anomalous" position in society as intellectual woman, Jew, and lesbian. Stein's relationship with Toklas was a "domestic precondition" of her writing, but she did not dare write directly about it. Her texts, like those of many other women who struggled with the "mind/body problem," are filled with coded language, vague metaphors, and "silence."

SARA TEASDALE
1884-1933

Teasdale was born in St. Louis, Missouri, to parents who both came from prominent New England families. As a young woman she wrote poems for *The Potter's Wheel*, a monthly literary magazine she and her friends printed by hand. These poems were then discovered by a publisher and collected in *Sonnets to Duse and Other Poems* (1907), Teasdale's first book. In 1910 Teasdale was invited to join the Poetry Society of America, where she met important editors and critics. The Society also brought her into contact with John Hall Wheelock, the young poet who became the unrequited love of her life and the subject of many of her best lyrics. Teasdale published *Helen of Troy and Other Poems* in 1911 and *Rivers to the Sea* in 1915. This last volume, one of Teasdale's most successful, followed her marriage to St. Louis businessman Ernst Filsinger. In 1916 the couple moved to New York City, where Teasdale continued to write popular verse. In 1917 she published *The Answering Voice*, an anthology of love poems by Elizabeth Barret Browning, Christina Rossetti, and other women writers. This was followed by *Flame and Shadow* (1920), *Rainbow Gold* (1922), *Dark of the Moon* (1926), and *Stars Tonight* (1930), a children's book. Teasdale's last book, *Strange Victory* (1933), was published posthumously.

Reissued Edition
Mirror of the Heart: Poems of Sara Teasdale. New York: Macmillan, 1984.

Biography and Commentary
Drake, William. *Sara Teasdale: Woman and Poet.* Knoxville: University of Tennessee Press, 1989.
  This reprint of the 1979 Harper & Row edition is a comprehensive illustrated biography with a bibliography appended. Drake traces how Teasdale's poetry grew out of her personal experience. In establishing the historical context for her work, he provides portraits of some of Teasdale's contemporaries, including Harriet Monroe and Vachel Lindsay, and of the city of St. Louis, the "Athens of the Middlewest."

Mannino, Mary Ann. "Sara Teasdale: Fitting Tunes to Everything." *Turn-of-the-Century Women* 5 (1990): 37-41.
  Mannino analyzes Teasdale's metrics in the context of turn-of-the-century experimentation and argues that the formal aspects of Teasdale's poetry deserve more attention than they have generally received.

Schoen, Carol B. *Sara Teasdale.* Boston: G. K. Hall, 1986.
  This volume in the Twayne Unites States Authors series includes a chronology and a bibliography. Schoen focuses on Teasdale's images and the development of her ideas about love, solitude, beauty, and

death. Teasdale was an extraordinary lyricist who created poetic melodies with the power to move the soul, Schoen concludes.

ELINOR WYLIE
1885-1928

Wylie was the oldest of five children born into a socially and politically prominent Philadelphia family. Her three marriages, the second to Horace Wylie, a Washington lawyer with whom she eloped in 1910, leaving behind her infant son, were the source of much gossip and scandal. Wylie began submitting her poems for publication with the encouragement of Sinclair Lewis and William Rose Benét, literary friends of her brother. She published her first volume of poetry, *Nets to Catch the Wine*, in 1921 and then moved to New York City to pursue a full-time literary career, at the same time divorcing Wylie and marrying Benét. In addition to writing poetry, Wylie served as a contributing editor of the *New Republic*, wrote four novels, short stories, and literary criticism.

Reissued Editions
Collected Poems. New York: Alfred A. Knopf, 1960.

The Last Poems of Elinor Wylie. Chicago: Academy Chicago Publishers, 1982.

Mr. Hodge and Mr. Hazard. Chicago: Academy Chicago Publishers, 1984.

The Venetian Glass Nephew. Chicago: Academy Chicago Publishers, 1984.

Biography and Criticism
Elfenbein, Anna Shannon, and Terence Allan Hoagwood. "'Wild Peaches': Landscapes of Desire and Deprivation." *Women's Studies* 15, no. 4 (1988): 387-397.

Though Wylie's poetry has often been judged superficial, Elfenbein and Hoagwood believe it contains "undercurrents" of discontent and violence and a subtle protest against conventional sex-roles. "Wild Peaches," an "ironic pastoral love idyll," dramatizes the "dialectic" of Wylie's life—a peaceful surface masking a secret history of abuse by a deranged husband.

Farr, Judith. "Elinor Wylie, Edna St. Vincent Millay, and the Elizabethan Sonnet Tradition," in *Poetic Traditions of the English Renaissance*, eds. Maynard Mack and George deForest Lord. New Haven: Yale University Press, 1982.

This is a study of Millay's *Fatal Interview* (1931), a sequence of fifty-two sonnets dedicated to Wylie, and Wylie's "One Person" (1928), a grouping of nineteen sonnets. Wylie's poems tell the story of an American woman attracted to a married middle-aged English aristocrat whom she idealizes. Elizabethan imagery and themes served Wylie well in expressing the impermanence of love with an "ardor and despair" uncommon in her other work. According to Farr, she was looking for a new way of writing which would allow her to associate her own personal experience with the great love lyrics of the past.

_____. *The Life and Art of Elinor Wylie.* Baton Rouge: Louisiana State University Press, 1983.

Farr explains Wylie's critical neglect as the result of "hostility" toward her person and the fact that she wrote classic lyrics rather than experimental poetry. Despite the legend of the "haughty Elinor," much of which she cultivated herself, the "excellence" of her achievement in the "open song" merits attention. Her themes are universal ones and her style has the intellectual and verbal sophistication of a Wharton or a James. Farr analyzes all of her work, poetry and prose, more or less chronologically, concluding with a discussion of her debt to Percy Bysshe Shelly in her late work.

Hoagwood, Thomas Allan. "Wylie's 'Beauty,'" *Explicator* 43, no. 1 (Fall 1984): 53-55, and "Wylie's 'The Crooked Stick,'" *Explicator* 44, no. 3 (Spring 1986): 54-57.

Hoagland interprets both of these poems as carefully constructed through the use of "doubling" devices and "a dialectical interplay of contraries." The first poem makes the point that "beauty" may embody contradictory values; the second emphasizes impermanence with its own "crooked lines," a sign of life's imperfection.

Jones, Phyllis M. "Amatory Sonnet Sequences and the Female Perspective of Elinor Wylie and Edna St. Vincent Millay." *Women's Studies* 10, no. 1 (1983): 41-61.

Jones argues for a tradition of women's love poetry which would include the work of Millay and Wylie as well as that of Christina Rossetti and Elizabeth Barrett Browning. Such a tradition would differ from the male form in both its cultural and literary conventions. Wylie herself used many of the themes of the male tradition, including the importance of physical beauty and courtly love, but also suggested that romantic love is "incomplete" and even "absurd." Her poems are often ironic and contain a "sober assessment" of reality despite her unquestioning acceptance of heterosexual love as the central experience in a woman's life.

Olson, Stanley. *Elinor Wylie: A Biography.* New York: Dial Press, 1979.

This biography highlights the problems and scandals associated with each of Wylie's marriages: her abandonment of her baby and her first husband, Philip Hickborn, who was deranged and probably abusive; her social disgrace following marriage to Horace Wylie, who was twenty years her senior and left behind a wife and four children; and her marriage to William Rose Benét following a messy divorce. Olson clarifies the reasons for Wylie's unhappy marriages and sees her writing as compensation for her failure as a woman. Apparently, Wylie was a cold and difficult woman who had a "fatal effect" on the many lives she touched. Olson bases his conclusion on extensive research, including family papers left to various institutions by Wylie's sister and second and third husbands. He has appended a bibliography, a family tree, and a lengthy list of source notes identifying the particular letter, diary entry, poem, or published commentary behind his observations.

Walker, Cheryl. "Women and Aggression: Elinor Wylie and the Woman Warrior Persona," in *Masks, Outrageous and Austere: Culture, Psyche, and Persona in Modern Women Poets*. Bloomington: Indiana University Press, 1991.

Wylie, according to Walker, was trapped by the female cycle of "rage and self-recrimination." Her poetry is both hostile and coy, both aggressive and despairing. Much of her poetry is about "degradation" described in the voice of a "gothic" persona. Wylie herself seemed to be living on the edge of hysteria late in her life. In addition to her analysis of representative poems, Walker considers Wylie's "disturbing" novel, *The Venetian Glass Nephew*, for evidence of the relationship between the woman warrior persona and the poet's own psychic repressions.

Chapter 4
INTELLECTUALS, REFORMERS, AND
JOURNALISTS

This chapter cannot possibly cover all the important women intellectuals, reformers, and journalists who wrote from 1848 to 1948. However, it does include representatives of diverse fields whose work is still available and who have been the subjects of biographies and critical studies published since 1980. This introduction also makes reference to women writers of particular significance and to the general historical situation that gave rise to the first generations of women publishing their work outside the "female" spheres of poetry and fiction.

The late nineteenth and early twentieth centuries were periods of impressive new opportunities for women seeking to enter professional careers and play more active roles in the nation's public life. Maria Mitchell, who discovered the comet which bears her name, was the first woman elected to membership in the American Academy of Arts and Sciences (1848) and helped found the Association for the Advancement of Women in 1873. Elizabeth Blackwell, America's first formally trained female physician, graduated from medical school in 1849 and established the New York Infirmary, a hospital staffed entirely by women, in 1857. Boston University graduated the country's first woman Ph.D. in 1877, and the United States Supreme Court admitted its first woman attorney in 1879. By 1920 ten percent of all Ph.D.'s were awarded to women, a percentage which steadily increased to fifteen percent in 1940 before beginning a thirty-year decline. By 1870 eight state universities accepted women; however, their enrollment was often limited to so-called ladies departments. Much of the success of women professionals in the nineteenth century can be directly attributed to the emergence of women's colleges; Vassar opened its doors in 1865, Smith and Wellesley in 1875. Mount Holyoke, which was founded as a female seminary in 1837, became a college in 1888. The women's colleges not only educated America's first generation of women professionals but also hired the first generations of female professors.

This first generation of women academics produced little scholarly research, partly because they were often segregated at women's colleges with scarce resources. Scholarly research in the German sense was a relatively new phenomenon in the late nineteenth century and, though women academics had often trained at the same universities as their male colleagues, they did not have access to the facilities and networks that made ongoing research possible. Alice Hamilton, the one scientist referenced in this chapter, conducted her research in factories rather than in academic laboratories and was thus able to create her own opportunities to some degree. By the twentieth century, there were more outlets for scholarship by women, but these might still depend on the whim of an individual department chair or mentor. For example, Franz Boas, chair of the anthropology department at Columbia University, is credited with encouraging several young women to pursue degrees and careers in anthropology, including Ruth Benedict and Zora Neale Hurston (chapter 5). Anthropology also provides an example of a field with enough women to allow for intergenerational influences, as Benedict was introduced to anthropology by Elsie Clews Parsons at the New School for Social Research and Benedict, in turn, helped inspire Margaret Mead to follow in her footsteps.

Many women academics with successful careers worked in fields and departments which were or became closely associated with women. Gordon Hamilton, author of *The Theory and Practice of Social Casework* (1940), used as a standard textbook into the 1960's, was hired as a faculty member by the New York School of Social Work in 1923. Dorothy Reed Mendenhall, one of the first doctors employed by the U.S. Children's Bureau, was a field lecturer on infant and maternal care for the University of Wisconsin's home economics department. Though most of her publications dealt with prenatal and infant care, she is best known today for having identified the cell responsible for Hodgkin's disease, research she did while an intern. Even the philosopher Susanne Langer, who published several pioneering texts in a male-dominated field, was a faculty member at a women's institution, Connecticut College. Langer is referenced here because her extensive scholarly work was widely studied through the 1980's.

The late nineteenth and early twentieth centuries also saw increasing numbers of women activists. The abolition, temperance, settlement, birth control, and women's rights movements all provided leadership opportunities for women. Several factors combined to encourage women to become involved in social and political organizations outside the home. Most important were higher levels of education for women and a substantial increase in the amount of leisure time available for outside activities. Moreover, the advent of women's magazines and women's clubs offered forums for discussion of important issues outside home and church. The growth of social work, in particular, as a career for women built on women's long history in missionary and charity work, and on their increasing awareness of the problems of the urban poor. Several of the women referenced in this chapter took advantage of the new climate for public involvement and became leaders of fields which they themselves created. Elizabeth Cady Stanton, included here as a representative of the suffrage movement, wrote the Declaration of Sentiments presented at the first women's rights convention at Seneca Falls in 1848. Mary Baker Eddy founded the Christian Science Association in 1876; Jane Addams created the nation's first settlement house in 1889; and from her base at Hull House, Alice Hamilton became the lead researcher in the new field of industrial disease. By

1921 Margaret Sanger had succeeded in organizing the first American Birth Control Conference. All these women were pioneers and all relied on the power of the spoken and written word to promote their causes. Two additional women included here played major roles in promoting political causes: the feminist Charlotte Perkins Gilman and the anarchist Emma Goldman. Both published their own journals in the years preceding World War I to help popularize their ideas; both became famous for their "radicalism" and their unconventional lifestyles. The lives and careers of both have been the subject of countless essays and books from the 1970's through the present.

By the time Gilman and Goldman decided to create their own periodicals, significant numbers of women had established careers for themselves in the growing field of journalism. In 1850, twenty-five magazines in America had women editors or associate editors. Though few women were welcome in the "grimy" world of daily newspaper offices, "literary ladies" regularly contributed poetry and "chatty" pieces on domestic topics to the daily press. The most successful of these, Sara Willis Parton, who published under the pseudonym Fanny Fern, wrote a weekly column for the *New York Ledger* which boosted the paper's circulation and made her the highest-paid columnist in the country. At the turn of the century, Ida Tarbell's investigative reports and serialized biographies for *McClure's* were considered the major source of that journal's commercial success. Tarbell was also credited with the breakup of the Standard Oil Trust following her published exposé of the company's history. Twenty years later, a very different writer, Dorothy Parker (chapter 3), helped establish a satirical tone for which the new magazine, *The New Yorker*, would soon be famous. Among the many women journalists not referenced here whose lives and careers are beginning to attract renewed critical attention are Elizabeth Cochrane Seaman (1865-1922), the globe-circling stunt reporter known as Nellie Bly; Jane Cunningham Croly (1829-1901), known as Jennie June, a pioneer in fashion and advice journalism and the first woman to work daily for a newspaper; and Anne O'Hare McCormick (1880-1954), the foreign correspondent who was the first woman to win a Pulitzer Prize for journalism, in 1937.

Despite the progress made by women in these very public arenas, many educated women worked out of their homes and financed their own research. Constance Rourke, for example, after teaching English at Vassar for a few years, resigned and returned home to live with her mother. Though she did write a few articles for the *New Republic* and other serious periodicals, most of her research was done independently as she collected artifacts from local attics and traveled through the country interviewing representatives of different ethnic groups for her studies of American folklore. The historian Mary Beard collaborated with her husband on major works of American history and had a separate writing career of her own which established her role as the first theorist of women's studies. Beard was both an intellectual and a political activist, both a scholar and a wife and mother; she wrote both standard textbooks and pioneering studies of women in history. There were evidently many other husband-wife teams working in many areas where the wife did not receive the recognition she deserved. Ariel Durant, for example, collaborated with her husband Will Durant on all seven volumes of the *Story of Civilization* (1935-1961), but her name did not appear as a joint author until the final volume. Fanny Bullock Workman, on the other hand, was known as the co-author of the five books she and her husband wrote based on their seven expeditions in the Himalayas and Karakoram ranges. Still, recognition by scholars and boards of geographical societies for her role in the mapping of uncharted areas and her many pioneering firsts came far more slowly to her than to William Workman.

Each day new studies appear on countless other scholars and activist-writers. Though not enough recent research (1970 on) exists yet to include them individually, I would like to mention several briefly as an indication of the numbers of women who made major contributions to the intellectual life of the United States from 1848 to 1948. Alice Morse Earle (1851-1911), the mother of four children, began her writing career with a family history, thus sparking an avocation that resulted in seventeen books and thirty articles about colonial times. Catherine Drinker Bowen (1897-1973), the mother of two children, wrote a children's book, a history of Lehigh University, and a novel before finding her niche as a biographer, writing books on Tchaikowsky, Anton and Nicholas Rubinstein, John Adams, Francis Bacon, and many other famous figures. Alice Hamilton's sister, Edith Hamilton (1867-1963), after many years as headmistress of Bryn Mawr School in Baltimore, moved to New York, where she was encouraged to contribute articles on ancient drama and culture to *Theater Arts Monthly*, a journal she edited. This work led to the writing of *The Greek Way* (1930) and many additional articles and books that are credited with reviving popular interest in Greek, Roman, and biblical antiquity. Many of Hamilton's enormously popular works have never gone out of print.

Among the activists and reformers not annotated here are three quite different women. Emily Greene Balch, who received the Nobel Peace Prize in 1946, wrote about problems of immigration and racism, the dangers of militarism, women's rights, and economic justice. She was one of countless Progressive Era activists and a leader in the antiwar movement. Ellen G. White, cofounder of the Seventh-day Adventist church in the 1840's, published several religious texts and is credited with saving her church from extinction. Adventist literature refers to her as the Lord's Messenger and the Spirit of Prophecy. She was also an important advocate for freedom of religion for everyone. Helen Keller, who blazed a miraculous trail from the isolation of a blind and deaf mute to a B.A. *cum laude* from Radcliffe College, is well-known to most American schoolchildren. Her autobiography, *The Story of My Life* (1902) never goes out of print and dozens of biographies focus on her relationship with her teacher, Annie Sullivan. Nonetheless, little serious scholarship exists yet on her activism as an advocate for the disabled.

Because this chapter collects such a diverse group of women writers, no general studies or journals apply to all of them. Each field, such as journalism, anthropology, history, social work, and medicine, has its own specialized journals and other sources of information. The Christian Science Publishing Society, for example, is the major source of information on Eddy. Included below are references to books that provide useful historical context for the lives and writings of women journalists, historians, intellectuals, scientists, suffragists, and radicals. Such feminist and general academic journals as *American Quarterly, Feminist Studies, Frontiers,* and *Signs* occasionally include articles on the writers referenced here. With the exception of literary pieces on the fiction of Gilman and Fern, the annotations in this chapter are primarily of book-length studies focused on a writer who is viewed as having made major contributions to women's rights or led a particularly interesting or controversial life. The large number of articles and books on Gilman, in particular, reflects the now "classic" status of her novella *The Yellow Wallpaper,* as well as the significance of her writings on "women and economics." To date, more research has been done on individual women poets and novelists than on women journalists, essayists, and writers of other work outside the realm of "belles lettres."

GENERAL STUDIES

Albertine, Susan, ed. *A Living of Words: American Women in Print Culture.* Knoxville: University of Tennessee Press, 1995.

This collection of biographical essays highlights women who were editors, patrons, publishers, printers, and booksellers. Though several were writers, their professional identity was defined more by their support of other authors than their own work. For example, Ida B. Wells-Barnett (chapter 5) owned, edited, and published newspapers; Harriet Moody (1857-1932) was a "self-effacing patron, salonière, and friend of the arts" whose financial and moral support enabled many important poets to flourish; Sylvia Beach (1887-1962) founded and ran the famous bookselling and lending business, Shakespeare and Company, on Paris's Left Bank; Mabel Loomis Todd (1856-1932) worked alongside Thomas Higginson in preparing Emily Dickinson's poems for publication. The text covers the lives of fourteen women in all and includes extensive notes and a bibliography.

Beasley, Maurine H., and Sheila J. Gibbons. *Taking Their Place: A Documentary History of Women and Journalism.* Washington, D.C.: American University Press, 1993.

This is a compilation of journalistic excerpts from colonial times through the 1990's. Each chapter provides a brief historical context for the writers whose works are included. There are chapters on the first women columnists, including Fanny Fern; on suffrage newspapers; on the first African American journalists, featuring Ida B. Wells (see chapter 5); on late nineteenth century stunt reporters and sob sisters; and on investigative reporting, featuring Ida M. Tarbell. The introduction reviews the history of women's participation in journalism from Margaret Fuller, the first woman to serve as a staff member on a major newspaper (she was hired by the *New York Tribune* in 1844), through Susan Faludi, the Pulitzer Prize-winning *Wall Street Journal* reporter who attacked the press's role in creating a "backlash" against women's rights in the 1980's. An annotated list of "additional resources" is appended.

Belford, Barbara. *Brilliant Bylines: A Biographical Anthology of Notable Newspaperwomen in America*. New York: Columbia University Press, 1986.

Among the twenty-four writers featured in this illustrated text, which begins with Margaret Fuller and ends with syndicated columnists from the 1980's, are at least a dozen who wrote between 1848 and 1948. In her introduction, Belford explains that most early newspaperwomen stumbled into journalism because they were suddenly forced to support themselves, yet ended up dedicating their lives to it. She also talks about the importance of Joseph Pulitzer and William Randolph Hearst in the development of "yellow journalism" with its stunt girls and sob sisters. Several sensational trials at the beginning of the century also made the women journalists who covered them famous.

Braude, Ann. *Radical Spirits: Spiritualism and Women's Rights in Nineteenth Century America*. Boston: Beacon Press, 1989.

This book includes chapters on Quaker abolitionists, spiritualists at Seneca Falls, changing attitudes about marriage and the family, criticism of orthodox medicine, and the relationship between Christian Science and spiritualism. Braude sees spiritualism as crucial to the development of radical individualism; in effect, it helped a generation of American women find their voice.

Conrad, Susan P. *Perish the Thought: Intellectual Women in Romantic America, 1830-1860*. New York: Oxford University Press, 1976.

Conrad considers the first generation of women who made intellectual contributions to social thought. Almost none had access to higher education; daughters of professional men, they used their fathers' libraries to educate themselves beyond the training in feminine arts they received at female academies. Most had children, yet still achieved a degree of personal freedom unavailable to the average wife. As a result, these women experienced less conflict between intellectual activity and "true womanhood" than later generations, whose members often chose not to marry. Elizabeth Cady Stanton, one of Conrad's major examples, is typical of these women who generally rejected roles as teachers or "scribblers" and sought other outlets for their boundless "mental energy." More than an activist and reformer, Stanton was a true intellectual involved in the kind of speculative thinking and analysis of ideas which leads to the development of new theories.

Cott, Nancy F. *The Grounding of Modern Feminism.* New Haven: Yale University Press, 1987.
  This is a comprehensive study of the women's movement between 1910 and 1930, its "promises and problems." Cott looks at the conflicting interests of diverse women who were active outside the home, but may or may not have been committed to feminist issues. She also considers the "persistence" of structures and ideologies which reinforced male dominance. The word "feminism" itself first came into general usage in 1913 and 1914; Cott explains the reasons for its emergence and how it was interpreted by those both inside and outside the women's movement. She also provides a history of The Woman's Party and other voluntary political organizations, and of women's employment and the debates surrounding the issue of married women and work. Among the many women whose contributions Cott cites are Addams, Beard, Gilman, Hamilton, and Stanton.

DuBois, Ellen Carol. *Feminism and Suffrage: The Emergence of an Independent Women's Movement in America, 1848-1869.* Ithaca, N.Y.: Cornell University Press, 1978.
  DuBois examines the relationship between the abolition and suffrage movements before and after the Civil War. It was the abolitionists' continued refusal to take suffrage seriously which led Stanton, Anthony, and others to form an independent movement. As a result, according to DuBois, the movement remained largely middle-class and white for the next fifty years. There is a bibliography with a list of manuscript collections appended.

Flexner, Eleanor. *The Women's Rights Movement in the United States* (originally published, 1959). New York: Atheneum, 1974.
  Flexner traces the history of the women's rights movement from its scattered beginnings early in the nineteenth century to the passage of the Nineteenth Amendment in 1920. She looks at the various issues of concern to women—education, employment, trade union organization, and the law—as well as the contributions of the key players—Anthony, Stanton, Sarah and Angelina Grimké, Lucy Stone, and many others. Much of the book focuses on the last twenty years of the suffrage struggle. Flexner also writes about those who opposed suffrage, about the opening of higher education to women, and about the growth of women's organizations. The preface and conclusion to the text relate this history to the women's movement of the 1960's.

Gacs, Ute, Aisha Khan, Jerrie McIntyre, and Ruth Weinberg, eds. *Women Anthropologists: Selected Biographies.* Urbana: University of Illinois Press, 1989.
  This text covers fifty-eight primarily British and American women

divided into two groups—those born between 1836 and 1901, including Parsons, Benedict, and Mead, and those born between 1902 and 1934, including Hurston. In addition to basic biographical information, each entry emphasizes where appropriate pioneering work dealing with gender, career difficulties or conflicts experienced by married women, relationships with colleagues, unusual circumstances surrounding fieldwork, and the achievement of first woman status for particular awards or honors. A bibliography follows each entry and general references and lists of fieldwork areas and birthdates appear at the end of the text.

Glazer, Penina Migdal, and Miriam Slater. *Unequal Colleagues: The Entrance of Women into the Professions, 1890-1940.* New Brunswick, N.J.: Rutgers University Press, 1987.

The authors look at the lives and careers of nine women—academics, physicians, research scientists, and social workers—as representative of the first generation of American women to attend graduate school. All nine came from middle-class Protestant backgrounds, seven of the nine attended eastern women's colleges, all were individuals of "extraordinary energy" and stamina, and all were prepared to live outside "conventional expectations" that they marry and have children (only two married and not until they were in their thirties). All achieved some success despite a "constellation of obstacles"; all experienced some degree of marginalization in their professions. Glazer uses the nine "comparative biographies" to analyze "the nature of inequality" and the ways in which highly accomplished women responded to discrimination. Included is the chapter on Alice Hamilton annotated below.

Gordon, Linda. *Woman's Body, Woman's Right: A Social History of Birth Control in America.* New York: Viking Press, 1976.

This comprehensive history of birth control is divided into three periods: the "voluntary" motherhood of late nineteenth century feminism, the development of contraception-oriented organizations from 1910 to 1920, and the liberal "planned parenthood" movement of the 1940's on. Gordon examines the terms of the debate on contraception, population control, and abortion, concluding that reproductive freedom is central to women's rights.

James, Janet Wilson, ed. *Women in American Religion.* Philadelphia: University of Pennsylvania Press, 1980.

This collection of essays looks at the history of women in Protestant, Catholic, and Jewish religious life. James's "overview" summarizes this history, noting, for example, the growth of a female majority as an active force in American Protestantism; the loosening of institutional structures as a result of the revival spirit which created leadership opportunities for women like Mary Baker Eddy; the role of Catholic immigrant women whose experience with religious education and charity work inspired Protestants to form volunteer groups; the rise of the Salvation Army and the Women's Christian Temperance Union (WCTU); and the shift to a "civil religion" of sorts in the settlement movement represented by Jane Addams. James also discusses the relationship between religion and social service in the black church, and the temple sisterhoods that developed in response to the mass immigration of Eastern European Jews.

Marzolf, Marion. "Sob Sister to War Correspondent," in *Up from the Footnote: A History of Women Journalists*. New York: Hastings House, 1977.
　　This chapter in Marzolf's history of women's participation in print, radio, and television journalism focuses on the growth of women's magazines and women's pages in daily and Sunday newspapers. Marzolf provides examples of "stunt" writers, advice columnists, and "muckrakers" whose "sensational" pieces were extremely popular at the turn of the century. Although such "yellow journalism" exploited the "novelty" of lady reporters, it also expanded the range of subject matter considered appropriate for women to cover. Stories about suffrage also helped women's news to be taken seriously. Two of the most important women in journalism history, Dorothy Thompson (1894-1961) and Anne O'Hare McCormick (1880-1954), began their careers in the 1920's; Thompson was the first woman to head a news bureau in Europe, McCormick the first woman on the *New York Times* editorial board.

Morantz-Sanchez, Regina Markell. *Women Physicians in American Medicine: Sympathy and Science*. New York: Oxford University Press, 1985.
　　This comprehensive history of women's participation in the practice of American medicine from colonial times to the present is supplemented by an extensive bibliography. Morantz-Sanchez notes that nineteenth and early twentieth century female physicians believed that they "belonged" in the profession because of their "natural gifts as healers and nurturers." Though studies of obstetrical procedures at male- and female-staffed hospitals reveal few significant differences, patients clearly received more attention from female physicians, who tended to believe in more "holistic" methods of care. Many female doctors attacked the "impersonal, dehumanized standards" of "scientific medicine" and supported social programs for women and children. By 1930, however, the medical world had done away with almost all female-run institutions and the liberal attitudes associated with them. The women who chose medical careers then were forced to accept the "prevailing values of the profession" without having the power to influence the system from within it.

Nies, Judith. *Seven Women: Portraits from the American Radical Tradition*. New York: Viking Press, 1977.

Nies looks at the lives and political activities of Sarah Grimké, Harriet Tubman, Elizabeth Cady Stanton, Mother Jones, Charlotte Perkins Gilman, Anne Louise Strong, and Dorothy Day for evidence of common experiences. Though each is chosen to represent a different radical movement—anti-slavery, suffrage, labor, anti-war, for example—all seven offer models of successful rebellion against the institutional relationships that dominated their lives. Nies's purpose is to establish a long tradition of radical women predating the women's movement of the 1970's. Her essay on Stanton is annotated below.

O'Connell, Agnes N., and Nancy Felipe Russo. "Psychology's Foremothers," in *Models of Achievement: Reflections of Eminent Women in Psychology.* New York: Columbia University Press, 1983.

The authors note that the growth of psychology coincided with a time of "vigorous expansion" for universities in America at the end of the nineteenth century. Though women were to be found throughout the discipline, the majority worked in "new" nontraditional specialties such as educational psychology, animal psychology, and the study of mental development. Margaret Floy Washburn (1871-1939), author of *The Animal Mind* (1908), was the first woman Ph.D. in 1894; by 1920 sixty-two American women had earned Ph.D.'s in psychology, fifteen of them from the University of Chicago, one of the few institutions to accept men and women on an equal basis. In addition to identifying "foremothers," O'Connell and Russo explain the barriers faced by women as students and professionals. They also discuss the role of minority women and the general evolution of the field of psychology at the beginning of the twentieth century.

Pleck, Elizabeth. "Feminist Responses to 'Crimes against Women,' 1868-1896." *Signs* 8, no. 3 (Spring 1983): 451-470.

Pleck looks at the beliefs and actions of four sets of reformers and organizations who lobbied on behalf of battered women and rape victims: liberal feminists Susan B. Anthony and Elizabeth Cady Stanton, conservative feminists Lucy Stone and Henry Blackwell, the Women's Christian Temperance Union, and Chicago's Protective Agency for Women and Children. Pleck also establishes the historical context which led to both the rise and the decline in the various campaigns on behalf of female victims. At first these reform movements were "moralistic, sexually prudish, and punitive," in some cases excessively so. However, with the disappearance of the worst rhetoric, the moral outrage which had fueled the campaigns also disappeared.

Reed, James. *From Private Vice to Public Virtue: The Birth Control Movement and American Society Since 1830.* New York: Basic Books, 1978.

This history of the birth control movement and of contraceptive technology emphasizes changes in medical attitudes and societal values. There are separate discussions of major figures, including Margaret

Sanger, of American concerns about both under- and overpopulation, and of development of the birth control pill. There are also illustrations and a bibliographic essay.

Rossi, Alice S., ed. *The Feminist Papers: From Addams to de Beauvoir*. Boston: Northeastern University Press, 1988.
This reprint of a 1973 collection includes excerpts from speeches, essays, and other documents of the women's movement from the eighteenth to mid-twentieth century. Rossi provides a general introduction as well as historical and social contexts for each section.

Rossiter, Margaret W. *Women Scientists in America: Struggles and Strategies to 1940*. Baltimore, Md.: The Johns Hopkins University Press, 1982.
Rossiter explains that women's historically subordinate "place" in science is directly attributable to the nineteenth century professionalization of science as a "tough" masculine discipline. Despite new opportunities for women in employment and higher education between 1820 and 1920, the narrow range of activities considered appropriate for women meant that a "woman scientist" was considered a "contradiction in terms." At the turn of the century, women increasingly took advantage of the wide diversity of new roles for scientists. At the same time, as the male establishment became more threatened by this apparent encroachment, it managed to exclude women from a variety of areas presumably because of new and more rigorous standards. By 1940 there were thousands of women working in a variety of scientific fields and institutions. This great growth, however, came at the "price of accepting a pattern of segregated employment and underrecognition." Rossiter, in documenting this "history," looks at women's colleges; the women's movement; employment patterns in academe, government, and industry; and the forms of public recognition that women scientists did and did not receive. She also traces the activities of hundreds of women, including Alice Hamilton and Ruth Benedict (see below), who contributed to the growth of American science despite the many obstacles they faced. The text includes illustrations, charts, and a bibliography.

Scott, Joan Wallach. "American Women Historians, 1884-1984," in *Gender and the Politics of History*. New York: Columbia University Press, 1988.
Scott looks at the participation of women historians in the American Historical Society, founded in 1884. This association was open to women academics because of its "democratic mission" and its "zeal" to make sure that the "new" history was taught everywhere in America, including at women's colleges, where almost all women historians taught. Two women, Nellie Neilson of Mount Holyoke and Lucy Maynard Salmon of Vassar, played important roles within the society but were never fully integrated into its activities, even though Neilson

was elected president in 1943. Scott also looks at the important role of the Berkshire Conference, which from 1929 on lobbied forcefully on behalf of women historians.

Seller, Maxine-Schwartz, ed. *Women Educators in the United States, 1820-1993.* Westport, Conn.: Greenwood Press, 1994.
This book profiles sixty-six women, including Jane Addams, Catherine Beecher, Anna Julia Cooper, and Mary Church Terrell. Each woman's career is summarized; then her life is described in a six- to ten-page essay which establishes her significance in the context of the historical period in which she lived and the educational field to which she contributed. A chronological listing of subjects by birthdate is appended.

Zinsser, Judith P. *History and Feminism: A Glass Half Full.* New York: Twayne, 1993.
Zinsser offers separate discussions of men's history, women's history, and the impact of feminism on each. In addition to her analysis of changes in the content of history and how it is taught, she looks at the development of academic departments of history and the role of women within them. The text contains extensive notes and references, including annotated suggestions for further reading.

JANE ADDAMS
1860-1935

Addams was born and raised in Cedarville, Illinois; the youngest of eight children, she was two when her mother died. Her father was a prominent community leader and businessman who served in the Illinois State Senate for many years. Addams attended the Rockford Female Seminary and the Women's Medical College of Pennsylvania, which she was forced to leave in order to have back surgery. During a trip to Europe with her friend Ellen Starr, Addams visited Toynbee Hall in London, the inspiration for Hull House, which the two women founded in 1889. Hull House, as conceived by Addams, was far more than a charitable mission; Addams's vision was for a cultural center where diverse ethnic groups and social classes could meet and exchange ideas. Addams devoted much of her energy to lecturing and writing on social issues; a collection of her essays, *Democracy and Social Ethics,* was published in 1902. This first book was followed by *Newer Ideals of Peace* (1907) and *The Spirit of Youth and the City Streets* (1909). Addams's best known work is *Twenty Years at Hull House* (1910), the autobiography she published at the age of fifty. She also published a study of prostitution, *A New Conscience and an Ancient Evil* (1912); a chronicle of her pacifist activities, *Peace and Bread in Time of War* (1922); and *The Second Twenty Years at Hull House* (1930). In addition to the fame associated with Hull House, Addams was well-known for her work in the international women's peace movement; she was named president of the International Congress of Women at The

Hague in 1915, and of the Women's International League for Peace and Freedom in 1919. Her many awards include an honorary degree from Yale University in 1910 and the Nobel Peace Prize in 1931.

Reissued Editions
Jane Addams on Education, ed. Ellen Condliffe Lagemann. New York: Teachers College Press, 1985.

Peace and Bread in Time of War. New York: Garland, 1972.

Twenty Years at Hull House (illustrated and with notes), ed. James Hurt. Champaign: University of Illinois Press, 1990.

Biography and Commentary
Conway, Jill. "Women Reformers and American Culture, 1870-1930." *Journal of Social History* 5, no. 2 (Winter 1971-1972): 164-177.
   Conway focuses on Jane Addams and Lillian Wald as examples of two different types of activists—the professional expert and the prophet who claims access to hidden wisdom by virtue of her feminine intuition. Addams, the "intuitive reformer," believed in women's special ability to empathize with the weak. By insisting on the "moral superiority" of women, Addams, according to Conway, failed to distinguish herself from Freud's irrational women. She also failed to see herself as the aggressive, hardworking individual she really was.

Davis, Allen F. *American Heroine: The Life and Legend of Jane Addams.* New York: Oxford University Press, 1975.
   Davis begins with a detailed description of the founding of Hull House, looking at both the personal and historical factors that may have influenced Addams. He then proceeds to study her reputation and public image, and the ways she has come to symbolize changing American attitudes toward poverty and reform. Davis credits Addams with helping make the public aware of urban problems but blames her for suggesting that her solution was the only one necessary. He himself sees her success as based on "administrative talent" despite her acquiescence to the feminine stereotype which evaluated her work as self-sacrificing and intuitive. Because of her pacifist ideas, Addams's writings were devalued and largely ignored in the twenty years following her death but again became fashionable in the reform-minded 1960's.

DeKoven, Marianne. "'Excellent Not a Hull House': Gertrude Stein, Jane Addams, and Feminist-Modernist Political Culture," in *Rereading Modernism: New Directions in Feminist Criticism,* ed. Lisa Rado. New York: Garland Publishing, Inc., 1994.
   DeKoven finds striking commonalities in the personal histories of Stein and Addams. Both were the youngest children in large families, both had complex relationships with charismatic fathers, both began but did not finish medical school, both suffered from prolonged periods of

depression, both relied on female companions for support and encouragement. Moreover, in their respective careers, both radically altered the "spaces" within which they worked. In creating Hull House Addams mediated between "traditional upper-class feminine charity work and radical socialist movements for political change." The history of Hull House, therefore, played an important role in bringing about the political, cultural, and gender changes associated with modernism.

Hovde, Jane. *Jane Addams.* New York: Facts on File, 1989.
    Part of the Makers of America series, this study of Addams's life and career includes photographs and a bibliography. Hovde begins with Addams's role at the 1912 National Progressive Party Convention where she was hailed "as one of the ten greatest citizens" of the country. Hovde then chronicles the founding and early years of Hull House in the context of the changing face of Chicago, Addams's increasing involvement in political activities, and the public response to Addams's role as a leader of the Women's International League for Peace and Freedom. Hovde concludes that Addams made a major political and intellectual contribution to the social reform movement in America.

Leffers, M. Regina. "Pragmatists Jane Addams and John Dewey Inform the Ethic of Care." *Hypatia* 8, no. 2 (Spring 1993): 64-77.
    Leffers uses Addams and Dewey to help demonstrate the moral significance of an ethic of caring for other people based on the premise that we are all radically connected to each other. Addams believed that respect for ourselves and others requires us to take responsive action to the perceived needs of self, other individuals, and the larger comunity. She was particularly critical of the way privileged young women were discouraged from active involvement in social causes and spoke passionately about the solidarity of the human race. Addams herself, according to Leffers, was gifted with an ability to see individuals as "interconnected and interrelated parts of ever larger wholes."

Lissak, Rivka Shpak. *Pluralism & Progressives: Hull House and the New Immigrants, 1890-1919.* Chicago: University of Chicago Press, 1989.
    Lissak looks at the history of Hull House in the context of liberal progressive attitudes and rhetoric about the perpetuation of ethnic and cultural differences. Addams and her fellow progressives opposed the Anglo-American nationalistic view of American culture but also believed in the "predominance" of more advanced cultures over less developed ones, according to Lissak. They wanted immigrant culture to contribute to the "melting pot," not to maintain a separate existence. Addams became reconciled to the persistence of ethnic identity only when faced with Hull House's failure in assimilating the new immigrants into the American mainstream. Nonetheless, Hull House

leaders' benign policies and tolerance for ethnic difference helped pave the way for the true pluralism of the 1930's.

Richards, Dell. "Jane Addams," in *Superstars: Twelve Lesbians Who Changed the World.* New York: Carroll & Graf, 1993.
   Richards offers a biographical essay and chronology of Addams's life and career which focuses on the influence of her two friends, Ellen Gates Starr and Mary Rozet Smith. Starr, a childhood friend, helped found Hull House, started its first cultural "club" and art classes, and helped "fire" mutual enthusiasm. Smith, a Chicago aristocrat, helped keep Hull House afloat financially and was a faithful friend until death. Whatever her "sexuality," Richards concludes, Addams turned to other women for "emotional and political support, for companionship, affection, and love."

Sklar, Kathryn Kish. "'Hull House in the 1890's': A Community of Women Reformers." *Signs* 10, no. 4 (Summer 1985): 658-677.
   Sklar focuses on the working relationships between Jane Addams, Julia Lathrop, and Florence Kelley as a "paradigm" for women's participation in Progressive reform activities. These women were able to develop and sustain their own institution, to blend mutual support and individual expression in creative ways, and to use Hull House to form alliances with male reformers which allowed them access to the political mainstream. Florence Kelley (1859-1932) was the key figure here whose leadership made them effective advocates for the rights and interests of women and children.
   See also: Kathryn Kish Sklar, "Jane Addams's Peace Activism, 1914-1922: A Modal for Women Today?" *Women's Studies Quarterly* 23, nos. 3-4 (Fall-Winter 1995): 32-47.

Stroup, Herbert. *Social Welfare Pioneers.* Chicago: Nelson-Hall, 1986.
   This collection of biographies highlights the contributions to social reform of the first generation of social workers. Its opening chapter is on Jane Addams.

Wheeler, Leslie A. *Jane Addams.* Englewood Cliffs, N.J.: Silver Burdett Press, 1990.
   This volume in the Pioneers in Change series for young adult readers includes photographs, a chronology, and a bibliography of primary and secondary sources. Wheeler reviews Addams's childhood and education, her political and reform activities, and the public reception of her major books. Wheeler emphasizes Addams's pioneering work both in helping the poor and in promoting peace. Though she fell out of public favor in the 1920's because of her opposition to World War I and was branded as a communist like many other social reformers whose work was considered radical, by the time of her death she was once again revered as a "national saint."

MARY RITTER BEARD
1876-1958

Beard was born in Indianapolis, the third of six children and the elder of two daughters. She studied political science, languages, and literature at DePauw, a Methodist university attended by her father and all her siblings, where she met her husband. The young couple moved to Oxford, England, where they became involved in reform movements for workers' rights and women's suffrage. Two years later they returned to New York and enrolled at Columbia University. Not long after the birth of her second child, Beard joined the National Women's Trade Union League and became increasingly involved in the suffrage movement. Her first books, *Woman's Work in Municipalities* (1915) and *A Short History of the American Labor Movement* (1920), focused on social reform and the working class. Beard and her husband moved to Milford, Connecticut, after he resigned his professorship at Columbia in 1917 and began their collaboration on high school textbooks and *The Rise of American Civilization* (1927-1942), their celebrated four-volume series on American history. At the same time, she began her own historical studies of women's neglected past, including *On Understanding Women* (1931) and *Woman as a Force in History* (1946). Beard also published two collections of women's writing: *America through Women's Eyes* (1933) and *Laughing Their Way: Women's Humor in America* (1934). In the 1930's Beard attempted to establish a World Center for Women's Archives, a project which ultimately failed. Into her seventies she continued to write and lecture on the need to transform higher education curricula so that they would reflect women's experience and perspectives.

Reissued Editions

Note: Several of the major works on which Beard collaborated with her husband, including the first three volumes of their series on American history, were reprinted in the 1960's.

On Understanding Women. Westport, Conn.: Greenwood Press, 1968.

A Short History of the American Labor Movement. Salem, N.H.: Arno Press, 1969.

Woman as a Force in History. New York: Octagon Books, 1986.

Woman's Work in Municipalities. Salem, N.H.: Arno Press, 1972.

Biography and Commentary

Cott, Nancy F. "Two Beards: Coauthorship and the Concept of Civilization." *American Quarterly* 42, no. 2 (June 1990): 247-300.

Cott offers a history of the Beards' relationship, including their activism while at Oxford and Columbia on behalf of suffrage and workers' causes. She then traces the evolution of their thinking,

Intellectuals, Reformers, and Journalists   **201**

individually and collectively. Both were skeptical about traditional higher education, both were critical of imperialistic capitalism, both were interested in finding a workable "collectivism" in response to the Depression. From 1921 until the late 1940's, they were almost always working together on U.S. history texts. His focus was constitutional history, hers women and women's history. The research she did probably led to their shared belief that "objective" history cannot be known.

_____, ed. *A Woman Making History: Mary Ritter Beard Through Her Letters*. New Haven: Yale University Press, 1991.
    This illustrated text with extensive source notes includes several hundred of Beard's letters written between the 1910's and the 1950's. Though Beard had objected to publication of private letters, Cott argues that few of the letters are truly personal and that their publication can help restore Beard's place in history. Though Mary Beard remained on the periphery of her husband's "limelight" and was effectively written "out of the record" by later historians, the letters make clear that the two Beards shared a "thorough and mutually supportive partnership in writing, politics, and life." Cott has grouped the letters chronologically with a brief introduction to each of the seven chapters.
    "Putting Women on the Record," Cott's sixty-page biographical introduction, traces the evolution of Beard's views on women's history, and analyzes in detail both her collaborative and individual work. Cott sees Beard as a "moralist and didact" who spoke directly to the people. Her approach to history was "holistic" in that she saw everything as related to everything else. She, like her husband, also insisted on the "subjectivity of historians." Beard believed that by writing women back into history and providing a fuller portrayal of their lives and experiences, she could help correct women's "underestimation of their own efficacy." She disagreed with feminists who emphasized women's victimization and who insisted on the importance of equality with men. Women had always worked, according to Beard, and a "world at risk" needed women who could offer something better than imitation of the worst excesses of capitalism and individualism.

Lane, Ann J., ed. *Mary Ritter Beard: A Sourcebook*. New York: Schocken Books, 1977.
    Lane includes a wide variety of selections from Beard's writings and speeches divided into sections: political activism, feminism as a theoretical world view, and feminism as a practical world view. Each section has a brief introduction and a bibliography of primary sources is appended.
    "Mary Ritter Beard: An Appraisal of Her Life and Work," Lane's seventy-page introduction, provides a comprehensive overview of Beard's career. Lane sees Beard's "thesis," that women have always been an important, though unrecognized, force in society, as based on her own personal experience. Despite the importance of her work,

including six books of her own and seven on which she collaborated with her husband, Beard has been neglected or "relegated to the status of Charles Beard's wife and collaborator." As a scholar, activist, wife, and mother, Beard offers a prototype of the kind of extraordinary woman who managed to combine a professional life with a commitment to home and family. Though her ideas were fully understood by only a few of her colleagues, her legacy lives on in women's studies programs, in feminist journals, and in that element of the women's movement focused on the needs of working-class women.

Lerner, Gerda. *The Majority Finds Its Past: Placing Women in History.* New York: Oxford University Press, 1979.
    Lerner credits Beard with creation of the modern concept of women's history and with raising critical issues which continued to concern later generations of feminists. Lerner's introduction highlights Beard's contributions; additional references to Beard appear throughout the text which also contains extensive notes and a bibliography.

Smith, Bonnie G. "Seeing Mary Beard." *Feminist Studies* 10, no. 3 (Fall 1984): 394-416.
    Smith traces Beard's development as a historian from the quite "normal" *Woman's Work in Municipalities* (1915) through the highly unconventional *Laughing Their Way* (1934). Beard came to reject a "unitary" interpretation of history based on raw facts in favor of a more anthropological approach which examined all aspects of history. As she began to use diary entries, poems, jokes, and cartoons on a wide diversity of topics to demonstrate the "multiplicity of voices" which she saw as women's history, her critics labeled her weird and ultimately deranged. Beard herself, having once established her authority as a historian, was happy to disappear into her anthologies of women's words and laughter; she never wanted to be "monumentalized."

Trigg, Mary. "'To Work Together for Ends Larger than Self': The Feminist Struggles of Mary Beard and Doris Stevens in the 1930's." *Journal of Women's History* 7, no. 2 (Summer 1995): 52-85.
    Trigg uses these two women to demonstrate that even during the Depression backlash years there were feminist leaders "of vision, inspiration, and perseverance" at work. Trigg offers an overview of Beard's life and ideas before focusing on her attempt to create a World Center for Women's Archives (WCWA). Begun in 1935 and dissolved in 1940, the WCWA was intended to be a "gathering place and clearinghouse of women's historical documents" representative of women in all their diversity. Beard hoped that these archives would inspire future generations of women to become "creative leaders" and would serve as a center for research on women. Trigg provides a history of Beard's efforts to raise funds for the WCWA and of the role of key supporters; she analyzes the reasons why Beard finally abandoned her dream. Ultimately, Beard's vision gave rise to both the Sophia Smith

Collection at Smith College and the Schlesinger Library at Radcliffe College. Thanks to Beard's work, according to Trigg, "women's history is now a rich and growing field of academic inquiry."

Turoff, Barbara K. *Mary Beard as Force in History.* Wright State University Monograph # 3. Dayton, Ohio: Wright State University, 1979.
This text has a generous selection of photographs, newspaper clippings, and excerpts from Beard's writings. There is also an extensive bibliography of primary and secondary sources. Turoff's stated objective is to provide an overview of Beard's activities as both a historian and a social reformer.

RUTH FULTON BENEDICT
1887-1948
Ruth Fulton was the first child of middle-class New York parents. Her father, a successful physician, died when she was twenty-one-months old. Throughout her life Benedict suffered from a severe hearing loss which made her quite shy and ultimately limited her professional career. She and her sister Margery attended Vassar College, their mother's alma mater, where Ruth developed an interest in literature and creative writing. Following graduation she worked as a teacher for several years until marrying Stanley Benedict at the age of twenty-seven. Perhaps because of her unhappiness with her marriage and her inability to have children, Ruth Benedict returned to school at the age of thirty-one and began studying anthropology under Franz Boas at Columbia. In 1934 she published *Patterns of Culture*, the culmination of years of research and thinking, which became known as a key text in the new field of culture and personality studies. Her two-volume work *Zuni Mythology* followed in 1934, *Race: Science and Politics* in 1940, and *The Chrysanthemum and the Sword* in 1946. This last work received high marks from both Japanese and Americans for helping to explain Japanese behavior during the war and for persuading American authorities to consider Japanese culture in planning occupation policies. In addition to her major works, Benedict published more than a hundred articles, served as editor of the *Journal of American Folklore,* chaired the American Anthropological Association, and, as a professor at Columbia, influenced countless students including Margaret Mead, who became a cherished friend and colleague. She also published poetry in literary journals under the pseudonym Anne Singleton.

Reissued Editions
The Chrysanthemum and the Sword: Patterns of Japanese Culture. Boston: Houghton Mifflin, 1989.

Patterns of Culture. Boston: Houghton Mifflin, 1989.

Biography and Commentary
Babcock, Barbara A. "'Not in the Absolute Singular': Re-reading Ruth Benedict." *Frontiers* 13, no. 3 (1992): 39-77.

Though Benedict's work was discounted in her own time because of its poetic and nonscientific qualities, according to Babcock, it anticipated many postmodern concerns. Benedict's relativism and anti-essentialism, and her "deconstruction" of the presumed scientific objectivity of anthropological discourse are particularly relevant today. Rather than a hindrance, Benedict's training in literary criticism allowed her to read cultures as "texts organized around tropes." Moreover, her deafness, though it did limit her fieldwork, forced her to go beyond the "minutiae" to see the larger picture holding the "rags and tatters" together. Babcock reviews Benedict's life, her major works, her most important relationships with other anthropologists, and concludes that her real contribution resulted from the combination of poet, philosopher, feminist, and anthropologist within her.

Caffrey, Margaret M. *Ruth Benedict: Stranger in This Land.* Austin: University of Texas Press, 1989.

Caffrey offers a comprehensive study of Benedict's life and work, including analysis of her poetry as well as her major articles and books. Throughout the biography she focuses on the intellectual environment in which Benedict developed her ideas and on the influence of particular individuals and historical trends. She traces Benedict's interest in the relationship of chaos and order to her feelings about her parents, her father's rationality and her mother's emotionalism. She traces her feminism to research she did as a young wife on the lives of Mary Wollstonecraft, Charlotte Perkins Gilman, and Olive Schreiner. Caffrey considers the important role of Franz Boas as mentor and colleague, and her deep intellectual and personal friendship with Margaret Mead. Anthropology, according to Caffrey, provided Benedict with a vehicle to think about social change in a way that made sense given her belief in the importance of culture and personality.

Mead, Margaret. *Ruth Benedict.* New York: Columbia University Press, 1974.

This biographical sketch builds on Mead's earlier study, *An Anthropologist at Work: Writings of Ruth Benedict* (1959). Mead intersperses her own commentary with Benedict's writings to establish the significance of her life and work.

Modell, Judith. *Ruth Benedict: Patterns of a Life.* Philadelphia: University of Pennsylvania Press, 1983.

Modell's biography, the first full-length study of the anthropologist, focuses on Benedict's major personal and professional relationships with Elsie Crews Parsons, Franz Boas, Edward Sapir, Margaret Mead, and Natalie Raymond, a research chemist with whom she shared an apartment following her separation from her husband. Modell quotes extensively from Benedict's poetry and diaries, finding in these evidence of a fundamental despair as well as an ongoing attempt to understand her feelings about her own life. She finds in Benedict's work a "distinct attitude" toward life; "a respect for individuality and a confidence in the power of individual imaginations to remake reality; a belief in the importance of comparison; a trust in the beneficial transmission of 'visions' from one person to another, one society to another." Modell also stresses Benedict's role as an observer with awareness of her own subjectivity and respect for the privacy and masks worn by others. Viewed from a distance, it is a life which demonstrates a woman's ability to resolve her own private conflicts through the pursuit of professional accomplishments. A bibliography is appended.

Shannon, Christopher. "A World Made Safe for Differences: Ruth Benedict's *The Chrysanthemum and the Sword.*" *American Quarterly* 47, no. 4 (December 1995): 659-680.

Shannon identifies Benedict's work as the precursor of the postwar doctrine of tolerance. He offers his own close reading of her study of Japanese culture to demonstrate both the value and the problems inherent in the ideology of cultural relativism as established by Benedict. Shannon agrees with Benedict's assessment of America's "neurotic fear of differences" and praises her refutation of stereotypes and her historical analysis of the apparent contradictions within Japanese culture. He is critical, however, of what he terms her unquestioned affirmation of the "very American value of individual freedom." Benedict assumes that once the Japanese are able to view their own culture with "anthropological detachment," they will reject all "restrictive" or "defining" cultural forms—irrational ties to family, for example—as external to the self. This reveals her own liberal bias against "normative" structures and the concept of a "national" or "dominant" culture, Shannon concludes.

MARY BAKER EDDY
1821-1910
Eddy was born in New Hampshire, the youngest of six children, and suffered throughout her childhood from illness. Her first husband died after six months of marriage while she was pregnant. Her only child, a son, was raised by relatives, since she was often too weak to care for him. After her relationship with her second husband declined, she turned for treatment to Phineas P. Quimby, a well-known healer in Portland, Maine. Eddy credited Quimby's use of "animal magnetism" and his belief that a patient's mental state had a direct impact on illness with curing her invalidism and inspiring her to become a healer herself. Divine revelation was said to aid her recovery from a serious spinal injury and to lead her to write *Science and Health* (1875). This was followed by formation of the Christian Science Association in 1876, the Church of Christ, Scientist in 1879, and the Massachusetts Metaphysical College in 1881. Eddy also married again in 1877. By

1900 a network of six hundred churches existed with the Mother Church in Boston, where Eddy served as pastor. She continued to play a leadership role in the organization and governance of the religious movement she had founded until her death at the age of eighty-nine. In addition to *Science and Health,* which went through four hundred editions in her lifetime, Eddy published several other books on Christian Science.

Reissued Editions
Manual of the Mother Church (1895). Boston: The Christian Science Publishing Society, 1976.

Science and Health, with a Key to Scriptures. Boston: The Christian Science Publishing Society, 1994.

Unity of Good: Rudimental Divine Science (1887). Boston: The Christian Science Publishing Society, 1971.

Biography and Criticism
Note: There is a three-volume official biography of Eddy by Robert Peel: *The Years of Discovery* (1966), *The Years of Trial* (1971), and *The Years of Authority* (1977), Austin, Tex.: Holt, Rinehart & Winston. Peel is Counselor on Publications for the Mother Church and writes of Eddy and the history of Christian Science from the perspective of a history of ideas.

Silberger, Julius, Jr. M. D. *Mary Baker Eddy: An Interpretive Biography of the Founder of Christian Science.* Boston: Little, Brown, 1980.
    Silberger, a psychiatrist with an interest in mental healing, sees Eddy as a "phenomenon" who can be understood only through appreciation of her unique talents, her ability to take advantage of both personal and external circumstances, and the role of divine inspiration. A woman of enormous intelligence, energy, and creativity, Eddy was a spoiled child who learned to get what she wanted by being helpless and avoiding any expression of anger or ambition. Her pains and trances progressed from an expression of her inner conflicts to a means of controlling others. With the death of her father and her healer, Quimby, her "hidden self" was able to emerge and lead to the creation of her church. Moreover, unlike most troubled visionaries who founded religions, Eddy possessed superb organizational skills and continued to head the church and to write its books until her death. This comprehensive biography chronicles the church's history, the controversies surrounding it and Eddy, and describes her friends and enemies, and especially her need for and use of the important men in her life.

Thomas, Robert David. *"With Bleeding Footsteps": Mary Baker Eddy's Path to Religious Leadership.* New York: Alfred A. Knopf, 1994.
This is a comprehensive biography based on ten years of research in the church archives. Thomas, a historian and psychoanalyst, and not a Christian Scientist, sees Eddy as a strikingly original thinker who, by synthesizing science and nurturance, emphasized what many people wanted to believe as they felt increasingly alienated by the materialism of a capitalist society. Despite the inconsistencies and complexities of her own personality, Eddy was neither the hysterical woman nor evil spider trapping innocent souls in her web that her detractors made her out to be. Many of these attacks were by male ministers, doctors, and other men who felt threatened by the power of a strong woman on the public stage. Christian Science as a religion was particularly attractive to women because it placed them beside men in the pulpit. Thomas looks at the psychological and social circumstances that led Eddy to found Christian Science. He also looks at the appeal of the church in the context of late Victorian values as he chronicles its rise within eight years of its founding into a "burgeoning organization" of twenty churches, ninety societies, and thirty-three teaching centers scattered across the country.

Washington, Peter. "The Source and the Key," in *Madame Blavatsky's Baboon: A History of the Mystics, Mediums, and Misfits Who Brought Spiritualism to America.* New York: Schocken Books, 1993.
Washington identifies two types of religious sects which developed in the late nineteenth century: the first was devoted to restoring the purity of the Christian doctrine, the second was based on personal revelation as embodied by the will of a charismatic individual. Eddy and her teachings grew out of the "purity" movements as influenced by the popular philosophy of Emanuel Swedenborg (1688-1772), who believed in the primacy of intuition and imagination as spiritual organs of perception, in the universe as a harmonious whole, and in a theory of correspondences according to which each material object was understood to be the sign of a higher divine meaning. Eddy, who had rejected Calvinism in favor of belief in a benevolent god and the kingdom of heaven as an immediate spiritual possibility, added to Swedenborg's tenets the concept of illness as an error arising from the mind's radical misunderstanding of reality. Like many women of her time, she was attracted to the notion that the Earth was an organism and part of a cosmic whole. Moreover, according to Washington, spirituality was one of the few domains outside of literature in which it was possible for Western women to play leadership roles.

FANNY FERN (SARA WILLIS PARTON)
1811-1872
Fern was born in Portland, Maine, and raised in Boston, where her father, Nathaniel Willis, published a religious newspaper. Following the

death of her first husband, Fern was reduced to relative poverty and forced to marry again to support herself and her family. When this marriage failed, she turned to writing in hopes of earning a living and by 1851 was placing her pieces in small Boston magazines. Her work was so popular that it drew the attention of major publishers and she was recruited by the *New York Ledger* to write a weekly column. For twenty years she never missed a column and was extraordinarily well-paid for her work. In the meantime, collections of her earlier work, *Fern Leaves from Fanny's Portfolio* (1853 and 1854), and *Little Ferns for Fanny's Little Friends* (1854) sold 180,000 copies in England and America. Fern also wrote two novels: *Ruth Hall* (1855) and *Rose Clark* (1856), both closely modeled on her own life. Most of Fern's columns were about everyday domestic topics and became increasingly satirical and less sentimental with time. By the late 1850's Fern had become a champion of women's rights and began to write about broader social problems. Fern published several additional books, raised two daughters, and enjoyed a good relationship with her third husband, James Parton.

Reissued Editions
Ruth Hall and Other Writings. New Brunswick, N.J.: Rutgers University Press, 1986.

Biography and Commentary
Berlant, Lauren. "The Female Woman: Fanny Fern and the Form of Sentiment," in *The Culture of Sentiment: Race, Gender, and Sentimentality in Nineteenth Century America,* ed. Shirley Samuels. New York: Oxford University Press, 1992.
    Berlant looks at Fern's popular newspaper columns and novels for evidence of the ambivalent politics of female sentimentalism as well as its contribution to a highly profitable "female culture industry." Fern was a practitioner of what Berlant terms "the female complaint," a journalistic form which provided consolation to women while attacking the dominant values of patriarchal structures. An expression of women's frustration, self-sacrifice, and even rage, these complaints did not challenge the basic tenets of the domestic sphere. While some of Fern's articles "validated" sentimentality, others used sarcasm to critique sentimentality. Fern was consistent in her attack on women's public embrace of stereotypes and used Margaret Fuller's concept of "femality" to urge women to wake up and actively engage their minds in analysis of their world, rather than retreat from it. As a coda to this essay, Berlant points out the interesting coincidence that Fern's brother, N. P. Willis, whose refusal to support her or her work she fiercely satirizes in *Ruth Hall*, was the same man who employed the fugitive slave Harriet Jacobs. Jacobs's letters reveal that she was forced to write her narrative (see chapter 5) at night because she mistrusted Willis. As publisher of the *Home Journal,* Willis was a national figure in the promotion of sentimental culture.

Warren, Joyce W. *Fanny Fern: An Independent Woman.* New Brunswick, N.J.: Rutgers University Press, 1992.
    This illustrated biography traces Fern's rise to worldwide fame as the most highly paid newspaper writer of her time and tells the story of her rebellious childhood, spirited youth, and three marriages. Warren explains Fern's popularity as based on the sharp humor and plain language she brought to the discussion of typical domestic concerns, as well as her willingness to address such taboo topics as prostitution, prison reform, and divorce. As a writer and social critic, she had a major impact on American literature and culture. She was, for example, the first woman who dared to praise in print Walt Whitman's controversial *Leaves of Grass.* Despite her celebrity during her own lifetime, Fern declined into oblivion soon after her death largely because she was considered to be a "sentimental nonentity" by academics who judged her by her flowery pseudonym (taken partly in jest) without ever reading her works.

——————————. "Fanny Fern's *Rose Clark.*" *Legacy* 8, no. 2 (Fall 1991): 92-103.
    This analysis of Fern's second novel focuses on its relationship to the biographical facts of Fern's second marriage to the abusive Samuel Farrington and her strategic decision to use two female protagonists, the sweet and gentle Rose Clark and the cynical Gertrude Dean. Warren also looks at how Fern's supporting characters undercut the conventional piety of the narrative voice and the affirmative ending. Though reviewers praised Fern's second novel as "more charitable" than her first, they still criticized her for portraying an abusive relationship; they did not want women writers to be angry and satirical. It is, therefore, not surprising, Warren concludes, that Fern never wrote another novel.

CHARLOTTE PERKINS GILMAN
1860-1935
    Gilman was born in Hartford, Connecticut; her father, a nephew of Harriet Beecher Stowe, left the family soon after Charlotte was born. Given the example of her long-suffering mother, Gilman by the age of twenty-one was writing poetry about the limitations placed on women, as well as working as an art teacher and governess. Gilman married Charles Stetson in 1894 and gave birth to a daughter ten months later. Following a nervous breakdown, perhaps partly the result of post-partum depression, Gilman and her baby moved to California, where she began a career as a feminist writer and lecturer. Gilman divorced her husband in 1894 and gave custody of her daughter to him and his new wife, who continued to be her good friend. Despite the fact that this decision seemed in the best interests of the child, it generated a great deal of negative publicity directed at Gilman. In 1898 Gilman published *Women and Economics,* which argued that women's dependence on men

was detrimental to the healthy emotional growth of both sexes. In 1899 she published *The Yellow Wallpaper*, a fictionalized version of the rest cure she had received following her breakdown. This work blames the several months of forced inactivity and isolation for truly driving her crazy. In 1900 she married her first cousin, George Houghton Gilman, whose support over the next three decades allowed her to continue her work. In 1909, Gilman began a seven-year editorship of her own periodical, the *Forerunner*, which published her essays, poems, and fiction, including serialized versions of three of her novels—*What Diantha Did* (1910), *Herland* (1915), and *With Her in Ourland* (1916). Gilman continued to write and speak about the need for communal services to aid women in the performance of domestic chores so that they might better utilize their talents for the benefit of society and themselves. After learning that she suffered from inoperable cancer, Gilman committed suicide because she could no longer be "of service," and believed in the "human right" to choose one's death.

Reissued Editions
A Charlotte Perkins Gilman Reader. Magnolia, Mass.: Peter Smith, 1992.

Herland. Magnolia, Mass.: Peter Smith, 1992.

The Living of Charlotte Perkins Gilman: An Autobiography (1935). Madison: University of Wisconsin Press, 1991.

A Non-Fiction Reader. New York: Columbia University Press, 1991.

The Yellow Wallpaper and Other Writings. New York: Bantam, 1989.

The Yellow Wallpaper: Texts and Contexts. New Brunswick, N.J.: Rutgers University Press, 1993.

Biography and Criticism
Note: Gilman's most famous work is sometimes considered a novella with its title italicized, sometimes a short story with its title in quotation marks.

Allen, Polly Wynn. *Building Domestic Liberty: Charlotte Perkins Gilman's Architectural Feminism.* Amherst: University of Massachusetts Press, 1988.
　　After establishing the social and personal context in which Gilman developed her ideas, Allen examines her writings on household organization and her attempts at developing a universal social ethic. Though Gilman herself felt her work on household organization was less important than her theology of world improvement, Allen disagrees and praises the former for its "crisp clarity" and reliance on real-life experience in contrast to the verbosity and abstract theorizing of the

latter. In proposing new kinds of residential spaces which allowed for shared domestic services, Gilman effectively made the case that women could not achieve autonomy as long as the physical setting for family life meant that they must spend countless hours on solitary domestic chores. Allen concludes with examples of residential communities inspired by Gilman's proposals.

Bak, John S. "Escaping the Jaundiced Eye: Foucaultian Panopticism in Charlotte Perkins Gilman's 'The Yellow Wallpaper.'" *Studies in Short Fiction* 31, no. 1 (Winter 1994): 39-46.

The "panoptican" was an eighteenth century prison reform that put inmates in clean, well-lighted, transparent cells where they were under constant surveillance without being able to see the prison warden or to know whether they were being observed. Such an "unscrupulous" method of interrogation led to extreme cases of paranoia. In Foucault's analysis of the panoptican, which Bak then applies to Gilman's story, the "faceless gaze" leads to a punishment worse than a dungeon, just as the rest cure, with its forced inactivity and isolation, can be worse than the disease. The "faceless gaze" Gilman's narrator suffers brings about the madness which is, paradoxically, her only escape.

Delamotte, Eugenia C. "Male and Female Mysteries in 'The Yellow Wallpaper.'" *Legacy* 5, no. 1 (Spring 1988): 3-14.

Delamotte uses comparisons with other gothic novels and stories to uncover hidden meanings in Gilman's work. In particular, she considers the nature of the narrator's imprisonment, the difficulty she has in making herself understood, and the claustrophobic circularity she experiences as typical of gothic fiction. The basic plot of a woman who cannot get out of the house is inverted here. Rather than depicting a "daylight world apprehended as nightmare," Gilman shows us "a nightmare world apprehended as merely ordinary."

Dock, Julie Bates. "'But One Expects That': Charlotte Perkins Gilman's 'The Yellow Wallpaper' and the Shifting Light of Scholarship." *PMLA* 111, no. 1 (January 1996): 52-65.

Dock reviews the critical history of Gilman's story for evidence that feminist scholars have not been as "watchful" about textual inconsistencies as they should be. Dock begins by noting that several major reprints claim to be based on the wrong editions, a not insignificant mistake given variations in wording and section breaks which have been used to justify particular interpretations. She then compares the two versions of the story's publication history—Gilman's own from her diary and that of William Dean Howells. Though it is not known which version is correct, feminist scholars have chosen to credit Gilman's. They have also accepted Gilman's assertion that her story led Dr. S. Weir Mitchell to change his treatment of nervous prostration, even though there is no evidence for this claim outside her autobiography. Finally, Dock notes repeated misinformation about the story's reception, which insists that its first readers saw it as a gothic thriller and did not appreciate its feminist message. Dock provides several examples of 1899 reviews which did discuss the story's sexual politics and the narrator's madness as the product of her narrow and isolated life. Dock concludes that once having cast Gilman in the role of "beleaguered heroine," it is not surprising that feminist scholars then looked for and found evidence to bolster their own biases.

Golden, Catherine, ed. *The Captive Imagination: A Casebook on The Yellow Wallpaper*. New York: The Feminist Press at City University of New York, 1992.

This volume contains the text of Gilman's novella, several essays on its historical sources, including "Fat and Blood," Dr. S. Weir Mitchell's description of his famous rest cure, and Gilman's own explanation for why she decided to dramatize her experience. There are also fifteen reprints of journal articles and book chapters, most originally published in the 1980's, including pieces by Golden, Kennard, and Shumaker annotated here.

_____. "The Writing of *The Yellow Wallpaper*: A Double Palimpsest." *Studies in American Fiction* 17, no. 2 (Autumn 1989): 193-201.

Building on previous analyses of the wallpaper pattern as a dominant text and the woman behind it as a subtext, Golden adds that the dramatic action of the story can also be seen as a dominant text and the writing of the story as a second, muted text in which the narrator fictionalizes herself. As the story unfolds, the narrator's writing ceases to match her thoughts and actions. By closely following the narrator's references to "I" and to "John" or "him," we can see a positive change in the narrator's self-presentation precisely when her actions appear the most insane. As the "fictionalized self creeps deeper into madness," the narrator defiantly banishes "him" to the "outer boundaries of her sentence!"

Hill, Mary A. *Charlotte Perkins Gilman: The Making of a Radical Feminist, 1860-1896*. Philadelphia: Temple University Press, 1980.

Hill sees Gilman as a "brilliant" and psychologically complex woman whose life and writings have great historical significance. The biography, which includes a bibliography and extensive source notes, focuses on the origins of Gilman's feminist convictions and the patterns of her early life, beginning with the intellectual influence of her Beecher relatives and the emotional impact of her parents' separation. At fifteen, Gilman was a "dynamo," academically and physically; a few years later she became moody and depressed with signs of the mental illness which would plague the early years of marriage and motherhood. Hill follows Gilman to California, detailing the development of new relationships and the progress of her growing career, leading to the publication of *Women and Economics*. At thirty-eight Gilman had become a well-known and inspiring public figure who had endured "public

condemnation for her unconventional behavior" and continued to be plagued by self-doubts.
Note: Hill has not yet published a planned second volume to the biography; however, she has edited and annotated *A Journey from Within: The Love Letters of Charlotte Perkins Gilman, 1897-1900*, Lewisburg, Pa.: Bucknell University Press, 1995, a compilation of the passionate twenty- to thirty-page letters Gilman wrote almost daily to Houghton Gilman in the years before they married.

Hume, Beverly A. "Gilman's 'Interminable Grotesque': The Narrator of 'The Yellow Wallpaper.'" *Studies in Short Fiction* 28, no. 4 (Fall 1991): 477-484.
Hume contrasts Gilman's autobiographical and fictional accounts of her rest cure experience to argue that the narrator of "The Yellow Wallpaper" is a grotesque figure Gilman intentionally characterized as a warning to her readers against becoming unduly obsessed with oppressive cultural or psychological circumstances. Gilman herself "survived" the rest cure. Apparently, she believed its brutality could best be dramatized through a darkly humorous treatment in which the husband is portrayed as a comic figure. Though the narrator is a writer, in failing to recognize the "grotesque proportions" of the wallpaper, she, unlike the true author of the story, becomes a madwoman.

Johnson, Greg. "Gilman's Gothic Allegory: Rage and Redemption in 'The Yellow Wallpaper.'" *Studies in Short Fiction* 26, no. 4. (Fall 1989): 521-530.
Johnson sees the story as haunted by the shadow text of *Jane Eyre*. The wallpaper represents the narrator's repressed desire; in trying to tear it down, she is attempting to eliminate the rebellious self which threatens her "ego ideal" rather than to free herself from male oppression. The story ends with the apparent victory of the "conforming self," which reduces the narrator to a helpless, infantile creature, who ironically triumphs over her husband. The husband then, like Rochester, will be chained to a madwoman, "the logical product of his own ideology." The real victory for readers is the survival of the text itself, which Johnson hopes can be kept "open" with "all possible meanings in play."

Karpinski, Joanne B. *Critical Essays on Charlotte Perkins Gilman.* Boston: G. K. Hall, 1992.
This volume contains early reviews and discussions of Gilman's work, plus excerpts from memoirs. There are also ten modern essays which include reprints and revisions of journal articles and book chapters as well as several new pieces written for this volume. It is an eclectic selection with essays on Gilman's poetry and journalism, on the diaries of her first husband, and comparisons of her work with *Gulliver's Travels* and the writings of Olive Schreiner.

Kennard, Jean E. "Convention Coverage of How to Read Your Own Life." *New Literary History* 13 (Autumn 1981): 69-88.

When originally written, "The Yellow Wallpaper" was considered a "Poesque tale of chilling horror" and a case study of developing insanity; in the 1970's readers and critics began to focus on the narrator and to interpret her "descent into madness as a way to health." Kennard elaborates on some of the feminist conventions which led to such a different reading: the concept of male power characterized by unimaginative and obsessively rational husbands and lovers, the concept of madness as a way to truth and a higher level of sanity, and the concept of female spiritual quest as a vertical journey in search of hidden truths rather than the traditional horizontal one across the wilderness. These conventions represent reversals of older ones perceived as "oppressive" because they clearly conflicted with the real-life experience of new communities of readers. Kennard examines how and why these conventions developed with reference to the work of Virginia Woolf, Margaret Atwood, Adrienne Rich, Ken Kesey, Doris Lessing, and many other twentieth century writers.

Kessler, Carol Farley. *Charlotte Perkins Gilman: Her Progress Toward Utopia with Selected Writings*. Syracuse, N.Y.: Syracuse University Press, 1995.

This text includes fourteen short utopian texts by Gilman following four chapters by Kessler in which she builds on her own previous work (see annotation above) in an attempt to place Gilman's utopian writing firmly in the context of her life. After a brief discussion of the significance of utopian writing and an overview of Gilman's personal history, Kessler traces the progression from Gilman's first "overtly utopian" essays, written in 1904, to her first full-blown utopian novel, *What Diantha Did*, published in 1910. She then considers the letters Gilman wrote her second husband for evidence of the process of healing which allowed her to see women as agents of social reform rather than victims.

_____. "Consider Her Ways: The Cultural Work of Charlotte Perkins Gilman's Pragmatopian Stories, 1908-1913," in *Utopian and Science Fiction by Women*, ed. Jane L. Donawerth and Carol A. Kolmerten. Syracuse, N.Y.: Syracuse University Press, 1994.

Gilman believed in the social function of literature and wrote stories which she hoped would accomplish "cultural work," that is, which would attempt to redefine the social order. Kessler looks at seven short stories, four novels, and the fragmentary "A Woman's Utopia" to demonstrate how Gilman used realism to present possible reconfigurations of gender boundaries. "Pragmatopias," unlike utopias, offer "realizable scenarios." Gilman's work pictures women filling a wide variety of roles within families, neighborhoods, and the work world to show how better use of women's abilities could benefit society as a whole.

Lancaster, Jane. "'I Could Easily Have Been an Acrobat': Charlotte Perkins Gilman and the Providence Ladies' Sanitary Gymnasium, 1881-1884." *American Transcendental Quarterly* 8, no. 1 (March 1994): 33-52.

Lancaster sees Gilman as a complex individual influenced by the spirit of the age, her own physical and psychological needs, and a range of male experts—among them two exercise gurus whose advice she followed in the three years immediately preceding her marriage. Lancaster provides background on the nineteenth century exercise movement and on the Providence Gymnasium Gilman attended. She also refers to Gilman's autobiography for evidence of how often she exercised and what kinds of exercises she did both at home and in the gym. Although she does not believe there was a direct connection between Gilman's post-marital depression and the cessation of her exercise program, Lancaster does argue that the exercise experts contributed to the mixed messages confusing Gilman and exacerbating a probable chemical imbalance. Ostensibly these experts preached autonomy, but they also promoted exercise as the path to sexual attractiveness and fertility.

Lane, Ann J. *To Herland and Beyond: The Life and Work of Charlotte Perkins Gilman.* New York: Pantheon Books, 1990.

This is a comprehensive biography based on Gilman's writings, letters, essays, published and unpublished autobiographies, and interviews with Gilman's daughter and grandchildren. The text, which includes illustrations and a bibliography, is structured around the major relationships in Gilman's life: her father and mother, her three closest female friends, her two husbands, and her daughter. There are also two chapters dedicated to Lane's analysis of Gilman's major works, including a summary of lecture topics and the main ideas in *Women and Economics*. Lane sees Gilman as the product of an extraordinary period of intellectual and political ferment and of her own personal struggle to maintain emotional stability. Ultimately, her marriage to her cousin, Houghton Gilman, enabled her to balance her need for autonomy and public recognition with her desire for a meaningful intimate relationship.

Meyering, Sheryl L., ed. *Charlotte Perkins Gilman: The Woman and Her Work.* Ann Arbor, Mich.: UMI Research Press, 1989.

This is a collection of fourteen essays, ten of which are reprints of journal articles and book chapters, almost all published between 1979 and 1986; annotations of the Kennard, Shumaker, and Wilson pieces are included here. The essays focus on Gilman's "seminal ideas," such as the importance of meaningful work for women, the suffocating effects of limiting women to a domestic sphere, and the double bind faced by women who would be artists.

Peyser, Thomas Galt. "Reproducing Utopia: Charlotte Perkins and *Herland.*" *Studies in American Fiction* 20, no. 1 (Spring 1992): 1-16.
 Peyser argues that *Herland* inverts patriarchal thought, rather than deconstructing it; that its ideals hold up a "discontented mirror" to patriarchy, rather than true opposition. The essential truth of humanity is preserved in the blood, according to Gilman, and threatened by historical contingencies which water it down over time. The oppression of women is wrong because it is against "nature." *Herland* leaves intact a center of power with women as producers; men are reduced to the role of onlookers because they cannot bear children. This is a "rearguard" view of the future, not a radical one, Peyser concludes.

Scharnhorst, Gary. *Charlotte Perkins Gilman.* Boston: Twayne, 1995.
 Scharnhorst offers a straightforward analysis of Gilman's poetry and fiction with a chronology of her life and an annotated bibliography.

Shumaker, Conrad. "'Too Terribly Good to Be Printed': Charlotte Perkins Gilman's 'The Yellow Wallpaper,'" in *Charlotte Perkins Gilman: The Woman and Her Work,* ed. Sheryl L. Meyering. Ann Arbor, Mich.: UMI Research Press, 1989.
 Shumaker focuses on Gilman's work both as a "complex work of art" and as an "effective indictment of the nineteenth century view of the sexes." Despite critics' insistence on the story's isolation from the dominant issues of the nineteenth century, Shumaker sees it as posing questions about the relationship between art and imagination which have a long history in American literature. Gilman, in effect, is warning her readers about the danger of identifying the useful and the practical as male, and devaluing the imagination as female and therefore weak. This message is conveyed with great skill, according to Shumaker, who analyzes Gilman's masterful use of "associations, foreshadowing, and even humor."

Smith, Marsha A. "The Disoriented Male Narrator and Societal Conversion: Charlotte Perkins Gilman's Feminist Utopian Vision." *American Transcendental Quarterly* 3, no. 1 (March 1989): 123-133.
 Smith analyzes Gilman's use of male narrators in her three utopias— *Moving the Mountain, Herland,* and *With Her in Ourland*—all of which depict women awakening to their own interior power and men renouncing the use of oppressive power. Because female subjectivity was understood as madness by most readers of *The Yellow Wallpaper,* Gilman may have turned to a male narrator as a safer, more acceptable literary position from which to tell a story. Moreover, a male narrator could demonstrate male comprehension of the female need for love and work, a male narrator could experience the change in the female gaze, and a male narrator could embody the role of the "new man" who was as important to Gilman's vision as the "new woman."

Wilson, Christopher P. "Charlotte Perkins Gilman's Steady Burghers: The Terrain of *Herland.*" *Women's Studies* 12 (1986): 271-292.
Wilson begins with the premise that Gilman's work is not very enjoyable as literature because she intentionally avoided adventure and romance, not because she did not care about aesthetics. Gilman wrote about aesthetics in *The Forerunner* and implemented her literary ideas in fiction. *Herland*, in particular, in terms of both style and content, establishes significant connections between Gilman's artistic practices and her ideological positions. For example, on one level the novel is a satire of expeditions with chapter titles functioning as puns on the "imperial and sexual designs" behind conventional narrative development. The novel also undermines conventional expectations about self-realization and individualism; names are unimportant, *Herland* women show very little ego, and mothers do not coo over their own babies. Moreover, the narrator's "near inability" to tell a tale reflects Gilman's distrust of "expressiveness" as a male trait. Gilman believed in a society of good worker bees whose selfhood would be subsumed by communal activity. She expressed this belief in a "plain," self-effacing style which rejected overtly literary affects.

EMMA GOLDMAN
1869-1940
Goldman was born in Russia; by the age of thirteen she was forced by poverty to work in St. Petersburg factories. Still, she found time to read European literature and to learn about the new political philosophies taking hold in intellectual circles. In 1886 Goldman joined her married sister in America and soon became active in anarchist circles. She wrote and lectured on workers' rights, birth control, the failure of American justice, and the social importance of contemporary European and British drama. She was arrested several times as a political agitator and forced into exile in 1919. Goldman's monthly publication, *Mother Earth* (1906-1917), published political and satirical pieces, poetry, literary excerpts, and book reviews. Following her deportation, Goldman returned to the Soviet Union, where her "disillusionment" led to a book on Russia (1923) and a political autobiography, *Living My Life* (1931). Repeatedly refused entrance to the United States, except for a brief lecture tour in 1934, Goldman died in Canada. However, she was allowed a burial in Chicago near the graves of her Haymarket "comrades," whose "unjust execution" she had used to begin her autobiography.

Reissued Editions
Anarchism and Other Essays. New York: Gordon Press, 1972.

Living My Life: An Autobiography of Emma Goldman. Irvine, Calif.: Reprint Services, 1991.

My Disillusionment in Russia. Irvine, Calif.: Reprint Services, 1991.

Red Emma Speaks: An Emma Goldman Reader, 3rd. ed. Atlantic Highlands, N.J.: Humanities Press, 1996.

The Social Significance of Modern Drama. New York: Applause Theater Books, 1987.

Biography and Commentary

Chalberg, John. *Emma Goldman: American Individualist.* New York: HarperCollins, 1991.
This volume in the Library of American Biography includes a bibliographic listing by types of sources. Chalberg sees Goldman as a passionate woman whose criticisms of everything from "corporate capitalism" to "marriage and family life" to all forms of both totalitarianism and democracy are still relevant today. Goldman was a very American anarchist who embraced the individualism of Jefferson and Thoreau and who had a lifelong love/hate relationship with the country to which she immigrated as a young girl. Goldman resisted commitments of any sort and paid for the resulting personal autonomy with periods of solitude and emptiness. Chalberg describes the main events, relationships, joys, and sorrows of Goldman's life, concluding that in both love and revolution it was an existence marked by extreme successes and defeats.

Falk, Candace Serena. *Love, Anarchy, and Emma Goldman.* New Brunswick, N.J.: Rutgers University Press, 1990.
This is a revision of a 1984 biography with illustrations and a bibliography. Falk's accidental discovery of Goldman's love letters to Ben Reitman led her on a six-year investigation and discovery of more than 40,000 documents by or about Emma Goldman in libraries and personal collections all over the world. Goldman wrote up to ten letters a day for much of her life; the letters reveal the daring and defiance with which she responded to political repression, in contrast to the desperation and sense of abandonment with which she responded to rejection from men she loved. Falk provides historical context for the letters she has chosen and fleshes out portraits of people and events referred to in the letters, but, for the most part, lets them speak for themselves. The book itself is organized around themes which highlight the relationships between gender, culture, politics, and love in Goldman's life.

Morton, Marian J. *Emma Goldman and the American Left: 'Nowhere at Home.'"* New York: Twayne, 1992.
This volume in Twayne's Twentieth Century American Biography series includes a chronology, bibliography, and a history of the Jewish roots of Russian radicalism. It is a political biography which connects Goldman's personal story to the history of anarchism within the context of the American left. Morton takes the title for her book from Goldman's autobiography, which she wrote in a spirit of loneliness as

an exile who had seen the anarchist movement to which she had dedicated her life in retreat following the defeat of the republicans during the 1936-1939 Spanish Civil War. Morton relies on Goldman's autobiography and her other published writings to trace the development of her political philosophy and to assess her aspirations and fears, friendships and accomplishments. Despite Goldman's own sense of self as a radical "nowhere at home," Morton sees her as a major figure who both defied and influenced the major political and social currents of her life.

Shulman, Alix Kates. "Dancing in the Revolution: Emma Goldman's Feminism." *Socialist Review* 62 (March-April 1982): 31-44.

Shulman sees Goldman as a sexual radical who denounced the "internal tyrants" that cripple women, yet opposed suffrage because she saw it as a diversion from the "real struggle." Goldman herself was a "stunning speaker" and a political leader of "immense energy and vitality." She was an important role model despite her impatience with women who could not or did not follow her example. Shulman notes that Goldman was far more sympathetic to the plight of prostitutes and working-class women than she was to the concerns of middle-class wives. Ultimately, she wanted women to take responsibility for their own lives instead of trying to improve or purify men.

Solomon, Martha. *Emma Goldman*. Boston: G. K. Hall, 1987.

This volume in Twayne's United States Authors series includes a chronology, annotated bibliography, and essays which discuss Goldman's political and philosophical essays, her autobiographical books, her analyses of European drama, and her lectures. Solomon provides an overview of Goldman's major writings and lecture tours with an evaluation of her individual successes and the reasons for her failures. Solomon believes that Goldman's sarcasm and obvious disdain for her audience antagonized many of the people she sought to convert. Though she won few recruits to anarchism as a political philosophy, Goldman did play a major role in increasing public awareness of pressing social problems.

Waldstreicher, David. *Emma Goldman*. New York: Chelsea House, 1990.

This illustrated volume in the Radcliffe American Women of Achievement series for young readers includes a chronology and brief bibliography. Waldstreicher begins with Goldman's arrest as a leading figure in the 1893 worker uprisings and ends with her efforts on behalf of a jailed anarchist threatened with deportation to Fascist Italy. The focus throughout the biography is on Goldman's political activities, the causes she embraced, and her most important writings and speeches, including the publication of *Mother Earth*. Waldstreicher calls Goldman the "queen of anarchy" and credits her "fierce commitment to the ideals of freedom and equality" with making it less likely that those in power will abuse the rights of workers, women, and minorities.

Wexler, Alice. *Emma Goldman in America*. Boston: Beacon Press, 1984.
This comprehensive biography includes illustrations and a bibliography. Wexler begins by describing Goldman's family background in the context of the persecution experienced by nineteenth century Russian Jews. She ends with Goldman's arrest and exile along with hundreds of other immigrant "radicals." Wexler sees Goldman as a woman who "never made peace either with the world or with herself." The focus of the biography is both on her personal struggles and on the legacy of a life dedicated to "free speech, free labor, free thought, free love."

_____. *Emma Goldman in Exile*. Boston: Beacon Press, 1989.
This sequel to the foregoing biography focuses on the last twenty years of Goldman's life. Wexler begins by describing Goldman's deportation and her two years of exile in Russia, where she became increasingly disillusioned by communism. She then looks at her anti-communist activities, her personal relationships, her on-going search for a meaningful public role, the writing of her autobiography as an attempt to create something "solid" out of the "ashes" of her life, and her involvement in the Spanish Civil War. Because of the extensive correspondence Goldman maintained during these years, Wexler was able to base her work on "mountains of letters" as well as personal interviews with many of Goldman's friends and acquaintances. Ultimately, according to Wexler, her book is a history of anarchism in America as well as the portrait of a lonely, older woman forced to live in exile.

ALICE HAMILTON
1869-1970
Hamilton, the second of five children, was born in New York City and raised in Fort Wayne, Indiana. She attended Miss Porter's School in Farmington, Connecticut, and the Fort Wayne College of Medicine before receiving her M.D. from the University of Michigan in 1893. Her scientific training included internships at the Northwestern Hospital for Women and Children and the New England Hospital for Women and Children, and a postgraduate year at the Johns Hopkins Medical School. She returned to Northwestern in 1897 as a professor of pathology and lived at Hull House where she soon became involved in discussions of trade unions and social programs to help the poor. In 1908 Hamilton was appointed to the Illinois Commission on Occupational Diseases, in 1910 she was named supervisor for a survey of industrial poisons, and in 1911 she was hired as a special investigator for the United States Bureau of Labor. By 1916, Hamilton was the leading American authority on lead poisoning and had earned a

reputation as a crusader for public health. After attending the second International Congress of Women in Zurich, Hamilton began her position as assistant professor of industrial medicine at the Harvard Medical School; she was the first woman faculty member ever hired by Harvard University. Her first book, *Industrial Poisons in the United States*, summarizing forty years of research, was published in 1934 and was followed by her autobiography, *Exploring the Dangerous Trades* in 1943. Despite forced retirement from Harvard in 1935, Hamilton remained politically active, serving a stint as president of the National Consumers' League (1944-1949), and continued to receive many honorary degrees and awards. Her most important legacies may prove to be the adoption of both the federal Mine Safety and Health Act in 1969 and the Occupational Safety and Health Act in 1970.

Reissued Editions
Exploring the Dangerous Trades: The Autobiography of Alice Hamilton. Boston: Northeastern University Press, 1985.

Hamilton and Hardy's Industrial Toxicology. Saint Louis, Mo.: Year Book Medical Publishers, 1985.

Biography and Commentary
Glazer, Penina Migdal, and Miriam Slater. "The Promise of New Opportunities in Science," in *Unequal Colleagues: The Entrance of Women into the Professions, 1890-1940.* New Brunswick, N.J.: Rutgers University Press, 1987.
    Alice Hamilton, as viewed by the authors, is representative of the first generation of women who wanted to move beyond the amateur societies where women scientists had previously gathered and claim their place among the professionals. Hamilton was led to research on industrial poisons partly because of the "accident" of moving to Chicago. When she eventually accepted an appointment as a federal investigator, Hamilton understood it meant never returning to laboratory science, with its prestige and financial rewards. Improving the conditions in America's factories was slow and difficult work, devalued as "socialism" or "feminine sentimentality for the poor." However, as industrial disease spread with the growth of the chemical and dye factories, the field of industrial medicine became increasingly important, with Hamilton as its undisputed leader. She was, therefore, the "only" possible candidate to fill a new position at Harvard University. Despite breaking new ground as the "first" woman faculty member at Harvard, she was unable to persuade the Medical School to admit women. The authors conclude that Hamilton understood fully the degree to which she was treated as a token superperformer whose presence, in a sense, made it even harder for the next generation to follow in her footsteps.

McPherson, Stephanie Sammartino. *The Worker's Detective: A Story about Dr. Alice Hamilton.* Minneapolis: Carolrhoda Books, 1992.

This is a children's book with hand-drawn illustrations and a bibliography. McPherson focuses on Hamilton as a doctor, social worker, and peace activist who saw herself as the person to get things done, and credits her with "single-handedly" improving the life and health of American workers.

Richards, Dell. "Alice Hamilton," in *Superstars: Twelve Lesbians Who Changed the World*. New York: Carroll & Graf, 1993.

Richards offers a biographical essay and chronology of Hamilton's life and career which emphasizes her relationship with her sister, Edith, and with the women of Hull House. Both Julia Lathrop, one of Hull House's original residents, and Jane Addams were important sources of inspiration to Hamilton. Addams was her "mentor," the person who most stimulated Hamilton's commitment to social justice; Lathrop taught her "negotiating and diplomatic skills," and the value of using facts rather than rhetoric to win supporters. Like many women of her era, Hamilton lived in a "female-only subculture." Unlike most women, however, all four of the Hamilton sisters chose careers over marriage, not even returning home to help care for an aging father.

Rosner, David, and Gerald Markowitz, eds. *Dying for Work: Workers' Safety and Health in Twentieth century America*. Bloomington: Indiana University Press, 1987.

This collection of essays establishes the historical climate in which Hamilton performed her research. Rosner and Markowitz's "A Gift of God? The Public Health Controversy over Leaded Gasoline During the 1920s" and Ruth Heifetz's "Women, Lead, and Reproductive Hazards: Defining a New Risk" deal directly with Hamilton's contributions.

Sicherman, Barbara. *Alice Hamilton: A Life in Letters*. Cambridge, Mass.: Harvard University Press, 1984.

Hamilton's voluminous correspondence with friends and colleagues is filled with "keen perceptions, intensity of feeling, and a wit that was sometimes wicked," thus providing a more personal view of her life and career than the carefully guarded public view of her autobiography. Early letters discuss her concern to find a true vocation in life and to balance ambition with family obligations. Other letters demonstrate her efforts to persuade businessmen to improve working conditions in their factories and document her involvement in a variety of social causes. We learn about her medical education, her debates with Felix Frankfurter over civil liberties, her work with Jane Addams, and her changing sense of self as she became more prominent, all in her own words. Sicherman describes her book as an "integrated work of biography and letters" for which the historian's job was to provide context and to interpret the "essential meaning" of Hamilton's life. Sicherman has also included an introductory biographical essay, extensive source notes, a Hamilton family tree, and a small selection of photographs.

JULIA WARD HOWE
1819-1910

Howe was born into a prominent New York family, the fourth of seven children. Her mother died of tuberculosis when Julia was only five. Primarily self-taught, as a young woman Howe published essays on German and French writers in the *New York Review* and *Theological Review*. At age twenty-three, Julia married a wealthy philanthropist and social activist in his early forties. The couple settled in Boston and had six children, the youngest of whom died of diphtheria at the age of three. Disenchanted with marriage and her husband's opposition to her writing, Howe turned inward and began to read religion and philosophy. She published two books of poetry anonymously, *Passion-flowers* (1854) and *Words for the Hour* (1857), and produced one play, *Leonora, or the World's Own* (1857), before achieving fame with "Battle Hymn of the Republic," for which quickly became known throughout the North following its 1862 publication in *The Atlantic Monthly*. It was after the war that Howe found her niche in the developing women's movement. She was a founder of the New England Women's Club, the New England Woman Suffrage Association, and the weekly *Woman's Journal*, which she served as editor for many years. Howe wrote articles in support of women in education, the arts, and the professions, and was a frequent speaker at conventions and legislative hearings. She founded women's clubs all over the United States and was an ardent promoter of international peace, serving as director and vice president of the American Peace Society. Many of Howe's lectures were later collected; in 1883 she completed a biography of Margaret Fuller, and in 1899 she published *Reminiscences*. By the time of her death Howe had become a national institution and unofficial poet laureate whose burial was attended by the governor of Massachusetts and other dignitaries. She was the first woman elected to the American Academy of Arts and Letters.

Reissued Editions
In 1990 and 1992, Reprint Services of Irvine, Calif., issued a fourteen-volume set of Howe's collected works.

Biography and Commentary
Clifford, Deborah Pickman. *Mine Eyes Have Seen the Glory; A Biography of Julia Ward Howe*. Boston: Little, Brown, 1979.

This comprehensive illustrated biography includes extensive source notes and a bibliography. Clifford offers a close look at Howe's stormy marriage and at the historical context behind her poetry and her mastery of the lecture platform.

Grant, Mary H. *Private Woman, Public Person: An Account of the Life of Julia Ward Howe from 1819 to 1868*. Brooklyn, N.Y.: Carlson, 1994.

This volume in Carlson's Scholarship in Women's History series offers a detailed analysis of Howe's private letters and journals. Grant also examines Howe's unpublished novel, *Eva and Raphael,* which dealt with taboo subjects such as rape, madness, and androgyny. In looking for the formative influences behind Howe's later commitment to women's causes, Grant uncovers a freer, more creative, and more powerful individual than the formal *persona* known by the public. Extensive notes and a bibliography are appended.

McCabe, Tracy. "Avenging Angel: Tragedy and Womanhood in Julia Ward Howe's *The World's Own.*" *Legacy* 12, no. 2 (1995): 98-111.
    McCabe offers her analysis of this 1857 play as a "tragedy" with a "remarkable female subtext." The ending of the play leaves the female protagonists—like Thelma and Louise, their contemporary cinema counterparts—with nowhere to go after they have taken revenge on the male characters and the male construction of womanhood.

Ream, Debbie Williams. "Mine Eyes Have Seen the Glory (J. W. Howe)." *American History Illustrated* 27 (January-February 1993): 60-64.
    This illustrated article provides a complete history of Howe's writing of her most famous poem and of its inspirational impact on the Civil War.

Schreiber, Mary Suzanne. "Julia Ward Howe and the Travel Book." *New England Quarterly* 62 (June 1989): 264-279.
    Schreiber examines Howe's role as one of the first women to write travel books, a popular nineteenth century literary form, and the empathy she expressed for women throughout the world who suffered from their status as second-class citizens.

Wallace, James D. "Hawthorne and the Scribbling Women Reconsidered." *American Literature* 62 (June 1990): 201-222.
    Wallace believes that Hawthorne's ambivalence about women writers and about Howe's poetry, in particular, reflects the complexity of his feelings about his own work. Hawthorne's evaluation of *Passion Flowers* ranged from "genuine delight" in Howe's exposure of family secrets to "righteous indignation" at her indiscretion. He saw her work as highly original, "impulsive, transgressive, and passionate." Wallace assumes Hawthorne was pleased by its break with the traditions of both English poetry and American domesticity.

SUSANNE K. LANGER
1895-1985
    Langer, one of five children, was raised in New York City in a highly intellectual and artistic environment. Both of her parents were born in Germany and spoke German at home. Langer graduated from Radcliffe College with a degree in philosophy in 1920 and married Willian Leonard Langer, a Harvard graduate student of history, the

following year. After a year spent studying in Vienna, Langer began graduate school and earned a Ph.D. from Harvard in 1926. Over the next fifteen years, Langer taught philsophy at Radcliffe and occasionally at Smith and Wellesley Colleges as well. Langer's first book was a study of myth and fantasy, *The Cruise of the Little Dipper, and Other Fairy Tales* (1924). Her first philosophical treatises were *The Practice of Philosophy* (1930) and *An Introduction to Symbolic Logic* (1937). With the publication of *Philosophy in a New Key: A Study in the Symbolism of Reason, Rite, and Art* (1942) and *Language and Myth* (1946), her translation of the German philosopher Ernst Cassirer's 1925 work, Langer became known as a leading figure in the field of aesthetics. From 1945 to 1950 Langer taught at Columbia University, where she received a Rockefeller Foundation Grant to write *Feeling and Form: A Theory of Art* (1953). This text further developed her theories of symbolism and logic in defining such terms as expression, creation, symbol, and intuition with respect to each of the various art forms. In 1954 Langer was named chair of the Philosophy Department at Connecticut College where she remained until her retirement in 1962. Her final project, the culmination of her life's work, was the three-volume *Mind: An Essay on Human Feeling* (1967, 1972, 1982). Langer received numerous awards and honorary doctorates throughout her career and in 1960 was elected to the American Academy of Arts and Sciences.

Reissued Edition
Mind: An Essay on Human Feeling (abridged edition). Baltimore: Johns Hopkins University Press, 1988.

Biography and Commentary
Curran, Trisha. *A New Note on the Film: A Theory of Film Criticism Derived from Susanne K. Langer's Philosophy of Art*. Salem, N.H.: Arno Press, 1980.

Curran makes use of three of Langer's key conceptions: the creation of an apparition, the achievement of organic unity, and the articulation of feeling. She suggests that film critics ask the same questions Langer proposed for drama critics—what has the artist done and how did s/he do it?

Danto, Arthur C. "Mind as Feeling, Form as Presence: Langer as Philosopher." *The Journal of Philosophy* 81 (November 1984): 641-646.

Danto traces the evolution of Langer's thinking on "feelings" which she originally defined as "nondiscursive urges" with rituals as their "outward forms." Later works by Langer look at a much more broadly conceived "empire of feeling," with thought, perception, imagination, understanding, and emotion among its many provinces. Langer's major contribution to philosophy, according to Danto, was to have recognized and begun analysis of complex relationships between self and world, feeling and thought, and sense and stimulus.

De Sousa, Ronald B. "Teleology and the Great Shift." *The Journal of Philosophy* 81 (November 1984): 647-653.
　　De Sousa compares Langer's analysis of the shift from animal behavior to human mentality with current ideas about the role of teleology in this shift. In particular, he focuses on the four principles Langer established to explain the shift and her explanation of the progression from "quasi-intentionality" to "full-fledged mentality."

Gill, Jerry H. "Langer, Language, and Art." *International Philosophical Quarterly* 34, no. 4 (December 1994): 419-432.
　　Gill praises Langer's construction of a "comprehensive and articulate" philosophy of art but warns of inconsistencies which result from the absolutist distinction she makes between "language" and "art" as the discursive as opposed to expressive functions of symbolic communication. Missing in her thinking, according to Gill, is a "conceptual bridge" between bodily gesture and onomatopoeia. As a result, her philosophy is more appropriate to analysis of dance than to that of poetry.

Hapberg, Garry. "Art and the Unsayable: Langers's Tractarian Aesthetics." *British Journal of Aesthetics* 24 (1984): 325+.
　　Hapberg reviews Langer's theory that art is a creation of forms which move beyond the limits of language in symbolizing human feeling.

Morawski, Stefan. "Art as Semblance." *The Journal of Philosophy* 81 (November 1984): 654-662.
　　Morawski evaluates the strengths and weaknesses of Langer's philosophy of art. He concludes that her analysis of "semblance" as the "main constituent of art" holds true in light of later theories.

MARGARET MEAD
1901-1978

　　Mead was born in Philadelphia to a family of educators. She began her undergraduate education at DePauw University, then transferred to Barnard College, where she met the anthropologists Franz Boas and Ruth Benedict. With their encouragement Mead began field work in American Samoa, where she used the participant observer method developed by the British anthropologist Stanislaw Malinowski to study adolescent girls. Upon returning to the United States, Mead completed her Ph.D. at Columbia University and published *Coming of Age in Samoa* (1928), which became an overnight success for its description of a world free of many of the stresses of Western adolescence, in which both boys and girls were taught to appreciate their own sexuality. *Sex and Temperament in Three Primitive Societies* (1935) and *Male and Female: A Study of the Sexes in a Changing World* (1949) continued Mead's work on the process by which cultures establish behavioral norms for men and women. In 1935 Mead divorced her second husband and collaborator, Reo Fortune, and married Gregory

Bateson, with whom she had worked in New Guinea. The two then went to Bali, where they pioneered the use of photographs and films as tools for anthropological research. Mead, along with other social scientists throughout the country, provided controversial intelligence work for government agencies during World War II and later joined Columbia University's Research in Contemporary Cultures think tank, funded by the Office of Navy Research. Mead also worked at the American Museum of Natural History from 1926 to 1969, becoming curator in 1964. In the last twenty-five years of her life she taught part-time at Columbia and held a variety of visiting professorships. She was elected president of the World Federation of Mental Health (1956-1957), the American Anthropological Association (1960), and the American Association for the Advancement of Science (1960). In addition to her scholarly achievements, Mead wrote a monthly column for *Redbook* magazine in which she discussed social problems, the future of the family, and child-rearing practices. During her celebrated lifetime, Mead made ten films and published thirty-four books, including her popular autobiography, *Blackberry Winter* (1972). She was awarded posthumously the Presidential Medal of Freedom.

Reissued Editions
Blackberry Winter: My Earlier Years. New York: Kodansha International, 1995.

Coming of Age in Samoa. Magnolia, Mass.: Peter Smith, 1978.

Growing Up in New Guinea. New York: Morrow, 1980.

Kinship in the Admiralty Islands. New York: Howard Fertig, 1992.

Letters from the Field 1925-1975. New York: Harper & Row, 1979.

Male and Female: A Study of the Sexes in a Changing World. Westport, Conn.: Greenwood Press, 1977.

Sex and Temperament in Three Primitive Societies. New York: Morrow, 1980.

Biography and Commentary
Bateson, Mary Catherine. *With a Daughter's Eye: A Memoir of Margaret Mead and Gregory Bateson.* New York: Morrow, 1984.
    This illustrated biography offers an intimate recollection of the author's parents. Bateson, herself an anthropologist, describes an extraordinary childhood marked by the pain of her parents' separation and divorce as well as the joys of the extended family and richly textured world in which she was raised. She also traces the separate paths taken by each of her parents and the complex ties that continued

to bind them together until their deaths. A brief bibliography of primary and secondary works is appended.

Cassidy, Robert. *Margaret Mead: A Voice for the Century.* New York: Universe Books, 1982.
   This is a relatively brief biography which surveys Mead's life and ideas and includes a bibliography of her major works. Cassidy sees Mead as an important role model and counselor for American women. Her popularity derived from her "uncanny ability" to provide commonsense solutions to problems which seemed overwhelming and to describe diverse cultures in terms of basic practices such as toilet training and paternal child-rearing roles.

Foerstel, Lenora, and Angela Gilliam, eds. *Confronting the Margaret Mead Legacy: Scholarship, Empire, and the South Pacific.* Philadelphia: Temple University Press, 1992.
   This is a collection of ten articles, including several by Pacific Islanders and an overview of Mead's career by the two editors. They criticize both Mead and Freeman (see below) for abstracting presumably "timeless" cultural practices from the reality of changing social contexts and for believing they could fully understand a complex culture after a few months of field work. Mead's legacy is ultimately a mixed one. She deserves credit for helping to debunk behavioral theories based on race and biology and encouraging serious study of the influence of culture on human behavior. She deserves blame for contributing to the stereotyping of Pacific peoples and betraying her own commitment to cultural autonomy with her uncritical support of U.S. government policies. In particular, Foerstel and Gilliam accuse Mead of "ignoring the devastating consequences" of nuclear testing in the Pacific and promoting "westernization" as the only path to progress.

Freeman, Derek. *Margaret Mead and Samoa: The Making and Unmaking of an Anthropological Myth.* Cambridge, Mass.: Harvard University Press, 1983.
   Freeman offers a detailed refutation of Mead's characterization of Samoan society. Based on this anthropologist's research, Samoan adolescence is a time of frequent stress and Samoan society is authoritarian rather than permissive, with restrictive regulations against premarital sex. Freeman explains Mead's misreading of Samoan life in the context of the debate betwen cultural and biological determinists and her relationships with her most important colleagues, Ruth Benedict and Franz Boas. He also asserts that Mead was unprepared for field work and undoubtedly misled by her adolescent informants.

Holmes, Lowell D. *Quest for the Real Samoa: The Mead/Freeman Controversy and Beyond.* South Hadley, Mass.: Bergin & Garvey, 1987.
   This book reports on Holmes's research in Samoa, where he recreated

the conditions and reexamined the conclusions of Mead's earlier work. He concludes that the validity of her research was "remarkably high" despite exaggerations typical of novice field workers. This conclusion is a direct challenge to the well-publicized critique of Mead in Derek Freeman's book (see foregoing entry).

Howard, Jane. *Margaret Mead: A Life*. New York: Simon & Schuster, 1984.

This is a comprehensive illustrated biography with primary and secondary source bibliographies and a listing of articles concerning the Mead-Freeman controversy. Howard sees Mead as an outrageous and extravagant woman who raced through life and whose work was sometimes insightful and sometimes naive. Howard quotes extensively from Mead's writings and from interviews with more than three hundred colleagues, critics, friends, and relatives. In Howard's own words, it is a "generalist" rather than an "academic" portrait.

Metraux, Rhoda. "Margaret Mead: A Biographical Sketch." *American Anthropologist* 82 (June 1980): 262-269.

This brief biographical essay was written by one of Mead's friends and collaborators from the American Museum of Natural History.

Newman, Louise M. "Coming of Age, but Not in Samoa: Reflections of Margaret Mead's Legacy for Western Liberal Feminism." *American Quarterly* 48, no. 2 (June 1996): 233-272.

Newman sees Mead as breaking with the tradition of evolutionary anthropology in her rejection of the concept of a "superior race," yet embracing belief in the cultural superiority of Western civilization. In a sense, Mead followed the nineteenth century tradition of women missionaries, explorers, and ethnographers represented by Alice Fletcher (1838-1923), a leader of the Indian reform movement. Like Fletcher and other women who worked in Africa and liberal feminists today, Mead maintained an authoritative, protective relationship with the primitive societies she studied and whom she hoped to help achieve progress in strictly "Western" terms.

ELSIE CLEWS PARSONS
1875-1941

Parsons, the first child of a wealthy New York family, graduated Phi Beta Kappa from Barnard College and earned a Ph.D. in sociology from Columbia University. In 1900, she married Herbert Parsons, a lawyer and Republican congressman, with whom she had six chldren. The children were educated by governesses and sent to private school, enabling Parsons to teach at Columbia (1899-1906), to travel extensively, and to pursue intellectual work and friendships. Parsons's first book, *The Family* (1906), was a textbook drawn from her class lectures. It was followed by *The Old Fashioned Woman* (1913), *Religious Chastity* (1913), *Fear and Conventionality* (1914), and *Social Freedom* (1915), books which focus on women's experience of social restraint in diverse cultures. While researching these works Parsons was active in radical intellectual groups and wrote articles for *The Masses, The New Republic,* and other leftist and liberal journals. Her growing interest in anthropology followed a 1910 trip to New Mexico, where she first came in contact with native peoples. Over the next thirty years Parsons returned frequently to the Southwest to gather ethnographic data about the Zuni, Laguna, Acoma, Jemez, Isleta, and Hopi Indians. Several books resulted from these studies, including the two-volume *Pueblo Indian Religion* (1939), considered her most significant contribution to anthropology. She also did research on Mexican Indian groups and on Caribbean and African American folktales. Parsons conducted some of her fieldwork with Franz Boas and is credited with advancing his methodology through her collection of large amounts of data on the Pueblo peoples. Her significance to anthropology was acknowledged with her election to the presidencies of the American Folklore Society (1918-1920), the American Ethnological Association (1923-1925), and the American Anthropological Association (1940-1941).

Reissued Editions
American Indian Life. Lincoln: University of Nebraska Press, 1991.

Educational Legislation and Administration of the Colonial Governments (1899). Salem, N.H.: Arno Press, 1991.

Isleta Paintings. Washington, D.C.: Smithsonian Institution Press, 1970.

The Old Fashioned Woman. Salem, N.H.: Arno Press, 1972.

Biography and Commentary
Babcock, Barbara. "Taking Liberties, Writing from the Margins, and Doing It with a Difference." *Journal of American Folklore* 100, no. 398 (October-December 1987): 390-411.

In her analysis of the intersections between folklore and feminist theory, Babcock looks at Helen Cordero, the Cochiti potter who invented the Storyteller doll in 1964; the Statue of Liberty as an example of a potent female body which has been used to embody an abstract male ideal; and the "indomitable" Elsie Clews Parsons. Parsons's work anticipated contemporary feminism in its recognition of the "seamless unified self at the center of patriarchal ideology." Despite the controversy generated by her life and career, Parsons's work, according to Babcock, was far more consistent than is generally acknowledged, particularly in its focus on the constraints of custom and culture on individual expression.

Friedlander, Judith. "Elsie Clews Parsons," in *Women Anthropologists: Selected Biographies,* eds. Ute Gacs, Aisha Khan, Jerrie

McIntyre, and Ruth Weinberg. Urbana: University of Illinois Press, 1989.

Friedlander notes that Parsons originally rose to fame because of her controversial sociological texts, which attacked the family for restricting individual freedom and called for trial marriages which could be easily dissolved in the absence of offspring. Today, however, she is best remembered for her detailed ethnographies of the Pueblos and Zapotecs and her collections of black folklore.

Hare, Peter H. *A Woman's Quest for Science: Portrait of Anthropologist Elsie Clews Parsons.* Buffalo, N.Y.: Prometheus, 1985.

This biography, written by Parsons's great-nephew, is credited with revitalizing research on the anthropologist. It quotes extensively from private papers not available elsewhere.

Lamphere, Louise. "Feminist Anthropology: The Legacy of Elsie Clews Parsons." *American Ethnologist* 16 (1989): 518-533.

Lamphere discusses Parsons's early feminism as separate from her anthropological work, and the important influence of Franz Boas on her thinking. She also compares Parsons's work with that of modern feminist anthropologists.

Zumwalt, Rosemary Levy. *Wealth and Rebellion: Elsie Clews Parsons, Anthropologist and Folklorist.* Urbana: University of Illinois Press, 1992.

This is a comprehensive illustrated biography with a bibliography appended. It draws extensively on Parsons's rich correspondence as well as her publications. Zumwalt looks at Parsons's work as an anthropologist, her fame as an eccentric philanthropist, and her role as the "nexus" of several important intellectual communities. The text is organized chronologically with fifteen chapters on topics including her childhood, her marriage, her feminist writings, her pacifist political activites, her anthropologist friends, her fieldwork experiences, and her contributions to the American Folklore and American Anthropology Societies.

CONSTANCE ROURKE
1885-1941

Rourke was born in Cleveland and raised in Grand Rapids, Michigan. She graduated from Vassar College in 1907 and then worked as a researcher for the Bibliothèque Nationale in Paris and the British Museum in London. Rourke taught English at Vassar from 1910 to 1915, before returning to Grand Rapids to be with her mother. Soon she began traveling through the country to collect examples of folk art for her free-lance research on American history and culture. Her first book, *Trumpets of Jubilee* (1927), examines the careers of five well-known individuals thought to have had a major impact on popular culture. *American Humor: A Study of the American Character* (1931), her most

One Hundred Years of American Women Writing

important book, is credited with legitimizing American culture as distinct from European and British, and establishing its roots in folk humor. Rourke's other books include *Troupers of the Gold Coast: Or the Rise of Lotta Crabtree* (1928), *Davy Crockett* (1934), *Audubon* (1936), and *Charles Sheeler: Artist in the American Tradition* (1938).

Reissued Editions
American Humor. Tallahassee: Florida State University Press, 1986.

Audubon. Irvine, Calif.: Reprint Services, 1993.

Troupers of the Gold Coast: Or the Rise of Lotta Crabtree. Irvine, Calif.: Reprint Services, 1992.

Biography and Commentary
Bellman, Samuel Irving. *Constance M. Rourke.* Boston: G. K. Hall, 1981.

This volume in Twayne's United States Authors series includes a chronology, bibliography, biographical essay, and analysis of all of Rourke's major works. There are chapters on Rourke's early journalistic sketches and on her last three books, each of which has an important place in "her developing picture of American cultural life," according to Bellman. Ultimately, he sees her as a "comic poet" whose lyricism, imagination, and "joyous attachment" to people of all types combined with her careful research and recording to call into being the spirit of the American character.

_____. "Where the West Begins: Constance Rourke's Images of Her Own Frontierland," in *Women and Western American Literature*, eds. Helen Winter Stauffer and Susan J. Rosowski. Troy, N.Y.: Whitston, 1982.

Bellman identifies four themes as central to the image of the Great West in Rourke's work: the impulse to "make all things new" which attracted religious and utopian reformers, the western prospect as a stimulus to the "creative imagination," the pioneering spirit in quest of open spaces, and the development of "mobile entertainers." *Trumpets of Jubilee*, which includes long biographical sketches of five easterners (Horace Greeley, P. T. Barnum, and Lyman Beecher and two of his children, Harriet and Henry Ward), considers the reasons behind their western migration and the impact it had on their beliefs and writings. *American Humor* looks at western folk stereotypes such as the "gamecock of the wilderness" exemplified by Davy Crockett and Mike Finn, and the "giant" earth mover and miracle worker; it also discusses "bands" of wandering actors, one of whom, Lotta Crabtree (1847-1924), Rourke further described in *Troupers of the Gold Coast.*

Rubin, Joan Shelley. *Constance Rourke and American Culture.* Chapel Hill: University of North Carolina Press, 1980.

This book-length study of Rourke's ideas begins with a biographical essay which identifies some of the sources behind her thinking, including the books she read and the controversies which interested her. Rubin pays particular attention to the new anthropological standards which influenced the way Rourke looked at culture. Rourke's own contribution was to show Americans as makers of their own mythology in response to the critique of the country as culturally barren. Rourke, in effect, created the notion of "American studies" and provided Americans with a sense of their own cultural unity. This "usable past" as presented by Rourke became the basis for concrete political action in the face of the growing fascism of the late 1930's and 1940's.

MARGARET SANGER
1879-1966

The sixth of eleven children, Sanger was born and raised in Corning, New York. Her mother died at the age of forty-nine, prematurely old, Sanger believed, because of the burdens of such a large family. After two years of training as a practical nurse, Sanger married an architect and had three children. The family moved to New York City in 1910 and became involved in radical politics; Margaret worked as a home nurse on the lower East Side and joined the Industrial Workers of the World (IWW), helping to organize strikes throughout the Northeast. She soon began to write articles on feminist issues and in 1914 founded the journal *The Woman Rebel*, which advocated the legalization of birth control. After the journal was confiscated, to avoid arrest Sanger fled to Europe, where she became an intimate friend of Havelock Ellis, author of *Studies in the Psychology of Sex*. She also studied the contraceptive advice centers she found in the Netherlands. When Sanger returned to the United States following the death of her daughter, she and her sister opened a birth control clinic in Brooklyn which lasted ten days before being shut down by the police. By 1921, with support from doctors and wealthy philanthropists, Sanger was able to organize the first American Birth Control Conference and establish the short-lived American Birth Control League. In the meantime, she had divorced her husband and married a millionaire manufacturer who was willing to help fund her cause. Sanger continued to fight the forces that opposed birth control throughout her life and to write about female sexuality and the problems of working-class women. Her best-known publications are listed below.

Reissued Editions

Note: Franklin Book Company of Elkins Park, Pa. in 1976 published an eight-volume set of Sanger's works including her autobiography (1938), *Happiness in Marriage* (1926), *Motherhood in Bondage* (1928), *My Fight for Birth Control* (1931), *The New Motherhood* (1934), *The Pivot of Civilization* (1922), *What Every Boy and Girl Should Know* (1927), and *Woman and the New Race* (1920). Also available are:

Happiness in Marriage. Bedford, Mass.: Applewood Books, 1993.

Margaret Sanger: An Autobiography. New York: Dover, 1971.

What Every Boy and Girl Should Know. New York: Scribner, 1980.

Biography and Commentary

Bachrach, Deborah. *The Importance of Margaret Sanger.* San Diego, Calif.: Lucent Books, 1993.

This text, one in a series of biographies for young readers about individuals who have made a "unique" contribution to history, includes photographs, a chronology, and a bibliography. Bachrach notes that Sanger's crusade "trod upon many of the most strongly held views" of the majority of Americans, and that she became increasingly "ruthless in her tactics" as she was personally threatened by hostile opposition. She also became more neglectful of her own health and more secretive about her personal life. Bachrach chooses to emphasize her struggles and her victories, rather than the dark, unconventional side to her personality, because of the "enormous contribution" she made to society. This contribution included making it acceptable to discuss publicly issues of sexuality and contraception, identifying the relationship between population growth and international conflict, and advocating for a birth control pill that would bring contraception to women in remote places.

Chesler, Ellen. *Woman of Valor: Margaret Sanger.* New York: Simon & Schuster, 1992.

This illustrated biography includes a bibliography and extensive source notes on the archival materials and interviews with family and friends on which it is based. Chesler considers both the personal and public dimensions of Sanger's life: her love affairs, her political strategies and changing political positions, her volatile temperament and the internal contradictions that made her such an interesting figure. Sanger, as described by Chesler, was both idealist and opportunist, bohemian and materialist, sexual adventurer and incurable romantic, socialist and registered Republican. In the 1920's and 1930's Sanger wrote best-selling books, published journals, and built a powerful voluntary organization. Then, as she saw the birth control movement she had created stall during the Depression and war years, Sanger became vehemently anti-Catholic and anti-Roosevelt. Above all, Sanger had a messianic faith in birth control as the best means to prevent labor unrest (by lowering the supply of workers, it would increase demand and hence wages), and to redistribute the balance of power in the bedroom, home, and larger community.

Dash, Joan. "Margaret Sanger," in *A Life of One's Own: Three Gifted Women and the Men They Married.* New York: Harper & Row, 1973.

Dash tells the story of Sanger's life and her crusade for birth control against the backdrop of her relationships with her father, her first and second husbands, and Havelock Ellis. Bill Sanger, the architect she married soon after her graduation from nursing school, tried his best to keep Margaret from divorcing him to the point of getting himself arrested for distributing her pamphlets while she was in exile in England. Noah Slee, whom she married in 1922 partly for his money and business acumen, continued to love her and to support her career, despite her indifference to his desires and needs. Marriage and motherhood were always sidelines in Sanger's life. Dash sees her as a rebellious woman dominated by a "will to power" which fortunately found a useful outlet in a worthwhile cause.

Gordon, Linda. *Woman's Body, Woman's Right: Birth Control in America*. New York: Penguin Books, 1990.

Gordon, in this revision of her 1976 text, offers a comprehensive overview of the struggle for reproductive rights. She faults Sanger for retreating from her early socialist politics and giving in to the demands of conservative groups whose support she sought.

Jensen, Joan M. "The Evolution of Margaret Sanger's *Family Limitation* Pamphlet, 1914-1921." *Signs* 6, no. 3 (Spring 1981): 548-567.

Jensen analyzes changes from the first to the tenth edition of this pamphlet (an annotated copy of the text is included) as indicative of changes in the women's movement. "Networks of left-wing women" helped produce and distribute the first version of the pamphlet, which emphasized the right of working-class women to use "family limitation" methods. In later editions Sanger replaced some of the language of class struggle, reflecting her own apparent move to the right and eventual ties to less radical middle-class women's groups. Jensen argues that the repression of the American Left during World War I may have led Sanger to more conservative supporters for pragmatic reasons; she continued to collaborate with leftists in Europe where socialists continued to dominate the women's movement.

Kennedy, David. *Birth Control in America: The Career of Margaret Sanger*. New Haven, Conn.: Yale University Press, 1970.

This is a highly critical interpetation of Sanger's work which focuses on the 1914 to 1940 period. Kennedy blames Sanger for the lack of cooperation between different groups with an interest in birth control reform.

AGNES SMEDLEY
1892-1950

Smedley was born in a two-room cabin in Missouri, the daughter of a tenant farmer, and raised in the mining district of southeastern Colorado. In 1912 she moved to San Francisco with her new husband, Ernest Brudin, and later completed her teaching education at the San Diego Normal School. While in San Diego she became interested in radical political movements after having attended lectures by Emma Goldman, the Indian nationalist Dr. Kesheva Shasti, and others. Following her divorce in 1916, she moved to Greenwich Village and was arrested two years later for her activities on behalf of both the Indian independence and birth control movements. In 1919 she traveled to Germany and the Soviet Union, where she visited Goldman. Her first major article as an aspiring journalist, "Starving Germany," was published in 1923 in *The Nation*. Her first trip to China came in 1928. Soon she was known as one of the most important journalists reporting on the Chinese Communist revolutionary movement and the Sino-Japanese War. She published hundreds of articles and worked tirelessly to obtain financial assistance for Chinese armies. Smedley's autobiographical novel, *Daughter of Earth*, was published in 1929 and soon translated into Chinese, Japanese, and German. It was followed by a collection of her articles, *Chinese Destinies* (1933), and several other books, including *China's Red Army Marches* (1934), *China Fights Back* (1938), and *Battle Hymn of China* (1943). In 1941 Smedley returned to the United States, where she joined Yaddo, the writers' colony at Saratoga Springs. Unil her death she continued to tour the country to publicize the war in China and to advocate on behalf of freedom from foreign domination for all peoples.

Reissued Editions
China's Red Army Marches. Westport, Conn.: Hyperion Press, 1977.

Chinese Destinies. Westport, Conn.: Hyperion Press, 1977.

Daughter of Earth. New York: Feminist Press of City University at New York, 1987.

Biography and Criticism
Graulich, Melodie. "Violence Against Women in Literature of the Western Family." *Frontiers* 7, no. 3 (1984): 14-20.
    Graulich identifies four texts which describe the prevalence of violence against women in the American West: Mari Sandoz's *Old Jules*, Meridel Le Sueur's *The Girl,* Tillie Olsen's *Yonnondio*, and Smedley's *Daughter of Earth*. Smedley emphasizes the economic dependence of women which obligates them to remain in violent marriages and compares the institution of marriage to prostitution. She also shows the conflict in her protagonist's mind between her love for her mother and her need to rebel against her mother's fate. Ultimately, she is so "damaged" by witnessing her mother's oppression that she rejects "love and tenderness" because she believes such female emotions can only result in "suffering and defeat."

MacKinnon, Janice R., and Stephen R. MacKinnon. *Agnes Smedley: The Life and Times of an American Radical*. Berkeley: University of California Press, 1988.

This is a comprehensive biography of Smedley which considers her private and public life in the context of feminism, radicalism, and world history. The authors, who are China scholars, draw extensively on Smedley's correspondence as well as her published writings and interviews with her contemporaries. In establishing the historical context for Smedley's ideas, they emphasize her independent thinking and her resistance to all labels. An extensive bibliography of Smedley's books and articles is appended.

Milton, Joyce. *A Friend of China.* New York: Hastings House, 1980.
   This illustrated biography for young readers provides a general introduction to Smedley's life and a clear assessment of her activities on behalf of communist revolutionaries in China.

Nichols, Kathleen L. "The Western Roots of Feminism in Agnes Smedley's *Daughter of Earth,*" in Helen Winter Stauffer and Susan J. Rosowski, eds. *Women and Western American Literature.* Troy, N.Y.: Whitston, 1982.
   Nichols identifies this work as an autobiographical novel celebrating the "daily loyalty and endurance" of women on the western frontier. She provides an overview of Smedley's life—the grim poverty of Colorado mining towns and rural Missouri, where she was raised, her first trip to China as a journalist in 1928, and the last twenty-two years of her life, when she was writing articles and books which attempted to persuade Americans to support the Chinese revolutionary cause.

ELIZABETH CADY STANTON
1815-1902
   Stanton was born in Johnstown, New York, the fourth of six children. She studied Greek and Latin as a young woman and graduated from Emma Willard's Troy Female Seminary. In 1840 she married Henry Brewster Stanton, an anti-slavery lecturer, and became involved in the abolition movement. In 1847 the couple moved to Seneca Falls, the site of the first women's rights convention, organized by Stanton and Lucretia Mott, whom Stanton had met in London. In 1851 Stanton met Susan B. Anthony, the lifelong friend who became her major collaborator in the struggle for women's rights; Stanton was the writer and speaker, Anthony the strategist and organizer. In 1868 the two published a magazine, *The Revolution*, to advocate for suffrage, more liberal divorce laws, and wider economic opportunities for women. In 1869, they founded the National Woman Suffrage Association, in which Stanton served as president for twenty-one years. To help finance the education of her seven children, Stanton traveled the country giving lectures for the New York Lyceum Bureau. Her popularity as a speaker also lent prestige to the suffrage cause. Stanton's writings include the Declaration of Sentiments, which she drafted for the 1848 convention; *The Woman's Bible* (2 vols., 1895-1898), her controversial analysis of derogatory references to women in the Bible; and *Eighty Years and*

More (1898), her autobiography. She and Anthony also coedited the three-volume *History of Woman's Suffrage* (1891-1896).

Reissued Editions
Note: A collection of Stanton's correspondence, writings, and speeches has been edited by Ellen Carol DuBois and published in 1981 by Schocken Books of New York, and in 1992 by Northeastern University Press. The *History of Woman's Suffrage*, written by Stanton, Anthony, and Matilda Joslyn Gage, was reprinted in 1985 by Ayer of Salem, N.H.

Eighty Years and More: Reminiscences of Elizabeth Cady Stanton.
Boston: Northeastern University Press, 1993.
The Woman's Bible. Boston: Northeastern University Press, 1993.

Biography and Commentary
Banner, Lois W. *Elizabeth Cady Stanton: A Radical for Woman's Rights.* Boston: Little, Brown, 1980.
   This comprehensive biography is based on extensive archival research in manuscript collections housed at academic libraries and historical societies throughout the country. Banner focuses on Stanton's life as a wife and mother, her friendships with Susan B. Anthony and Victoria Woodhull, and the evolution of her philosophy and her political activities. Included are discussions of her major writings—her work on the three-volume *History of Woman's Suffrage* and *The Woman's Bible*, her radical feminist commentary on scripture—and of individuals and works that influenced her thinking.

Cullen-DuPont, Kathryn. *Elizabeth Cady Stanton and Women's Liberty.* New York: Facts on File, 1992.
   This illustrated text for young readers is part of the Makers of America series. It begins with Stanton's objection to the word "obey" as part of the marriage ceremony and ends with her 1902 letter to President Roosevelt requesting that he immortalize himself by bringing about the emancipation of women. The author focuses throughout on such dramatic moments in Stanton's life enhanced by a wide selection of excerpts from her speeches and writings. An epilogue on passage of the Nineteenth Amendment and an annotated bibliography on suffrage and Stanton are also included.

Griffith, Elisabeth. *In Her Own Right: The Life of Elizabeth Cady Stanton.* New York: Oxford University Press, 1984.
   Griffith offers a psychological analysis of Stanton's life in terms of a progression of behavior patterns based on role models. Despite criticism by many people, Stanton's behavior was supported by those who mattered most to her. Once she had "internalized" a belief in female autonomy and "self-sovereignty," she was able to persevere in the roles she had chosen for herself without further reinforcement from others. As a child and young woman, Stanton sought the approval of important

men in her life—her father, her brother-in-law, her husband. Eventually women, including Elizabeth Smith Miller, Lucretia Mott, and Susan B. Anthony, displaced men as her most influential mentors. Stanton, of course, was a complex woman whose humor, energy, and appetites cannot be explained simply in terms of such models. In old age she acted as she pleased, despite the disapproval of her former friends. The text includes illustrations, a family tree, and a "phrenological" study of her character done in 1853.

Jelinek, Estelle C. "Traditional Autobiography Liberated: The Ordinary and Superwoman Elizabeth Cady Stanton," in *The Tradition of Women's Autobiography: From Antiquity to the Present*. Boston: G. K. Hall, 1986.
    Jelinek demonstrates that Stanton had two objectives in writing *Eighty Years and More*. On the one hand, she wanted to educate her readers about women's rights and convert them to the cause of suffrage. On the other hand, she believed she must earn their trust by persuading them that she was an "ordinary" person, cheerful and healthy, with varied domestic interests in addition to her political ones. The resulting narrative is filled with "paradox, contradictions, and ambivalence." Stanton offers many domestic anecdotes which seem to provide personal information but in effect are intended only to demonstrate her "oneness" with all women. The narrative does not reveal Stanton's fears, conflicts, or any other intimate information about her life.

Nies, Judith. "Elizabeth Cady Stanton," in *Seven Women: Portraits from the American Radical Tradition*. New York: Viking Press, 1977.
    This biographical essay portrays Stanton as a "fresh and creative thinker" on many topics, including children and child-rearing. Nies credits Stanton's failed campaign to change women's fashion with teaching her how deep-seated and irrational were many of society's attitudes about women. As a result Stanton also began to use traditional forms to communicate new ideas, most famously in the Declaration of Sentiments she wrote for the first women's rights convention. Stanton had strong political instincts and enjoyed working a crowd. Nies also describes Stanton's relationship with her father and husband and highlights the role of Lucretia Mott in freeing Stanton from dependence on male authority. She chronicles Stanton's writings for the "revolution," the controversy over her refusal to support the Fifteenth Amendment, and her friendship with Frederick Douglass. Stanton's greatest gift, according to Nies, was her ability to articulate complex issues and orchestrate the reform agenda of the women's movement.

Waggenspack, Beth M. *The Search for Self-Sovereignty: The Oratory of Elizabeth Cady Stanton*. New York: Greenwood Press, 1989.
    Following an introductory biographical essay, Waggenspack groups Stanton's speeches by broad topical categories. Each section includes

texts of several representative speeches and an analysis of their significance. A detailed description of primary sources is also included.

IDA M. TARBELL
1857-1944

Tarbell was born and raised in Erie County, Pennsylvania, an important oil center. She studied biology at Allegheny College, where she was the only woman in her class, then taught at a seminary in Ohio before moving home to join the staff of the *Chautauquan*, a monthly magazine published by the Methodist Church. At the age of thirty, Tarbell quit her job and went to Paris, where she researched and wrote a biography of a French revolutionary, *Madame Roland: A Biographical Study* (1896), and articles for *McClure's, Scribner's*, and *American Magazine*. Her serialized biography of Napoleon Bonaparte (1894-1895) is credited with boosting *McClure's* circulation. It was followed by several volumes of work on Abraham Lincoln's life and career and *A History of the Standard Oil Company* (1904). This two-volume exposé of "commercial sin" proved powerful enough to persuade the Supreme Court to dissolve the Standard Oil Trust. For twenty-one years Tarbell continued to produce the kind of investigative reporting which made her famous as one of the nation's "muckrakers." Her autobiography, *All in the Day's Work* (1939), was written at the age of eighty-two.

Reissued Editions
All in the Day's Work: An Autobiography. Boston: G. K. Hall, 1985.

The Historical and Political Preparation of Lincoln for the Presidency of the United States. Albuquerque, N. Mex.: American Classical College Press, 1991.

A History of the Standard Oil Company. Cutchogue, N.Y.: Buccaneer Books, 1987.

Biography and Commentary
Brady, Kathleen. *Ida Tarbell: Portrait of a Muckraker*. Seaview, N.Y.: Putnam, 1984.

This comprehensive biography includes a selected bibliography of primary and secondary sources and is based on newly discovered letters and firsthand interviews as well as the published record of Tarbell's writing. Brady sees Tarbell as a tragic figure who never appreciated the extent of her own achievement. She was a researcher who studied history books and statistical records, counted the number of women with registered patents, but "never dared look within herself." As a woman in a male-dominated world, she thought herself inferior and a failure for having forged an independent existence rather than a domestic one. Brady gives Tarbell high marks for her "groundbreaking" biographies of Lincoln and Napoleon, her "seminal studies" of labor issues and tariff controversies, and the power of the exposé that finally forced the Supreme Court to dissolve the Standard Oil monopoly. She also chronicles Tarbell's interviews with many of her time's most important figures and the comments made about her by famous friends and enemies, including Teddy Roosevelt, Jane Addams, Henry James, and Herbert Hoover.

Kochersberger, Robert C., Jr., ed. *More than a Muckraker: Ida Tarbell's Lifetime in Journalism.* Knoxville: University of Tennessee Press, 1994.
This collection of twenty-six pieces is divided into four groups: biographical writings, business writings, essays on women's issues, and essays on general topics, including religion, poverty, and old age. Kochersberger's introduction takes the form of a biographical essay which identifies the key influences in Tarbell's life and traces her professional development. Kochersberger sees a clear progression from the fact-filled studies of Tarbell's early career to the more thoughtful essays on broader social issues of her later years. He has organized the collection chronologically and provided a separate introduction for each of his four groups, with useful background on the selections he has chosen.

Stinson, Robert. "Ida M. Tarbell and the Ambiguities of Feminism." *The Pennsylvania Magazine of History and Biography* 51, no. 1 (January 1977): 217-239.
Stinson looks at Tarbell's anti-feminist writings, which urge women to marry despite her own example to the contrary, and offers two interpretations of her conservatism. She may have resented being pushed into a professional career that made domestic life impossible. Or, she may have been projecting her own ambivalence about women's social roles. *The Business of Being a Woman* (1912), with its praise of motherhood and its attack on feminism, seems a personal refutation of her own career. Many of her friends were shocked by its arguments and what they perceived to be her reactionary conversion. Stinson concludes that almost all female intellectuals were torn between marriage and independence, but most resolved the conflict by turning more forcefully toward feminism.

Tomkins, Mary E. *Ida M. Tarbell.* Boston: G. K. Hall, 1974.
This volume in Twayne's United States Authors series includes a chronology, bibliography, biographical essay, and discussion of Tarbell's major work. Tomkins establishes the connections between significant events in Tarbell's life and her writings, tracing the development of her career as a journalist for *McClure's* and *The American Magazine* and as a lecturer on the Chautauqua circuit. Despite being best known as the female muckraker who bested the robber barons of Standard Oil, Tarbell's most significant writings, according to Tomkins, are her portrait of Abraham Lincoln as frontiersman, which generated a new American myth, and her descriptions of selfless

business leaders dedicated to public service and selfless housewives dedicated to the rearing of the next generation, which affirmed key middle-class beliefs. Tarbell was not a great stylist but her work reflected clear thinking, respect for facts, and a sincere moral indignation, which made her enormously popular with the magazine-reading public she served as a kind of "national maiden aunt."

Chapter 5
AFRICAN AMERICAN WOMEN WRITERS

African American women have written poetry, drama, fiction, essays, children's stories, and newspaper articles; their work spans all genres. They have been grouped together here based on a literary-historical assumption that their work is best understood in the context of a racial identity inescapable for African Americans, especially those writing in the years immediately preceding and following the Civil War and Reconstruction. Though the Harlem Renaissance or New Negro Movement of the 1920's and 1930's is usually identified as the first period of intense African American creativity in art and literature, in fact it was the decade of the 1890's which represented the first major flowering of Black intellectual life with establishment of increasing numbers of black-owned newspapers and magazines and the publication of hundreds of works by black novelists, journalists, and poets. This decade, marked by recognition of the terrible failure of Reconstruction and its legacy of Jim Crow laws and the Ku Klux Klan, inspired both the angry anti-lynching rhetoric of Ida B. Wells and the "racial uplift" novels of Frances Harper and Pauline Hopkins. It also saw the publication of Anna Julia Cooper's *A Voice from the South* (1892), the first feminist text by an African American. These writers and many others whose work is still being recovered helped pave the way for later generations of novelists and poets, including Jessie Redmon Fauset, Nella Larsen, and Zora Neale Hurston, the three best-known women writers of the Harlem Renaissance. From Harriet Wilson's *Our Nig* (1859), the first known novel by an African American woman, and Harriet Jacobs's *Incidents in the Life of a Slave Girl* (1861), to Hurston's *Their Eyes Were Watching God* (1937), now considered a classic, the literature of African American women has confronted the racism and sexism its authors experienced in their own lives and has attempted to correct stereotypical images fostered by sentimental novels and the popular press.

Despite the historical importance of the writers discussed in this chapter and the recognition many of them received in their own time, most of their work was forgotten or dismissed as trivial until rediscovered by feminists and students of African American studies in the 1970's. It took the popular and critical success of African American women writers, culminating in Toni Morrison's 1993 Nobel Prize in Literature, to motivate the search for foremothers. Alice Walker's own delightful account of her search for Zora Neale Hurston's unmarked grave stands as a metaphor for the work that would be done by a new generation of scholars in "unearthing" and reassessing nineteenth and early twentieth century texts. Though important research has been done by both female and male scholars, both black and white, the major pioneers have been African American women themselves with a strong interest in establishing a personal legacy and heritage with which they could identify and which would help ground their own historical position as black feminists. Three works, in particular, are usually credited with inaugurating the new field: Barbara Smith's groundbreaking essay "Toward a Black Feminist Criticism" (1977), Barbara Christian's *Black Women Novelists: The Development of a Tradition, 1892-1976* (1980), which was the first attempt to articulate the existence of such a tradition, and Mary Helen Washington's *Black-Eyed Susans* (1975), the first anthology dedicated to stories by African American women.

The existence of a black feminist critical tradition has been solidified and legitimized through countless essays and book-length studies. Included in this chapter are those which make specific reference to the first generations of African American women writers; many others focus primarily on such contemporary writers as Toni Cade Bambara, Jamaica Kincaid, Paule Marshall, Toni Morrison, Gloria Naylor, and Alice Walker. Though by far the bulk of criticism has been done on writers of fiction, attention to other genres is beginning to result in significant scholarly work. Moreover, as the work of recovery proceeds, consideration has been given to women who, despite their limited literary output, can help establish a larger historical context for the major figures. Examples of such studies are included in this chapter to help provide an overview of the field.

Let me conclude by calling the reader's attention to the thirty-volume *Schomburg Library of Nineteenth Century Black Women Writers*, published in 1988 by Oxford University Press, and its sequel, *African American Women Writers, 1910-1940,* a projected thirty-one volume series which G. K. Hall began to publish in 1995. Both series make available new editions of works that have been out of print for decades and are generally unknown to readers. Useful historical information is also contained in the sixteen-volume encyclopedia *Black Women in the United States*, published by Carlson in 1990.

Readers should also be aware of four scholarly journals: *African American Review* (formerly *Black American Literature Forum*), *Black Scholar, Callaloo,* and *CLA Journal,* which regularly publish essays on many of the writers discussed in this chapter. Please note that in he annotations that follow I have tried to respect authors' preferences for racial descriptors—Black, African American, or Afro-American—and for capitalization of "black" and "white." One final comment: many of the general studies listed below are also annotated as critical and biographical studies of individual writers; this overlap reflects the importance of identifying "intertextual" connections in "constructing" a traditon. Most journal articles included here built on these earlier book-length general studies and were, therefore, published more recently, most in the 1990's.

GENERAL STUDIES
Ammons, Elizabeth. *Conflicting Stories*. New York: Oxford University Press, 1991.
Ammons sees the period between 1890 and 1920 as one which produced some of America's "most talented and accomplished women writers," many of whom were African American. Ammons considers the life situation of these women—their education, whether or not they married and had children, their personal experience of sexism and racism—to establish commonalities and differences in their literary concerns. She examines, for example, the impact of the "cult of true womanhood" on both African American and white women. This text may, in fact, be the only study of turn-of-the-century American literature which provides thorough analysis of the literary history of both women of color and white women writers.

Braxton, Joanne, and Andrea McLaughlin, eds. *Wild Women in the Whirlwind: Afra-American Culture and the Contemporary Literary Renaissance*. New Brunswick, N.J.: Rutgers University Press, 1990.
This is a collection of essays on black cultural, literary, and political foremothers (Phillis Wheatley, Sojourner Truth, Harriet Wilson, Charlotte Forten Grimké, Angelina Grimké, and Fannie Lou Hamer). It also includes discussions of contemporary fiction, autobiography, and poetry.

Carby, Hazel V. *Reconstructing Womanhood: The Emergence of the Afro-American Woman Novelist*. New York: Oxford University Press, 1987.
Carby identifies four major "concerns" for her text: to consider how writers adapted and transformed nineteenth century ideologies of womanhood for their own purposes, to identify the boundaries that separated white and black women and prevented any real solidarity between them, to reestablish the existence of a "first flowering" of black women's autonomous organizations and intellectual activity during the late nineteenth and early twentieth centuries, and finally to provide a cultural history of their work with particular attention to the specific impact of gender, race, and class. To support this program Carby offers extensive analysis of the life and work of Wilson, Harper, Larsen, and Hopkins, in particular, with reference to dozens of other important figures.

Dearborn, Mary V. *Pocahontas's Daughters: Gender and Ethnicity in American Culture*. New York: Oxford University Press, 1986.
Dearborn's premise is that those who seem to be on the margins of American culture may best represent what happens within that culture. Ethnicity is then a crucial aspect of the national character. Dearborn focuses on two topics of particular relevance for this bibliography: the struggles of African American women writers with the politics of

"Black Art" and the theme of miscegenation as a locus for concerns about the meaning of inheritance in the American identity.

DuCille, Ann. *The Coupling Convention: Sex, Text and Tradition in Black Women's Fiction.* New York: Oxford University Press, 1993.
DuCille looks at how African American writers have made "unconventional use" of the so-called marriage plot to explore issues of female identity and sexuality as well as race. She focuses on two periods: the 1890's, including the work of Hopkins and Harper, and the 1920's to 1940's, including the work of Fauset, Larsen, and Hurston. In her analysis of how these authors make use of the "coupling convention," DuCille also attempts to "unread" previous interpretations and to demonstrate how different generations of critics have, in effect, rewritten these texts to fit their own interpretive purposes.

Foster, Frances Smith. *Written by Herself: Literary Production by African American Women, 1746-1892.* Bloomington: Indiana University Press, 1993.
Foster looks at a broad range of women who managed to "testify" to their experiences, and considers the impact of race, gender, and class on their achievements. She also uses a variety of theoretical considerations as appropriate examining, for example, the effect both of nineteenth century audience reception on Harriet Jacobs, and the intense political and cultural racism of the post-Reconstruction era on late nineteenth century writers.

Fox-Genovese, Elizabeth. *Within the Plantation Household: Black and White Women of the Old South.* Chapel Hill: University of North Carolina Press, 1988.
Fox-Genovese argues that the institution of slavery made it impossible for black and white women to form any kind of "sisterly" bonds. To support her argument she quotes from published and unpublished writings by black and white women. These writers discuss such topics as "ladylike" behavior, women's rights, sexual abuse, abolitionism, and slavery. Illustrations and an extensive bibliography are included.

Gates, Henry Louis, Jr., ed. *Reading Black, Reading Feminist: A Critical Anthology.* New York: Meridian, 1990.
This collection of interviews and essays, several of which are annotated here, includes pieces by Hazel Carby, Elizabeth Fox-Genovese, Valerie Smith and Molly Hite on Larsen, Jacobs, and Hurston.

Giddings, Paula. *When and Where I Enter: The Impact of Black Women on Race and Sex in America.* New York: William Morrow, 1984.
Giddings uses the speeches, diaries, essays, and fiction of black

women, including most of the writers referenced in this bibliography, to establish their intellectual response to the double burden of American racism and sexism.

Gwin, Minrose C. *Black and White Women of the Old South: The Peculiar Sisterhood in American Literature.* Knoxville: University of Tennessee Press, 1985.
    In order to demonstrate the complexity of interracial female relationships, Gwin examines dozens of nineteenth century autobiographies by both black and white women, three modern novels by William Faulkner, Willa Cather, and Margaret Walker, and *Uncle Tom's Cabin* (1852), as well as a pro-slavery response, *Aunt Phillis's* (1852). In particular, she identifies the ways in which white women projected their own repressed selves on a symbolic "other" and how the legacy of slavery continues to affect our "literary and cultural consciousness" today.

Hamalian, Leo, and James V. Hatch, eds. *The Roots of African American Drama: An Anthology of Early Plays, 1858-1938.* Detroit: Wayne State University Press, 1991.
    This collection of thirteen plays includes five by women: *The First One* (1927) by Hurston, *Peculiar Sam, or, the Underground Railroad* (1879) by Hopkins, *Aunt Betsy's Thanksgiving* (1914) by Katherine D. Chapman Tillman, *Aftermath* (1929?) by Mary Burill, and *Tom-Tom* (1932) by Shirley Grahman. The introduction to the text provides background on each play and its author.

Harris, Trudier, and Thadious M. Davis, eds. *Afro American Writers from the Harlem Renaissance to 1940. Dictionary of Literary Biography,* vol. 51. Detroit: Gale Research, 1987.
    This volume contains essays on seven women poets, playwrights, and novelists, including Jessie Fauset, Zora Neale Hurston, and Nella Larsen.

Harris, Will. "Early Black Women Playwrights and the Dual Liberation Motif." *African American Review* 28, no. 2 (Summer 1994): 205-221.
    This article discusses the plays of Angelina Weld Grimké, Georgia Douglas Johnson, Mary Burrill, Zora Neale Hurston, Eulalie Spence, May Miller, Marita Bonner, Shirley Graham, and Alice Childress. Harris provides a brief history of pre-1950 drama by African American women, noting the absence of black men as authority figures and the frequent focus on the black woman's role as domestic servant. These plays continued the program of racial uplift while also dramatizing the strength and independence of black women.

Hine, Darlene Clark, ed. *Black Women in America.* Brooklyn, N.Y.: Carlson, 1993.

This two-volume encyclopedia includes extensive biographical information about all the writers in this bibliography.

Hull, Gloria T. "Afro-American Women Poets: A Bio-Critical Survey," in *Shakespeare's Sisters: Feminist Essays on Women Poets*, eds. Sandra M. Gilbert and Susan Gubar. Bloomington: Indiana University Press, 1979.
    Hull argues that black women poets gave birth to their own "Anglo-African" tradition rather than simply accepting Western ideas and conventions. After discussing Phillis Wheatley's life and poetry, Hull turns to Frances Harper, the "key" female poet of the nineteenth century, and discusses her early anti-slavery poetry and last volume of poems, *Sketches of a Southern Life* (1872). No more "queens" appeared on the poetry throne until Margaret Walker and Gwendolyn Brooks began publishing in the 1940's and 1950's (they are not included in this bibliography since most of their work was completed after 1948), but at least seven women were active in the Harlem Renaissance. Georgia Douglas Johnson published three volumes of poems between 1918 and 1938, Anne Spencer—a less prolific but more "arresting" poet—wrote quite dramatic and experimental poetry, and Helene Johnson dealt most explicitly with "racial protest" themes. The other four—Angelina Grimké, Jessie Fauset, Effie Newsome, and Gwendolyn Bennett—published very little poetry and have been relegated to "footnotes and appendixes."

_____. *Color, Sex, and Poetry: Three Women Writers of the Harlem Renaissance*. Bloomington: Indiana University Press, 1987.
    This biographical study of Angelina Weld Grimké, Alice Dunbar-Nelson, and Georgia Douglas Johnson is based on unpublished letters, diaries, and manuscripts. Hull, in her introduction, provides a history of the role of women in the Harlem Renaissance from the "leisured wives and daughters" of successful businessmen to factory workers and domestics, from progressive activists to conservative schoolteachers. Though women writers participated fully in the intellectual life of their times, their publications were limited by lack of access to important male networks and lack of geographic mobility. Hull has chosen these three poets, in particular, because all had "considerable contemporary reputations" and enough of their work has survived to allow for serious study. All three were schoolteachers educated to lead traditional lives; all three were torn by a complex racial consciousness resulting from their obvious mixed blood. Hull's stated aim is to correct their reputations as nothing more than poet-housewives or appendages to more famous relatives.

Hull, Gloria T., Patricia Bell Scott, and Barbara Smith, eds. *All the Women Are White, All the Blacks Are Men, but Some of Us Are Brave: Black Women's Studies*. Old Westbury, N.Y.: Feminist Press, 1982.
    This collection of essays is considered a landmark in the

establishment of Black women's studies as an academic discipline. Many of the essays look at the political situation of Afro-American women and present a radical, feminist point of view. The text includes a section on Black women's literature as well as bibliographic essays and recommended syllabi.

Knopf, Marcy, ed. *The Sleeper Wakes: Harlem Renaissance Stories by Women.* New Brunswick, N.J.: Rutgers University Press, 1993.

This anthology includes little-known stories by well-known writers such as Fauset, Hurston, and Larsen, as well as stories by less well-known figures. Some of these stories were never published; most appeared in popular African American magazines but were never reprinted.

Lerner, Gerda, ed. *Black Women in White America: A Documentary History.* New York: Random House, 1973.

This is a collection of writings by and about black women from 1811 to the 1970's. Topics include slavery, work, education, politics, and racism. There are introductions to each section, and bibliographic and source notes.

McCaskill, Barbara. "The Folklore of the Coasts in Black Women's Fiction of the Harlem Renaissance." *CLA Journal* 39, no. 3 (March 1996): 273-301.

Noting that seacoasts are used as metaphors by many American writers, McCaskill focuses on three stories—"Sanctuary" (1930) by Nella Larsen, "John Redding Goes to Sea" (1921) by Zora Neale Hurston, and "The Sleeper Wakes" (1920) by Jessie Fauset—to demonstrate their particular significance in the work of African American women writers. Coasts in these works are "signatures of losses and gains" in a culture "baptized by imprisonment and pain." They represent the terrible legacy of enslavement and the isolation of the bourgeois from folk culture.

McDowell, Deborah E. "New Directions for Black Feminist Criticism." *Black American Literature Forum* 14 (1980): 153-159.

After noting the absence of Black women writers from literary criticism by both white feminists and African American male scholars, McDowell sets an agenda for a new Black feminist criticism. In addition to the resurrection of forgotten writers and the revision of "misinformed" critical opinions, critics should provide contextual information to help clarify "problems" in the work of early writers, such as Fauset, Larsen, and Hurston; they should attempt to identify through close reading "thematic, stylistic, and linguistic commonalities" and, eventually, they should move beyond "separatism" to a consideration of the parallels in the work of both male and female writers.

McLendon, Jacquelyn Y. *The Politics of Color in the Fiction of Jessie Fauset and Nella Larsen.* Charlottesville: University Press of Virginia, 1995.

McLendon "interrogates" the work of well-known critics of African American literature to argue that they have misread the appraisal of black middle-class values in the work of Fauset, Larsen, and other writers. According to McLendon, these authors do not subscribe to a color caste system that devalues blackness. Rather, they celebrate blackness and traditional southern black culture and use the figure of the mulatto to question traditional assumptions about color and class.

Peterson, Carla L. *"Doers of the Word": African American Women Speakers and Writers in the North (1830-1880).* New York: Oxford University Press, 1995.

A substantial body of writing by black women first emerged in 1830 because of the rise of both abolitionism and a variety of organizations—literary, anti-slavery, and mutual aid societies—which helped create a new elite black audience. Women during this period gave lectures, wrote for newspapers, produced evangelical and travel pieces, and published poetry and fiction. Peterson provides examples of all of these "genres" and devotes one chapter to Harriet A. Jacobs, Harriet E. Wilson, and Frances Ellen Watkins Harper, whom she classifies as writers countering official historical accounts by defining African American identity in their own terms.

Pryse, Marjorie, and Hortense J. Spillers, eds. *Black Women, Fiction, and Literary Tradition.* Bloomington: Indiana University Press, 1985.

This collection, like the more recent one edited by Gates, is part of a general project to establish the literary history of black women writers. It includes essays by Minrose Gwin, Claudia Tate, and Deborah E. McDowell on Wilson, Jacobs, Hopkins, and Fauset.

Roses, Lorraine Elena, and Ruth Elizabeth Randolph, eds. *The Harlem Renaissance and Beyond: The Literary Biographies of 100 Black Women Writers, 1900-1945.* Boston: G. K. Hall, 1990.

This reference work contains biocritical sketches of writers of fiction and nonfiction with a selective bibliography for each. There is also an extensive general bibliography, photos of twenty-five of the writers, and four appendices which list writers by genre, place of birth, dates, and titles. The editors explain that they have included very minor writers with few publications to help fill the "uncharted spaces" between their better-known peers.

Shine, Ted "Opportunities for African-American Women Playwrights," in *American Women Playwrights, 1900-1950,* by Yvonne Shafer. New York: Peter Lang, 1995.

Shine notes that during the Harlem Renaissance there was hope that the creation of "true" black characters by African American playwrights would drive the old Negro stereotypes off the stage. Unfortunately, original plays presented at community theaters interested in promoting the work of black playwrights were rarely published and, prior to the 1960's. only a very few African Americans were able to earn a living exclusively in theater. The greatest support for young playwrights came from campus-based groups founded in the 1920's, including the Howard University Players, the Negro Intercollegiate Dramatic Association, and the Southern Association of Dramatic and Speech Arts.

Shockley, Ann Allen. *Afro-American Women Writers, 1746-1933: An Anthology and Critical Guide*. Boston: G. K. Hall, 1988.

Shockley traces the history of African American women writers from colonial days to the Depression, provides an historical overview of each of four major periods, and attempts to cover all genres, including poetry, biography, autobiography, essays, short stories, novels, diaries, and journals. More than forty authors who published books or serialized novels are discussed, and there are useful listings of both primary and secondary sources.

Sterling, Dorothy, ed. *We Are Your Sisters: Black Women in the Nineteenth Century*. New York: W.W. Norton, 1984.

This is a compilation of original source materials from letters, interviews, diaries, and other writings by nineteenth century African American women, many of whom are referenced here. Entries discuss life before, during, and after the Civil War, in both the North and the South. Illustrations and a selected bibliography are included.

Stetson, Erlene, ed. *Black Sister: Poetry by Black American Women, 1746-1980*. Bloomington: Indiana University Press, 1981.

This comprehensive anthology has selections by fifty-eight writers, divided into two sections—eighteenth and nineteenth century poets, and twentieth century poets—followed by a bibliography of anthologies, criticism, and primary sources organized by poet. An introduction to each section highlights the contributions of a small group of the most significant poets, and a general introduction identifies the general themes and poetic techniques common to African American women poets. Stetson argues that black women writers have had to contend with two large issues in their poetry—how to assert their identity in a world that does not acknowledge their existence, and how to balance their rage in order to express the full range of human emotions.

Tate, Claudia. "Allegories of Black Female Desire: Or, Rereading Nineteenth century Sentimental Narratives of Black Female Authority," in *Changing Our Own Words: Essays on Criticism, Theory and Writing by Black Women*, ed. Cheryl A. Wall. New Brunswick, N.J.: Rutgers University Press, 1989.

Tate examines black women's postbellum sentimental fiction, including the work of Frances Harper and Pauline Hopkins, to consider how these writers dealt with the apparent contradiction between liberation and marriage which shows up in more modern work. For nineteenth century blacks, according to Tate, voting and marriage were the two most important newly acquired civil rights. Nonetheless, black women novelists did question many of the gender conventions of white sentimental fiction and insisted on the significance of their own points of view; marriage was not the ultimate goal of their lives but the promise of a new beginning.

_____. *Domestic Allegories of Political Desire: The Black Heroine's Text at the Turn of the Century.* New York: Oxford University Press, 1992.

Tate argues for "an historicized interpretive mode" to read writers of the post-Reconstruction era. The "maudlin" novels of writers like Pauline Hopkins must have appealed to ambitious black Americans who sought to enjoy their own middle-class lives despite the common experience of racial oppression and the reality of lynchings and widespread political disenfranchisement. Tate focuses on the "cultural contexts" of eleven novels by Harper, Hopkins, and several other writers as evidence of the stresses and communal anxieties which marked black American life at the turn of the century. She also notes that the "genteel domestic feminism" of these works makes them the direct precursors of Hurston's *Their Eyes Were Watching God.* The text includes a bibliography and extensive source notes.

Wade-Gayles, Gloria. "Black Women Journalists in the South, 1880-1905: An Approach to the Study of Black Women's History." *Callaloo* 4, nos. 1-3 (February-October 1981): 138-152.

Wade-Gayles offers a composite portrait of fourteen of these journalists. Most were active in "colored women's clubs" and began their careers writing for church newspapers. Eventually, they became regular contributors to nationally recognized papers, including *The New York Age, The Boston Advocate, The New York Freeman, The Richmond Planet,* and many others. Most were married and also worked as teachers, since they were not paid for their journalism. They wore "long dresses with high necklines" wherever they went and were clearly recognized as "women of prestige and influence" who played important leadership roles in their communities. Thanks to the rapid rise of the black Southern press in the 1880's and 1890's, more than half of the black women journalists of the time were, in fact, from the South.

Wall, Cheryl, ed. *Changing Our Own Words: Essays on Criticism, Theory, and Writing by Black Women.* New Brunswick, N.J.: Rutgers University Press, 1989.

This is a collection of essays by women critics who participated in a 1987 symposium and includes explanatory readings of several writers discussed here (Frances Harper, Harriet Jacobs, and Harriet Wilson). Wall's introduction offers a survey of the recent history of literature by and about African American women.

Washington, Mary Helen. *Invented Lives: Narratives of Black Women, 1860-1960.* Garden City, N.Y.: Anchor Press, 1987.

This book is part of Washington's continuing effort to piece together a coherent literary tradition in which black women are fully represented. She focuses on ten writers from Harriet Jacobs to Gwendolyn Brooks. The excerpts are preceded by essays on topics such as "The Slave Woman's Voice," "Uplifting the Women and the Race," and "The Mulatta Trap." Washington's concern throughout is how each writer challenged contemporary conventions of what was possible for women characters. Brief bibliographic notes are also included.

Watson, Carol McAlpine. *Prologue: The Novels of Black American Women, 1891-1965.* Westport, Conn.: Greenwood Press, 1985.

This is a short and very straightforward discussion of fifty-eight novels written by African American women writers between 1891 and 1965. Watson sees these texts as works of social protest and racial appeal which were written for didactic rather than artistic purposes. The book includes a chart of major themes and the percentage of their appearance in each of three periods: 1891-1920, 1921-1945, and 1946-1965. It also includes an appendix with plot summaries of each novel discussed in the text.

Werner, Craig. *Black American Women Novelists.* Pasadena, Calif.: Salem Press, 1989.

This annotated bibliography of criticism features articles on the individual novels of writers from Harriet Wilson to Toni Morrison. Jacobs, Fauset, Larsen, Harper, and Hopkins are included.

Yellin, Jean Fagan, and Cynthia D. Bond. *The Pen Is Ours: A Listing of Writings by and about African American Women Before 1910 with a Secondary Bibliography to the Present.* New York: Oxford University Press, 1991.

This bibliography is intended as a supplement to the *Schomburg Library of Nineteenth century Black Women Writers.* It includes five sets of listings: individual publications by and about African American women, dictated slave narratives, articles in periodicals and collections by and about African American women, notable African American women who were subjects of writings, and selected contemporary writings about but not by African American women.

ANNA JULIA COOPER
1859-1964

Cooper was born in Raleigh, the child of a slave mother and a father presumed to have been her mother's master. As a child she was awarded a scholarship to attend St. Augustine's, a missionary school for future teachers and clergymen. In 1877 she married her Greek teacher, the theology student George A. C. Cooper, who died two years later. She left St. Augustine's in 1881 to attend Oberlin College, graduating as one of the first few black women to complete a four-year degree in a traditional "gentlemen's" curriculum. Cooper taught for a year at Wilberforce College in Ohio before returning to St. Augustine's. Then, in 1887, she was invited to join the faculty at M Street (now Paul Laurence Dunbar) High School in Washington, D.C., where she was named principal in 1901. During these years, Cooper became well known for her essays and lectures on race and gender issues. Considered a leading intellectual and spokeswoman for her race, Cooper was invited to address a special meeting of the 1893 Women's Congress in Chicago and was the only woman elected to membership to the American Negro Academy, a late nineteenth century black research institution. She was also invited to address the first Pan-African Conference in London. Cooper began doctoral studies at Columbia University, completing her Ph.D. at the Sorbonne after raising five greatnieces and greatnephews whose mother had died. Cooper's early essays were collected in *A Voice from the South by a Black Woman of the South* (1892), which is often cited as the first feminist text by an African American.

Reissued Essays and Books
"The Colored Woman Should Not Be Ignored," in *Black Women in White America*, ed. Gerda Lerner. New York: Random House, 1972.

"The Higher Education of Women," in *Black Women in Nineteenth century American Life: Their Words, Their Thoughts, Their Feelings*, eds. Bert James Loewenberg and Ruth Bogin. University Park: Pennsylvania State University Press, 1976.

Slavery and the French Revolutionists, 1788-1805, ed. and trans. Frances R. Keller. French Civilization Series, 1. Lewiston, N.Y.: The Edwin Mellen Press, 1988.

A Voice from the South. New York: Oxford University Press, 1988.

Biography and Commentary
Note: Though few contemporary sources focus in any detail on Cooper's works, quotations from her essays are found in many discussions of late nineteenth- and early twentieth century African American history and literature.

Alexander, Elizabeth. "'We Must Be about Our Father's Business': Anna Julia Cooper and the In-corporation of the Nineteenth century African-American Woman Intellectual." *Signs* 20, no. 2 (Winter 1995): 336-356.
　　Alexander provides a detailed analysis of Cooper's "textual

strategies"—her liberal use of the first person, her "corporeal metaphors," her occasional sarcasm, the anecdotes she tells, the expertise she demonstrates, even her use of quotation marks—to demonstrate the complex and diverse structure of her essays. Such a mix of "allegory, autobiography, history, oratory, poetry, and literary criticism" creates the public space in which an African American female intellectual first establishes her "voice." In effect, Cooper "valorizes" her own individual experience while also emphasizing her oneness with other African American women; what matters most is not her actual words, but the fact that an African American female voice is speaking and being heard.

Giddings, Paula. *When and Where I Enter: The Impact of Black Women on Race and Sex in America*. New York: William Morrow, 1984.

Giddings takes the title for her narrative history of black women from an essay of Cooper's and continues to refer to her work for insights into such topics as education, suffrage, and female fulfillment. Cooper spoke of the pivotal role black women would play in the regeneration of the race and of the "patient and silent toil of mothers to gain title to the bodies of their daughters." Giddings quotes Cooper on women's desire for education and for means of self-actualization outside love and marriage, and hails *A Voice from the South* as one of the best-written books of its period.

Hutchinson, Louise Daniel. "Anna Julia Haywood Cooper," in *Black Women in America*, Vol. 1, ed. Darlene Clark Hine. Brooklyn, N.Y.: Carlson, 1993.

Hutchinson emphasizes Cooper's passion for learning, her tough-minded approach to difficult decisions and issues, and her leading role in the intellectual life of her times. Cooper was in the "vanguard of the struggle for human rights," to which she brought more than fifty years of activism. She was a "consummate teacher" and a much-sought-after speaker who continued her work as an educator well into her eighties.

Shockley, Ann Allen. "Anna Julia Haywood Cooper," in *Afro-American Women Writers, 1746-1933: An Anthology and Critical Guide*. Boston: G. K. Hall, 1988.

Shockley cites Cooper's life as "the impressive chronicle of a woman moving from slavery to leadership" and emphasizes her commitment to equality and education for women. She received her Ph.D. at the "amazing age" of sixty-five and after retirement accepted a position as the second president of Frelinghuysen University, a nontraditional institution with the mission of offering a variety of services to working-class blacks, a concept to which Cooper remained dedicated in her remaining years. Included is Cooper's best-known essay, "The Higher Education of Women."

Washington, Mary Helen. "Anna Julia Cooper: The Black Feminist Voice for the 1890's." *Legacy* 4, no. 2 (Fall 1987): 3-15.

Cooper has never received the recognition she deserved as the nineteenth century's most articulate black feminist, according to Washington. This may be because her role as a scholar was limited, and she presumed to speak for black women, rather than to them. In this brief biographical essay, Washington highlights Cooper's "forceful" statements about sexual and racial politics. Though she found it too risky to identify with issues of concern to poor black women, Cooper did speak out on education and "racial uplift."

JESSIE REDMON FAUSET
1882-1961

Jessie Fauset was born in New Jersey and raised in Philadelphia, where her father moved following the death of her mother shortly after her birth. She was the only African American in her class at Philadelphia High School for Girls and one of the first black women to attend Cornell University, where she majored in classical languages. Fauset was the first black woman in America to graduate Phi Beta Kappa. She later studied at the Sorbonne and led literary groups to Europe. Her professional life included teaching languages, writing, and editing. Widely recognized as one of the "midwives" of the Harlem Renaissance, Fauset was the first literary editor of *Crisis,* the journal of the National Association for the Advancement of Colored People (NAACP). She also edited the *Brownies Book,* a monthly magazine for children for which she wrote hundreds of signed and unsigned stories, poems, biographies, and essays. Fauset published her first novel, *There Is Confusion* (1924), at the age of forty-two; it is generally considered the first novel to depict the black middle class. This was followed by *Plum Bun: A Novel without a Moral* (1929), *The Chinaberry Tree: A Novel of American Life* (1931), and *Comedy, American Style* (1933).

Reissued Editions
The Chinaberry Tree and Selected Writings. Boston: Northeastern University Press, 1994.

Comedy, American Style. College Park, Md.: McGrath Publishing, 1969.

Plum Bun. Boston: Beacon Press, 1990.

There Is Confusion. Boston: Northeastern University Press, 1989.

Biography and Commentary
Ammons, Elizabeth. "Plots: Jessie Fauset and Edith Wharton," in *Conflicting Stories.* New York: Oxford University Press, 1991.

Ammons discusses the similarities and differences between the "scripts" according to which these two women were expected to live their lives, and then looks at the way they depict the problems faced by women artists in their fiction. According to Ammons, Fauset's *There Is Confusion* deals with some of the same issues of "control, freedom and sexual conflict" found in Wharton's work, but has far more significant similarities to Hopkins's *Contending Forces* and Harper's *Iola Leroy* in terms of "context." Like Wharton, Fauset was a realist who asked difficult questions: How, for example, can Angela in *Plum Bun* make art if she does not "prostitute" herself to the white world, which offers training and production?

Carby, Hazel V. "The Quicksands of Representation: Rethinking Black Cultural Politics," in *Reconstructing Womanhood: The Emergence of the Afro-American Woman Novelist.* New York: Oxford University Press, 1987.

    Carby describes Fauset as a basically conservative woman who subscribed to a "middle-class code of morality and behavior." In *The Chinaberry Tree*, for example, Fauset shows how professional black men save their women from isolated lives as unmarried mothers. She disagrees with more sympathetic readings of Fauset and argues that her work "adapts but does not transcend" the conventional romance.

Christian, Barbara. "The Rise and Fall of the Proper Mulatta," in *Black Women Novelists: The Development of a Tradition, 1892-1976.* Westport, Conn.: Greenwood Press, 1980.

    Christian criticizes Fauset for her uncritical acceptance of the American dream but praises her for her "incisive analysis" of the Black as "funny man" in her essay "Gift of Laughter." Fauset was one of several female novelists of her day who "chose" for their heroines middle-class, fair-skinned women of "taste and refinement." Her mistake was to suggest that the lives of these women were representative, resulting in what Christian terms "bad fairy tales" which neglect the depressing reality of most black people's lives.

Davis, Thadious M. "Jessie Redmon Fauset," in *Black Women in America*, Vol. 1, ed. Darlene Clark Hine. Brooklyn, N.Y.: Carlson, 1993.

    Davis begins his biographical essay with the assertion that "race" was the "driving force" behind Fauset's fiction. He praises critics such as Carolyn Sylvander for identifying Fauset's "modern" treatment of sexism and female socialization and blames older critics such as Robert Bone for labeling her as one of the old-fashioned "Rear Guard." Davis credits Fauset with shaping the cultural agenda for the *Crisis* and for showing black authors how to take control of their own representation in fiction. He believes she used "passing" in all of her novels as a "means of representing the arbitrariness and destructiveness of racial constructions in the United States."

DuCille, Ann. *The Coupling Convention: Sex, Text and Tradition in Black Women's Fiction.* New York: Oxford University Press, 1993.

DuCille argues that the novels of both Fauset and Nella Larsen, like those of Kate Chopin, anticipate the franker depiction of female sexuality to be found in more recent feminist texts. Their novels "transcend" the theme of "passing" to critique the conventions of sentimental romance. *Comedy, American Style,* for example, offers a complex and highly ironic picture of the "mixed blessings" experienced by middle-class black women in a patriarchal, racist society.

See also: Ann DuCille, "Blue Notes on Black Sexuality: Sex and the Texts of Jessie Fauset," in *Journal of the History of Sexuality* (January 3, 1993): 418-444.

Lewis, Vashti Crutcher. "Mulatto Hegemony in the Novels of Jessie Fauset." *CLA Journal* 35, no. 4 (June 1992): 375-386.

Lewis sees Fauset's heroines as variations on the tragic mulatto archetype of antebellum antislavery fiction. Though her light-skinned characters are overly class and color conscious, Fauset portrays them with sympathy and understanding and must, therefore, be credited with humanizing stereotypical "caricatures."

Lupton, Mary Jane. "Bad Blood in Jersey: Jessie Fauset's *The Chinaberry Tree.*" *CLA Journal* 27, no. 4 (June 1984): 383-392.

Lupton credits Fauset with the creation of "authentic female lives" seen as entrapped within the narrow confines of room, house, and backyard. She notes that only Fauset's women suffer from the moral curse of "bad blood" brought about by incest and miscegenation. Critics who fault Fauset as "insipid" misunderstand the nature of her protest, Lupton concludes.

See also: Mary Jane Lupton, "Clothes and Closure in Three Novels by Black Women," *Black American Literature Forum* 20, no. 4 (Winter 1986): 409-421, for a comparison of Fauset's *Comedy: American Style* with Alice Walker's *The Color Purple* and Toni Morrison's *Tar Baby* in terms of clothing as a "vehicle for transformation."

McCoy, Beth A. "'Is this really what you wanted me to be?' The Daughter's Disintegration in Jessie Redmon Fauset's *There Is Confusion.*" *Modern Fiction Studies* 40, no. 1 (Spring 1994): 101-118.

McCoy challenges the common assumption that Fauset was an "accommodationist" and that the "false" happy ending of *There Is Confusion* reflects her conservatism. The novel traces its heroine's shift from "questing subject" to racialized "sexual object" in McCoy's reading. Joanna experiences, but does not recognize, her exploitation. Rather than subscribing to the Harlem Renaissance belief in "art" as a weapon against racial stereotypes, Fauset may have been demonstrating that the American myth of individual transcendence does not work for everyone, and is especially problematic for black women.

McDowell, Deborah E. "The Neglected Dimension of Jessie Fauset," in *Conjuring: Black Women, Fiction, and Literary Tradition*, eds. Marjorie Pryse and Hortense J. Spillers. Bloomington: Indiana University Press, 1985.

McDowell argues that Fauset's reliance on the "novel of manners" and her use of fairy-tale patterns were conscious "stratagems" to mask her real topic: "the black woman's struggle for democratic ideals in a society whose sexist conventions assiduously work to thwart that struggle." McDowell analyzes in depth an early short story, "The Sleeper Wakes" (1920), and Fauset's first novel, *There Is Confusion* (1924), to demonstrate that Fauset's work was far more "progressive" than acknowledged by those critics who continue to see her as a "prim and proper Victorian."

Shockley, Ann Allen. "Jessie Redmon Fauset Harris," in *Afro-American Women Writers, 1746-1933: An Anthology and Critical Guide*. Boston: G. K. Hall, 1988.

Shockley summarizes the key events in Fauset's life and the plots of her four novels, and also includes an excerpt from *Plum Bun*. She emphasizes the difficulty Fauset had finding publishers for her first novels; most believed that white readers would consider middle-class black characters to be unrealistic. Shockley takes to task those critics who blame Fauset for writing about what she knew best: "the snobbery, hypocrisy, pettiness, clannishness and narrow mindedness" of people whose lives resemble their own. As a sophisticated world traveler, Fauset herself represented the "new breed" of African American woman.

Showalter, Elaine. "The Other Lost Generation," in *Sister's Choice*. New York: Oxford University Press, 1991.

Showalter identifies Fauset as one of "the most gifted women" of the Harlem Renaissance, one whose work challenged the stereotypes of black male readers despite being dismissed as "fastidious and precious" by its critics. Showalter argues that Fauset's work was more "innovative" than most male critics acknowledged, particularly in its refusal of the "cult of primitivism" and the "limits" that white publishers set on the portrayal of blacks in fiction. Moreover, the novels are about "sexual politics" as well as "racial tensions," and demonstrate the interaction of race and gender in determining power relationships.

Sims, Janet L. "Jessie Redmon Fauset: A Selected Annotated Bibliography." *Black American Literature Forum* 14, no. 4 (Winter 1980): 147-150.

Sims provides a comprehensive list of Fauset's writings and contemporaneous reviews plus annotated biographical and bibliographical references to her and her work.

Sylvander, Carolyn Wedin. "Jessie Redmon Fauset (1882-1961)," in *Afro American Women Writers from the Harlem Renaissance to 1940*, Vol. 51, in *Dictionary of Literary Biography*, eds. Trudier Harris and Thadious M. Davis. Detroit: Gale Research, 1987.

This biographical essay is a distillation of Sylvander's book-length biography, which traces Fauset's life and career and offers commentary on each of her novels. Sylvander considers Fauset "a minor, though pivotal" figure in the Harlem Renaissance whose critics have ignored significant elements in her work because of their exclusive focus on her depiction of her own middle-class Philadelphia background.

See also: Carolyn Wedin Sylvander, *Jessie Redmon Fauset: Black American Writer*. Troy, N.Y.: Whitston, 1981.

Wall, Cheryl A. "Jessie Redmon Fauset." *Black American Literature Forum* 20 (Spring/Summer 1986): 97-111.

Wall praises Fauset for demonstrating the interconnectedness of race, class, and sex and for her subversive use of the tragic mulatto convention.

Watson, Carol McAlpine. "Race Consciousness and Self-Criticism, 1921-1945," in *Prologue: The Novels of Black American Women, 1891-1965*. Westport, Conn.: Greenwood Press, 1985.

Watson sees *There Is Confusion* as a novel which both promotes middle-class achievement and warns of the price to be paid for middle-class ambitions. *Comedy, American Style* focuses on the contradictions inherent in "color mania." The novel criticizes the importance paid to color, while at the same time seeming to suggest that it is best to be "as white as possible," given the realities of life in America.

FRANCES ELLEN WATKINS HARPER
1825-1911

Harper was born in Baltimore; her parents died when she was three, leaving her to be raised by her aunt and uncle, who were abolitionists and ran a school for "free" children. Harper is best known as the author of *Iola Leroy* (1892), which for many years was thought to be the first novel written by an African American woman. However, recent scholarship has identified *Our Nig* (1859; see entry under Harriet E. Wilson) as the more probable first novel and has discovered three additional works by Harper serialized between 1869 and 1889. Prior to Paul Laurence Dunbar, Harper was the most popular and best-known poet of her day; she published the first of ten books of poetry in 1846. She was also an exceptionally effective speaker. An activist all her life—abolitionist, social reformer, and feminist—she gave her first public lecture, "Education and Elevation of the Colored Race," in 1854 and helped support the Underground Railroad.

Reissued Editions
The African-American Novel in the Age of Reaction: Three Classics: Iola Leroy (1892), The Marrow of Tradition (1901), The Sport of the Gods (1902), ed. William L. Andrews. New York: Penguin, 1992.

A Brighter Coming Day: A Francis Ellen Watkins Harper Reader, ed. Frances Smith Foster. New York: Feminist Press, 1990.

The Complete Poems of Frances E. W. Harper. New York: Oxford University Press, 1988.

Iola Leroy. Boston: Beacon Press, 1987.

Minnie's Sacrifice; Sowing and Reaping; Trial and Triumph: Three Rediscovered Novels by Frances E. W. Harper, ed. Frances Smith Foster. Boston: Beacon Press, 1994.

Biography and Commentary
Bell, Bernard W. "The Early Afro-American Novel: Historical Romance, Social Realism and Beyond," in *The Afro-American Novel and Its Tradition.* Amherst: University of Massachusetts Press, 1987.
  Bell compares *Iola Leroy* to William Dean Howells's *An Imperative Duty* (1892), which also emphasizes the moral duty of mulattos to uplift their race. Bell notes that *Iola Leroy* was the first Afro-American novel to treat the heroism of blacks during and after the Civil War.

Boyd, Melba Joyce. *Discarded Legacy: Politics and Poetics in the Life of Frances E. W. Harper, 1825-1911.* Detroit, Mich.: Wayne State University Press, 1994.
  Boyd, a black female poet herself, sees Harper as a writer who addressed all the crucial issues of her times. Her varied career as abolitionist, social reformer, feminist activist, and creative writer brought her in contact with the best-known abolitionists and women's rights activists of the nineteenth century. Boyd considers Harper's work with both the white-dominated Women's Christian Temperance Union and the Black Women's Club Movement. The text includes primary and secondary bibliographies and extensive quotations from Harper's poetry and other writings.

Carby, Hazel V. "'Of Lasting Service for the Race': The Work of Frances Ellen Watkins Harper," in *Reconstructing Womanhood: The Emergence of the Afro-American Woman Novelist.* New York: Oxford University Press, 1987.
  Carby offers a detailed analysis of *Iola Leroy* in order to consider its relationship to Harper's life and experience. In effect, Carby deconstructs the notion that this novel, undertaken when Harper was sixty-seven years old, was the author's "least successful project." As Carby sees it, Harper intentionally wrote the work "to intervene in and

to influence political, social and cultural debate concerning the status of 'the Negro.'" The novel predated W. E. B. Du Bois's concept of "the talented tenth" and served as a textbook of sorts for black intellectuals. Carby disagrees with critics who blame Harper for trying to appeal to a white audience and suggests that her use of the mulatta figure underscores the separateness of the races despite their evident sexual interaction.

Christian, Barbara. "Shadows Uplifted," in *Black Women Novelists: The Development of a Tradition, 1892-1976*. Westport, Conn.: Greenwood Press, 1980.
    Christian discusses the historical context of *Iola Leroy* and its relationship to William Wells Brown's *Clotel* (1861). By the time Harper's novel was published, the country had gone through Reconstruction, "as tumultuous a time as the Civil War," which resulted in a "steady stream of defeats" for black abolitionists. Harper, an "abolitionist elder" and a founder of anti-lynching societies, used the beautiful octoroon heroine of antebellum abolitionist novels to make her story palatable to white readers. The tone is one of "uplifting the race," the mulatta "no longer tragic or melancholy but a source of light for those below and around her."

Dearborn, Mary V. "Strategies of Authorship: Midwiving and Mediation," in *Pocahontas's Daughters: Gender and Ethnicity in American Culture*. New York: Oxford University Press, 1986.
    Dearborn considers Harper's work as an example of ethnic writing which attempts to mediate between different cultures. Harper uses "subversive communication" and "trickster" motifs to convey her criticism of white middle-class culture to her black readers while at the same time generating sympathy for black suffering among her white readers. The novel both encourages "race pride" and urges other blacks to write, an act that can ultimately lead to "power."

DuCille, Ann. *The Coupling Convention: Sex, Text and Tradition in Black Women's Fiction.* New York: Oxford University Press, 1993.
    DuCille argues that the near-white heroines of Hopkins and Frances Harper, no matter how passionless and sickeningly pious they seem today, served important political and literary functions in their own day. Moreover, the marital relationship in *Iola Leroy* is clearly depicted in sensual terms; Iola and Frank are passionate about both the work of racial uplift and their love for each other.

Ernest, John. "From Mysteries to Histories: Cultural Pedagogy in Frances E. W. Harper's *Iola Leroy*." *American Literature* 64, no. 3 (September 1992): 497-518.
    Ernest considers *Iola Leroy* to be a "subtle and intricate" novel of historical importance for what it reveals about Harper's response to racism. Key to the novel is its emphasis on "shadows," "the shadows

of cultural confusion, miscomprehension, and racial tension that threaten the nation's future." These shadows will be lifted only when education becomes a "mutual effort," not just the socialization of one culture by another.

Foster, Frances Smith. "Frances Ellen Watkins Harper," in *Black Women in America*, Vol. 1. Brooklyn, N.Y.: Carlson, 1993.

Foster begins her biographical essay by describing Harper as a writer committed to the "utility of beauty" whose works were designed "to delight" and "to teach." She then provides a positive portrait of an independent, courageous woman who firmly believed that the twentieth century held the hope of a "brighter day" for African American women and that her own writing and work would help usher in the new era.

Hill, Patricia Liggins. "'Let Me Make the Songs for the People': A Study of Frances Watkins Harper's Poetry." *Black American Literature Forum* 15, no. 2 (Summer 1981): 60-65.

Hill argues that Harper's reputation as a poet "rests on her excellent skills in oral poetry delivery" and not on technique. Her poetry depends on "vivid, striking imagery" and "simplistic language" which give it a mass appeal not unlike the social protest poetry of Nikki Giovanni, LeRoi Jones (Amiri Baraka), or, more recently, Sonia Sanchez. The majority of her poems are appeals for "freedmen's rights, suffrage and racial equality." Hill identifies Harper as the "first black feminist poet" and stresses how in her Aunt Chloe poems (*Sketches of Southern Life*, 1891) she teaches the black woman how to "uplift her race." Hill concludes that, despite the disappearance of Harper's poetry from print, it is worthy of "serious literary/critical attention" and should be considered as "the foundation upon which much of contemporary black poetry is based."

Peterson, Carla L. "'Further Lifting of the Veil': Gender, Class, and Labor in Frances E. W. Harper's *Iola Leroy*," in *Listening to Silences: New Essays in Feminist Criticism*, eds. Elaine Hedges and Shelley Fisher Fishkin. New York: Oxford University Press, 1994.

Peterson uses new archival discoveries to argue that the novel is far more than a portrayal of an elite black heroine. Iola's uncle Robert Johnson also plays a central role in the novel's discussion of labor and leadership issues within the black community.

Shockley, Ann Allen. "Frances Ellen Watkins Harper," in *Afro-American Women Writers, 1746-1933: An Anthology and Critical Guide*. Boston: G. K. Hall, 1988.

Shockley describes Harper's public career following the death of her husband as a "majestic testament" to the intelligence and talents of African American women. She highlights her feminism and her leading role in the Women's Christian Temperance Union, and shows how her concerns about the evils of alcohol and the pressing needs of women were expressed in both her poetry and her lectures. Shockley includes the poem "A Double Standard" and an excerpt from *Iola Leroy*.

Washington, Mary Helen. "Uplifting the Women and the Race: The Forerunners—Harper and Hopkins," in *Invented Lives: Narratives of Black Women, 1860-1960*. Garden City, N.Y.: Anchor Press, 1987.
   Washington acknowledges that Harper supported the values associated with the "cult of true womanhood," but believes that she still rejected the concept of marriage as an emotional and economic refuge for women. She highlights Harper's concern to defend black men and women against vicious stereotypes.

Watson, Carol McAlpine. "Uplift and Protest, 1891-1920," in *Prologue: The Novels of Black American Women, 1891-1965*. Westport, Conn.: Greenwood Press, 1985.
   Watson emphasizes the "inspirational" quality of Harper's work and her creation of positive black role models worthy of emulation. She also discusses her involvement with the Women's Christian Temperance Union.

Young, Elizabeth. "Warring Fictions: *Iola Leroy* and the Color of Gender." *American Literature* 64, no. 2 (June 1992): 273-297.
   Harper's novel was the first to address black participation in the Civil War. Young analyzes the way in which it "foregrounds" the role of both black soldiers and the black family. Harper used "civil war" as a metaphor for a variety of racial and gender conflicts, including Iola's own struggle for identity. Like many white writers, Harper also connected the themes of war and rape; however, she inverted the southern practice of using rape plots for racist and misogynistic purposes, and instead equated rape with the antebellum oppression of slaves.

PAULINE ELIZABETH HOPKINS
1859-1930

Hopkins was born in Portland, Maine, and raised in Boston, where she graduated from the Boston Girls High School. She later studied stenography and worked for the Bureau of Statistics. Hopkins's first literary work was a musical drama written for the Hopkins Colored Troubadours, of which she was a member. She wrote her first short story, "The Mystery within Us" (1900), for the maiden issue of *The Colored American,* a monthly magazine for which she served as editor, shareholder, and member of the board. She continued to write fiction, social commentary, and biographical sketches of prominent African Americans for this and other journals, though she later returned to stenography to support herself. Hopkins's first novel, *Contending Forces: A Romance Illustrative of Negro Life North and South,* was published in 1900. Her three other novels, *Hagar's Daughter, Winona,* and *Of One Blood*, were serialized in *The Colored American* during the years 1901 to 1903.

Reissued Editions
Contending Forces: A Romance Illustrative of Negro Life North and South. New York: Oxford University Press, 1988.
The Magazine Novels of Pauline Hopkins. New York: Oxford University Press, 1988.

Biography and Commentary
Campbell, Jane. "Pauline Elizabeth Hopkins," in *Black Women in America*, Vol. 1, ed. Darlene Clark Hine. Brooklyn, N.Y.: Carlson, 1993.
  Campbell sees Hopkins as a "remarkably prolific" and talented writer of popular romances which capture the heroism and drama inherent in the black struggle against racial oppression. In summarizing Hopkins's life and accomplishments, Campbell stresses the important role she played for *The Colored American* as writer, editor, and promoter, and the continued relevance of her work for today's readers.

Carby, Hazel V. "'Of What Use Is Fiction?' Pauline Elizabeth Hopkins" and "'All the Fire and Romance': The Magazine Fiction of Pauline Hopkins," in *Reconstructing Womanhood: The Emergence of the Afro-American Woman Novelist*. New York: Oxford University Press, 1987.
  Carby devotes two full chapters to Hopkins's career, the history of *The Colored American*, and analysis of *Contending Forces*. Given the magazine's stated objective of reaching a comprehensive black readership, Carby considers just who its readers might have been in terms of education and occupation. Hopkins's own political agenda was to use fiction to help improve race relations. Unfortunately, according to Carby, she was unable to reconcile her faith in New England progressivism with her experience of the reality of northern racism. Hopkins has been accused of expressing her own implicit desire to "lighten the race" through her mulatto and octoroon characters. Carby disagrees, arguing rather that Hopkins's characters show the consequences of white supremacy and rape and the absurdity of concepts of racial purity. She goes on to identify *Contending Forces* as a "detailed exploration of the parameters of black womanhood and the patriarchal limitations of black womanhood" and to term Hopkins's fiction in general a "cathartic response" to a fundamentally pessimistic view of black life in America.

Clark, Edward. "Boston Black and White." *Black American Literature Forum* 19 (Summer 1985): 83-89.
  Clark refers to two of Hopkins's novels, *Contending Forces* and *Of One Blood*, to demonstrate that her depiction of Boston, like that of

other black novelists, contrasts sharply with the liberal image of the city projected by white writers.

Dearborn, Mary V. "Miscegenation and the Mulatto, Inheritance and Incest: The Pocahontas Marriages, Part II," in *Pocahontas's Daughters: Gender and Ethnicity in American Culture.* New York: Oxford University Press, 1986.

Dearborn focuses on Hopkins's two less well-known novels, *Winona* and *Of One Blood,* because their excessive melodrama reveals the "remarkable contradictions" of interracial romances. In *Of One Blood,* in particular, Hopkins turns to the gothic genre to explore the "fluidity of boundaries" in interracial relationships. Dearborn believes Hopkins wrote these novels to protest "the refusal of white males to acknowledge their mulatto children."

DuCille, Ann. *The Coupling Convention: Sex, Text and Tradition in Black Women's Fiction.* New York: Oxford University Press, 1993.

DuCille argues that the near-white heroines of Hopkins and Frances Harper, no matter how passionless and sickeningly pious they seem today, served important political and literary functions in their own day. *Contending Forces,* in particular, exposed the horrors of white male supremacy while providing a positive portrait of black patriarchy. The utopian marriage Hopkins describes is intended to exemplify a "partnership in race work" rather than submission to a cult of domesticity.

Gillman, Susan. "The Mulatto, Tragic or Triumphant: The Nineteenth century American Race Melodrama," in *The Culture of Sentiment: Race, Gender, and Sentimentality in Nineteenth century America,* ed. Shirley Samuels. New York: Oxford University Press, 1992.

Gillman uses Hopkins's *Of One Blood* as a case study of the kind of romantic story about a black family with an interracial genealogy which flourished at the same time that institutional racism was solidifying. These stories, by both white and black writers, showed parents, children, and lovers representative of different races or classes coming together in the service of racial and national unity. The search for kinship in Hopkins's novel takes the conventional story further and refigures it "globally" as a metaphor for the history of the black diaspora and a pan-African future.

Otten, Thomas J. "Pauline Hopkins and the Hidden Self of Race." *ELH* 59, no. 1 (Spring 1992): 227-256.

Otten analyzes Hopkins's use of W. E. B. Du Bois's theories on race and William James's on human psychology. In *Of One Blood,* Hopkins dramatized their ideas as a way of revealing the artificiality of conventional assumptions about the differences between blacks and whites. James, in particular, proved a "congenial source" who made it possible for Hopkins to identify a "hidden power," preserved in folk medicines and other folk practices, which harked back to ancient Africa. This ancient culture, through Moses, is presented by Hopkins as the origin of a racially mixed Western heritage.

Shockley, Ann Allen. "Pauline Elizabeth Hopkins," in *Afro-American Women Writers, 1746-1933: An Anthology and Critical Guide*. Boston: G. K. Hall, 1988.
   Shockley reviews Hopkins's life and work as editor, writer, novelist, playwright, and singer. She concludes that throughout this versatile career Hopkins placed the welfare of her people above all else, and that she has not received the recognition she deserves for her work as a literary editor in particular. "The Sewing Circle," an excerpt from *Contending Forces*, is included.

Tate, Claudia. "From Domestic Happiness to Racial Despair," in *Domestic Allegories of Political Desire: The Black Heroine's Text at the Turn of the Century*. New York: Oxford University Press, 1992.
   Tate uses Hopkins's fiction to demonstrate that the "racial optimism" which dominated novels of the 1890's, including *Contending Forces*, slowly disappeared in later works. *Hagar's Daughter*, for example, replaces the protest for racial equality of the earlier novel with "generational tests of interracial true love." *Winona* and *Of One Blood* also have plots which revolve around tests of true love, but with slightly more "explicit" racial polemics. Moreover, the heroines of the later works are less central, their function limited to inciting sympathy for their "racial plight," rather than admiration for their brilliance. Hopkins apparently lost faith in the effectiveness of "black female authority" as an agent of positive social reform.

——————. "Pauline Hopkins: Our Literary Foremother," in *Conjuring: Black Women, Fiction, and Literary Tradition*, eds. Marjorie Pryse and Hortense J. Spillers. Bloomington: Indiana University Press, 1985.
   Tate surveys the history of Hopkins's critical reception, quoting from Vernon Loggin, Hugh Glouster, Robert Bone, and Judith Berzon, none of whom deals with the full body of Hopkins's work. Tate then summarizes the plot and thematic concerns of Hopkins's serial novels, concluding that, despite their "excessively episodic and melodramatic techniques," all of Hopkins's works are worthy of our consideration given the overall importance of her career as both novelist and journalist.

Washington, Mary Helen. "Uplifting the Women and the Race: The Forerunners—Harper and Hopkins," in *Invented Lives: Narratives of Black Women, 1860-1960*. Garden City, N.Y.: Anchor Press, 1987.
   Hopkins, like Harper, used her fiction to counteract the negative images of blacks and women typical of the times. Both "foreground" women's lives and feelings and reverse the image of the tragic mulatta,

transforming her into a social and political activist. Hopkins is less militant and progressive than Harper and more ambivalent about female roles. Washington includes two chapters from *Contending Forces* and the short story, "Bro'r Abr'm Jimson's Wedding: A Christmas Story" (1901).

ZORA NEALE HURSTON
1891-1960

Hurston was born in Eatonville, Florida, an all-black town of which her father was mayor. She attended Howard University, where she began her writing career. Her second short story, "Spunk" (1925), and her first play, *Color Struck* (1926), won literary prizes and were quickly recognized by leaders of the Harlem Renaissance, who encouraged Hurston to move to New York. She continued writing while studying anthropology at Barnard College and later compiled two volumes of folklore: *Mules and Men* (1935) and *Tell My Horse* (1938). Hurston wrote four novels—*Jonah's Gourd Vine* (1934), loosely based on her father's life; *Their Eyes Were Watching God* (1937), now considered a feminist classic; *Moses, Man of the Mountain* (1939); and *Seraph on the Suwanee* (1948)—and a controversial autobiography, *Dust Tracks on a Road* (1942). Despite this impressive record of publication, Hurston died virtually penniless and unknown after returning to Florida in the 1950's. Her Fort Pierce grave remained unmarked until Alice Walker searched for and discovered it in 1979, as recounted in *In Search of Our Mothers' Gardens* (1983).

Reissued Editions
Note: Almost all of Hurston's fiction and folklore is available in both hardback and paperback editions. There are also audiocassettes of her most popular work and librettos of stage adaptations.

The Complete Stories. New York: HarperCollins, 1994.

Folklore, Memoirs and Other Writings. New York: Library of America, 1995.

Jonah's Gourd Vine. New York: HarperCollins, 1990.

Moses, Man of the Mountain. New York: HarperCollins, 1991.

Mule Bone: A Comedy of Negro Life in Three Acts (written with Langston Hughes). New York: HarperCollins, 1991.

Mules and Men: A Treasury of Black American Folklore. New York: HarperCollins, 1990.

Novels and Stories. New York: Library of America, 1995.

Seraph on the Suwanee. New York: HarperCollins, 1991.

Spunk: The Selected Stories of Zora Neale Hurston. Berkeley, Calif.: Turtle Island Foundation, 1985.

Tell My Horse: Voodoo and Life in Haiti and Jamaica. New York: HarperCollins, 1990.

Their Eyes Were Watching God. New York: HarperCollins, 1990.

Three Classic Works by Zora Neale Hurston: Their Eyes Were Watching God, Dust Tracks on a Road, Mules & Men. New York: HarperCollins, 1991.

Biography and Commentary
Ashe, Bertram D. "'Why don't he like my hair?' Constructing African-American Standards of Beauty in Toni Morrison's *Song of Solomon* and Zora Neale Hurston's *Their Eyes Were Watching God.*" *African American Review* 29, no. 4 (Winter 1995): 579-592.
    Both Morrison and Hurston clarify the politics of black hairstyles. Though Janie Crawford is sought after by a variety of men because she approximates the white ideal of beauty with her light skin and long, silky hair, she herself refuses to put down "kinfolks" who are "black" rather than "yaller," and struggles against all her husbands who try to keep her apart from "the greater black community." Ashe notes that Joe Stark tries to control Janie by making her wear a headrag; she in turn exerts her freedom by letting her hair down.

Awkward, Michael, ed. *New Essays on Their Eyes Were Watching God.* New York: Cambridge University Press, 1990.
    This volume in the American Novel series includes a bibliography, an introductory overview of Hurston criticism, and essays by Robert Hemenway, Nellie McKay, Hazel Carby, Rachel Blau DuPlessis, and Awkward himself.

Christian, Barbara. "The Rise and Fall of the Proper Mulatta," in *Black Women Novelists: The Development of a Tradition, 1892-1976.* Westport, Conn.: Greenwood Press, 1980.
    Christian summarizes the key elements of Hurston's life and career and then considers *Their Eyes Were Watching God* as a transitional work in terms of the image of the black woman in literature. Janie is the first black girl or woman whose experiences are described from "within." Moreover, as one of the first writers "to use folk images and speech," Hurston anticipates more recent African American women writers. Her heroine's "cultural values" and sense of self stand worlds apart from those of the more conventional mulatta, Iola Leroy, in Frances Harper's novel. In the end, Hurston (like Nella Larsen) "fell prey" to "racial and sexual stereotypes," a victim of unjust criticism

and innuendo indicative of the "vulnerable" position of all black
women writers of her time.

Davie, Sharon. "Free Mules, Talking Buzzards, and Cracked Plates: The
Politics of Dislocation in *Their Eyes Were Watching God.*" *PMLA*
108, no. 3 (May 1993): 446-459.
  Davie discusses the ways in which the novel undercuts rational,
dualistic, hierarchical thinking and therefore encourages readers to see
beyond traditional boundaries. The free mule stories, for example,
"playfully upset the man-animal hierarchy." Moreover, Janie's
comparison of Joe Stark and the helpless, pathetic mule undermines his
master status and reveals her sexual power. The buzzard tale "challenges
the domination of realistic fiction over black folk forms" and
underscores the meaninglessness of hierarchies in the face of death.
Finally, Hurston's use of bodily metaphors emphasizes tactile, physical
reality and the inadequacy of language to express fully human
experience. Janie's joy in the "playful sensuality of her relationship
with Teacake" parallels Hurston's own love for the "adorned, active,
physical language of black folk expression."

Davies, Kathleen. "Zora Neale Hurston's Politics of Embalmment:
Articulating the Rage of Black Women and Narrative Self-Defense."
African American Review 26, no. 1 (Spring 1992): 173-182.
  Beginning with the observation that in her autobiography Hurston
was quite kind in her description of a lover who abused her, Davies
notes that in her novels Hurston kills off "oppressive black men" while
also preserving them in the "sweet balm of memory." *Their Eyes Were
Watching God* can be read as a black woman's desire "to merge her
quest for liberation with that of the black man while maintaining her
right to live without his abuse." Both author and heroine "construct"
the truth in order to protect themselves and their dreams.

Dearborn, Mary V. "Black Women Authors and the Harlem
Renaissance," in *Pocahontas's Daughters: Gender and Ethnicity in
American Culture.* New York: Oxford University Press, 1986.
  Dearborn identifies Hurston, along with Fauset and Larsen, as one of
the key female figures in the Harlem Renaissance. Hurston was blamed
by her peers for being too dependent on white patronage, for not being
bitter enough about the black condition, and for using folklore too
obtrusively in her fiction, thereby contributing to "cultural
colonialism." Dearborn looks closely at Hurston's relationship with
Mrs. Mason, her Park Avenue patron, and concludes that Hurston, "in
classic trickster fashion," used this relationship to her own advantage.
Hurston, like Langston Hughes—also a Mason prodigy—called Mrs.
Mason her "godmother." This was a complex relationship at best,
especially given Hurston's real need for a surrogate mother. Despite
Hurston's own ambivalence about the proper relationship between
folklore and fiction, despite the controversy surrounding her career,

Their Eyes Were Watching God, argues Dearborn, stands on its own as a "wholly self-sufficient and unmediated" text superior to the work of most of her contemporaries.

DuCille, Ann. *The Coupling Convention: Sex, Text and Tradition in Black Women's Fiction.* New York: Oxford University Press, 1993.

DuCille traces the many influences on Hurston, including folklore, slave narratives, blues singers, her literary precursors Harper and Hopkins, and her contemporaries Fauset, Larsen, Dunbar-Nelson, and Bonner. In particular, DuCille focuses on Hurston's depiction of marital relations in *Their Eyes Were Watching God* and *Seraph on the Suwanee*. The use of white characters in the latter novel allowed Hurston to deal with issues of misogyny and violence against women without feeding racist stereotypes of black men as rapists. DuCille concludes that the supposed submissiveness of Hurston's female protagonists is actually a clever strategy that allows them to "win" at the game of love.

Dutton, Wendy. "The Problem of Invisibility: Voodoo and Zora Neale Hurston." *Frontiers* 13, no. 2 (1992): 131-152.

Dutton provides her own brief history of voodoo, an overview of Hurston's career as an anthropologist, and a summary of her comments about the voodoo industry in New Orleans in *Mules and Men*, before turning to *Tell My Horse*, Hurston's attempt to demystify Haitian voodoo. This was a particularly difficult task for Hurston because of her own ambivalence about voodoo practices; the book itself is a strange mix of fiction and anthropology which tells the story of Hurston's active participation in voodoo rituals as well as the results of her more objective observations. Though her research was incomplete, Hurston prepared the way for later researchers who understood the necessity to immerse themselves in voodoo practices in order to understand them. She herself was the first person to photograph a zombie, which led to the later discovery of the drugs used to create the deathlike state.

Gates, Henry Louis, Jr. "Color Me Zora: Alice Walker's (Re)Writing of the Speakerly Text," in *The Signifying Monkey: A Theory of Afro-American Literary Criticism.* New York: Oxford University Press, 1988.

For Gates, Janie's "ultimate moment of self-awareness" comes with "her ability to name her own divided consciousness." Hurston's use of "free indirect discourse" and her "valorization of oral narration" make *Their Eyes Were Watching God* an exemplary text in the black literary quest to find an authentic voice for its speaking subjects. Janie's "movement from object to subject" begins when she fails to recognize her "colored" self in a photograph; her self-consciousness is finally affirmed in the "ritual speech act," where she is able to tell Phoeby her own version of events. Alice Walker, in writing *The Color Purple*, "has turned to a black antecedent text to claim literary ancestry" for both the content and structure of her work. Gates traces the ways in which Walker lovingly revises Hurston's text, casting Shug as a "figure for Hurston herself."

Gates, Henry Louis, Jr., and K. A. Appiah, eds. *Zora Neale Hurston: Critical Perspectives Past and Present.* New York: Amistad, 1993.
This collection includes contemporaneous reviews of Hurston's major works, fourteen critical essays, a bibliography, and a chronology of Hurston's career.

Hemenway, Robert. *Zora Neale Hurston: A Literary Biography.* Urbana: University of Illinois Press, 1977.
This full-length biography of Hurston is considered a standard work which provides most of the key information about her life now used by other critics. Hemenway looks at Hurston's Florida childhood, her role in the Harlem Renaissance and her controversial relationship with her patron, Mrs. Mason, and the relatively obscure final years of her life. He also offers analysis of her major works, emphasizing her use of folklore, and discusses how they were received in their own time. The biography includes an introduction by Alice Walker.

Hite, Molly. "Romance, Marginality, and Matrilineage: *The Color Purple* and *Their Eyes Were Watching God,*" in *Reading Black, Reading Feminist: A Critical Anthology,* ed. Henry Louis Gates, Jr. New York: Meridian, 1990.
Hite argues that what is often perceived as "marginal" in conventional Western realism and romance is treated by Hurston as "central," thus freeing her to use the novel to serve her own purposes. In particular, the "story" of Janie telling her story, rather than framing the novel, actually "supplants" what seems to be the main plot—the search for the right man to marry and love. Hite also comments on Hurston's use of the "muck," the fertile Florida bottomland where Teacake takes Janie, as a kind of Shakespearean green world with magical powers. However, she sees this as a "transitory stage," not the "culmination of the plot"; again it is the theme of finding a voice, of Janie's becoming "author" and "mother" of her own story, that the novel is truly about, states Hite.

Howard, Lillie P. "*Seraph on the Suwanee,*" in *Zora Neale Hurston.* New York: Macmillan, 1980.
Despite the fact that its characters are white, Hurston's last novel deals with the same themes and has the same focus on the "feminine psyche" as her other novels, according to Howard. Though "less lively" than *Their Eyes, Seraph on the Suwanee* is not necessarily an assimilationist novel, as it has been called by other critics.

_____. ed. *Alice Walker and Zora Neale Hurston: The Common Bond.* Westport, Conn.: Greenwood Press, 1993.

This collection includes a bibliography, an introduction by Howard, and eight essays which look for evidence of Hurston's influence on Walker and compare the fiction of the two writers.

Jones, Evora. "Ascent and Immersion: Narrative Expression in *Their Eyes Were Watching God.*" *CLA Journal* 39, no. 3 (March 1996): 369-379.

Building on an earlier analysis of the novel in Robert Stepto's *Beyond the Veil* (1979), Jones notes that Janie's journey fulfills the plots of both ascent and immersion stories. Her quest which takes her on symbolic trips North and South leads to self-knowledge and heroic stature as an "articulate survivor." However, she uses her freedom not just to assert her individuality, but also to take her place in a stable and familiar community.

Lowe, John. *Jump at the Sun: Zora Neale Hurston's Cosmic Comedy.* Champaign: University of Illinois Press, 1994.

Lowe looks at the entire body of Hurston's work in the context of her life and the cultural and historical events she experienced to demonstrate the sources and nature of her humor. He also shows how Hurston drew on African and African American religious imagery, particularly in *Moses, Man of the Mountain,* a "remarkable" book in its comic and satirical revisions of scripture. Ultimately, Hurston used humor as a vehicle both for subversive commentary on oppressive conditions and for joyous celebrations of a resilient folk culture. The "verve" with which she addresses serious topics may very well be the source of her continuing popularity. The text includes a list of works cited and extensive endnotes to each chapter.

McDowell, Deborah E. "Lines of Descent/Dissenting Lines," intro. to *Moses, Man of the Mountain.* New York: HarperCollins, 1991.

McDowell considers *Moses* in light of other African American versions of the exodus story, Hurston's own interest in the "problematics of liberation," and the inevitable impact of Nazi theories of "racial purity" on her thinking. The novel is proof that Hurston is not just a "regional" writer, but one whose work deserves consideration in a more "global context of cultural production and exchange."

Paquet, Sandra Pouchet. "The Ancestor as Foundation in *Their Eyes Were Watching God* and *Tar Baby.*" *Callaloo* 13, no. 3 (Summer 1990): 499-515.

The protagonists of both novels are orphans alienated from their roots who become romantically involved with men embodying important aspects of African American folk culture. Both authors call for a "roots-directed redefinition of self as a means to psychic wholeness." Hurston's heroine, Janie, completes her education and becomes a role model for others; her namesake, Jadine, in Morrison's novel, does not. Hurston sees "reconnection with the folk," not as a "permanent condition," but as a "means to an end" which helps Janie grow stronger, more creative, and more independent.

Patterson, Tiffany. "Zora Neale Hurston," in *Black Women in America,* Vol. 1, ed. Darlene Clark Hine. Brooklyn, N.Y.: Carlson, 1993.

Patterson calls Hurston "a colorful and flamboyant figure" and emphasizes the controversy that surrounded her career because she rejected the prevailing notion that blacks needed to be "uplifted" and that their culture was inferior. As an anthropologist she believed in the "value and legitimacy" of all cultures. She disagreed with the 1954 Supreme Court desegregation decision, which she saw as an insult to African American teachers. Patterson briefly discusses each of Hurston's works and concludes that all reinforce her belief that "real freedom can only occur in a whole, self-actualized community."

Peters, Pearlie M. "'Ah Got the Law in My Mouth': Black Women and Assertive Voice in Hurston's Fiction and Folklore." *CLA Journal* 37, no. 3 (March 1994): 293-302.

Peters focuses on three characters—Janie in *Their Eyes Were Watching God,* Delia in the story "Sweat," and Big Sweet in *Mules and Men*—to demonstrate Hurston's belief that women are the "real and essential storytellers of the race" because of their "honesty" and the "clarity" of their expression. Peters also discusses the influence of Hurston's mother and her Aunt Caroline, two women who used their assertive voices to help bring peace and harmony to their communities and homes.

Sadoff, Dianne. "Black Matrilineage: The Case of Alice Walker and Zora Neale Hurston." *Signs* 11, no. 1 (1985): 4-26.

Sadoff writes about the sources of "nurturance" Walker and other African American women writers have found in the work of Hurston by inadvertently idealizing and "misreading" her texts. She also describes the ways Hurston's novels fictionalize material omitted from her autobiography for political and personal reasons. Sadoff's analysis of *Their Eyes Were Watching God* suggests that the novel's flaws can be explained as a product of Hurston's own ambivalence about the compatibility of love and creativity. She may have had Janie kill Teacake out of subconscious rage at male domination; this act then symbolically frees both protagonist and author.

Walker, Alice. "Zora Neale Hurston: A Cautionary Tale and Partisan View" and "Looking for Zora," in *In Search of Our Mothers' Gardens.* New York: Harcourt Brace Jovanovich, 1983.

"Looking for Zora" is Walker's lively and moving account of her successful search for Hurston's unmarked grave. "A Cautionary Tale" is Walker's paean to Hurston's achievement as part of a trinity of "foremothers," including Billie Holiday and Bessie Smith.

Wall, Cheryl A. "Zora Neale Hurston: Changing Her Own Words," in *American Novelists Revisited: Essays in Feminist Criticism,* ed. Fritz Fleischmann. New York: G. K. Hall, 1982.

Wall credits recent feminist and African American criticism for correcting the old, distorted view of Hurston's use of folklore as "charming and quaint." Hurston's respect for the "cultural traditions of black people" is, according to Wall, the thread that ties together all of her work. Her appreciation of the "richness of black verbal expression" was learned through listening to her father's powerful sermons. Wall summarizes several of the most important folktales in *Mules and Men,* identifying it as the first collection of Afro-American folklore published by an Afro-American. She then goes on to praise the "sustained beauty of Hurston's prose" in *Their Eyes Were Watching God,* a literary "triumph" in which the folk material complements the basic plot.

Washington, Mary Helen. "'I Love the Way Janie Crawford Left Her Husbands': Zora Neale Hurston's Emergent Female Hero," in *Invented Lives: Narratives of Black Women, 1860-1960.* Garden City, N.Y.: Anchor Press, 1987.

Washington sees *Their Eyes Were Watching God* as a novel about "women's exclusion from power" as compared to *Jonah's Gourd Vine,* with its articulate male folk hero, John Pearson; excerpts from both works are included. While Janie is, in effect, silenced at key points in her own story, John Pearson "unambiguously" occupies the heroic center of his. Though Hurston is clearly critical of patriarchal norms, she is also somewhat uncomfortable with her own questing female hero and, therefore, endows her with many of the trappings of the romantic heroine, from her beautiful hair to the "tall, dark, mysterious stranger" who rescues her. Still, Janie's resistance to her community's values and her status as "outsider" affirm her individual potential, whereas the eulogy presented at John's funeral is more a tribute to the "male story" than to the man himself.

Willis, Susan. "Wandering: Zora Neale Hurston's Search for Self and Method," in *Specifying: Black Women Writing the American Experience.* Madison: University of Wisconsin Press, 1987.

Willis analyzes the way Hurston transforms the name-calling or "specifying" of folk culture into the kind of literary metaphor she needs to mediate between the "deeply polarized worlds" of South/North, black/white, and rural/urban America. In much of her work, including *Mules and Men,* Hurston creates images which stand halfway between "specifying" and metaphor. With *Their Eyes Were Watching God,* however, she achieves a more sophisticated narrative form which "transcends" the split between text and context and prepares the way for the "highly condensed, multireferential figures" found in the later work of Paule Marshall and Toni Morrison.

HARRIET ANN JACOBS
1813-1897

Jacobs was born a slave in North Carolina, where she was taught to read by a kind mistress who unfortunately died when Harriet was eleven or twelve years old. She then became the property of her mistress's niece and later fled what became an unbearable situation to the home of her freed grandmother, where she hid for seven years. In 1842 she finally escaped to the North, where she found work as a housekeeper for a family that bought her freedom for $300. The autobiography *Incidents in the Life of a Slave Girl*, which Jacobs wrote under the pseudonym Linda Brent, was published in 1861 with the help of Lydia Maria Child, a well-known white abolitionist. It was not until the publication of Yellin's 1987 annotated edition that Jacobs was fully credited with the actual writing of the narrative, which had previously been assumed to be the work of a white collaborator.

Reissued Editions

Brent, Linda. *Incidents in the Life of a Slave Girl.* New York: Harcourt Brace Jovanovich, 1973.

Jacobs, Harriet Ann [Linda Brent]. *Incidents in the Life of a Slave Girl, Written by Herself,* edited and with an introduction by Jean Fagan Yellin. Cambridge: Oxford University Press, 1987.

Biography and Commentary

Bartholomaus, Craig. "'What Would You Be?' Racial Myths and Cultural Sameness in *Incidents in the Life of a Slave Girl.*" *CLA Journal* 39, no. 2 (December 1995): 174-194.

Bartholomaus believes that Jacobs consciously made use of coventional language and of the values of "true womanhood" in order to counter prevailing stereotypes about African "nature" and to demonstrate her own "humanity." The text, therefore, does not include folktales or other "exclusive" cultural references, and the heroic family members and friends Jacobs portrays never speak in "vernacular discourse."

Becker, Elizabeth C. "Harriet Jacobs's Search for Home." *CLA Journal* 35, no. 4 (June 1992): 411-421.

Becker sees Jacobs's search for a "home" as proof of the influence on her of the "cult of true womanhood." In effect, Jacobs's decision to sacrifice her own freedom in order to "stay home," virtually imprisoned with her children, makes her the "consummate mother." Though she hopes for a sisterhood of white and black women, she ends up a domestic rather than a woman with a home of her own. As a result of her failed efforts to create homes, Jacobs ultimately developed her own voice, a voice of defiance rather than apology.

Braxton, Joanne. "Harriet Jacobs's *Incidents in the Life of a Slave Girl:* The Re-Definition of the Slave Narrative Genre." *Massachusetts Review* 27 (Summer 1986): 379-387.

Braxton examines Jacobs's autobiography in the context of dominant scholarship on slave narratives. This scholarship focuses almost exclusively on "heroic males" and not on their less heroic wives or sisters. Braxton suggests that scholars need to ask different questions about women's narratives and wonders how inclusion of women will ultimately change the shape of the genre as we now understand it.

Carby, Hazel V. "'Hear My Voice, Ye Careless Daughters': Narratives of Slave and Free Women before Emancipation," in *Reconstructing Womanhood: The Emergence of the Afro-American Woman Novelist.* New York: Oxford University Press, 1987.

Carby responds to the charge of "inauthenticity" made by critics who find the melodrama of Jacobs's work proof that it is fiction. She points out that slave stories of "miscegenation, unrequited love, outraged virtue and planter licentiousness" are corroborated in the diaries of southern white women, though absent from the records of their planter husbands. Carby goes on to explain Jacobs's use of a pseudonym and her rejection of Harriet Beecher Stowe's offer to include her story in *The Key to Uncle Tom's Cabin.* As Carby sees it, the writing of this autobiography enabled Jacobs to "reconstruct" the meaning of her own life as woman and mother against the ideological definition of true womanhood from which she was necessarily excluded.

Fox-Genovese, Elizabeth. "My Statue, My Self: Autobiographical Writings of Afro-American Women," in *The Private Self: Theory and Practice of Women's Autobiographical Writings,* ed. Shari Benstock. Chapel Hill: University of North Carolina Press, 1988.

Fox-Genovese defines autobiographies of black women as a genre with certain identifiable characteristics. Both Harriet Jacobs and Harriet Wilson, for example, wrote for white readers who could authenticate their work and, presumably, be positively influenced by it. Both use the metaphor of the journey, both use some of the conventions of literary domesticity and, most important, both "subvert" the promise of candor in order to make their writing palatable to its intended audience. Thus, the battle of wills between Jacobs and her master is recast as a conflict between virtue and licentiousness.

Gates, Henry Louis, Jr., and K. A. Appiah, eds. *Harriet Jacobs: Critical Perspectives Past and Present.* New York: Amistad, 1994.

This book-length collection of articles and reviews, part of the Amistad Literary series, includes essays by Mary Helen Washington, Cheryl A. Wall, Deborah E. McDowell, and Lillie P. Howard, a chronology, and a bibliography.

Gwin, Minrose C. "Green-Eyed Monsters of the Slavocracy: Jealous Mistresses in Two Slave Narratives," in *Conjuring: Black Women, Fiction, and Literary Tradition*, eds. Marjorie Pryse and Hortense J. Spillers. Bloomington: Indiana University Press, 1985.

Gwin discusses Jacobs's autobiography in the context of a sexual mythology that denied white women their sexuality and reduced black women to identification with theirs. In the mistress-slave relationship which resulted, the white woman, "powerless against a lustful husband and blind to the harsh realities of chattel slavery," often turned against the black victim whom she could at least control. Gwin emphasizes the rage and ironic tone of much of Jacobs's autobiography and shows how she uses the power of her own language to get back at and ultimately gain power over her cruel mistress.

Nudelman, Franny. "Harriet Jacobs and the Sentimental Politics of Female Suffering." *ELH* 59, no. 4 (Winter 1992): 939-964.

Nudelman disagrees with interpretations of Jacobs's work as an "outsider's heroic refashioning of convention." She believes that Jacobs, like Stowe, consciously made use of abolitionist rhetoric aimed at mobilizing the political implications of sentimentality. This then required that she describe her "sexual suffering" as both an exceptional case and representative of female suffering in general. Similarly, she herself was both victim and agent, sufferer and speaker of her own story.

Shockley, Ann Allen. "Harriet Ann Jacobs/Linda Brent," in *Afro-American Women Writers, 1746-1933: An Anthology and Critical Guide*. Boston: G. K. Hall, 1988.

Shockley summarizes the key events of Jacobs's life, pointing out that she was one of the few ex-slaves who wrote her own narrative. She concludes with a quotation from a letter Jacobs wrote to Lydia Maria Child expressing her joy at the Emancipation Proclamation and with an affirmation of the good work she continued to do "helping her people" in Washington, D.C. An excerpt entitled "The Jealous Mistress" is included.

Smith, Valerie. "'Loopholes of Retreat': Architecture and Ideology in Harriet Jacobs's *Incidents in the Life of a Slave Girl*," in *Reading Black, Reading Feminist: A Critical Anthology*, ed. Henry Louis Gates, Jr. New York: Meridian, 1990.

Smith uses Jacobs's ambiguous phrase "loopholes of retreat" to demonstrate how, at various points in her story, Jacobs chooses a place of confinement to escape the inevitability of persecution. Similarly, as a writer, Jacobs had to express her experiences within the literary confines of the sentimental novel, the only form available to her. It is therefore not surprising that the work is filled with ironies and with "both literal and figurative enclosures." Unlike the sentimental heroine, she "plays for different stakes"—freedom, not marriage. With this atypical ending and with the narrative silences which surround "those aspects of her

own sexuality for which the genre does not allow," Jacobs "triumphs" over the limits of the sentimental novel.
See also: Valerie Smith, "Form and Ideology in Three Slave Narratives," in *Self-Discovery and Authority in Afro-American Narrative*, Cambridge: Harvard University Press, 1987.

Soristo, Carolyn. "There Is Might in Each Conception of Self in Harriet Jacobs's *Incidents in the Life of a Save Girl, Written by Herself.*" *Legacy* 13, no. 1 (1996): 1-18.
Soristo discusses Jacobs's use of both the sentimental genteel tradition and Emersonian individualism. The text raises questions as to the possibility of situating one's own identity in relation to and apart from others. Its message is that one may remain pure though fallen, that the most powerless can win freedom, and that every version of the self has room for subversion.

Washington, Mary Helen. "Meditations on History: The Slave Woman's Voice," in *Invented Lives: Narratives of Black Women, 1860-1960*. Garden City, N.Y.: Anchor Press, 1987.
Washington stresses the difficult circumstances in which Jacobs wrote her narrative. Apparently, she was only able to find the time and the privacy to write after first completing her exhausting duties for the Willis family. Moreover, in order to describe fully the oppressive circumstances of her life, she had to discuss her sexual exploitation and thus reveal herself to be a "scandalous woman with a disgraceful past" in terms of Victorian moral codes. The result may be, according to Washington, the only slave narrative to deal with what it was really like to be a female slave.

Yellin, Jean Fagan. "Harriet Jacobs's Family History." *American Literature* 66, no. 4 (December 1994): 565-567.
Yellin uses recently uncovered information about Jacobs's father to correct previous biographies. This new information leads to new questions about choices Jacobs made in writing her slave narrative, which must now be understood as a "carefully constructed" narrative that intentionally omits discussion of her father's family.

NELLA LARSEN
1891-1964

Nella Larsen was born in Chicago, the daughter of a Danish woman and a West Indian man. She was educated at Fisk University and the University of Copenhagen. Her first novel, *Quicksand* (1928), received rave reviews and quickly established her reputation as a writer. Following the publication of *Passing* (1929), she received a Guggenheim fellowship to support her creative writing, the first African American woman to receive such an award. She later divorced her husband, Dr. Elmer S. Hines, a Ph.D. physicist. After traveling in Europe for several years, Larsen apparently stopped writing, perhaps because of a charge of plagiarism leveled against one of her short stories or perhaps because the Harlem Renaissance was in decline. Larsen returned to her nursing career to support herself; she had worked as both a nurse and a librarian prior to her brief literary successes. Larsen died of heart failure, having lived the last thirty years of her life in relative obscurity.

Reissued Editions
An Intimation of Things Distant: The Collected Fiction of Nella Larsen. New York: Anchor Books, 1992.

Quicksand and Passing. New Brunswick, N.J.: Rutgers University Press, 1986.

Biography and Commentary
Barnett, Pamela E. "'My Picture of You Is, After All, the True Helga Crane': Portraiture and Identity in Nella Larsen's *Quicksand.*" *Signs* 20, no. 3 (Spring 1995): 575-600.
    Barnett sees Helga Crane as a work of art in search of an appropriate setting. In each environment that she tests she serves as a spectacle for the other characters and the novel's readers. Barnett interprets *Quicksand* as a critique of both "fascist depictions" of black female sexuality and "reactionary portraits" of a "desexualized" middle class. Though, at first, marriage seems to offer Helga the frame she needs to legitimize her sexuality, the limitations of the relationship and the burdens of motherhood soon determine her ultimately unhappy fate—a "deliberately constructed failure" on Larsen's part, concludes Barnett.

Beemyn, Brett. "A Bibliography of Works by and about Nella Larsen." *African American Review* 26, no. 1 (Spring 1992): 183-188.
    This includes listings of editions of the novels, criticism of both novels and of each separately, and biographic and bibliographic information.

Blackmer, Corinne E. "The Veils of the Law: Race and Sexuality in Nella Larsen's *Passing.*" *College Literature* 22, no. 3 (October 1995): 50-67.
    Blackmer notes that legally sanctioned racial separatism led to the kind of "racial panic" that is at the core of Larsen's novel. She also notes that the psychological predicament faced by African Americans who were able to "pass" for white in the 1920's is "structurally analogous" to that faced by homosexuals today who try to "pass" as straight. The "strategies of self-disguise and masquerade," perhaps both sexual and racial, used by Clare Kendry represent a carefully calculated response to social prejudice and legal prohibitions.

Brody, Jennifer DeVere. "Clare Kendry's 'True' Colors: Race and Class in Nella Larsen's *Passing.*" *Callaloo* 15, no. 4 (Fall 1992): 1053-1065.

Brody sees Irene Redfield and Clare Kendry as representatives of two competing ideologies. A romanticized Africa as "constructed" during the Harlem Renaissance offers "liberation" for Clare and "denigration" for Irene. Brody also compares the two women to the protagonists of Toni Morrison's *Sula*; Irene, like Nel, is mostly concerned with climbing the social ladder, while Clare, like Sula, invents and reinvents herself.

Carby, Hazel V. "The Quicksands of Representation: Rethinking Black Cultural Politics," in *Reconstructing Womanhood: The Emergence of the Afro-American Woman Novelist*. New York: Oxford University Press, 1987.

Carby focuses her discussion on *Quicksand*, contrasting the work of both Larsen and Jessie Fauset with that of Zora Neale Hurston, and praising Larsen, in particular, for writing the first text by a black woman which depicts a woman's life in the context of "capitalist social relations." According to Carby, Larsen was able neither to accept the "world view of the new black middle-class" nor to "romanticize the people as folk." Her novels undermined both romantic conventions and the ideology of racial uplift. As such they are the precursors to the urban narratives of Richard Wright, Ralph Ellison, and Ann Petry.

Christian, Barbara. "The Rise and Fall of the Proper Mulatta," in *Black Women Novelists: The Development of a Tradition, 1892-1976*. Westport, Conn.: Greenwood Press, 1980.

Christian sees *Quicksand* as a critical work which brings to "bitter fruition" the pathos inherent in the depiction of tragic mulattas in abolitionist novels. Larsen's heroines, unlike Fauset's, are at home in neither Black nor White worlds, in neither primitive rural America nor urban upper-class society. Rather, they are "doomed" to self-centered, neurotic lives, not unlike Larsen's own.

Davis, Thadious M. *Nella Larsen, Novelist of the Harlem Renaissance: A Woman's Life Unveiled*. Baton Rouge: Louisiana State University Press, 1994.

Davis has written the first full-length biography of Larsen based on fifteen years of detective work searching through school transcripts, employment records, fellowship applications, and other documents, and interviewing old friends and colleagues in Chicago, New York, and Nashville. The resulting 492 pages clarify previous confusion about Larsen's family and reveal the shocking information that her white mother and stepfather may have institutionalized her for a few years and later sent her to prep at Fisk so that they could live free from the racism to which they were subject because of their mulatta daughter. Davis sees the "drama" in Larsen's fiction as an attempt to "hide" her even more dramatic personal history. However, unlike other biographers, he views her post-literary career, not as a "defeat," but as evidence of professional success in still another field.

DuCille, Ann. *The Coupling Convention: Sex, Text and Tradition in Black Women's Fiction.* New York: Oxford University Press, 1993.
DuCille argues that the novels of both Larsen and Jessie Fauset, like those of Kate Chopin, anticipate the franker depiction of female sexuality to be found in later feminist texts. Their novels "transcend" the theme of "passing" to critique the conventions of sentimental romance. *Passing*, in particular, dramatically dissects the "dialectics of desire" and offers its readers a complex analysis of the female body which is open to a variety of interpretations depending on whether Clare or Irene is seen as the main character.

Horton, Merrill. "Blackness, Betrayal, and Childhood: Race and Identity in Nella Larsen's *Passing*." *CLA Journal* 38, no. 1 (September 1994): 31-45.
Horton summarizes the novel's plot and reviews its critical reception over the years. He himself sees Larsen's childhood experience of race as the key to the novel. For both Clare and Irene, who seduce and betray each other, the game of "passing" has yielded spiritual and sexual bankruptcy. Clare ends up dead as a result of trying to rejoin black culture; Irene suffers continuing ambivalence about her own racial identity.

Hostetler, Ann E. "The Aesthetics of Race and Gender in Nella Larsen's *Quicksand*." *PMLA* 105, no. 1 (January 1990): 35-46.
Hostetler sees *Quicksand* as a "meditation on color." The novel's protagonist, Helga Crane, through her own sensitivity to tone and hue and her own love of the nuances of color, attempts to create "a palette that will unify her life rather than leave it divided." Hostetler looks at the parallels between the novel and the author's own life and concludes that Larsen has created a "startlingly original" portrait of the black bourgeoisie and the problems of cultural identity and assimilation it faced.

Larson, Charles R. *Invisible Darkness: Jean Toomer & Nella Larsen.* Iowa City: University of Iowa Press, 1993.
This an illustrated biography of the two writers with a bibliography appended. The author sees both as enigmatic figures who once led "dazzling lives" and published brilliant first novels, then disappeared into relative obscurity. Larsen, in particular, seems to have "sought obscurity" and to have deliberately distorted the facts of her life. Unlike Toomer, who died a defeated and unhappy man, Larsen compensated for her own lonely life by helping the "sick and the downcast," the author concludes.

Little, Jonathan. "Nella Larsen's *Passing* and the Critics." *African American Review* 26, no. 1 (Spring 1992): 173-182.
Though the novel has been criticized for its lack of positive role models, Little sees it as the most sophisticated and internally consistent

novel on the subject of "passing." Larsen's irony is a brilliant tool, according to Little, which allows her to delve into the ambiguous and self-deceiving nature of human behavior and expression. Irene ultimately embodies "writer and reader, defendant and advocate, prosecutor and judge" as she becomes increasingly alienated from herself.

McDowell, Deborah E. "'That nameless . . . shameful impulse': Sexuality in Nella Larsen's *Quicksand* and *Passing*." *Studies in Black American Literature* 3 (1988): 139-167.
      McDowell credits Larsen for being a trailblazer in her depiction of female sexuality and notes that there may even be an implicit lesbian subplot in *Passing*. Though her plots revolve around the lives of presumably "genteel" middle-class women, this gentility is revealed to be a "mask" which hides the more "dangerous" story of female desire.

Madigan, Mark J. "Miscegenation and 'The Dicta of Race and Class': The Rhinelander Case and Nella Larsen's *Passing*." *Modern Fiction Studies* 36, no. 4 (Winter 1990): 523-528.
      The Rhinelander case referred to in the novel was a sensational trial in which a wealthy New Yorker tried to get an annulment of his marriage to a mulatto chambermaid on the grounds that she had deceived him about the race of her father, who she had said was Cuban rather than African American. This case was widely covered by both the white and African American press and was used to define issues related to miscegenation and racial "passing" during the period of the Harlem Renaissance.

Shockley, Ann Allen. "Nella Marian Larsen Imes," in *Afro-American Women Writers, 1746-1933: An Anthology and Critical Guide*. Boston: G. K. Hall, 1988.
      Shockley provides relatively detailed biographical information and a lengthy summary of Larsen's two novels. An excerpt from *Quicksand* is included. She also reviews the critical reception of both novels in their own time and in recent years, agreeing with feminist readings that interpret Larsen's novels as "a coming out of the Victorian closet for black women in reckoning with their sexuality."

Silverman, Debra B. "Nella Larsen's *Quicksand*: Untangling the Webs of Exoticism." *African American Review* 27, no. 4 (Winter 1993): 599-615.
      Silverman considers three works—Phyllis Rose's biography of Josephine Baker, Gertrude Stein's *Three Lives*, and Nella Larsen's *Quicksand*—in order to expose historical misrepresentations of black female sexuality. Larsen's work both complicates issues of sexuality and racial identity and challenges stereotypic portrayals of the black woman as "exotic."

Tate, Claudia. "Nella Larsen's *Passing*: A Problem of Interpretation."
Black American Literature Forum 14, no. 4 (Winter 1980): 142-146.

Tate argues that *Passing* is much more than a conventional depiction
of the tragic mulatta, that it also includes a complex and ambiguous
psychological portrait of its major characters; the meaning of their lives
must, in effect, be "pieced together" by the reader. The novel's central
conflict, according to Tate, is based on jealousy, not on race. Exclusive
focus on the latter and on the novel's melodrama has led many critics to
miss the novel's subtlety and intrigue.

Washington, Mary Helen. "Nella Larsen: Mystery Woman of the
Harlem Renaissance." *Ms.* 9, no. 6 (December 1980): 44, 47-48, 50.

Washington discusses Larsen's novels and her life in terms of what
she sees as the particular plight of the middle-class black woman, both
in the 1920's and now, who is "unwilling to conform to a
circumscribed existence in the black world and unable to move freely in
the white world." Larsen's "preoccupation" with the theme of
marginality predates Ralph Ellison's *Invisible Man* (1952) and helps us
to understand the further estrangement of a "colored woman in a white,
male world." Washington shows us how the "carefully manicured
exterior" of the middle-class black woman masks the emotional and
psychological extremes she experiences, how the appearance of security
belies the reality of her walled existence.

IDA B. WELLS
1862-1931

Wells was born a slave in Holly Springs, Mississippi, the eldest of
eight children. Her parents believed in the importance of education and
sent their children to school as soon as possible. Both parents died in
the 1878 yellow fever epidemic, leaving Ida to raise the five brothers
and sisters still living. She was able to support herself through
teaching, first in Holly Springs, later in Memphis, where she moved in
with a widowed aunt. She continued her education at Fisk University
and became editor of a local church paper and then of a weekly, the
Living Way. Under the pen name Iola, her popularity grew and she
began to contribute articles to national publications such as the
Chicago Conservator and *New York Age*. Called the "Princess of the
Press," she was the first woman to attend the Afro-American Press
Convention in Louisville. Wells is best known for her powerful
protests against lynching and against the barring of blacks from the
1893 World's Fair in Chicago. In addition to her writing, Wells was a
social and political activist who founded both the Negro Fellowship
League, which provided housing and employment services to migrant
blacks, and the Alpha Suffrage Club, the first black women's suffrage
group in Illinois. In 1895 she married Ferdinand Barnett, the owner of
the *Conservator* and a widower with two children, and had four
children of her own. Throughout her life she continued to do
investigative reporting and to urge African Americans to organize

themselves to fight more effectively for their own rights. The first federally funded low-income housing project in Chicago was named after Wells in 1940, and her house has been designated a National Historic Landmark.

Reissued Essays and Books
Crusade for Justice: The Autobiography of Ida B. Wells, ed. Alfred M. Duster. Chicago: University of Chicago Press, 1970.

The Memphis Diary of Ida B. Wells, ed. Miriam Decosta-Willis. Boston: Beacon Press 1995.

"A Red Record (1895)" and "Let the African-American Depend but on Himself," in *Black Women in White America*, ed. Gerda Lerner. New York: Random House, 1972.

Selected Works of Ida B. Wells, ed. Trudier Harris. New York: Oxford University Press, 1991.

"U.S. Atrocities" [London 1892], in *Black Women in Nineteenth century American Life: Their Words, Their Thoughts, Their Feelings*, eds. Bert James Loewenberg and Ruth Bogin. University Park: Pennsylvania State University Press, 1976.

Biography and Commentary
Boyd, Melba Joyce. "Canon Configuration for Ida B. Wells-Barnett." *The Black Scholar* 24, no. 1 (Winter 1994): 8-13.
　　Boyd reviews the reissued editions of Wells's essays and autobiography, a biography by Mildred Thompson, and the documentary *Passion for Justice* to explain interest in Wells one hundred years after her anti-lynching campaign. Boyd sees Wells's canonization as the direct result of black women's studies and the "contemporary need for her ideological integrity and tenacity." Study of Wells's life and writings in the context of her own times can provide insight into the racism and sexism of the 1980's and 1990's, Boyd concludes.

Davidson, Sue. *Getting the Real Story: Nellie Bly and Ida B. Wells*. Seattle: Seal Press, 1992.
　　Davidson's book is an "imaginary reconstruction" of the lives of Wells and Bly (the globe-circling stunt reporter) written for fourth-through sixth-graders. She looks at how both Wells and Bly used journalism in their fight for social justice, and how their own life experiences were shaped by the fact of being born either "black" or "white."

Davis, Simone W. "The 'Weak Race' and the Winchester: Political Voices in the Pamphlets of Ida B. Wells-Barnett." *Legacy* 12, no. 2 (1995): 77-97.

Davis credits Wells with a "double-sightedness" which allowed her to look at herself and her own writings as they would be seen by others. This led her to adopt several key strategies, including the use of quotations from the white press which could be turned around to alert readers about "the nature and power of politically loaded language." Wells, for example, would take common dichotomies such as the virgin and the whore, the civilized man and the savage, and order versus anarchy to present the violence being done to Black men. Though Wells aligned herself with the concerns of men, her own powerful voice was itself a challenge to existing notions about gender as well as race.

Giddings, Paula. "'To Sell My Life as Dearly as Possible': Ida B. Wells and the First Antilynching Campaign," in *When and Where I Enter: The Impact of Black Women on Race and Sex in America.* New York: William Morrow, 1984.

Giddings offers a detailed account of the lynching of three black businessmen and of Wells's own lawsuit against the Chesapeake and Ohio Railway, two "stunning" experiences which motivated her career as a journalist. She discusses Wells's career alongside that of her good friend, Mary Church Terrell; these two women were to "dedicate their lives to the fight against lynching and the malevolent impulses that underlined it." Giddings later considers the impact of Wells's international campaign against lynching and the response of the British to it. She credits Wells with the decline in the number of lynchings from 1893 on.

Hendricks, Wanda. "Ida Bell Wells-Barnett," in *Black Women in America*, Vol. 2, ed. Darlene Clark Hine. Brooklyn, N.Y.: Carlson, 1993.

Hendricks emphasizes Wells's "fearless devotion" to civil and economic rights for African Americans. She emphasizes the dramatic events that encouraged Wells's political activism, beginning with her own refusal to move to a segregated railroad car in 1884 (she sued for damages and was awarded $500, but the Tennessee state supreme court overturned the decision). In 1892, following the lynching of three Black businessmen, whose "only crime was economic prosperity," she wrote "scathing" editorials that attacked white women and urged the Black citizens of Memphis to leave town. She also traveled through England and Scotland to gain international support for her crusade against lynching. Hendricks goes on to discuss Wells's involvement in the formation of the National Association for the Advancement of Colored People (NAACP), which she later criticized for its timidity in confronting racial issues, and her alliance with Marcus Garvey, which resulted in her being branded "a dangerous radical" by the U.S. Secret Service.

Shockley, Ann Allen. "Ida Bell Wells-Barnett [Iola, pseud.]," in *Afro-American Women Writers, 1746-1933: An Anthology and Critical Guide*. Boston: G. K. Hall, 1988.

Shockley summarizes the key events in Wells's life and career and includes "The Case Stated," a chapter from *A Red Record: Tabulated Statistics and Alleged Causes of Lynchings in the United States, 1892-1893-1894*. Shockley concludes that Wells-Barnett was a "dynamic, bold, and strong-minded woman" who spoke her mind and was therefore often opposed, not only by whites, but also by some of her fellow blacks.

Sterling, Dorothy. "Ida B. Wells: Voice of a People," in *Black Foremothers: Three Lives*. New York: Feminist Press, 1988.

Sterling's book looks at the lives and work of three nineteenth century women: Ellen Craft, who grew up an unlettered slave, Ida B. Wells, who scrimped pennies for her education, and Mary Church Terrell, the daughter of the South's first black millionaire. Wells, as Sterling describes her, was a serious young woman who worked very hard to support herself. The lynching of Thomas Moss "changed the whole course of her life"; Sterling recounts in detail the "crusade" which followed. She then reviews Wells's political activities crisscrossing the country to give lectures and organize anti-lynching societies, and her dispute with Frances Willard, head of the Women's Christian Temperance Union, which Susan B. Anthony tried unsuccessfully to mediate. Wells purchased the *Conservator* from her husband and his associates shortly before her marriage and continued to work as its editor, publisher, and business manager. It was a most unconventional marriage for the time. Wells had little interest in domesticity but was determined to be a good mother; "she was equally determined not to give up public life" and therefore brought her babies with her wherever she went. Even in "retirement," Wells continued to be politically effective and ran for state senate at the age of sixty-seven. She died literally pen in hand as she was working on her autobiography.

Van Steenwyk, Elizabeth. *Ida B. Wells-Barnett: Woman of Courage*. London: F. Watts, 1992.

This biography written for young adults establishes the political and social climate of the late nineteenth and early twentieth centuries, including the rise of lynching and the founding of the National Association for the Advancement of Colored People (NAACP). Wells is portrayed as an "unconventional woman" who devoted her life singlemindedly to the cause of civil rights.

HARRIET WILSON
1807 or 1827-1870

Little is known for sure about the life of Harriet Wilson other than that she entered the copyright of her novel at the Clerk's Office of the

District Court of Massachusetts in 1859. In the novel's preface she explains that she has written the book in hopes of earning enough money to support herself and her son, who apparently died within six months of the book's publication. The son's death certificate has been used to establish the racial identity of the author and hence to document the probable status of *Our Nig* as the first novel published by an African American in the United States. Given recent detective work and the testimony of the three witnesses whose statements appear in the appendix to corroborate the work's authenticity, much of the novel is apparently autobiographical. Wilson was hired out as a young child to a family that worked her so hard that her health was permanently impaired. She later married a Thomas Wilson, who went to sea, abandoning her when she was pregnant. He returned briefly thereafter only to depart again.

Reissued Edition

Our Nig: Or, Sketches from the Life of a Free Black. In a Two-Story White House, North. Showing That Slavery's Shadows Fall Even There. New York: Random House, 1983.

Biography and Commentary

Breau, Elizabeth. "Identifying Satire: *Our Nig.*" *Callaloo* 16, no. 2 (Spring 1993): 455-465.

Breau argues against an autobiographical reading of *Our Nig*, pointing out that the three appended letters testifying to the text's integrity may very well be parodies written by Wilson herself. Much of the novel's "impudent" tone suggests a satirical intention aimed at condemning the hypocrisy of northerners who probably found the book "ungrateful."

Carby, Hazel V. "'Hear My Voice, Ye Careless Daughters': Narratives of Slave and Free Women before Emancipation," in *Reconstructing Womanhood: The Emergence of the Afro-American Woman Novelist.* New York: Oxford University Press, 1987.

Carby views *Our Nig* as a slave narrative set in the North. She sees the two-story white house in which Frado is held captive as the equivalent of a southern plantation with its own evil mistress.

Davis, Cynthia. "Speaking the Body's Pain: Harriet Wilson's *Our Nig.*" *African American Review* 27, no. 3 (Fall 1993): 391-404.

Most nineteenth century novels depict black women as either "disembodied saints or wanton bodies." *Our Nig* is a significant work precisely because of its protest against physical abuse and pain, rather than rape. When Frado finally stands up to her cruel mistress, she discovers her own voice and, therefore, establishes her own humanity. Davis surmises that this powerful narrative may itself have been silenced because the story of pain it tells was not one that readers wanted to hear.

Ernest, John. "Economies of Identity: Harriet E. Wilson's *Our Nig*." *PMLA* 10, no. 3 (May 1994): 424-438.
Ernest analyzes *Our Nig* in terms of the "economic motives" which "predominate" in the text. He provides examples of the ways in which Frado exposes and subverts the economy of the Bellmonts, initiating a "more active system of exchange." In order to escape from the corner into which she has been backed by ethical, racial, and sexual oppression, Frado, like Wilson herself, has to transfrom her own cultural identity and take charge of her own "self-purchase."

Fox-Genovese, Elizabeth. "My Statue, My Self: Autobiographical Writings of Afro-American Women," in *The Private Self: Theory and Practice of Women's Autobiographical Writings*, ed. Shari Benstock. Chapel Hill: University of North Carolina Press, 1988.
Fox-Genovese compares Wilson's autobiography with that of Harriet Jacobs in terms of the literary conventions it uses and its attempt to appeal to a white audience. Wilson's story is more "problematic" than Jacobs's, according to Fox-Genovese, because it is "cast as a fiction" and because Wilson's villain "represents the world of female domesticity" from which her readers would be drawn.

Gardner, Eric. "'This Attempt of Their Sister': Harriet Wilson's *Our Nig* from Printer to Reader." *The New England Quarterly* 66, no. 1 (March 1993): 226-246.
Gardner researched the seventeen names he found in the thirty-four existing copies of *Our Nig*; apparently the book was owned by white young people who lived not far from where it was published. There is no evidence that it was read by blacks or that it was publicized by abolitionists, who must have known of its existence. Gardner believes that the book was printed as an "act of charity" and marketed as a tale of "moral improvement."

Gates, Henry Louis, Jr. "Harriet E. Wilson," in *Black Women in America*, Vol. 2, ed. Darlene Clark Hine. Brooklyn, N.Y.: Carlson, 1993.
Gates argues that Wilson, in effect, created a new literary form by combining the structure of the sentimental novel with key conventions of the slave narrative. Unfortunately, this extraordinary achievement was lost to future generations of black writers who might have benefited from its example. Gates also calls attention to the novel's preface where Wilson warns her readers that the book is not about slavery in the South, but about the horrors of racism in the North. The book may very well have been condemned to obscurity precisely because of its direct and unequivocal depiction of racism even on the part of northern white women.

Jones, Jill. "The Disappearing 'I' in *Our Nig*." *Legacy* 13, no. 1 (1996): 38-53.
Jones notes that the text "slips and slides" between first and third

person narration and between the particular authority of both slave narratives and the sentimental novel. Apparently, Wilson is attempting to find an "authoritative voice" for her narrator/protagonist/author who is "disempowered" by race, class, and gender.

Shockley, Ann Allen. "Harriet E. Adams Wilson," in *Afro-American Women Writers, 1746-1933: An Anthology and Critical Guide.* Boston: G. K. Hall, 1988.
Shockley summarizes what was known of Wilson's life at the time of *Our Nig*'s reissue in 1982 and includes an excerpt from the book. She calls the work "a tragic Dickensian tale of social, racial and economic dehumanization" which demonstrated the prejudice and fact of black bondage in the North even while abolitionists were attacking slavery in the South.

Stern, Julia. "Excavating Genre in *Our Nig*." *American Literature* 67, no. 3 (September 1995): 439-461.
Stern sees the novel as truer to the "brutal vision of maternity" typical of gothic narratives than to the "syrupy language of sentimental fiction." Mother love in *Our Nig* consistently operates according to the logic of economic conditions with no place for bonds of reciprocal affection. Critics who have focused on the novel's sentimentality have often missed its "overarching atmosphere of maternal violence and filial terror." The private realm, especially the kitchen, is a place of mortal danger, rather than the haven of domestic fiction; the public realm, especially school, is where Frado finds the only sustenance she receives. Ultimately, domestic space offers no solution to the problems of race and gender; Wilson herself was forced because of poverty to relinquish custody of her own son and turned to the public with the hope of earning enough money to get him back.

White, Barbara A. "*Our Nig* and the She Devil: New Information about Harriet Wilson and the 'Bellmont' Family." *American Literature* 65, no. 1 (March 1993): 19-52.
New research shows that the Bellmont family corresponds closely with the Haywards on which it was based, with the important exception that Jonas Hayward was an active abolitionist while his mother was mistreating a slave in her own home. White raises the issue of whether or not *Our Nig* should be considered as autobiography. Though much of what Wilson wrote was literally true, she had a strong aesthetic consciousness, according to White, which led her to shape a dramatic storyline.

Chapter 6
ETHNIC WOMEN WRITING

This chapter focuses on Asian American, Hispanic/Latina, Jewish American, and Native American women writers. These broadly construed ethnic and racial groupings each include a diversity of cultures and literary traditions. Each has become the object of serious academic studies, most dating from 1980, by scholars interested both in exploring the relationship between historical experience and written texts and in enlarging the scope of American literature. The result is a more inclusive view of American literature which encompasses diverse forms, languages other than English, and all countries of origin within the Americas, not just the United States. In its first five chapters this bibliography has dealt with United States authors writing in English in traditional published genres. Chapter 6 adds references to cultural antecedents and foremothers from a broader literary spectrum that may have particular significance to an understanding of major U.S. authors.

The years covered by this bibliography, 1848 to 1948, were critical ones in the ethnic and racial history of the United States. The Indian Removal Act of 1830 began a long series of coercive policies which resulted in the forced resettlement of thousands of Indian peoples west of the Mississippi. By 1887, after a series of gruesome wars, almost all Native Americans were living on reservations. The building of the railroads brought thousands of Chinese laborers to the West Coast beginning in the 1850's.. The Mexican American War ended in 1848 with annexation of much of California and Texas; the Spanish American War ended in 1898 with the ceding of Puerto Rico to the United States. By 1880 immigration from the British Isles and northern and western Europe had begun to fall off, to be replaced by immigration from eastern Europe and Asia. Pogroms in Russia brought hundreds of thousands of Jews to Ellis Island in the 1890's.

With late nineteenth century industrialization, urbanization, multiethnic immigration, and the African American migration north, the face of America was rapidly changing. Still, with a few notable exceptions, until the post-World War II explosion of the middle class, literary production remained primarily in the hands of an educated elite with access to the urban centers, mostly on the East Coast, which dominated American publishing and intellectual life. Nonetheless, almost every immigrant group and every generation of immigrants have left a record of their experiences in America. Most public libraries include among their holdings bibliographies of local ethnic groups whether Irish American, German American, Italian American, Norwegian American, or Croatian American. These list writings drawn from diaries, newspapers, published and unpublished autobiographies, and other sources.

The four "groups" discussed here have been the object of greater scholarly attention than other "ethnicities" for a variety of reasons, most obviously their ongoing identification as "minorities" and the persistent stereotypes and "racial" associations from which they continue to suffer. Each has a particularly complex interrelationship with mainstream North American culture, understood to derive primarily from English and Northern European origins. Moreover, as the "melting pot" metaphor of cultural assimilation has gradually given way to an image of America as a land of cultural pluralism, scholarly interest has turned to those cultures in which ethnic differences have proved the most powerful and enduring. This is especially true of African American literature, which is discussed separately in chapter 5 because it has an older, more coherent history of published writing in English. Asian American, Jewish American, Native American, and Latina literature in English did not become firmly established in most cases until well into the twentieth century, with most major figures emerging after 1948. Hence the references here are primarily to studies of "groups" of writers rather than individuals.

Native American literature is, of course, our oldest literary tradition, with a long history of ceremonial and popular forms, as pointed out by Paula Gunn Allen and other contemporary scholars. Moreover, great diversity exists among the hundreds of tribes and cultures understood to make up "Native Americans." Many traditional Indian stories were originally introduced to Euro-American readers as translations and undoubtedly reflected the biases of the anthropologists who worked with the Native speakers in recording them. Of particular interest to the study of Native American literature in English are the first captivity narratives and oral autobiographies recorded by white scholars. The earliest written autobiographies include Sarah Winnemucca Hopkins's *Life Among the Paiutes: Their Wrongs and Claims* (1883), edited by Mrs. Horace Mann; and Zitkala-Sa's recollections of her life on a Sioux reservation and at a missionary school, published in *The Atlantic Monthly* (1900-1902). The plight of American Native peoples following their forced removal to reservations beginning in 1831 and the nullification of the treaties which presumably guaranteed their land claims came to the attention of the public in such crusading works as Helen Hunt Jackson's *A Century of Dishonor* (1881), discussed in chapter 1. It was not until the late 1970's, however, that Native American oral and written work came to be considered as "American" rather than "aboriginal" literature. Much of the recent scholarship on early Native American written literature by women has been inspired by the popularity of Leslie Silko, who published *Ceremony* in 1977 to rave reviews, and Louise Erdrich, whose first "novel," *Love Medicine*, (1984) and its sequels have also been very well received.

Hispanic, Chicano, and Latino literature exists in an even more complex historical context. The term "Hispanic" is generally used to refer to Mexican Americans, Cuban Americans, Puerto Ricans, and other Spanish-speaking groups residing in the United States. "Chicano" is used specifically for Mexican Americans, who make up almost two-thirds of Hispanics living in the United States and whose culture predates the Mexican-American War (1846-1848). "Latino" and its feminine form "Latina" are more recent terms used to refer to all the peoples of Central and South America, including the Portuguese-speaking Brazilians, as well as the hundreds of thousands of immigrants from "Latin" America who have come to the United States for economic or political reasons. Given the diversity of cultural, historical, and geographical backgrounds encompassed by this large group, it is not surprising to find a variety of secondary sources reflecting the differing agendas of various recovery projects. The search for forgotten women writers who published in English or in Spanish has been given greater impetus recently by the success of such contemporary writers as Sandra Cisneros, the first Chicana writer to receive a major contract in the United States after publication of *The House on Mango Street* (1984); Julia Alvarez, the Dominican writer whose first novel, *How the Garcia Girls Lost Their Accents* (1991), was a critical and popular success; Julia Ortiz Cofer, a poet and educator best known for *Silent Dancing* (1990), a lyrical account of childhood summers in Puerto Rico and winters in New Jersey; and Isabel Allende, the Chilean writer whose first book, *La Casa de los espiritus* (1982), was made into a movie and whose novels have all been translated into English.

The term "Asian American" also refers to a wide variety of ethnic and national backgrounds, including Korean, Filipino, Indonesian, Vietnamese, and natives of Hawaii and the Pacific Islands, as well as the Chinese and Japanese who were the earliest Asian immigrants to the United States. By 1870 there were more than 60,000 Chinese in America, the majority in San Francisco, with a twelve-to-one ratio of men to women. Chinese immigration was at first encouraged to provide a labor force for the railroads, but then abruptly halted, with the Chinese Exclusion Act of 1882 ushering in the most regressive and racist phase in U.S. immigration history. Though Japanese and Korean immigrants continued to enter the United States following the Gentlemen's Agreement of 1907, the 1924 Oriental Exclusion Act terminated labor immigration from all of mainland Asia and instituted a quota system to limit immigration to a fixed percentage of the numbers of people of that origin already living in the United States. World War II was, of course, an important watershed in U.S. attitudes about Asians and resulted in greater sympathy for the Chinese and increased racism against the Japanese, culminating in their forced relocation and internment. Amy Ling, the foremost scholar on Chinese women writers, credits both Pearl Buck and the Japanese attack on Pearl Harbor, as well as several popular war novels by Eurasian women born in China but raised in the West, for these changing sympathies. Two popular autobiographies—*Fifth Chinese Daughter* (1945), by Jade Snow Wong, and *Nisei Daughter* (1952), an account of life in a Japanese internment camp, by Monica Sone—were also published right after the war. The best-known Asian writer in recent years has been Amy Tan, whose *Joy Luck Club* (1989) was made into a Hollywood movie. Although Americans seem to be fascinated by Chinese culture in particular, the aftermath of the Vietnam War, the influx of immigrants from other Asian countries, and the "economic miracle" of Japan, Taiwan, and Korea have all led to new interest in the literary legacy of other Asian minorities as well.

Jewish American writers from diverse socioeconomic and educational backgrounds have a long and interesting history of publication in the U.S. They include English-speaking Jews who were to varying degrees assimilated into mainstream Euro-American culture and those who continued to speak and write in Yiddish. Lillian Hellman, Edna Ferber, and Gertrude Stein (chapters 2, 3) achieved "mainstream" status as playwrights and novelists in contrast to Anzia Yezierska (chapter 2), who has been categorized as a Jewish "ethnic" writer. *Hungry Hearts* (1920), a collection of stories about lower East Side life, was turned into a Hollywood movie which catapulted Yezierska into fame. It was not, however, until the 1980's that scholarly interest in ethnicity led to serious study of Yezierska's work as part of a Jewish American tradition and representative of ethnic, immigrant, and working-class literature. Emma Lazarus and Mary Antin are also the subject of increasing scholarly attention, though far less than Yezierska. Lazarus is known today because her sonnet, "The New Colossus" (1883), with its stirring reference to America's "tired and poor/[its] huddled masses yearning to breathe free," is inscribed on the base of the Statue of Liberty. She also wrote many poems on classical and Jewish themes and was a regular contributor to the Jewish press. Antin's novel *The Promised Land* (1913) has been rediscovered as a classic immigration tale. Both Antin and Lazarus, like other Jewish writers of the late nineteenth and early twentieth centuries, spoke out against the horrors of the bloody pogroms which forced hundreds of thousands of destitute Jews to flee Russia, and warned of growing anti-Semitism in the United States. As with other ethnic and racial groups, the popularity of contemporary writers, in this case almost exclusively male writers such as Saul Bellow, Bernard Malamud, and Philip Roth, has led to a search for forefathers. Only Cynthia Ozick is regularly referenced in "standard" discussions of contemporary Jewish American literature, although several other women writers, most notably Hortense Calisher, Grace Paley, Tillie Olsen, and Marge Piercy, are frequently referenced in feminist journals and studies.

The foregoing brief discussions of Native American, Latina, Asian American, and Jewish American literature indicate that only recently have Americans begun to appreciate their multicultural heritage and have significant numbers of "minority" women felt empowered to tell their stories. As Toni Morrison stated in her Nobel Prize acceptance speech, conventional wisdom about the Tower of Babel no longer makes sense. The belief that "one monolithic language would have expedited the building and heaven would have been reached" begs the question of "whose heaven" and "what kind." "Perhaps the achievement of Paradise" would have been "premature," she concludes, "if no one could take the time to understand other languages, other views, other narratives." This chapter, in particular, reflects the historical reality that it has taken to the end of the twentieth century for students of literary history to find the time to learn about "other" literary voices and to encourage their expression.

GENERAL STUDIES AND ANTHOLOGIES OF MINORITY AND MULTICULTURAL LITERATURE

Note: The secondary sources listed below reflect recent interest in the literary legacy, the historical context, and the ethnic roots behind the work of contemporary writers. I have indicated only those sources which contain significant information on writers who published before 1948. Each ethnic group has its own literary journals, though most focus on contemporary works; *World Literature Today* and *MELUS, The Journal of the Society for the Study of the Multi-Ethnic Literature of the United States,* founded in 1974, regularly publish articles on earlier works.

Ammons, Elizabeth, and Annette White-Parks, eds. *Tricksterism in Turn-of-the-Century American Literature: A Multicultural Perspective.* Hanover, N.H.: University Press of New England, 1994.
  Some essays discuss the trickster as a culturally specific folk hero, others focus on the ethnic writer as a kind of trickster or the trickster as a feminist icon. Represented authors include Sui Sin Far, Onoto Watanna, Mourning Dove, Frances Harper (chapter 5), and Zitkala-Sa.

Baker, Houston A., Jr., ed. *Three American Literatures: Essays on Chicano, Native American, and Asian American Literature for Teachers of American Literature.* New York: Modern Language Association, 1982.
  This collection of essays offers overviews of the three traditions represented and two to three critical studies of each.

Dearborn, Mary V. *Pocahontas's Daughters: Gender and Ethnicity in American Culture.* New York: Oxford University Press, 1986.
  Dearborn discusses Native American, African American, and other "ethnic" women writers, as well as miscegenation as a theme in American literature. Her premise is that those who seem to be on the margins of American culture may best represent what happens within that culture. Ethnicity, for Dearborn, is a crucial aspect of the national character.

Fisher, Dexter, ed. *The Third Woman: Minority Women Writers of the United States.* Boston: Houghton Mifflin, 1980.
  This text includes a broad selection of poetry and short stories by

African American, Native American, Asian American, and Chicana writers, with introductions to each writer and a bibliography.

Harris, Susan K. "Problems of Representation in Turn-of-the-Century Immigrant Fiction," in *American Realism and the Canon*, eds. Tom Quirk and Gary Scharnhorst. Newark: University of Delaware Press, 1994.

Though most of this essay focuses on Abraham Cahan's story "The Imported Bridegroom" (1898), Harris also considers autobiographical novels by Mary Antin, a Polish Jew; Zitkala-Sa, a Dakota Sioux; and Sui Sin Far, a Chinese Eurasian. Harris notes how each writer consciously structures her stories around myths familiar to mainstream readers. These multicultural "voices" mark "watersheds" in the consciousness of their own communities about their position within the United States. Harris believes that inclusion of these voices in the American literary canon can help bring about positive social change.

Hoobler, Dorothy, and Thomas Hoobler. *American Family Albums*. New York: Oxford University Press, 1994-1995.

This series for young readers includes African Americans, Chinese Americans, Japanese Americans, Jewish Americans, Mexican Americans, and other minority groups. Each volume contains period photographs, selections from diaries, letters, memoirs, newspapers, and a timeline and bibliography.

Holte, James Craig. *The Ethnic I: A Sourcebook for Ethnic American Autobiography*. Westport, Conn.: Greenwood Press, 1988.

Holte sees much of American literature as an "obsessive inquiry into what it means to be American" with autobiography therefore a key genre. Twenty-nine writers of autobiographies chosen from a broad section of ethnic backgrounds and generations, eight of them women, are included. For each entry there is a brief biography of the author, an introduction to the autobiography and an overview of its critical reception.

Payne, James R., ed. *American Lives: Multicultural Autobiography*. Knoxville: University of Tennessee Press, 1991.

The text includes essays on African American, Native American, Asian American, Chicano, European American, Italian, and Jewish autobiographies.

Peck, David R. *American Ethnic Literatures: Native American, African American, Chicano/Latino, and Asian American Writers and Their Backgrounds*. Pasadena, Calif.: Salem Press, 1992.

This annotated bibliography includes chapters on the history of ethnic groups and on the teaching of ethnic literature. Each of the four major chapters contains a listing of primary sources, annotations of literary reference works and critical studies divided by genre and gender.

Of special interest to this bibliography are the sections on anthologies of Latina, Black, Native American, and Asian American women writers.

Ruoff, A. LaVonne Brown, and Jerry W. Ward, Jr., eds. *Redefining American Literary History*. New York: Modern Language Association, 1990.
This collection includes essays, lists of journals, and bibliographies on multicultural literature in general and on African American, Native American, Asian American, Chicano, and Puerto Rican literature in particular. Essays include "Orality and Hispanic Literature," "The Native American Trickster," a study of canonization in Chicano literature, and Amy Ling's discussion (see below) of Chinese women writers who preceded Maxine Hong Kingston. Though several articles mention nineteenth and early twentieth century writers, most focus on the post-World War II period.

Singh, Amritjit, Joseph T. Skerrett, and Robert E. Hogan, eds. *Memory, Narrative, and Identity: New Essays in Ethnic Literature*. Boston: Northeastern University Press, 1994.
This collection includes pieces on nineteenth century Mexican American autobiography and Jewish American immigrant narratives. Most of the essays deal with topics such as the politics of rembrance; collective, generational, and mythic memory; and the construction and narration of the past.

Sollors, Werner, ed. *The Invention of Ethnicity*. New York: Oxford University Press, 1989.
This is a collection of essays which challenge the concept of ethnicity as a "fixed encyclopedia of supposed cultural essentials." In his introduction Sollors argues for an understanding of the historical factors that contribute to the "invention" of ethnicity and an appreciation of the complex interplay between the idioms of a specific group and a larger shared cultural context. Essay topics include nineteenth century German Americans, ethnic trilogies such as the work of Josephine Herbst (chapter 2), definitions of race from 1890 to 1930, and the creation of Anzia Yezierska's ethnic identity (an essay annotated in chapter 2).

Thernstrom, Stephan. *The Harvard Encyclopedia of American Ethnic Groups*. Cambridge: Belknap Press, 1980.
This standard reference provides a wealth of information about ethnic life and culture.

ASIAN AMERICAN WRITERS
Note: Since the 1970's the United States has received an influx of immigrants of South Asian descent from India, Pakistan, Sri Lanka, Bangladesh, and Nepal and of Southeastern Asian descent from Vietnam and Cambodia, primarily. The books referenced here, because they deal

with earlier generations of women, focus almost exclusively on Japanese and Chinese Americans.

Asian Women United of California, ed. *Making Waves: An Anthology of Writings by and about Asian American Women.* Boston: Beacon Press, 1989.
This is a collection of autobiographical writings, short stories, poetry, essays, and photographs by Asian American women and about their experiences and history. Though most of the pieces were written expressly for this volume, many deal with the experiences of previous generations. There is also a chronology of Asian American history which begins in 1565 with Spanish colonial rule of the Philippine Islands and a "woman-centered" essay on Asian American history which begins with the experiences of late nineteenth century immigrants.

Chan, Sucheng. *Asian Americans: An Interpretive History.* Boston: G. K. Hall, 1991.
This illustrated text has a chronology and bibliographic essay. Two chapters—"Immigration and Livelihood, 1840's to 1930's" and "Women, Families, and the 'Second Generation Dilemma,'"—have pertinent information on pre-1948 writers.

Glenn, Evelyn Nakano. *Issei, Nisei, War Bride: Three Generations of Japanese American Women in Domestic Service.* Philadelphia: Temple University Press, 1986.
This text provides a useful history of the process of labor migration and settlement of northern California by Japanese immigrants from 1890 to 1960. Glenn notes that Japanese workers were at first welcomed as replacements for Chinese, but soon faced the same kind of hostility. The first period of Japanese immigration (1890-1910) was marked by the arrival of young single men who took jobs as unskilled laborers. The second period (1910-1924) saw the arrival of women recruited as wives and the establishment of permanent settlements. Almost half of these women ended up working as domestics, as was typical of most immigrant women in American from the mid-nineteenth century through the 1930's. Glenn considers their attitudes about domestic work, the internal dynamics of their family life, and the differing expectations and experiences of each new generation.

Kim, Elaine H. *Asian American Literature: An Introduction to the Writings and Their Social Context.* Philadelphia: Temple University Press, 1982.
This comprehensive reference work is organized thematically and chronologically, with a detailed bibliography appended. Topics include "Images of Asians in Anglo-American Literature," the "Japanese American Family," with chapters on early Asian immigrant writers. The

text ends with a discussion of "New Directions in Asian American Literature."

Lim, Shirley Geok-Lin. "Twelve Asian American Writers in Search of Self-Definition." *MELUS* 13, nos. 1-2 (Spring-Summer 1986): 57-78.
Lim discusses Jade Snow Wong's *Fifth Chinese Daughter* (1945), Lin Yutang's *Chinatown Family* (1948), and Monica Sone's *Nisei Daughter* (1953), as well as several contemporary works by Asian American male and female writers. Her focus is on the writers' awareness of racial and patriarchal myths, and their understanding of their own status in relation to mainstream culture.

Ling, Amy. *Between Worlds: Women Writers of Chinese Ancestry.* New York: Pergamon Press, 1990.
Ling identifies two sisters as the first Asian American writers of fiction. Edith Maud Eaton (1865-1914), who wrote under the pseudonym Sui Sin Far, embraced her Chinese identity; Winnifred Eaton (1875-1945), who wrote under the pseudonym Onoto Watanna, attempted to "pass" for Japanese in order to escape American prejudice which viewed the Chinese as the least "civilized" of Asian immigrants. Edith taught English to immigrants in Seattle, wrote newspaper articles on racism, and published gently ironic stories for children. Winnifred published two dozen popular romances, illustrated by a Japanese artist, and worked in Hollywood (1924-1931) as a screenwriter and an editor of several famous movies, including *Phantom of the Opera* and *Showboat.* Ling analyzes the writings of both women and their sense of self as reflected in their autobiographies.
Ling also discusses the work of five Chinese women living in Europe and America whose novels about World War II launched literary careers. These women, the best known of whom is the Belgian-raised Han Suyin, all had educated Western fathers. Ling credits Pearl Buck and Pearl Harbor for changing Western attitudes about the Chinese and allowing these women to find a reading public. Earlier generations of Chinese immigrants came from the working class and had neither the leisure nor the education to write.
See also: Amy Ling "Chinese American Women Writers: The Tradition behind Maxine Hong Kingston," in *Redefining American Literary History*, eds. A. LaVonne Brown Ruoff and Jerry W. Ward, Jr. New York: Modern Language Association, 1990.

Matsumoto, Valerie. "Desperately Seeking 'Deirdre': Gender Roles, Multicultural Relations and Nisei Women Writers of the 1930's." *Frontiers* 12, no. 1 (1991): 19-32.
Before their internment during World War II, there was a very active literary community of Japanese Americans. Mary "Mollie" Oyama Mittwer, who wrote under the pen-name Deirdre, was one of its best-known journalists. She wrote articles, interviews, poetry and regular columns for most of the major Japanese American newspapers, and from

1935 to 1941 had a popular advice column in the *New World Sun*. Matsumoto sees this column as an important aid in helping Nisei (the first generation of Japanese born in America) negotiate between white social standards and the mores of their own culture. The columns focused on family affairs, love, sex problems, and social etiquette, with special attention to the complexities of interracial dating. Matsumoto provides examples of these columns as evidence of the issues facing Japanese Americans and to establish Deirdre's role as a writer in a tradition which stretches from *Godey's Lady's Book* to Dear Abby and Miss Manners.

Nakano, Mei. *Japanese American Women: Three Generations: 1890-1990*. Berkeley, Calif.: National Japanese American Historical Society and Mina Press, 1990.

This illustrated text was written to accompany the museum exhibit by the same name. Nakano notes that the first group of picture brides were never at home in the U.S. Their daughters had greater expectations as second-generation Japanese Americans and, therefore, suffered more from racism. Most of the book focuses on this generation's experiences—their education, their religious practices, and their job opportunities—and on their role as a bridge between two cultures.

Ng, Franklin, ed. *The Asian American Encyclopedia*, 6 vols. New York: Marshall Cavendish, 1995.

These illustrated texts contain 2,000 entries which range from brief definitions to 4,000-word essays on topics such as U.S. immigration policy. Included are overviews of the history of the six largest groups, detailed chronologies, lists of research centers and libraries, dozens of tables and graphs, and several useful bibliographies. There are individual entries for all of the Asian American writers discussed in this chapter.

Niiya, Brian, ed. *Japanese American History: An A to Z Reference from 1868 to the Present*. New York: Facts on File, 1993.

The text opens with a narrative historical overview and a chronology of Japanese American history. The dictionary entries which follow cover individuals and topics such as alien land laws, Asian American theater, and the "yellow peril," the term used by anti-Japanese agitators.

White-Parks, Annette. *Sui Sin Far/Edith Maude Eaton*. Urbana: University of Illinois Press, 1995.

This comprehensive illustrated biography is a portrait of both the author and her times. Building on the work of Amy Ling (above), the author credits Sui Sin Far for giving "voice" to Chinese American women and children as she responded to social divisions and discrimination. Her use of "trickster" characters and tools of irony is typical of writers coping with the marginalization resulting from their race, class, or gender.

Yung, Judy. *Unbound Feet: A Social History of Chinese Women in San Francisco.* Berkeley: University of California Press, 1996.
This text is organized chronologically from the mid-nineteenth century to World War II. Yung bases her study on first-person accounts from letters and personal interviews, countless unpublished manuscripts, private papers, local Chinese- and English-language newspaper articles, and her own experience.

JEWISH AMERICAN WRITERS
Note: Anzia Yezierska is referenced in chapter 2 because of the widespread attention her work is now receiving; Gertrude Stein and Lillian Hellman are referenced in chapter 3 and Emma Goldman in chapter 4 as mainstream writers.

Baskin, Judith R., ed. *Women of the Word: Jewish Women and Jewish Writing.* Detroit: Wayne State University Press, 1994.
This collection of essays, several of which are annotated here, includes pieces on Israeli women writers, Jewish women writers in Latin America, female heroines in the works of male authors, and Holocaust literature.

Burstein, Janet. "Mother at the Center: Jewish American Women's Stories of the 1920's," in *Women of the Word: Jewish Women and Jewish Writing,* ed. Judith R. Baskin. Detroit: Wayne State University Press, 1994.
Burstein credits three works—Rebekah Bettelheim Kohut's autobiography *My Portion* (1925), Elizabeth G. Stern's largely fictive *I Am a Woman—and a Jew* (1926) written under the pseudonym Leah Morton, and Emanie Sach's novel *Red Damask* (1927)—with establishing the significance of the Jewish mother as a major figure in American literature. Though not as radical as Kate Chopin and Charlotte Perkins Gilman, these authors raised questions about the restrictive ideals of maternal service and duty to others and thus prepared the way for the later work of Tillie Olsen and Grace Paley.

Cohen, Sarah Blacher, ed. *From Hester Street to Hollywood: The Jewish-American Stage and Screen.* Bloomington: Indiana University Press, 1983.
Though most of the articles in this collection focus on contemporary male writers such as Clifford Odets, Paddy Chayefsky, and Woody Allen, there are chapters on the entertainers Sophie Tucker and Fannie Brice, and on the playwright Lillian Hellman (this last essay is annotated in chapter 3).

Fried, Lewis, ed. *Handbook of American Jewish Literature: An Analytical Guide to Topics, Themes, and Sources.* Westport, Conn.: Greenwood Press, 1988.
This collection contains a bibliography, a list of relevant journals

and magazines, and a variety of essays on diverse topics related to the rise of modern American Jewish letters from 1880 to the present. Included are Kathryn Hellerstein's "A Question of Tradition: Women Poets in Yiddish," Stephen J. Rubins's "American Jewish Autobiography, 1912 to the Present" with discussions of Yezierska and Mary Antin, and Asher Z. Milbauer's "Eastern Europe in American Jewish Writing" with discussions of Antin, Lazarus, and Yezierska.

Guttmann, Allen. *The Jewish Writer: Assimilation and the Crisis of Identity.* New York: Oxford University Press, 1971.

Guttmann's analysis of literature about America as "the promised land" includes a detailed description of the work of Antin, Lazarus, and Yezierska.

Kessner, Carole S. "Matrilineal Dissent: The Rhetoric of Zeal in Emma Lazarus, Marie Syrkin, and Cynthia Ozick," in *Women of the Word: Jewish Women and Jewish Writing,* ed. Judith R. Baskin. Detroit: Wayne State University Press, 1994.

All three women considered themselves assimilated Jews and aspired to careers in English literature; all became ardent supporters of Zionism and other Jewish causes in their thirties and, in the process, became well-known writers. Kessner offers a biographical essay on Lazarus and on Syrkin to emphasize their similarities with Ozick, their literary daughter. Syrkin was editor-in-chief of the *Jewish Frontier,* a journal of labor Zionists, and author of *Blessed Is the Match* (1947), a book on the Jewish Resistance. She was also the first female professor of an academic subject hired by Brandeis University.

Lichtenstein, Diane. *Writing Their Nations: The Tradition of Nineteenth Century American Jewish Women Writers.* Bloomington: Indiana University Press, 1992.

This is a study of Sephardic and German Jewish women who wrote in English as early as 1815. Lichtenstein looks at poems, letters, diaries, stories, and other pieces of "literature" to show how Jewish women transformed American and Jewish cultural myths into usable forms. Despite the difficulties they faced in daring to write, the act of writing proved a vehicle to explore their American, Jewish, and female identities and to establish their own respectability. Lichtenstein sees these women as "subjects" worthy of our attention precisely because they wrote from the margins of society; she attempts to define an ethnic tradition based on the common myths—the Mother in Israel, the specialness of the Jews, the True Woman, and the unique Jewish family—which inform Jewish women writers' sense of the world. The book also contains a chapter on well-known published writers Emma Lazarus and Edna Ferber, and a detailed bibliography.

Marovitz, Sanford E. "Romance and Realism: Children of the New Colossus and the Jewish Struggle Within," in *American Realism and the Canon*, eds. Tom Quirk and Gary Scharnhorst. Newark: University of Delaware Press, 1994.

   Marovitz discusses the commonalities in the work of Emma Lazarus, who came from a wealthy Portuguese family, one of the oldest Sephardic families in America; and Abraham Cahan, the Ashkenazic immigrant who arrived in New York in 1882 and achieved literary fame with *The Rise of David Levinsky* (1917). Marovitz also refers to the novels of Anzia Yezierska, Mary Antin, author of *The Promised Land* (1912), and Emma Wolf, author of *Heirs of Yesterday* (1900). Jewish realism as it appears in the work of these and other early twentieth century writers is marked by "emotionally laden" descriptions of suffering, a celebration of "social ideology," and an "emphasis on hope and dream." It deals with the effects of increasing mass immigration, the constant presence of anti-Semitism, and controversies surrounding the desire for assimilation.

Pratt, Norma Fain. "Culture and Radical Politics: Yiddish Women Writers in America, 1890-1940," in *Women of the Word: Jewish Women and Jewish Writing*, ed. Judith R. Baskin. Detroit: Wayne State University Press, 1994.
   Pratt focuses on approximately ten of the fifty East European women she identifies as regular writers for the Jewish communist presses. These women were among the first generation to receive a formal education before leaving Europe. Once in America, they published poems, short stories, and essays on gender, class, and immigrant issues, and thus became spokeswomen for a radical Jewish subculture.

Shapiro, Ann R. *Jewish American Women Writers: A Bio-Bibliographical and Critical Sourcebook.* Westport, Conn.: Greenwood Press, 1994.
   For each writer there is a biographical summary, an analysis of major work, a survey of criticism, and a bibliography of primary and secondary sources. Included are entries on Gertrude Stein and Lillian Hellman (chapter 3), Anzia Yezierska (chapter 2), and Mary Antin, Edna Ferber, Fannie Hurst, Emma Lazarus, and Tess Slesinger. Shapiro, in reviewing Jewish anthologies, notes the absence of women writers. Her concern is to "revision" female experience as seen by women themselves and to correct stereotypes of Jewish women created by male authors.

Walden, Daniel, ed. *Twentieth Century American-Jewish Fiction Writers. Dictionary of Literary Biography*, vol. 28. Detroit: Gale Research, 1984.
   This standard reference contains biographical essays on Ferber, Yezierska, and Laura Z. Hobson.

Zaborowska, Magdalena J. *How We Found America: Reading Gender through East European Immigrant Narratives.* Chapel Hill: University of North Carolina Press, 1995.
    Zaborowska looks at works by Mary Antin, Elizabeth Stern, and Anzia Yezierska against more recent texts by Maria Kuncewicz and Eva Hoffman. Despite the diversity of writing by female immigrants and expatriates, she finds a common resistance in their work to the status of "otherness" to which women were relegated in both Old and New Worlds. Zaborowska also considers the ways in which these writers "problematize" the conventional narrative of female assimilation.

LATINA WRITERS

Note: Though earlier chapters of this bibliography only cover writers from the United States who published works in English, the term "American" rightly refers to writers from Canada, Central America, and South America as well. Recent interest in Spanish-speaking writers from throughout the Americas is reflected in several of the sources listed below. I have also listed a few of the best known of these women in the appendix.
    The U.S. Hispanic Literary Heritage Project, which supports the Arte Público Press in Houston, Texas, continues to reprint forgotten works, for example, the 1872 satiric novel *Who Would Have Thought It?* (1995) by Maria Amparo Ruiz De Burton, a native of Baja, California, birthdate unknown. The Texas Pan American Series also publishes updated English translations, such as *House of Mist and The Shrouded Woman: Two Novels by María Luisa Bombal* (1995), one of the best-known Chilean writers of the early twentieth century.

Candelaria, Cordelia Chávez. "Latina Women Writers: Chicana, Cuban American and Puerto Rican Voices," in *Handbook of Hispanic Cultures in the United States: Literature and Art,* eds. Nicolás Kanellos and Claudio Esteva-Fabregat. Houston: Arte Público Press, 1993.
    Candelaria sees Latina writing in the United States as focused on a "dynamic web" of interrelationships between gender, genre, and geography. Although most of the women she discusses began publishing after 1948, she does identify a few important early writers, including the Mexican American novelist Josephina Niggli, the Cuban folklorist Lydia Cabrera, and the Puerto Rican poet Julia de Burgos.

Chevigny, Bell Gale, and Gari Laguardia. "Introduction," in *Reinventing the Americas: Comparative Studies of Literature of the United States and Spanish America.* Cambridge, England: Cambridge University Press, 1986.
    The authors provide a comparative political and literary history from colonization through the 1960's, contrasting, for example, the legal status of slaves and the rise of a middle class in Spanish America and the United States. They also contrast the literary treatment of nature, the encounter between Native Americans and whites, and the role of black

culture in various writers' works, and consider the differing literary histories of various genres. The novel achieved prominence in the United States in the late nineteenth century and in Spanish America in the 1940's after a period of "consolidation of previous forms and thematics." The growing "convergence" of American literatures advanced rapidly in the 1970's with Spanish American narrative techniques transforming U.S. and European narrative conventions. Chevigny and Laguardia hope the "unexpected elements of reciprocity," despite historical discontinuities, will lead to better understanding of our various American selves.

Fabre, Genvieve, ed. *European Perspectives on Hispanic Literature in the United States.* Houston: Arte Público Press, 1988.

This collection of essays includes two that deal with early Chicano writings: "The Recovery of the Nineteenth Century Chicano Autobiography" by Genaro Padilla and "Cultural Ambivalence in Early Chicana Literature" by Gloria Velásquez.

Horno-Delgado, Asuncíon, ed. *Breaking Boundaries: Toward a Critical Practice of Latina Writing.* Amherst: University of Massachusetts Press, 1989.

Though this collection of essays primarily deals with contemporary writers, its stated scope is the more than one hundred years following United States acquisition of Mexican and Puerto Rican national territory.

Jehenson, Myriam Yvonne. *Latin-American Women Writers: Class, Race, and Gender.* Albany: State University of New York Press, 1995.

Though the emphasis here is on the second half of the twentieth century, chapters two and three identify several important "foremothers": the Argentine Victoria Ocampo, the Venezuelan Teresa de la Parra, and two Chileans, Marta Brunet and María Luisa Bombal. These writers come from diverse cultural and socioeconomic backgrounds and write with a variety of "literary strategies." Each is discussed in a brief bio-critical essay which analyzes her work in the context of race, gender, and class.

Kanellos, Nicolás. "Literature," in *The Hispanic American Almanac.* Detroit: Gale Research, 1993.

Kanellos notes that much of the early Spanish-language literature published in the Southwest before and after it became part of the United States has been lost or not yet collected and studied. In the years following the Mexican-American War and up to 1910, Spanish-language newspapers laid the foundation for a vital literature. The late nineteenth century also saw a flowering of essays, poetry, and short stories by Puerto Rican writers living in New York while they worked for independence. Among the Chicana writers Kanellos discusses are the novelist Pilar Ruiz de Burton, the poet Sara Estela Ramírez, and the novelist Josephina Niggli. He also cites the contributions of Lola Rodríguez de Tío, one of Puerto Rico's most important literary and patriotic figures, and Franca de Armiño, a prolific poet-playwright whose work has been lost with the exception of *Los hipócritas: comedia dramática social*, self-published in 1937.

Lomelli, Francisco A., and Carl R. Shirley, eds. *Chicano Writers. Dictionary of Literary Biography*, vol. 122. Detroit: Gale Research, 1992.
   This standard reference work contains biographical essays on Fabiola Cabeza de Baca Gilbert and Cleofas M. Jaramillo, although the bulk of the entries are on contemporary writers.

Martin, Diane E., ed. *Spanish American Women Writers: A Bio-Bibliographic Source Book*. Westport, Conn.: Greenwood Press, 1990.
   This reference work includes biographical essays on fifty women writers from the seventeenth century to the present, approximately twenty of whom wrote between 1848 and 1948. Each entry includes a bibliography and an overview of basic career information, major themes in the writer's work, and her critical reputation. Appendices list authors by genre, nationality, and birthdate.

Robelledo, Tey Diana. *Women Singing in the Snow: Cultural Analysis of Chicana Literature*. Tucson: University of Arizona Press, 1995.
   Robelledo provides a social, cultural, and historical context for Chicana writers from the earliest oral stories centered on home and food preparation to the sexual politics embedded in late twentieth century novels. The first chapter covers oral and written texts in both English and Spanish produced between 1848 and 1910, a period when only women from wealthy families were able to read and write. The second chapter discusses three writers—Fabiola Cabeza de Baca Gilbert, Nina Otero-Warren, and Cleofas Jaramillo—who worked to preserve the Hispanic culture of New Mexico from the 1930's to the 1950's. The text includes a bibliography and a list of published sources.

Rodríguez, Carla E. *Puerto Ricans: Born in the U.S.A.* Boston: Unwin Hyman, 1989.
   The text is supplemented by a bibliography and many useful charts and tables. Though the focus is primarily on the post-World War II period, discussions of the literature of migration and the politicization of women provide historical information pertinent to the work of earlier writers.

Telgen, Diane, and Jim Kamp, eds. *Notable Hispanic American Women*. Detroit: Gale Research, 1993.
   This encyclopedia of almost three hundred entries offers brief biographical essays on the lives and careers of a wide range of women activists, artists, educators, business and professional women, social and

religious workers, scientists, and television show hosts who come from Spanish-speaking cultures. Indexes list subjects by ethnicity and by occupation, including author/writer, dramatist/playwright, historian, journalist, novelist, poet, and storyteller. The majority of writers referenced published their work after 1948; among the few discussed who published between 1848 and 1948 are the poet Sara Estela Ramírez, the folklorist Lydia Cabrera, and the home economist Fabiola Cabeza de Baca Gilbert.

NATIVE AMERICAN WRITERS
Note: The three Native American women writers most frequently referenced who published works under their own names in the United States between 1848 and 1948 are Zitkala-Sa (1876-1938), who gained widespread prominence as a "Native" intellectual and activist; E. Pauline Johnson (1861-1913), the Canadian Mohawk who became famous for her dramatic readings of her poetry and stories; and Humishima or Mourning Dove (1888-1936), the author of *Coyote Stories*, who wrote the first known novel by a Native American woman, *Cogewea: The Half-Blood* (1927).

Allen, Paula Gunn. "The Word Warriors," in *The Sacred Hoop: Recovering the Feminine in American Indian Traditions.* Boston: Beacon Press, 1986.
Gunn explains the major differences between "traditional" Native American literature and Western literature, which derive from the very different realities they reflect. For example, the Western distinction between nature and the supernatural is "foreign" to Native American thought. Native American literature is essentially mystical and psychic. It includes ceremonial and popular forms, each with its own distinctive characteristics; Western distinctions between prose and poetry do not apply. Gunn criticizes those who categorize Native American literature as "folklore" without a true appreciation of its "complexity" and of the "unity and harmony of symbol, structure, and articulation" that is "peculiar" to the Native American world.

_____, ed. *Spider Woman's Granddaughters: Traditional Tales and Contemporary Writing by Native American Women.* Boston: Beacon Press, 1989.
This collection of traditional tales, biographical writings, and contemporary short stories includes excerpts from the works of Pretty Shield, Zitkala-Sa, E. Pauline Johnson, Humishima, and Ella Deloria, told or written in the early twentieth century. A glossary and bibliography are appended.
Bataille, Gretchen M., and Kathleen Mullen Sands. *American Indian Women: Telling Their Lives.* Lincoln: University of Nebraska Press, 1984.
This is a comprehensive study of oral and written Native American women's autobiography which includes an annotated bibliography of

primary and secondary sources. The authors see these autobiographies as particularly useful in correcting misconceptions about the status of Native American women in their own societies. In their introduction they provide an overview of the history of Native American autobiography, noting that early captivity narratives recorded by ethnographers are generally more exotic in their depiction of Native American life than later narratives written by Native Americans themselves. They also comment on the similarities between slave narratives and Native American autobiographies, and contrast the focus on everyday life and personal growth in autobiographies by women with the focus on heroic individualism in those by men. *Papago Woman*, originally published in the 1930's and narrated by Maria Chona, the daughter of a Papago chief, is discussed in detail as the prime example of a successful collaboration between a strong and independent-minded Native American woman and a sensitive and insightful recorder-editor, Ruth Underhill. Also referred to are Sarah Winnemucca Hopkins's *Life Among the Paiutes: Their Wrongs and Claims* (1883), Ruth Landes's *The Ojibwa Woman* (1938), *Pretty Shield, Medicine Woman of the Crows* (1932, original title *Red Mother*), and *Waheenee: An Indian Girl's Story, Told by Herself* (1921).

Bernardin, Susan K. "Mixed Messages: Authority and Authorship in Mourning Dove's *Cogewea, the Half-Blood.*" *American Literature* 67, no. 3 (September 1995): 487-509.
   Bernardin explores the complex relationship between Mourning Dove and Lucullus V. McWhorter, the editor who made possible the publication of *Cogewea* but whose editorial assistance ended up demoralizing her and compromising her credibility as author. McWhorter's objective in insisting on key changes was to distance the work from the Western romances it imitated and to heighten its authenticity through the addition of ethnographic and historical footnotes. Mourning Dove saw herself as a mixed-blood Indian with the mission of writing stories to mediate between two worlds. Bernardin, in her analysis of the novel, demonstrates that despite its "ambivalent narrative resolutions," it does, in effect, offer a "fusion of Okanogan orality" with mainstream plots and genres. McWhorter, however, steered Mourning Dove away from the future novels she wanted to write and toward the collection of Okanogan stories, later published as *Coyote Stories* (1933), which he believed would better serve as cultural mediators. Ultimately, the novel itself and the history of its co-authorship reveal the "predicament of early marginalized writers who attempted to translate and legitimize their culture to a predominantly Euro-American audience."

Brown, Alanna Kathleen. "Legacy Profile: Mourning Dove." *Legacy* 6 (1989): 51-56.
   Brown reviews the key facts of Mourning Dove's life. She managed

to obtain a few years of formal schooling while being raised in a small community in Washington and on the Flathead Reservation. The 1912 federally ordered round-up and evacuation of the buffalo on her reservation inspired her to write a novel for "her people, for herself and for the Euro-Americans who understood so little about those they had conquered." McWhorter, the white advocate of Indian rights to whom she first showed the book, had trouble finding a publisher for it and, therefore, decided to add more political and ethnographic material without asking Mourning Dove's permission. It took fifteen years for Mourning Dove to see her novel in print, a work that she wrote at night in tents after long days in the field as a migrant worker. When she actually read the published version, she stated it felt like someone else's book and not hers at all.

Fisher, Dexter. "The Transformation of Tradition: A Study of Zitkala-Sa and Mourning Dove, Two Transitional American Indian Writers," in *Critical Essays on Native American Literature*, ed. Andrew Wiget. Boston: G. K. Hall, 1985.
   Fisher identifies Zitkala-Sa and Mourning Dove as two of the first Indian writers to attempt to bridge the gap between tradition and assimilation. Both combined firsthand knowledge of the language and traditions of their tribes with fluency in English acquired at off-reservation schools. Both felt an obligation to help preserve their culture, as well as a need to express their own unique points of view. Both became darlings of the white world, which romanticized and objectified their accomplishments. Zitkala-Sa is best known for her autobiographical work *American Indian Stories* (1921), which chronicles the pain and difficulty of growing up "Indian" in a white man's world; she also published a collection of traditional Sioux tales, *Old Indian Legends* (1901). Mourning Dove is best known for her translations of Okanogan folklore, *Coyote Stories* (1933), and is also the author of one of the first Native American novels, *Cogewea* (1927). Fisher provides a brief biographical sketch of each woman and a discussion of her writings, political activities, and personal relationships with Indians and whites.

Green, Rayna. "Native American Woman: Review Essay." *Signs* 6, no. 2 (Winter 1980): 248-267.
   This chronological study of scholarship and popular literature on the American Indian woman traces the evolution of images and mainstream attitudes from the seventeenth century to the present in the United States and Canada. Green identifies Ruth Landes's "flawed and male-centered" book, *The Ojibwa Woman* (1933), as the first to establish the possibility of publishing full-length studies of tribal women. It would take another thirty to forty years for a true "flowering" of scholarly articles on Native American women.

Okker, Patricia. "Native American Literatures and the Canon: The Case of Zitkala-Sa," in *American Realism and the Canon*, eds. Tom Quirk and Gary Scharnhorst. Newark: University of Delaware Press, 1994.

Okker notes that Zitkala-Sa is now included in several major anthologies of American literature, but that her work is represented by a very "Euro-American" autobiographical essay, rather than by a short story that might be more typical of Native American literature. Okker compares Zitkala-Sa's story "The Soft-Hearted Sioux" with Jack London's "Law of the Land" to show how her portrait of a stoic Indian suffering from "cultural displacement" differs from the stereotypic romanticized version popularized by London and others. Zitkala-Sa's story is also less "realistic" than literature of its time was supposed to be. Okker concludes that in order to establish Zitkala-Sa's and other Native Americans' real place in literary history, we need to look at their work in the context of their own historical experience and their own literary traditions.

Ruoff, A. LaVonne Brown. *American Indian Literatures: An Introduction, Bibliographic Review, and Selected Bibliography.* New York: Modern Language Association, 1990.

This comprehensive reference work credits a 1977 seminar on contemporary Native American literature jointly sponsored by the National Endowment for the Humanities and the Modern Language Association with establishing the legitimacy of Native American oral and written work as "American" rather than "aboriginal" literature. Ruoff provides a history of Native Americans before and after the arrival of western Europeans and offers an overview of their oral literature, ritual dramas, songs, storytelling, life histories, and autobiographies. Among the many annotated bibliographies included is a listing of relevant sources in women's studies.

_____. "Justice for Indians and Women: The Protest Fiction of Alice Callahan and E. Pauline Johnson." *World Literature Today* 66, no. 2 (Spring 1992): 249-255.

Callahan and Johnson were both "acculturated, well-read, independent daughters" of Indian fathers active in tribal affairs. Ruoff summarizes the plots of their novels and provides a brief biographical essay for each woman. Both combine protest fiction with domestic romance and effectively describe the oppression of Indians and women. Their works are important to the history of American Indian literature because of the "bicultural voices" of these two women and their testimony to the strength of individuals in the face of sexism and racism.

Warrior, Robert Allen. "Reading American Indian Intellectual Traditions." *World Literature Today* 66, no. 2 (Spring 1992): 236-240.

Warrior discusses the political positions of prominent Native

American intellectuals during the key period, 1890-1930, particularly in terms of their response to the 1890 massacre at Wounded Knee. He criticizes Gertrude Bonnin (Zitkala-Sa) and her husband for their staunch support of the "antipeyote campaign" but praises her opposition to the paternalism of non-Native education.

Wiget, Andrew. *Native American Literature*. Boston: G. K. Hall, 1985.
   This text includes a bibliography and a chronology which begins in 50,000 b.c. and ends in 1977 with the publication of Leslie Silko's *Ceremony*. Individual chapters focus on oral narrative and poetry, the autobiographical tradition of the nineteenth century, the poetry of E. Pauline Johnson, and modern fiction. Wiget also provides an overview of major Native American myths and the writings of seventeenthcentury men who attended Harvard Indian College.

Appendix A
Selected Women Writers by Birthdate
Who Published 1848-1948

Sarah Josepha Hale
1788-1879

Woman's Record: Sketches of All Distinguished Women from the Beginning to A.D. 1850 (1853). Novelist, essayist, editor, *Godey's Lady's Book* (1837-1877).

Lydia Sigourney
1791-1865

Illustrated Poems (1849). Poetry.

Catharine Beecher
1800-1878

The American Woman's Home (1869). Education, home economics.

Caroline Kirkland
1801-1864

The Evening Book (1852). Short stories, essays.

Elizabeth Palmer Peabody
1804-1894

Lectures in Training Schools for Kindergartners (1888). Education reform.

Harriet Wilson
1807?-1870

Our Nig: Or Sketches from the Life of a Free Black (1859). Novel.

Sara Willis Parton
(Fanny Fern) 1811-1872

Fern Leaves from Fanny's Portfolio (1853), *Ruth Hall* (1855). Novels, newspaper columns, and sketches.

Harriet Beecher Stowe
1811-1896

Uncle Tom's Cabin (1852). Domestic novels.

Harriet Ann Jacobs
1813-1897

Incidents in the Life of a Slave-Girl (1861). Autobiography/slave narrative.

Elizabeth Cady Stanton
1815-1902

The Woman's Bible (1898), *Eighty Years and More* (1898). Autobiography, articles on feminist issues and suffrage.

Julia Ward Howe
1819-1910

"Battle Hymn of the Republic" (1862). Poetry, articles on women's rights.

E. D. E. N. Southworth
1819-1899

The Hidden Hand (1888). Novels.

Susan Warner
1819-1885

The Wide, Wide World (1850). Novels, children's stories.

Mary Baker Eddy
1821-1910

Founder, Church of Christ, Scientist (1879). Religious treatises.

Lydia Folger Fowler
1822-1879

Second American woman to receive an M.D.; first to teach at a medical school; essays on child care, poetry, a temperance novel.

Mary Boykin Chesnut
1823-1886

A Diary from Dixie (1905). Civil war diaries.

Jessie Benton Fremont
1824-1902

Far-West Sketches (1890). Travelogues, short stories, reminiscences.

Lucy Larcom
1824-1893

As It Is in Heaven (1893). Poetry, articles on education, Christian novels.

Frances Watkins Harper
1825-1911

Iola Leroy (1892). Novels, poetry, social criticism.

Matilda Joslyn Gage
1826-1898

Woman, Church, and State (1893). Suffrage literature, women's history.

Rose Terry Cooke
1827-1892

Somebody's Neighbors (1881). Short stories, poetry.

Maria Cummins
1827-1866

The Lamplighter. Novels.

Ellen G. White
1827-1915

Co-founder, Seventh-day Adventist church. Religious treatises.

Jane Cunningham Croly
(Jennie June) 1829-1901

Advice journalism.

Emily Dickinson
1830-1886

First published collection—1890. Poetry.

Helen Hunt Jackson
1830-1885

Ramona (1894). Novel, treatises on Indian rights.

Mary Terhune
1830-1922

Common Sense in the Household (1871). Novels, advice books.

Rebecca Harding Davis
1831-1910

Life in the Iron Mills (1861). Novels, short stories.

Louisa May Alcott
1832-1888

Little Women (1868, 1869). Novels.

Celia Thaxter
1835-1894

An Island Garden (1894). Poetry, children's stories, essays on gardens.

Marietta Holley
1836-1926

Betsey Bobbett (1873). Humorous novels.

Constance Fenimore Woolson
1840-1894

"Miss Grief" and other stories (1890's). Novels, short stories.

Elizabeth Stuart Phelps
1844-1911

The Silent Partner (1971). Novels about career women.

Alice James
1848-1892

Alice James: Her Brothers—Her Journal (1934). Diary on impressions of British and American society.

Frances Hodgson Burnett
1849-1924

A Little Princess (1905), *The Secret Garden* (1911). Children's stories.

Emma Lazarus
1849-1887

"The New Colossus" inscribed on Statue of Liberty (1903). Poetry, plays, translations, essays on Jewish themes.

Sarah Orne Jewett
1849-1909

The Country of the Pointed Firs (1896). Novels, short stories.

Kate Chopin
1850-1904

The Awakening (1899). Novels, short stories.

Alice Morse Earle
1851-1911

Child Life in Colonial Days (1899). Colonial history.

Mary Wilkins Freeman
1852-1930

"A New England Nun," and other stories (1880's). Novels, short stories.

Grace King
1852-1932

"Monsieur Motte" (1886), "The Little Covenant Girl" (1893). Novels, history, stories about New Orleans.

Gertrude Atherton
1857-1948

Black Oxen (1923), *Adventures of a Novelist* (1932). Novels, chronicles of California.

Fannie Merritt Farmer
1857-1915

Boston Cooking-School Cook Book (1896). Cookbooks.

Ida Tarbell
1857-1944

The History of the Standard Oil Company (1902). Biography, autobiography, investigative reporting.

Julia C. Lathorp
1858-1932

First woman to head a federal agency, U.S. Children's Bureau. Social reform; *Hull House Maps and and Papers* (1895).

Marion Talbot 1858-1948	*More than Lore* (1936), on experience as first dean of women, University of Chicago; home economics, education.
Katharine Lee Bates 1859-1929	"America the Beautiful" (1895). Poetry, literary commentary, textbooks, translations.
Anna Julia Cooper 1859-1964	*A Voice from the South* (1892). Essays on race and gender.
Pauline Hopkins 1859-1930	*Contending Forces* (1900). Novels, social commentary, biographical sketches.
Florence Kelley 1859-1932	*Hull House Maps and Papers* (1895). Social reform.
Fanny Bullock Workman 1859-1925	*Two Summers in the Ice-wilds of Eastern Karakoram* (1917). Geography, accounts of mountain-climbing treks.
Jane Addams 1860-1935	*Twenty Years at Hull House* (1910). Autobiography and social criticism.
Charlotte Perkins Gilman 1860-1935	*The Yellow Wallpaper* (1892), *Women and Economics* (1898). Novels, science fiction, economic and feminist treatises.
Henrietta Szold (Sulamith) 1860-1945	First president, Hadassah, American women's Zionist group. Translations, essays.
E. Pauline Johnson 1861-1913	*The Moccasin Maker* (1913). Poetry and short stories.
Ida B. Wells 1862-1931	*A Red Record: Tabulated Statistics and Alleged Causes of Lynchings in the United States* (1895). Autobiography and social commentary.
Edith Wharton 1862-1937	*The House of Mirth* (1905), *The Age of Innocence* (1920). Novels, short stories, travelogues.
Mary Church Terrell 1863-1954	First president, National Association of Colored Women. Essays.
Elizabeth Cochrane Seaman (Nellie Bly) 1864-1922	Most famous stunt—around the world in 75 days. Investigative reporting.
Edith Maud Eaton (Sui Sin Far) 1865-1914	*Mrs. Spring Fragrance* (1912). Autobiography, children's stories, articles on racism.

Margaret Armstrong 1867-1944	*Western Wild Flowers* (1915). Book design and illustration.
Emily Greene Balch 1867-1961	*Our Slavic Fellow Citizens* (1910). Nobel Peace Prize (1946). Social reform.
Edith Hamilton 1867-1963	*The Greek Way* (1930). Studies of Greek, Roman, and biblical antiquity.
Laura Ingalls Wilder 1867-1957	*The Little House on the Prairie* (1935). Children's stories.
Emma Goldman 1869-1940	Founder of *Mother Earth* (1906), anarchist journal. Political and literary commentary.
Alice Hamilton 1869-1970	*Exploring the Dangerous Trades* (1943). Autobiography and scientific studies.
Anne Warner French 1869-1913	*Susan Clegg and Her Friend Mrs. Lathorp* (1904). Humorous novels.
Rachel Crothers 1870-1958	*When Ladies Meet* (1932). Playwright.
Willa Cather 1873-1947	*My Antonia* (1918), *Death Comes for the Archbishop* (1927). Novels.
Ellen Glasgow 1873-1945	*Barren Ground* (1925), *Vein of Iron* (1935). Novels.
Emily Post 1873-1960	*Etiquette in Society, in Business, in Politics, and at Home* (1922). Etiquette books and newspaper columns.
Zona Gale 1874-1938	*Miss Lulu Bett* (1920). Short stories, drama, journalism.
Amy Lowell 1874-1925	*Sword Blades and Poppy Seeds* (1914). Poetry, literary commentary.
Dorothy Reed Mendenhall 1874-1964	"Child Care and Child Welfare: Outlines for Study" (1921). Medical research, essays on child care and maternal health.
Gertrude Stein 1874-1946	*The Autobiography of Alice B. Toklas* (1933). Experimental fiction, biography, and drama.
Etsu Sugimoto 1874-1950	*Daughter of the Samurai* (1934). Autobiography.
Alice Dunbar-Nelson 1875-1935	*The Goodness of St. Rocque and Other Stories* (1899). Poetry, short stories.

Winnifred Eaton
(Onoto Watanna) 1875-1945

Miss Nome of Japan (1899).   Popular romance, screenplays.

Elsie Clews Parsons
1875-1941

Pueblo Indian Religion (1939).   Anthropology.

Gertrude Simmons Bonnin
(Zitkala-Sa) 1876-1938

American Indian Stories (1921).   Autobiography, short stories, collections of Sioux tales.

Mary Beard
1876-1958

On Understanding Women (1931), *Woman as a Force in History* (1946).   American history studies and textbooks.

Susan Glaspell
1876-1948

Trifles (1916).   Drama, novels, short stories.

Mary Roberts Rinehart
1876-1958

The Circular Staircase (1908).   Detective fiction.

Georgia Douglas Johnson
1877-1966

The Heart of a Woman and Other Poems (1918).   Poetry, drama.

Cleofas Jaramillo
1878-1956

The Genuine New Mexico Tasty Recipes (1939).   Folklore, autobiography.

Louise Beebe Wilder
1878-1938

Color in My Garden (1918). Garden writing.

Dorothy Canfield Fisher
1879-1958

Understood Betsy (1917). Children's stories, poetry, textbooks, educational treatises, translations.

Margaret Sanger
1879-1966

Autobiography, essays on feminist issues and birth control.

Angelina Grimké
1880-1958

Rachel: A Play in Three Acts (1920). Poetry, drama.

Georgia Douglas Johnson
1880-1966

Plumes (1927).   Drama, poetry.

Helen Keller
1880-1969

The Story of My Life (1902). Autobiography, social reform.

Anne O'Hare McCormick
1880-1954

Pulitzer Prize for Journalism (1937). Foreign correspondence.

Mary Antin
1881-1949

The Promised Land (1912).   Autobiography.

Sara Estela Ramirez
1881-1910

El Beso de un Angel (1908). Poetry, poetic essays in Spanish.

Florence Guy Seabury
1881-1951

Love Is a Challenge (1935).   Humorous
novels and stories.

Jessie Redmon Fauset
1882-1961

There Is Confusion (1924).   Novels.

Nina Otero-Warren
1882-1965

Old Spain in Our Southwest (1936).
Folklore.

Anne Spencer
1882-1975

"Before the Feast at Shushan" (1920). Poetry.

Anzia Yezierska
1883-1970

Hungry Hearts (1920). Novels, short stories,
autobiography.

Edith Summers Kelley
1884-1956

Weeds (1923).   Novels.

Sara Teasdale
1884-1933

Love Songs (1917).   Poetry.

Edna Ferber
1885-1968

So Big (1924).   Novels, screenplays.

Constance Rourke
1885-1941

American Humor (1931).   Studies of
American culture.

Sophie Treadwell
1885?-1970

Machinal (1928).   Drama.

Elinor Wylie
1885-1928

Collected Poems (1932). Poetry, novels,
short stories, literary criticism.

Zoe Akins
1886-1958

Déclassée (1919).   Drama.

H. D. (Hilda Doolittle)
1886-1961

Collected Poems of H. D. (1925).   Poetry.

Ruth Fulton Benedict
1887-1948

Patterns of Culture (1934).   Anthropology.

Frances Marion
1887-1973

*How to Write and Sell Motion Picture
Stories* (1937). Screenwriter.

Marianne Moore
1887-1972

Selected Poems (1935). Poetry.

Mourning Dove
(Humishima) 1888-1936

Coyote Stories (1933). Novel, translations of
Okanogan folklore.

Anita Loos
1888-1981

Gentlemen Prefer Blondes (1925).
Scriptwriter and novelist.

Ella Deloria 1889- ?	*Dakota Texts* (1932), *Waterlily* (1944). Native American folklore, novel.
Fannie Hurst 1889-1968	*Imitation of Life* (1933). Novels.
Gabriela Mistral (Chile) 1889-1957	Nobel Prize for Literature (1945). Poetry.
Elizabeth Stern 1889-1954	*My Mother and I* (1917). Fictionalized autobiographies.
Teresa de la Parra (Venezuela) 1889-1936	*Las Memorias de Mama Blanca* (1929; *Mama Blanca's Memoirs*) *Iphigenia* (1924; *The Diary of a Young Lady Who Wrote Because She was Bored*).
Victoria Ocampo (Argentina) 1890-1979	*Testimonios* (10 vols., 1935-1977). Autobiography, essays, journalism.
Katherine Anne Porter 1890-1980	*Pale Horse, Pale Rider* (1939). Short stories.
Zora Neale Hurston 1891-1960	*Their Eyes Were Watching God* (1937). Autobiography, anthropology, novels.
Nella Larsen 1891-1964	*Quicksand* (1928). Novels.
Djuna Barnes 1892-1982	*Nightwood* (1936). Novels, drama.
Pearl S. Buck 1892-1973	*The Good Earth* (1931). Nobel Prize for Literature (1938). Novels, essays on China and on women's issues.
Gordon Hamilton 1892-1967	*Theory and Practice of Social Casework* (1940). Social work—textbooks and studies.
Josephine Herbst 1892-1969	*Rope of Gold* (1939). Political novels.
Edna St. Vincent Millay 1892-1950	*Renascence, and Other Poems* (1917), *The Ballad of the Harp Weaver* (1922). Poetry, drama.
Agnes Smedley 1892-1950	*Daughter of Earth* (1929), autobiographical novel. Reportage (books, articles) on Chinese revolution.
Dorothy Parker 1893-1967	"Big Blond" (1929), *A Star is Born* (1937). Poetry, short stories, humorous sketches, screenplays.

Dorothy Thompson 1893-1961	*Let the Record Speak* (1939). Syndicated political journalism.
Genevieve Taggard 1894-1948	*Collected Poems, 1918-1938* (1938). Poetry.
Rose Franken 1895-1988	*Another Language* (1932). Drama, screenplays, novels.
Susanne K. Langer 1895-1985	*Philosophy in a New Key: A Study in the Symbolism of Reason, Rite, and Art* (1942). Philosophy.
Helen Merrell Lynd 1896-1982	*Middletown: A Study in Contemporary American Culture* (1929). Sociology, education.
Mari Sandoz 1896-1966	*Old Jules* (1935), *Crazy Horse* (1942). Historical novels and biography.
Louise Bogan 1897-1970	*The Blue Estuaries: Poems 1923-1968* (1968). Poetry, short stories, literary criticism.
Catherine Drinker Bowen 1897-1973	*"Beloved Friend": The Story of Tchaikowsky and Nadeja von Meck* (1937). Biography.
Marta Brunet (Chile) 1897-1967	*Aguas abayos* (1943; *Downstream*). Novels.
Elizabeth Seifert 1897-1983	*Young Doctor Galahad* (1938). Medical romances.
Ariel Durant 1898-1981	*The Story of Civilization* (7 vols., 1935-1961). History.
Fabiola Cabeza de Baca Gilbert 1898- ?	*Historic Cookery* (1939). Home economics.
Marita Bonner 1899-1971	"On Being Young—A Woman—And Colored" (1925). Drama, essays, short stories.
Marie Syrkin 1899-1989	*Blessed Is the Match* (1947). Journalism, books on Zionism and Jewish Resistance.
Lydia Cabrera (Cuba) 1900-1991	*Cuentos negros de Cuba* (1936; *Black Tales of Cuba*). Folklore.
Laura Z. Hobson 1900-1986	*Gentleman's Agreement* (1947). Novels.

Meridel Le Sueur 1900-1996	*Salute to Spring and Other Stories* (1940). Political novels, short stories.
Margaret Mitchell 1900-1949	*Gone with the Wind* (1936). Novels.
Laura Riding Jackson 1901-1991	*Collected Poems* (1938). Poetry.
Margaret Mead 1901-1978	*Coming of Age in Samoa* (1928). Anthropology.
Clare Boothe Luce 1903-1987	*The Women* (1936). Drama, journalism, politics.
Lillian Hellman 1905-1984	*The Little Foxes* (1939). Playwright and screenwriter.
Tess Slesinger 1905-1945	*The Unpossessed* (1934). Novels, short stories, screenplays.
Mary Oyama Mittwer 1907-	"Deirdre" (1935-1941). Advice columns.
Maria Luisa Bombal (Chile) 1910-1980	*La última niebla* (1935; *The House of Mist*). Novels, short stories.
Margaret Wise Brown 1910-1952	*Goodnight Moon* (1947). Children's books.
Josephina Niggli 1910-	*Mexican Village* (1945). Romance.
Dorothy West 1910-	*The Living is Easy* (1948). Novels, short stories, sketches.
Ann Petry 1911-	*The Street* (1946). Novels, short stories.
Elizabeth Bishop 1911-1979	*North and South* (1946). Poetry.
Julia de Burgos 1914-1953	*Poemas en veinte surcos* (1938; *Poems in Twenty Furrows*). Poetry.
Gwendolyn Brooks 1917-	*A Street in Bronzeville* (1945). Poetry.
Carson McCullers 1917-1967	*The Member of the Wedding* (1946). Novels, short stories.
Jade Snow Wong 1922-	*Fifth Chinese Daughter* (1945). Autobiography.

Appendix B
Selected Women Writers by Ethnicity
Who Published 1848-1948

African American Writers
Bonner, Marita
1899-1971

Brooks, Gwendolyn
1917-

Cooper, Anna Julia
1859-1964

Dunbar-Nelson, Alice
1875-1935

Fauset, Jessie Redmon
1882-1961

Grimké, Angelina
1880-1958

Harper, Frances Watkins
1825-1911

Hopkins, Pauline Elizabeth
1859-1930

Hurston, Zora Neale
1891-1960

Jacobs, Harriet Ann
1813-1897

Johnson, Georgia Douglas
1877-1966

Larsen, Nella
1891-1964

Petry, Ann
1911-

Spencer, Anne
1882-1975

Terrell, Mary Church
1863-1954

Wells, Ida Barnett
1862-1931

West, Dorothy
1910-

Wilson, Harriet
1807?-1870

Asian American Writers
Eaton, Edith Maud
1865-1914

Eaton, Winnifred
1875-1945

Sugimoto, Etsu
1874-1950

Mittwer, Mary Oyama
1907-

Wong, Jade Snow
1922-

Jewish American Writers
Antin, Mary
1881-1949

Ferber, Edna
1885-1968

Goldman, Emma
1869-1940

Hellman, Lillian
1905-1984

Hobson, Laura Z.
1900-1986

Hurst, Fannie
1889-1968

Lazarus, Emma
1849-1887

Slesinger, Tess
1905-1945

Stein, Gertrude
1874-1946

Stern, Elizabeth
1889-1954

Syrkin, Marie
1899-1989

Szold, Henrietta
1860-1945

Yezierska, Anzia
1883-1970

Latina Writers
Bombal, María Luisa
1910-1980

Brunet, Marta
1897-1967

Cabrera, Lydia
1900-1991

de Baca Gilbert, Fabiola
1898-?

de Burgos, Julia
1914-1953

de la Parra, Teresa
1889-1936

Jaramillo, Cleofas
1878-1956

Mistral, Gabriela
1889-1957

Niggli, Josephina
1910-

Ocampo, Victoria
1890-1980

Otero-Warren, Nina
1882-1965

Ramírez, Sara Estela
1881-1910

Native American Writers
Deloria, Ella
1889-?

Hopkins, Sarah Winnemucca
1844-1891

Humishima (Mourning Dove)
1888-1936

Johnson, E. Pauline
1861-1913

Zitkala-Sa
1876-1938

INDEX

Index

Index

Index

Smith, Paul. 160
Smith, Valerie. 278
Smith-Rosenberg, Carroll. 13
Sollors, Werner, ed. 297
Solomon, Martha. 219
Soristo, Carolyn. 279
Souhami, Diana. 180
Spaeth, Janet. 125
Stanbrough, Jane. 170
Stange, Margit 38
Stapelton, Laurence. 174
Stauffer, Helen Winter. 112
Steiner, Wendy. 180
Stendhal, Renate. 180
Stephenson, William. 107
Stepto, Robert B. 66
Sterling, Dorothy. 251, 287
Stern, Julia. 290
Stern, Madeleine B. 31
Stetson, Erlene, ed. 137, 251
Stewart, Veronica. 69
Stimpson, Catharine R. 180
Stinson, Robert. 241
Stiriling, Nora. 85
Stout, Janis P. 104
Strickland, Charles. 31
Stroup, Herbert. 199
Stuckey, William J. 92
Sundquist, Eric J. 66
Susina, Jan. 126
Sutherland, Cynthia. 146
Sylvander, Carolyn Wedin. 260
Szczesiul, Anthony E. 67

Tate, Claudia. 251, 267, 284
Taylor, Helen. 57
Telgen, Diane, and Jim Kamp,
    eds. 306
Thernstrom, Stephan. 297
Thesing, William B. 170
Thiebaux, Ellen. 97
Thomas, Robert David. 207
Thomson, James C., Jr. 85
Tinter, Adeline R. 120
Tomkins, Mary E. 241
Tompkins, Jane. 24, 67
Torsney, Cheryl B. 73

Toth, Emily. 38, 176
Toth, Susan Allen. 24
Trigg, Mary. 202
Turoff, Barbara K. 203

Unrue, Darlene Harbour. 105

Van Steenwyk, Elizabeth. 287
Vendler, Helen. 174
Villiger, Laura R. 112

Wade-Gayles, Gloria. 252
Waggenspack, Beth M. 239
Wagner-Martin, Linda. 80, 97,
    121, 160
Waid, Candace. 121
Walden, Daniel, ed. 303
Waldstreicher, David. 219
Walker, Alice. 274
Walker, Cheryl. 49, 137, 167,
    184
Walker, Nancy 38
Wall, Cheryl A. 252, 260, 275
Wallace, James D. 224
Walsh, Thomas F. 105
Ward, Susan. 60
Wardrop, Daneen. 152
Warren, Joyce W. 24, 209
Warren, Robert Penn, ed. 106
Warrior, Robert Allen. 310
Washington, Mary Helen. 253,
    256, 264, 267, 275, 279, 284
Washington, Peter. 207
Wasserman, Loretta. 92
Waterman, Arthur E. 155
Watson, Carol McAlpine. 253,
    260, 264
Watts, Emily Stipes. 138
Weimer, Joan Myers. 73
Weir, Sybil. 82
Welter, Barbara. 13
Werner, Craig. 253
Westbrook, Perry D. 47
Wexler, Alice. 220
Wexler, Laura. 25, 129
Wheeler, Kenneth W., and
    Virginia Lee Lussier. 14
Wheeler, Leslie A. 199
Whitaker, Rosemary. 50
White, Barbara A. 121, 290
White, Isabelle. 70
White-Parks, Annette. 300
Wiget, Andrew. 311

Wilentz, Gary. 129
Williams, Cynthia Schoolar. 70
Williams, Susan S. 70
Williamson, Marilyn L. 14
Willis, Patricia C., ed. 174
Willis, Susan. 275
Wilson, Christopher P. 217

ABOUT THE AUTHOR

Jane Missner Barstow is associate professor of English and chair of women's studies at Hartford College for Women, University of Hartford, and she serves as director of research and nominations for the Connecticut Women's Hall of Fame. Dr. Barstow earned a B.A. in English from Smith College and a Ph.D. in comparative literature from the University of Michigan. She also did graduate work at the University of Paris and has spent two years teaching at the Aristotelian University of Thessaloniki, Greece, as a Fulbright scholar.

At Hartford College for Women, Professor Barstow teaches courses on the nineteenth century heroine, African American women writers, and contemporary women writers from around the world. She has lectured and taught seminars on the works of Edith Wharton and Toni Morrison. Dr. Barstow is the author of many articles on contemporary women writers, including articles on Joyce Carol Oates, Doris Lessing, Margaret Atwood, and Marguerite Yourcenar for Salem Press. She has also led several workshops on integrating African American and women writers into the high school English curriculum.

Dr. Barstow's honors include the Rackham Prize for doctoral research, an NEH summer fellowship, and the educational equity award from the American Association of University Women. She is a daughter, sister, wife, and mother.